KASHMIR IN CONFLICT

Kashmir
IN CONFLICT

India, Pakistan and the Unending War

VICTORIA SCHOFIELD

I.B. TAURIS

LONDON · NEW YORK

New edition published in 2003 by I.B.Tauris & Co Ltd
6 Salem Road, London W2 4BU
175 Fifth Avenue, New York NY 10010
www.ibtauris.com

In the United States of America and in Canada distributed by Palgrave Macmillan, a division of
St Martin's Press, 175 Fifth Avenue, New York NY 10010

ISBN 1 86064 898 3

A full CIP record for this book is available from the British Library
A full CIP record for this book is available from the Library of Congress

Library of Congress catalog card: available

Typeset in Monotype Garamond by Wyvern 21 Ltd, Bristol
Printed and bound in Great Britain by Mackays of Chatham plc, Chatham, Kent

Contents

Maps

Acknowledgements

'A country of such striking natural beauty must, surely, at some period of its history have produced refined and noble people,' writes Sir Francis Young-husband in his *History of Kashmir*. So indeed, and during my own journey through Kashmir's contemporary history, I have been privileged to make contact with some of them. In the present day, I am grateful to the three main protagonists in the current struggle: the Indians, Pakistanis and the Kashmiris and, by this, I include all the inhabitants of the once princely state. My thanks also go to the Governments of India and Pakistan, whose representatives have always received me openly, as well as their respective High Commissions in London; in addition, I should like to thank the members of the Government of the state of Jammu and Kashmir, the members of the All Parties Hurriyat Conference, the 'Azad' Government of Jammu and Kashmir and numerous officials and private individuals.

No book is written single-handedly. All those I interviewed, often at short notice, could not have been more willing to open their hearts and homes to me in order for me to understand their story. Where they have not been able to resolve their differences at the negotiating table, I have attempted to sit with them independently, listen to their grievances and share their dreams. They, too, are contributors to this book. I am also grateful for permission to quote from numerous works listed in the bibliography; I have done so with special attention to those first-hand accounts which capture an event far better than it is sometimes possible to do with the wisdom of hindsight. In quoting the views and opinions of others, I have also wanted to give the reader the benefit of their analyses as well as my own.

I am grateful to all those who assisted me during my long years of research on Kashmir, especially David Page, who gave me invaluable advice. I am also grateful to Lord Ahmed, the late Lynne Ali, Lord Avebury, Rahul Bedi, Gulam Butt, Brian Cloughley, Alexander Evans, M.J. Gohel, Irfan Husain, Professor Alastair Lamb, Margot Norman, Dr Rashmi Shankar, Leslie Wolf-Phillips and Malcolm Yapp, as well as Philip Armstrong and Russell Townsend for drawing the maps.

My thanks go to the staff of the British Library and the Oriental and India Office Collection for the many hours I have spent researching in these libraries. I am grateful for permission to quote from the books and manuscripts I have used from their collections. I am also grateful to the London Library for its liberal lending policy, the United Nations Library and the Royal Geographical Society, whose collection of maps I have consulted. Finally, I should like to thank my agent, Sara Menguc, my publisher,

Iradj Bagherzade, and his colleagues at I.B.Tauris, my husband, Stephen Willis, my children, Alexandra, Anthony and Olivia and my friends, all of whom have supported me emotionally and practically while I have been trying to understand the complexities of Kashmir. Unless otherwise stated, all views and conclusions expressed in this book are my own.

Preface

Who has not heard of the Vale of Cashmere,
With its roses the brightest that earth ever gave,
Its temples and grottos, and fountains as clear
As the love-lightened eyes that hang over the wave?[1]

In 1846, under the terms of the Treaty of Amritsar, the British sold the beautiful valley of Kashmir to the Hindu Dogra ruler, Gulab Singh. As Maharaja of Jammu and Kashmir, he was at last able to include Kashmir as the 'jewel' among his other territorial possessions, which included Jammu, Ladakh, Baltistan and numerous hill states, through which flowed the river Indus and its tributaries to the east. Thus, people of different linguistic, religious and cultural traditions were all brought under the jurisdiction of one ruler. The inclusion of the predominantly Muslim, and more densely populated, valley meant that Hindus, Sikhs and Buddhists were in the minority. When, a century later, the sub-continent was partitioned at independence in 1947, Maharaja Hari Singh, Gulab Singh's great-grandson, could not decide whether to join the new dominion of Pakistan or India. For over two months, his state remained 'independent'. In October, after large numbers of tribesmen from Pakistan's North-West Frontier invaded the state, he finally agreed to join India. His decision was immediately contested by Pakistan on the basis of the state's majority Muslim population. War between India and Pakistan was finally halted in 1949 by a ceasefire supervised by the recently founded United Nations.

For over fifty years, India and Pakistan have fought over Jammu and Kashmir both on the battlefield and at the negotiating table; both countries wanted to absorb it within their borders, neither of them has succeeded in doing so entirely. One-third of the former princely state is administered by Pakistan, known as 'Azad' (Free) Jammu and Kashmir and the Northern Areas; two-thirds, known as the state of Jammu and Kashmir, are controlled by India; this area includes the regions of Ladakh, Jammu and the prized valley of Kashmir. Since 1949, the ceasefire line has been monitored by a small force of the United Nations Military Observer Group in India and Pakistan (UNMOGIP). Although hostilities broke out again in 1965, the ceasefire line remained the de facto border. Following the 1971 war, when East Pakistan seceded to become independent Bangladesh, under the terms of the 1972 Simla[2] agreement between Pakistan and India, the ceasefire line was renamed the line of control (LOC). Subsequently India requested UNMOGIP's withdrawal from the Indian side of the LOC on the grounds that its mandate had lapsed.

In the north-east, China lays claim to a section of uninhabited land, the Aksai Chin, through which, in the 1950s, it constructed a road linking Tibet to Sinkiang (Xinjiang). The boundary – called the 'line of actual control' (LAC) – between Indian and Chinese-held territories has never been delimited. To complicate the issue further, the ceasefire line between Indian and Pakistani-administered Jammu and Kashmir, also stopped short at the Siachen glacier (at map coordinate NJ9842) which extends for forty miles to the de facto border with China. In 1984 Indian troops took control of part of the glacier; since then Indian and Pakistani forces have confronted each other in the world's highest war zone. Although bilateral discussions regarding the glacier were begun in 1986, they were suspended after six rounds without agreement in 1992.

What distinguishes the Kashmir conflict from other regional disputes is that, in order to effect the ceasefire, in 1948 the Indian government made a formal complaint to the Security Council of the United Nations against Pakistan's 'aggression'. The complaint against Pakistan in an international forum turned a dispute between two countries into an issue which demanded international attention. The recommendations of the United Nations, formulated into three resolutions passed in 1948 and 1949, also formalised the presence of a third party into the debate: the wishes of the people who lived in the land over which India and Pakistan were fighting. All three resolutions recommended that India and Pakistan should proceed with holding a plebiscite, as already agreed by the Governments of India and Pakistan, so that the people themselves could decide their future.[3]

That the plebiscite was never held should perhaps be no surprise. Firstly as a prerequisite, Pakistan was required to withdraw its forces from the territory which they had occupied. Secondly, it was clear that the Indian government only agreed to hold a plebiscite at a time when it was confident that the majority would confirm union with India. In the event, Pakistan's reluctance to vacate the territory it had occupied gave India the excuse to renege on its commitment to hold a plebiscite; the *de facto* divison of the state which India and Pakistan had achieved militarily was therefore neither reversed nor confirmed. But although successive Indian governments may have regretted the fact that an international body was ever involved in discussing the future of the state of Jammu and Kashmir, the UN resolutions remain on the agenda. Whatever India or Pakistan may have subsequently agreed between themselves at later summits – Tashkent in 1966, Simla in 1972 and Lahore in 1999 – the tripartite nature of the issue, with the plebiscite as a means of determining the political allegiance of the inhabitants of the state, was already confirmed by the United Nations in 1948.

But, as Sir Owen Dixon, UN representative for India and Pakistan, noted in 1950, the difficulty of resolving the future of the state was compounded by the fact that it was 'not really a unit geographically, demographically or economically' but 'an agglomeration of territories brought under the political power of One Maharaja.' On the Pakistani-administered side of the ceasefire line, the peoples of the Northern Areas, including the former kingdoms of Hunza, Nagar, Gilgit and Baltistan, are culturally distinct not only from each other, but from the inhabitants in the rest of the state; so too are the people of Azad Jammu and Kashmir, centred on the districts of Kotli, Poonch, Mirpur and Muzaffarabad. All are Muslim, but whereas Shia Muslims predominate in the Northern Areas, Sunnis are in the majority in Azad Jammu and Kashmir.[4] In the two-thirds of the territory administered by India, the majority of the valley's inhabitants are Kashmiri Muslims, with a small percentage of Hindus and Sikhs. In Jammu approximately two-thirds of the population are Hindu, one-third Muslims, who live primarily in the Doda and Rajauri areas bordering Pakistani-administered AJK. Ladakh is sparsely populated. Over half its population are Buddhist, less than half are Shia Muslim with a small percentage of Hindus.[5] What Owen Dixon noticed from the outset was that with peoples of such diverse origins nominally united under one political authority, whatever the outcome of a unitary plebiscite, there was bound to be disappointment from amongst the minority. He therefore suggested, as have future commentators, that a regional plebiscite might provide a more equitable outcome, even though it would undoubtedly lead to the division of the state. As the Indian writer, Sumantra Bose, has recognised, the challenge was always to find a middle ground between 'communal compartmentalisation and the chimera of a non-existent oneness'.[6]

In 1989 a significant number of the Muslim inhabitants of the valley began a movement of protest, which was both an armed struggle and a political rejection of their continuing allegiance to the Indian Union. The difficulty which they faced, and which was always inherent in any debate about their collective will, was the lack of obvious unanimity of objective in their movement. Some were still fighting for the plebiscite to be held so that the valley could join Pakistan; others wanted a plebiscite which would include a 'third option' – independence of the entire state, as it existed in 1947, including the area controlled by Pakistan.[7] The pro-independence activists found legal justification in the UN resolution adopted on 13 August 1948 which recommended that a final decision on the status of Jammu and Kashmir 'shall be determined in accordance with the will of the people' without reference to a choice between either India or Pakistan. Other inhabitants of the state – the Buddhist Ladakhis and the Shia Muslims of the Kargil area – did not support the movement of protest. Nor did the formerly nomadic Gujar and Bakherwal Muslims. The Hindus and Sikhs of the Jammu region also traditionally regarded themselves as part of the Indian Union and resisted the dominant will of the numerically superior Muslims of the valley. The Pakistani government, however, which had made no secret of its disappointment that the state had not acceded to Pakistan at independence, was only too happy to support the movement 'morally and diplomatically'; unofficially, Pakistan was also prepared to assist in reviving the spirit of the 1947 'jihad' in a covert war to assist the

Kashmiri insurgents, which might eventually achieve militarily what it had failed to gain through negotiation. That what began as a more secular movement in the valley for greater political liberty became one with 'Islamist' overtones arose directly from the changes occurring within Pakistani society and influences from Afghanistan.

To the outside observer, Pakistan's deliberate encouragement of the Kashmiris to fight for their self-determination may appear inconsistent with its own national objective to include the state of Jammu and Kashmir as part of Pakistan. But reading between the lines of Pakistani statements, no government accepted a definition of 'self-determination' to be anything other than a choice between India and Pakistan. Recently Pakistan has unofficially modified its position in two significant respects. Firstly, the government no longer realistically expects to include the whole of the state (including Ladakh and Jammu) within its borders; secondly, it has been obliged to recognise that a movement for independence does exist among the valley Kashmiris. Pending any other agreement regarding the resolution of the issue, it still adhers to the relevance of the UN resolutions as drafted in 1948 and 1949, without which it fears it would lose its locus standi in the issue. In order not to 'sabotage' their movement, the disaffected Kashmiris have also agreed not to resolve the dilemma of their dual – and what would eventually be – competing objectives. Likewise, despite statements insisting that legally the whole of the state of Jammu and Kashmir belongs to India, the Indian government does not realistically expect to include Azad Jammu and Kashmir and the Northern Areas as part of India. The bone of contention between the two countries is, as it has always been, the status of the valley of Kashmir.

Ever since 1947, the international community has watched the situation in Jammu and Kashmir with foreboding, lest the conflict escalate into another war. The contribution which it has been able to make has, however, been limited. After the UN resolutions in 1948 and 1949 were passed, successive governments in India have attempted to distance themselves from any attempts at international mediation, either by the UN or any other body or individual country. The 1972 Simla agreement with Pakistan provided the opportunity for India to claim that the issue was no longer an 'international' but a bilateral one. But even bilateral talks with Pakistan over Jammu and Kashmir have led to a stalemate of rhetoric. Whenever Pakistan called for third party mediation, India reacted against the 'internationalisation' of the issue.

On 11 September 2001, the terrorist attacks on the World Trade Center in New York and the Pentagon in Washington had immediate repercussions in South Asia. The Pakistani government agreed to assist the United States in 'a war against terrorism' which came right to its borders with neighbouring Afghanistan. As a result, the Indian government saw this as an opportunity to point out to the world community the continuing assistance which Pakistan was giving to the militancy in Jammu and Kashmir. Pakistan therefore found

itself applauded for confronting terrorism in Afghanistan at the same time as being condemned for supporting it in Jammu and Kashmir. When, in December 2001, there was a bomb attack on the Indian Parliament in New Delhi, India began to talk more seriously than ever before about putting an end to 'cross-border terrorism'. The international border between the two countries was closed and by the Spring of 2002, India and Pakistan again appeared to be on the brink of war. The prospect had horrendous overtones because both governments talked about using the nuclear weapons they had tested in 1998.

The Kashmiri conflict remains both a struggle for land as well as about the rights of people to determine their future. To date, no consensus has been reached between India and Pakistan, nor with the people, on the future of the state, merely an unacknowledged status quo, to which there appears to be a curious attachment lest any alteration cause even greater trauma to the region. In addition, there is still no obvious 'collective' will amongst the heterogeneous inhabitants of the entire state of Jammu and Kashmir, whose state has now been divided for over half as long as it was ever a unified whole. In the crossfire of multiple objectives remain the lives, and sadly often violent deaths of men, women and children who have been caught up in a deadly war of words and weapons, which seems unending. As I have often been told during my years of research on Kashmir. 'You cannot talk about Kashmir as a dispute between two nations. It is a conflict because we – the Kashmiris – are in the middle.'

Notes

1. Thomas Moore, *Lalla Rookh*, London, 1986, p.256.

2. Shimla. For consistency, I have retained the original name, Simla, as it was in 1972.

3. One resolution was passed by the Security Council (21 April 1948); two by UNCIP, the United Nations Commission in India and Pakistan, set up by the Security Council, to oversee the holding of the plebiscite (13 August 1948 & 5 January 1949).

4. Shia Muslims believe that the Prophet chose his son-in-law and cousin, Ali, as his successor. Sunnis believe that the Prophet's role in revealing God's laws and guiding the people ended with him. The differences are fundamental and have caused major strife between the two communities.

5. Population figures for the state of Jammu and Kashmir in 1981: Kashmir valley 3 million, of which 95% were Muslim, 4% Hindu; Jammu 2.7 million, of which 66% Hindus, 30% Muslims; Ladakh 134,000 of which over half were Buddhist, 46% Shia Muslim, less than 3% Hindu. Total population of J & K for 2001: 10,069,917. Source: Jammu and Kashmir 2001, Information Department. Azad Jammu and Kashmir: 2,915,567; Northern Areas: 870,347 (in 1998). Source: Pakistan High Commission, London, August 2002.

6. Sumantra Bose, *The Challenge in Kashmir*, Delhi, 1997, p. 177.

7. There were also Kashmiri Muslims in the valley who did not challenge Indian authority.

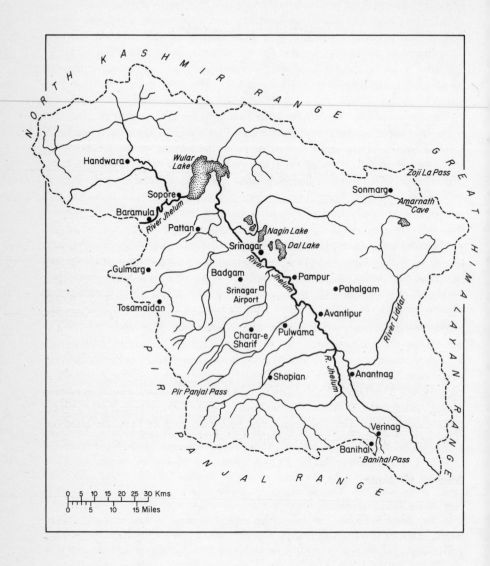

1. The Valley of Kashmir
(Source: Raghubir Singh, *Kashmir: Garden of the Himalayas*, London, 1983)

CHAPTER I

Introducing Kashmir

Small indeed the country may seem by the side of the great plains that extend in the south, and confined the history of which it was the scene. And yet, just as the natural attractions of the valley have won it fame beyond the frontiers of India, thus too the interest attaching to its history far exceeds the narrow geographical limits.

Sir Aurel Stein, 1900[1]

The valley of Kashmir, an irregular oval of land, is one of the most beautiful places in the world. On a map the valley appears remote and landlocked, extending for no more than ninety miles, isolated by successive ranges of the Himalayan mountains high above the plains of the sub-continent. Its apparent impregnability is, however, illusory. Over twenty passes provide points of entry, making the valley both a crossroads and a place of refuge. A unique record of the history of Kashmir, the *Rajatarangini* (Chronicle of Kings), written in the 12th century by the poet Kalhana, describes how, since legendary times, the valley's rulers came into contact and conflict with their neighbours.[2] Sometimes the valley formed part of a great empire, at others it comprised a kingdom in its own right. At all times, its peoples have retained a strong attachment to their Kashmiriyat – their cultural identity – which transcends religion. The Kashmiri language is also distinct from the Hindi or Urdu spoken by the inhabitants of the plains.[3]

Ancient Kashmir

Kashmir's first period of 'imperial' history begins in the third century BC with the rule of Asoka, whose empire extended from Bengal to the Deccan, Afghanistan to the Punjab, and included Kashmir. Originally a devout Hindu, Asoka turned to Buddhism and sent Buddhist missionaries to the valley. When he died, Kashmir once more regained its independence. In the first century AD, the valley was invaded by the Kushans from north-west China who had succeeded in conquering the whole of northern India. King Kanishka, who converted to Buddhism, also loved Kashmir and often held his court in the valley. The Kushan kings were renowned for their love of art, architecture and learning and the period was marked by intellectual resurgence. Traders, who traversed the famed Silk route, brought not only merchandise but also literary

and artistic ideas. In the decades which followed, Kashmir is remembered as
enjoying a 'golden age'. The economic life of the people was simple. They
worked the land, and were expected to pay a proportion of what they
cultivated to the ruler. Kashmiris became famous throughout Asia as learned,
cultured and humane and the intellectual contribution of writers, poets,
musicians, scientists to the rest of India was comparable to that of ancient
Greece to European civilisation.

Lalitaditya, who ruled in the early 8th century, is still regarded as one of the
most celebrated Hindu kings. A predecessor of the European emperor,
Charlemagne, he epitomised the type of conquering hero upon which
Kashmiri pride in their ancient rulers is founded. He also made a significant
contribution as an administrator. Avantivarman, who lived in the 9th century,
is another of the great Hindu kings after whom the town of Avantipur is
named, and who earned praise from Kalhana for his internal consolidation of
the state. From the 10th century onwards, however, struggles for power in
Kashmir intensified. The isolationist policy adopted by the later Hindu kings
to counter emergent Islam in north India meant that the resources of the
kingdom were insufficient to sustain the population.

The first great king of the Muslim period was Shahab-ud Din who came to
the throne in 1354. With peace restored after the devastation of the Mongols,
Shahab-ud Din devoted his attention to foreign expeditions, conquering
Baltistan, Ladakh, Kishtwar and Jammu. Shahab-ud Din also loved learning
and patronised art and architecture. He was married to a Hindu, Laxmi, and
had great regard for the religious feelings of all his subjects. During the reign
of his successor, Qutb-ud Din, the pace of conversion to Islam increased.
Hinduism persisted, however, and the administration remained in the hands of
learned men, the Brahmins[4], who were recognised as the traditional official
class; Sanskrit also remained the official court language. In 1420 another great
king, popularly called Bud Shah (meaning 'great king') came to the throne. The
grandson of Qutb-ud-Din, he took the name Sultan Zain-ul Abidin. During
his long reign, which lasted until 1470, the valley prospered. Bud Shah's court
was full of poets and musicians. He also patronised scholars and intellectuals.
He was tolerant towards the Brahmins and rebuilt the temples, which had
been destroyed during his father's reign. Many Hindus, who had left, returned.
Persian became the new official language and those who learnt it were offered
government appointments. Bud Shah also introduced the art of weaving and
papier mâché making, which have made Kashmiri handicrafts famous to this
day. His reign, however, was not free from the usual power struggles. For the
last eighteen years of his life, a war over the succession raged between his
three sons.

In the years to come, the fame of Kashmir attracted the Mughals but they
failed in their early attempts to dominate the valley. It was, however, only a
matter of time before the Mughal emperor, Akbar, who had succeeded to the
throne of Delhi in 1558, sought to take advantage of yet another power

struggle. In 1586 he sent an expedition to conquer the valley. Kashmir's last king died in exile. With the incorporation of Kashmir into the Mughal Empire, the valley of Kashmir's long history as a kingdom in its own right came to an end. When Kashmiris point to their political heritage, they remember with pride the Hindu dynasties and the Muslim Sultanates. Most importantly, although the lives of the people were undeniably harsh, none of their rulers was answerable to some alien power in Kabul, Lahore or Delhi; accordingly, their actions form part of a history which Kashmiris regard as undeniably their own.

Mughals and Afghans 1586–1819

The conquest of the valley by the Mughals is generally regarded as marking the beginning of Kashmir's modern history. For nearly two centuries, Kashmir was the northernmost point of an empire whose power base was situated in Delhi. Once master of Kashmir, Akbar, adopted a policy of conciliation and entered into marriage alliances with the Kashmiri nobility. His rule, both throughout India and in the valley, was known for its liberalism. Of all the rulers of Kashmir, Akbar's son and successor, Jehangir, who ascended the throne in 1605, is perhaps best remembered for his love of the valley. During his reign Jehangir beautified Kashmir with over 700 gardens. On his deathbed, he was reportedly asked if there was anything he wanted, to which he replied: 'Nothing but Kashmir.' His son, Shah Jehan, who succeeded him in 1624, also loved Kashmir and the valley became a popular place of refuge for the Mughal nobility away from the plains of India during the hot summers.

With Mughal rule, a pattern of government began, which was to become only too familiar to the Kashmiri people. A governor was sent to administer the province and demand taxes. Yet even though Kashmir was dominated by an outside power and once more comprised part of a great empire, early Mughal rule is generally remembered as a period of relative stability and prosperity. Poets and scholars came to Kashmir. Land reforms were also undertaken. Those who visited Kashmir in later years retained the belief that Mughal rule was also a golden age.

Aurangzeb, who came to the throne in 1658, was the last of the Mughal Emperors to make any impact on Kashmir's history. When he made his first and only visit to Kashmir in 1665, he was accompanied by the French doctor, François Bernier, whose enthusiasm for Kashmir undoubtedly influenced future travellers. 'I am charmed with Kachemire. In truth, the kingdom surpasses in beauty all that my warm imagination had anticipated.' Bernier wrote favourably of people who 'are celebrated for wit, and considered much more intelligent and ingenious than the Indians.'[5] By this time the shawl industry, begun by Bud Shah, was coming into its own and Bernier took note of the great number of shawls which the local people manufactured.

Towards the end of Aurangzeb's reign, an event occurred which had special significance for later generations of Kashmiri Muslims. In 1700 a strand of the beard of the Prophet Muhammad, the Mo-i Muqaddas, was brought by the servant of a wealthy Kashmiri merchant to Kashmir. It was originally displayed in a mosque in Srinagar, but the mosque was too small for the crowds who came to see it. The relic was therefore taken to another mosque on the banks of Upper Dal lake, which was known first as Asar-e-Sharif – shrine of the relic – and then Hazratbal – the lake of the Hazrat, or the Prophet. It has remained there ever since, with one brief interlude in 1963 when it mysteriously disappeared. Unlike Akbar, Aurangzeb was intolerant of other religions and the memory of his reign is tarnished by his persecution of Hindus and Shias Muslims. Brahmins were, however, still retained within the administration and opportunities existed for both Muslims and Hindus to prosper on merit and learning. The end of Aurangzeb's rule and the war of succession between his three sons after his death in 1707 led to a steady decline of Mughal rule in Kashmir.

In the early 18th century, the number of Hindus leaving the valley increased. Although it was believed this was due to persecution, it is also possible that the Brahmins left because of the opportunities presented by contacts made while Kashmir was part of the Mughal empire.[6] When the Persian king, Nadir Shah, invaded Delhi in 1738, the Mughal hold on Kashmir was weakened still further. This in turn left Kashmir to the mercy of further invaders. In 1751, the Afghans, ruled by Ahmed Shah Durrani, absorbed Kashmir into their expanding empire. The names of the Afghan governors who ruled Kashmir are all but forgotten but not their cruelty, which was directed mainly towards the Hindus. Oppression took the form of extortion of money from the local people and brutality in the face of opposition. Both Kashmiri men and women lived in fear of their lives. Many were captured and sent as slaves to Afghanistan. After Ahmed Shah Duranni's death in 1772, the Afghan kingdom never again reached the heights to which it had risen under his leadership but Afghan control of the valley of Kashmir lasted another 47 years. During Afghan dominance, the shawl industry declined, probably due to heavy taxes. By the 1780s there were 16,000 shawl looms in use compared with 40,000 in the time of the Mughals; by the beginning of the 19th century the demand for shawls in Europe meant that the number of looms rose to 24,000 by 1813.[7] Despite the religious oppression, to which many Hindus were subjected, they were, however, useful to the Afghans because of their administrative experience. Kashmiri Pandits were not prevented from entering into government service and there were some families whose names consistently appear in public service – the Dhars, Kauls, Tikkus and Saprus.[8]

To the south of Kashmir, the Sikh ruler, Ranjit Singh, son of Mahan Singh, head of one of the twelve Sikh confederacies, known as 'misls', was extending his empire in the Punjab at the expense of the declining Afghan empire. In 1799 he had acquired Lahore and the title of maharaja from Zaman Shah, King of Afghanistan. In 1802 Ranjit conquered Amritsar. In 1809, the British and Sikhs concluded a treaty of 'Amity and Concord' by which the Sikhs acknowledged British supremacy in Sindh and the British agreed that their territory would stop at the river Sutlej. In 1819, the 'Lion of the Punjab', as Ranjit Singh became known, finally succeeded in taking Kashmir, initially to the relief of the local people who had suffered under the Afghans.

Sikh rule

As was customary practice under the Mughals and Afghans, control of Kashmir was carried out by a series of governors. Several measures, which demonstrated the assertion of Hindu belief over that of the Muslims, were enacted. Cow slaughter was made punishable by death. The picture painted by the Europeans who began to visit the valley more frequently was one of deprivation and starvation. In 1823 William Moorcroft travelled throughout Kashmir on his way to Bokhara. His objective was to locate a better breed of horse from amongst the Turkman steeds for the East India Company's military stud. Before becoming a veterinary surgeon, he had trained as a doctor and while in Srinagar, he treated the local people:

> Everywhere the people were in the most abject condition, exorbitantly taxed by the Sikh Government and subjected to every kind of extortion and oppression by its officers. The consequences of this system are the gradual depopulation of the country.[9]

Moorcroft estimated that no more than one-sixteenth of the cultivable land surface was under cultivation; as a result, the starving people had fled in great numbers to India. Moorcroft's mission was never completed because he died of fever in 1825 but his journals, edited by H.H. Wilson, provide a valuable insight into the condition of the people in the early years of Sikh rule. The Kashmiris, he said, were treated as 'little better than cattle'.[10] In 1831 Victor Jacquemont, a French botanist, arrived in the valley. The appearance of Srinagar, he said, was the 'most miserable in the world ... nowhere else in India are the masses as poor and denuded as they are in Kashmir.'[11] Godfrey Vigne who travelled throughout Kashmir in the late 1830s had a similar story to tell. 'Not a day passed whilst I was on the path to Kashmir, and even when travelling in the valley, that I did not see the bleached remains of some unfortunate wretch who had fallen a victim either to sickness or starvation.'[12] There were, however, some benefits arising from the contact with Europeans: detailed studies were made of the area and Captain Wade's map, presented to Ranjit Singh, was the first up-to-date map of Kashmir. A rudimentary postal system was also set up.

Ranjit Singh never visited the valley of Kashmir; but there is a well-known

story which relates how he once wrote to one of his governors, Colonel Mian
Singh: 'Would that I could only once in my life enjoy the delight of wandering
through the gardens of Kashmir, fragrant with almond-blossoms, and sitting
on the fresh green turf!' To please the maharaja, the governor ordered a
special Kashmiri carpet to be woven with a green background, dotted with
little pink spots and interspersed with tiny little pearl-like dots. When he
received it, Ranjit was delighted and rolled himself on it as though he were
rolling in Kashmiri grass.[13] A shawl was also prepared for Ranjit Singh
depicting a map of the Kashmir valley; but by the time it was completed
thirty-seven years later, the Lion of the Punjab was dead.

On the sidelines of Kashmir, in the neighbouring plains of Jammu, the
Dogra Rajputs were keenly interested in events in the valley. They had settled
around the lakes of Mansar and Siroinsar in the tract of land rising from the
plains of the Punjab to the mountains in the north and they took their name
from Dogirath, which, in Sanskrit, means 'two lakes'. In the 1820s, the ruler of
Jammu, a feudatory of Ranjit Singh, was Raja Gulab Singh, born in 1792. With
his two younger brothers, Dhyan and Suchet, Gulab had succeeded in making
himself indispensable at the court of the Sikh ruler. As Ranjit Singh's vassals,
the three brothers succeeded in amassing land and wealth both in the plains
and hill states to the north of the Punjab. Created Raja of Jammu by Ranjit
Singh in 1822,[14] Gulab Singh also expanded his lands in the name of the Sikh
kingdom still further to include Ladakh which bordered China. When Ranjit
Singh died in 1838, in the chaos of the Sikh succession, Gulab Singh was well-
placed to control events not only in the heart of the Sikh empire in Lahore
but also in Kashmir and its neighbouring states.

Until Ranjit Singh's death, the East India Company had maintained
cordial relations with the Sikhs; they in turn did not wish to upset the
British. After his death, the relationship fell apart. On 11 December 1845, in
the First Anglo-Sikh war, the Sikh army moved across the river Sutlej. Two
encounters – at Mudki and Firuzshar – left the Sikhs defeated although not
conclusively. The following year, on 10 February 1846, the Sikhs once more
engaged the British in battle at Sobraon, a small village on the banks of
the Sutlej. Gulab Singh remained on the sidelines, offering to help his
overlords but failing to give it, at the same time as keeping in regular contact
with the British. Without his support, Sikh defeat was inevitable.
Representatives from both sides met at Kasur, where the two armies had
halted, about thirty miles from Lahore. The British, recognising that Gulab
Singh's neutrality had tipped the balance of the war in their favour, treated
him as a welcome ambassador.

The terms of the settlement embodied in the Treaty of Peace, ratified at
Lahore on 9 March 1846, between the young Sikh Maharaja, Dulip Singh, and
the British, were designed to reward Gulab Singh. Instead of paying an
indemnity of one crore of rupees, the Sikhs were required to cede to the East
India Company the provinces of Kashmir and Hazara. The Sikhs were also

obliged to recognise the independent sovereignty of Gulab Singh in territories which were to be made over to him by a separate agreement. A week later, on 16 March, the British signed the Treaty of Amritsar with Gulab Singh. He was to pay the exact sum in lieu of which the British had taken possession of Kashmir one week earlier: one crore of rupees towards the indemnity. Twenty-five lakhs were later waived because the British retained some territory across the river Beas.[15] By the terms of the Treaty of Amristar, Gulab Singh was able to sever his allegiance from the Sikhs; henceforward, he was no longer their feudatory but, as Maharaja of Jammu and Kashmir, a counterpoise against them. Gulab Singh's estate included not only his native Jammu but also the Himalayan kingdom of Kashmir, Ladakh and Baltistan, which Gulab Singh's famous general, Zorawar Singh, had conquered on behalf of the Sikhs in 1840.[16]

Dogras

Despite Gulab Singh's status as a maharaja, he still came under suspicion when, once again the Sikhs confronted the British in 1848, in the second Anglo-Sikh war. Gulab Singh, however, did not turn on his new overlords, as the British feared he might. Instead, when the British demanded his support, as they were entitled to do under the terms of the Treaty of Amritsar, he gave it. Sikh defeat at the battle of Gujrat on 21 February 1848 led to the total dismemberment of the Sikh empire and the annexation by the British of the Punjab.

Although the valley of Kashmir had been added to the Dogras' possessions, the Kashmiris always felt that the Dogras considered Jammu as their home and the valley as a conquered territory. The British, who came under severe criticism for the sale of the valley, could not do much to improve the lot of the Kashmiris, since they had no mandate to interfere in the conduct of the state. They were concerned, however, to pressurise Gulab Singh to dispense with suttee, female infanticide and the killing of illegitimate children. Gulab Singh also continued to allow universal freedom of worship and, although he did not approve of Hindu-Muslim marriages, he did not prevent them. In 1856, after ten years as maharaja, Gulab Singh's health began to fail. He had had diabetes since 1851 and was also suffering from dropsy. In order to smooth the succession and prevent rival claims to the throne from the sons of his brothers, Dhyan and Suchet, he asked the Governor-General to install his third son, Ranbir Singh, as maharaja on 8 February 1856. Although Gulab Singh had formally abdicated, he became governor of the province and retained full sovereignty until his death on 7 August 1857.

The general uprising of sepoys, the local troops used in the army of the East India Company – known by the British as 'the Indian Mutiny' and by the Indians as 'the war of independence' – started in Meerut, near Delhi, on

Attempts to establish Dogra control c. 1850-90. A part leased from Kashmir by the British in 1935

Gilgit
Gilgit Agency

1864 – Dogra effort to gain foothold in Southern Sinkiang

Baltistan

Skardu

Conquered 1840

Ladakh

Vale of Kashmir

Srinagar

Leh

Poonch

Purchased from the British 1846

1841 – Attempted Dogra Invasion of Western Tibet

Poonch

A Buddhist kingdom conquered by the Dogras in 1834

Dogra heartland

Jammu

Jammu

☐ Muslim majority

▨ Hindu Sikh majority

▧ Buddhist majority

Note on population: The 1941 census gives a total population of 4,021,616 of whom 77 per cent were Muslims, 20 per cent Hindus, 1.64 per cent Sikhs and 1 per cent Buddhists. By 1981 the total population was estimated at 8,529,389.

2. The Creation of the State of Jammu and Kashmir with Communal Groupings (Source: Alastair Lamb, *Crisis in Kashmir*, London, 1966)

10 May 1857. It soon spread to other towns and hundreds of Europeans were massacred. The titular head of the former Mughal empire, Bahadur Shah II, supported the mutineers. The rebellion, which lasted for over a year, not only undermined British confidence in their rule in India, but it also called for loyal allies. The state of Jammu and Kashmir, under the joint leadership of the ailing Gulab Singh and his son, Ranbir, responded favourably to British appeals for help. They sent a large amount of money to the Punjab for the troops whose pay was in arrears. The mutineers were also forbidden to seek asylum in Kashmir which, after British annexation of the Punjab, now bordered British India. Shelter in the valley was also provided to English women and children, seeking refuge from the plains. Most importantly, the Dogras agreed to send a Kashmiri force to assist the British in the siege of Delhi, although continuing doubts about their loyalty to the British kept the soldiers inactive for several months. Only after Gulab Singh's death in August 1857, was the force allowed to depart. It saw only limited action, but the psychological significance of the decision to commit Kashmiri troops on the side of the British outweighed their possible contribution in the fighting.[17] After the mutiny, the Governor-General became the Queen's representative, the Viceroy, and the administration was no longer enacted through the East India Company but through the Government of India.

By amending the terms of the Treaty of Amritsar, in 1860 His Highness Maharaja Sir Ranbir Singh, Indar Mahindar, Sipar-i-Saltanat, General, Asakir-i-Inglishia, Mushir-i-Khas-i-Qaisara-i-Hind, Grand Commander of the Star of India, Grand Commander of the Indian Empire was rewarded for his loyalty and assistance during the Indian mutiny by being allowed to adopt an heir from a collateral branch of the family. This was confirmed by George Canning in 1862 that 'on failure of natural heirs, the adoption of an heir into your Highness' House, according to its usage and traditions will be willingly recognised ... so long as your House is loyal to the Crown.'[18] This would secure the succession of the Dogras in perpetuity, in the event he or his successors did not have an heir. Queen Victoria conferred on Maharaja Ranbir Singh the title of the Most Exalted Order of the Star of India and his gun-salute was raised from 19 to 21. Rather more popular – and less formidable – than his father, Ranbir was not, however, able to improve conditions for the people. The country remained in the hands of officials, who were neither motivated nor intellectually equipped to undertake any reforms.

Colonel Ralph Young visited Kashmir in 1867. As he travelled along the road to Srinagar he found 'that it had all been once under cultivation but it is now desolate. Certainly the country is not now flourishing.' During his travels he met Frederick Drew, who had come to work for Ranbir Singh in the forestry department, exploring the geology of the mountains and later became Governor of Ladakh. From Drew, Young formed the impression that all ranks were 'discontented with the Jummoo rule, and that they would rebel but for

the belief that the English would interfere to put down the rebellion.'[19] Robert
Thorp, who openly expressed his outrage at the sale of Kashmir to the Dogras
in 1846, believed that the British had some responsibility to 'the people whom
it sold into the slavery of Gulab Singh.' He described a people 'whose
characteristics (both intellectual and moral) give evidence of former greatness,
trampled upon by a race in every way inferior to themselves and steadily
deteriorating under the influence of an oppressive despotism, which bars the
way to all improvement, whether social, intellectual or religious.' Death or
migration was the only escape from this form of servitude. The shawl makers
worked for a pittance. 'Of almost everything produced by the soil, the
Government takes a large proportion and the numerous officials who are
employed in collecting it are paid by an award of so much grain from the
share of the landlords.'[20]

Ranbir Singh's twenty-eight year reign was marked by a combination of
indifference to local government and a series of natural disasters. In 1884 Lord
Kimberley, Secretary of State for India, wrote to the Government of India: 'As
to the urgent need for reforms in the administration of the State of Jammu
and Kashmir, there is, unfortunately, no room for doubt.' He went on to say
that, given the circumstances under which the Dogras came to rule over
Kashmir, 'the intervention of the British government on behalf of the
Mohammedan population has already been too long delayed.'[21] But, concerned
as the British were by the internal situation in the state, there was a more
important reason why the Government of India chose to intervene more
assertively in Kashmiri affairs. The state of Jammu and Kashmir effectively
constituted the northern frontier of Imperial India.

Kashmir: the frontier state

British imperial policy towards the state of Jammu and Kashmir in the
late 19th century was guided primarily by fear of a Russian advance towards
India through the Pamir mountains, as well as by events in the expanse of
land north of the Hindu Kush and Himalayas, known as Turkestan, the
eastern part of which was under the nominal rule of China. In addition, the
British were continually troubled by the independent policy adopted by the
Amir of Afghanistan, whose lands also extended as far as the north-western
frontier of the sub-continent. On account of its strategic location, the state of
Jammu and Kashmir appeared to be an ideal buffer against potential
incursions from Russia, Afghanistan and China into the sub-continent.
Provided the British could maintain a workable alliance with the maharaja they
would not be obliged to incur the expense of fortifying the northern frontier
themselves.

Such a policy, however, implied a degree of control over the maharaja
which the British did not have. The Treaty of Amritsar made no provision
for a British representative at Gulab Singh's court. Although technically a

feudatory of the British, there was no clause preventing the maharaja from conducting his own independent diplomatic relations. Since the Treaty of Amritsar was vague regarding the boundary of the state west of the Indus in the area known as Dardistan, the maharaja was interested in bringing the neighbouring border states under his control. Chilas, on the route to Gilgit, already paid nominal tribute to Kashmir. Just before Gulab Singh's death, the Dogras had been obliged to give up the strategically placed area of Gilgit, bordering the independent kingdoms of Hunza and Nagar. In 1860 Ranbir Singh had sent a force which recaptured Gilgit and it was annexed to the state of Jammu and Kashmir. By the end of the decade Hunza and Nagar, traditional rivals, both paid tribute to the maharaja, in return for which they received an annual subsidy.

In view of these developments, the late 19th century saw a period of intense British interest in the sub-continent's northern frontier. Lord Mayo, who became viceroy in 1869 directed his policy towards Kashmir with Britain's imperial considerations firmly in mind. His successor, Lord Northbrook, did not object to permitting the maharaja to extend Kashmiri influence if, at the same time, it served British interests; Northbrook's thinking was accepted by Lord Lytton who took over as viceroy in 1876. Ranbir Singh, however, was most alarmed when the British proposed to station an Officer on Special Duty (OSD) in Gilgit, who would report directly to the British Government on border developments. When the viceroy and the maharaja met at Madophur in November 1876, their discussions nearly broke down. Only when Lord Lytton assured Ranbir Singh that the British would not interfere in the domestic management of the state, did he agree. Colonel John Bidduph was sent to Gilgit as the first British OSD in 1877.

Lytton had, however, also been exploring the possibility of redefining British relations with Afghanistan. He believed that the obvious estrangement of Sher Ali, the Amir of Afghanistan, from the British was due to their own neglect of him. Lytton proffered friendship and, in 1877, the British and Afghans met in Peshawar. Had their negotiations been successful, Britain's perceived need to rely on the maharaja of Jammu and Kashmir to safeguard the northern frontier might have diminished. As relations deteriorated with Sher Ali, however, leading to war in 1878, British reliance on the maharaja became more significant. Ranbir Singh was also playing his own game. Biddulph was not welcomed in Gilgit and the maharaja never fully co-operated with him. The ruler of Chitral, the Mehtar, who was obliged to accept Kashmiri suzerainty in 1878, was also an unwilling partner in the relationship. He was far more disposed to treat with his fellow Muslims in Afghanistan than with Hindus and 'Kafirs' on his eastern borders. In 1881 the Gilgit Agency was withdrawn. It had not proved to be a particularly valuable listening post and the maharaja was left to guard the northern frontier on his own. The premise of Lytton's policy was also that Kashmir was completely loyal to the British Government in preference to both Russia and Afghanistan. The maharaja, however, was found to have had dealings with both.

The significance of Kashmir, as the guardian of India's northern frontier, lay not only in its western border areas of Gilgit and Hunza, but also in the east because of Ladakh, which Gulab Singh had acquired in 1834. From Srinagar access to Leh led onwards to Khotan, Yarkand, and Kashgar in Turkestan. After the creation of the state of Jammu and Kashmir, one of the Boundary Commission's tasks was to define the borders of the new state, which was the first time Britain became officially aware of a route through Ladakh to China. As the Russian empire moved ever closer to the north-west frontier, the British became concerned that Russian interests might extend still further to Chinese Turkestan, which would deprive Britain of the opportunity of expanding their own commercial links in the region. The Manchu dynasty was in decline and Chinese rule over its Muslim subjects in Central Asia was greatly weakened after Chinese Muslims in Gansu had rebelled in 1861.

Ranbir Singh was not oblivious to the fluid situation on his northern frontier and attempted to take advantage of it to expand his trading links with eastern Turkestan. The maharaja's independent initiatives were, however, watched with concern by the British, who were still making up their minds as to the extent to which they would permit him to conduct an independent foreign policy. But, although in the decades to come, Central Asia became the arena for intense rivalry, Ladakh remained outside the field of immediate conflict for the rest of the century. Subsequent British attempts to define the border in the Aksai Chin were not reciprocated by the Chinese.[22] Thus the border and the area still under dispute between India and China was left ill-defined at the Kunlun range of mountains.

In 1882, Ranbir Singh had considered nominating his youngest son, Amar Singh, as his successor, since he was considered to be 'wiser' than his brothers Pratap or Ram. The maharaja repeated the request to the British again in 1884, but, when he died on 15 September 1885, the British chose to let his eldest son, Pratap Singh, ascend the throne; they stipulated, however, that a Resident Political Officer would be appointed, who would act as his adviser in the reform of the administration. On the same day Pratap Singh was installed as maharaja, Colonel O. St John was appointed resident. At the Darbar in 1885, the maharaja announced a series of reforms, which included abolition of state monopolies, reorganisation of the financial administration of the state, rationalisation of taxes, construction of roads and the removal of restrictions on emigration. But the reforms envisaged were, as later commentators observed, beyond the ability of the maharaja, whose officials were incapable and corrupt.[23]

The view expressed by St John after four months as resident, that the maharaja was unfit to rule, persisted throughout Pratap Singh's long reign. In 1886 the Government of India obliged the maharaja to appoint a new council which included his younger brothers Amar and Ram Singh. In 1887 a land settlement was instituted in order to redress the inequities which had existed in land tenure since the time of the Afghans and Sikhs. Walter Lawrence came to Kashmir in 1889 and was appointed settlement commissioner. He described the position of the people as worse than that of the Third Estate in France before the French Revolution.[24]

At the end of 1888 the residency disclosed that it had discovered over thirty letters of a treasonable nature from the maharaja to the Tsar. Although the maharaja denied having written them and it was subsequently proved they were forgeries, the episode was sufficient to undermine the last vestiges of confidence which the British had in the maharaja. On 1 April 1889, Pratap Singh was divested of all but nominal powers. The Council was comprised of his two brothers, two ministers and an English member 'specifically selected by the Government of India.' Amar Singh became prime minister, then president of the Council and executive head of the administration; the real power, however, lay with the British resident.

For the rest of the century, the major concern of the British was the possibility of a Russian invasion into the sub-continent. In 1888 Colonel Algernon Durand went to Gilgit to work out a defensive strategy which would utilise the recently formed Kashmir Imperial Service Troops. The viceroy, Lord Dufferin, had decided to make all the rulers of the princely states share in the defence of the Empire by contributing both men and money. When Durand returned from Gilgit, he reported to his brother, the foreign secretary of the Government of India, Sir Mortimer Durand, that he had heard that a Russian officer, Captain Grombchevsky, had been in Hunza. This news added to British fears that the Russians could pass through the Pamir mountains and that India was within range of their forces. The following year, in July 1889, Durand was sent back to Gilgit to re-establish the Gilgit Agency.

No sooner, however, had the British established themselves at Gilgit, than their position was once more threatened by the activities of the rulers of Hunza and Nagar, who made a temporary alliance and challenged the authority of the British. In one of the most famous actions of British imperial history, at the end of 1889, British troops succeeded in breaching the defences of the heavily fortified Hunza-Nagar forces along the Hunza river. Hunza and Nagar then became absorbed into the Gilgit Agency, over which the British subsequently obtained direct control. In peace time, the Gilgit garrison was manned by about 2000 Jammu and Kashmir state troops, paid for mostly by the Jammu and Kashmir State Treasury. It was not until 1913 that local troops were found to man the garrison with the foundation of the Corps of Gilgit Scouts.

In the late 19th century, Kashmir was already becoming famous for the rest and relaxation which it afforded European visitors from the heat of the plains. One of Srinagar's great attractions was the beautiful lake, Dal lake, on which people used to stay in boats, which developed into the houseboats of today. A century later, there were estimated to be fifteen hundred houseboats on Dal lake. Makers of shawls, embroidery, carpets, papier mâché boxes all benefited from the influx of holidaymakers, officers, with their wives and children, who arrived in the valley every summer. The presence of light-hearted holidaymakers was, however, in total contrast to the harshness of the lives of the local people, most of whom lived in abject poverty. Only a small minority, centred around the Dogra rulers, enjoyed unparalleled affluence. Europeans also made their presence felt as doctors and teachers. As in other parts of the Empire, under the direction of the Church Missionary Society, the British founded mission schools and hospitals. Canon Tyndale Biscoe, who arrived in Srinagar in 1890, took over as headmaster of the Mission School, founded by the Reverend Doxey in 1882. He remained in Kashmir for fifty years and made himself famous by sending the boys onto the streets to put out fires, which occurred regularly. He also insisted that the boys learn to swim, which had been considered improper, so that they could help save lives during frequent flooding.

Ever since his deposition, Pratap Singh held his brother, Amar Singh, responsible for all his problems. In 1889 he wrote to the viceroy, Lord Lansdowne, begging to be reinstated and if that was not possible, for the viceroy to shoot him 'through the heart with your Excellency's hands, and thus at once relieve an unfortunate prince from unbearable misery, contempt and disgrace for ever.'[25] Although the viceroy declined to reinstate Pratap Singh or to shoot him, other Indian princes were not happy with the unprecedented British interference in Kashmir. The Indian press had also taken up the cause of Pratap Singh and had requested Charles Bradlaugh, a well-known exponent of free speech, to attend the recently formed Indian National Congress in 1889 in order to focus attention on the deposition of Pratap Singh. Although Bradlaugh was criticised for pleading the cause of a Hindu 'despot', rather than focusing on the plight of the poor Muslims, the maharaja was gradually rehabilitated. Successive residents and viceroys did not, however, have any faith in his administrative ability. When, in 1891 the council was reconstituted and the maharaja was offered the presidency, Amar remained as prime minister. Only when Amar Singh died in 1909, did the long feud between the brothers finally end. In 1905 the viceroy, Lord Curzon, abolished the council and nominal power was restored to the Maharaja. The Government of India retained control over the finances of the state, the armed forces, tax, appointments to administrative services and foreign relations. The maharaja also had to follow the advice of the British resident whenever it was offered to him.

In order to improve the administration of the Kashmiri government, the Government of India had prescribed the appointment of 'respectable' officials amongst the principal measures of reform. The lack of educated or trained Kashmiris to fulfil these positions meant that Bengalis and Punjabis from British India were introduced into the administration, which upset the local Kashmiris. While the poor people were burdened with taxes, the middle classes felt resentful. When the Kashmiri Pandits benefited from better education, the Muslims, although numerically superior, remained excluded. As Canon Tyndale Biscoe had noted: 'the Mohammedan did not send their sons to school as all government service was closed to them.'[26] The All India Muslim Kashmiri Conference, formed in 1896 and supported by many Muslim Kashmiris who had settled mainly in the Punjab, was, however, beginning to support Kashmiris in the state, both morally and financially, by offering scholarships for them to study in British India. In 1905 the Mirwaiz, the religious leader of the Muslims of the valley, formed an association, the Anjuman-i Nusrat-ul Islam, whose objective was to improve the condition of the Muslims, especially in education.

Initially, political awareness in the state of Jammu and Kashmir was not linked to the movement for 'responsible' government which was making itself increasingly evident to the British in the opening decades of the 20th century, spearheaded by the activities of the Indian National Congress, founded in 1885, and the Muslim League, which was established in 1906. The 1906 reforms, sponsored by the Earl of Morley, as secretary of state, and Lord Minto, the viceroy, were designed to give the people of British India wider opportunities of expressing their views on how they should be governed, but this did not apply to the 565 states, some of which were no larger than a landed estate, others of which, like Jammu and Kashmir, were as large as some European countries.[27]

During the 1914–1918 World War, the Indians from both British India and the princely states had demonstrated their loyalty to the British Crown by their willing support of the war effort. 'They have shown that our quarrel is their quarrel ... they were a profound surprise and disappointment to the enemy; and a cause of delight and pride to those who knew beforehand the Princes' devotion to the Crown.'[28] Throughout the war, Pratap Singh placed all the forces of the state of Jammu and Kashmir at the disposal of the British. Contingents of Kashmiri forces fought in East Africa, Egypt, Mesopotamia and France. They also took part in operations which led to the defeat of the Turks in Palestine. While the Indians fought on behalf of the British Empire overseas, within British India, the Indian politicians were exerting pressure to increase the pace of change. In response, on 20 August 1917, the secretary of state for India announced in the House of Commons that the policy of the government was for 'increasing association of Indians in every branch of the administration and the gradual development of self-governing institutions with a view to the progressive realisation of responsible government in India as an integral part of the British Empire'.[29]

The implementation of this declaration was subsequently embodied in the Montagu-Chelmsford reforms, effected by an Act of 1919. In their report the secretary of state and the viceroy recognised that the rulers of the princely states would undoubtedly want a share in any control, 'if control of matters common to India as a whole is shared with some popular element in the government.' They also pointed to 'a stronger reason why the present stir in British India cannot be a matter of indifference to the Princes. Hopes and aspirations may overleap frontier lines like sparks across a street … No one would be surprised if constitutional changes in British India quickened the pace in the native states as well.'[30] The Montagu-Chelmsford recommendation was for all the important states, of which Jammu and Kashmir was one, to have direct political relations with the Government of India since 'the trend of events' would inevitably draw the princely states still closer into the 'orbit of empire'. The recommendation was to set up a consultative body, the Chamber of Princes.

Within Jammu and Kashmir, Pratap Singh was trying to reassert full power over his state. In October 1918 he made another request and, the following year, a few procedural changes were agreed. In 1920 he appealed again, pointing out that it was 'high time' – after nearly thirty years – that the restrictions were removed. On 4 February 1921 the maharaja was restored full powers, on condition only that the resident's advice would be accepted by the maharaja whenever it was offered. A new executive council was established, of which Hari Singh, his nephew and heir, the son of Amar Singh, became a member. Yet another scheme for reform was introduced. Amongst those who also gave vocal support to the Kashmiri Muslims was the influential and widely respected poet, Allama Sir Muhammad Iqbal. He first visited Kashmir in 1921 and put to verse his distress at the poverty of the people:

'In the bitter chill of winter shivers his naked body
Whose skill wraps the rich in royal shawls.'[31]

Leading Muslim newspapers in India continued to point to the progress of the Kashmiri Pandits at the expense of the Muslims. In the Spring of 1924 the predominantly Muslim workers of the state-owned silk factory demanded an increase in wages and the transfer of a Hindu clerk, whom they alleged was extorting bribes. Although the workers were given a minimal wage increase, some of their leaders were arrested, which led to a strike. As later reported in a representation to the viceroy, Lord Reading: 'Military was sent for and most inhuman treatment was meted out to the poor, helpless, unarmed peace-loving labourers who were assaulted with spears, lances and other implements of warfare.' The representation, signed by the two chief religious leaders, and submitted to the viceroy, also referred to other grievances:

'The Mussulmans of Kashmir are in a miserable plight today. Their education needs are woefully neglected. Though forming 96 per cent of the population, the percentage of literacy amongst them is only 0.8 per cent…. So far we have patiently borne the State's indifference towards our grievances and our claims and its high-handedness towards our rights, but patience has its limit and resignation its end…. the Hindus of the state, forming merely 4 per cent of the whole population are the undisputed masters of all departments.'[32]

When the viceroy, Lord Reading, forwarded the representation to Pratap Singh, an inquiry was made, but the conclusion of the Kashmir Darbar was that the protesters were 'sedition mongers'. The signatories of the representation were reprimanded; some were banished from the state, while others apologised. For its part, the Government of India saw no reason to interfere with the discretion of the Kashmir Darbar or the resident.[33]

The last Maharaja

By the time Pratap Singh died on 25 September 1925, he was 'a courteous tho' opium sodden old gentleman.'[34] When Lieutenant-General His Highness Inder Mahander Rajrajeshwar Maharajadhiraj Sir Hari Singh succeeded to the throne, there was cautious optimism that he would prove a more effective ruler than his uncle. The peoples' enthusiasm for the new ruler, however, was at once dampened by his lavish coronation costing millions of rupees. The alienation of the Kashmiris to Hari Singh was heightened by the continuing presence of 'outsiders' in government service, which led to a movement known as 'Kashmir for the Kashmiris', sponsored by the more educated Kashmiri Pandits. In 1927 a law defining a 'Hereditary State Subject' was passed forbidding the employment of non-state subjects in the public services; they were also not allowed to purchase land (hence the attraction of the houseboats to British holidaymakers). But, to the disappointment of the Kashmiris, the top positions were invariably filled by people from Jammu, especially the ruling class of the Dogra Rajputs. When the Pandits also began to improve their status in government service, this aggravated the Muslims still further. No Muslim in the valley was allowed to carry a firearm and they were not allowed in the army. The only Muslims who were recruited, normally under the command of a Dogra officer, were the Suddhans of Poonch and the Sandans from Mirpur; culturally and linguistically distinct from the Kashmiris of the valley, the maharaja believed he could depend on them to suppress whatever trouble might arise in the valley.

Soon after Hari Singh became maharaja, a campaign against his autocratic rule was orchestrated by both the Hindus and Muslims. The Lahore Muslim press had been consistently highlighting the condition of the Muslim Kashmiris and newspapers critical of the maharaja were sent into the state. At the same time, small groups joined together to discuss their grievances. In 1929 Ghulam Abbas, a Muslim from Jammu, who had obtained a law degree in Lahore, reorganised the Anjuman-i Islam into the Young Men's Muslim Association of Jammu, to work for the betterment of Muslims. In Srinagar the Reading Room Party, comprising a number of graduates from Aligarh Muslim University[35] in British India, rose to prominence. Prem Nath Bazaz, Ghulam Abbas, Muhammad Yusuf Shah were all active in discussing their grievances. In 1931 Yusuf Shah succeeded his uncle as Mirwaiz in Srinagar. He used his position in the mosque to organise a series of meetings, which protested against the maharaja's government. After being educated at Aligarh, another rising political activist, Sheikh Mohammad Abdullah, returned to the valley in 1930, just as the political turmoil in Kashmir was beginning. He too became a member of the Reading Room Party and rose to prominence as the 'Lion of Kashmir'.

Kashmir was already like the proverbial powder keg. The spark was provided by a butler in the service of a European, Abdul Qadir, who, in July 1931, made a fiery speech calling for the people to fight against oppression.[36] When he was arrested, crowds mobbed the jail, and several others were also arrested. There were further protests at which point the police fired on the crowd. Twenty-one people died. Their bodies were carried in procession to the centre of the town. Hindu shops were broken into and looted. The government retaliated with further arrests. 'Our Dogra rulers unleashed a reign of terror,' recalled Abdullah, who was amongst the many hundreds of young protesters arrested after what became known as the 'Abdul Qadir incident'.[37] Under pressure from the British resident, Hari Singh appointed a commission, headed by Sir Bertrand Glancy, a senior officer in the political department of the Government of India, to inquire into the complaints of the people. In April 1932 Glancy presented his report which recommended reforms for the development of education, the appointment of government servants and the establishment of industries to create employment opportunities. Glancy's recommendations were later supplemented by the Reform Conference, which proposed that a legislative assembly should be set up. Known as the Praja Sabha, it was to have seventy-five members, but, of its sixty non-official representatives, only thirty-three were to be elected, leaving the maharaja with the majority vote.

While Sheikh Abdullah and the other political leaders were detained in Srinagar Central Jail, they discussed the formation of a political party, which they decided to call the 'Muslim Conference.' Released from prison in June 1932, Abdullah became President and Ghulam Abbas the first General Secretary. A hallmark of Abdullah's political struggle was his insistence that the fight was against the oppression of both the Muslim and Hindu poorer classes. His continuing emphasis on secularism, however, eventually led to an internal disagreement, which also had some foundation in religious differences amongst the Muslims. Several of the prominent Muslim leaders, including Mirwaiz Muhammad Yusuf Shah, broke away.

While Maharaja Hari Singh was being made increasingly aware of a new more vociferous discontent within his state, he was also actively participating in the discussions which the British had instigated to determine how best to answer the clamour for 'responsible' government throughout India. Following the Montagu-Chelmsford recommendation for a consultative body to be set up, the Chamber of Princes was instituted, which included 108 rulers in their own right and 12 representatives of 127 smaller States. When the first Round Table Conference met in the House of Lords in London from November

1930 to January 1931 to discuss the future of the sub-continent, all the princes, including Hari Singh endorsed the statement of the Maharaja of Bikaner for an all-India federation. The starting point for their future relationship, he said, 'must be sought, not in the dead land of an impossible uniformity, but in an associated diversity.' A unitary state would be impossible and would 'crack under its own ponderability.'[38] Two further Round Table Conferences elaborated on the scheme for federation.

By the early 1930s the British had once more become alarmed at the activities of the Soviet Union in Sinkiang, which they perceived threatened Gilgit directly. Even though much of their anxiety was without foundation, certain British officials, among them Olaf Caroe, the deputy secretary in the Indian foreign department, argued forcefully for resuming direct control over Gilgit. There was also the belief that, so long as the British had maintained exclusive control over the maharaja's foreign affairs, as they had during the reign of Pratap Singh, they could be sure that the Jammu and Kashmir forces could be relied upon to act on behalf of the Government of India in an emergency over the northern frontier. Since the maharaja was now conducting his own foreign policy and did not appear to regard the frontier as 'sacrosanct' as the British, the time seemed right for a reassessment both of the costs of maintaining the agency and its direction. After over two years of discussion, the maharaja suggested that he would either take over responsibility for the defence of Gilgit, provided he did not have to share administration with the political agent; alternatively, he was prepared to hand over all responsibility to the Government of India. Despite their concerns of the financial costs, the British favoured the second alternative. The result of subsequent negotiations was the lease by the British of the Gilgit Agency north of the Indus for a period of sixty years from 26 March 1935.

In 1935 the suggestion made at the Round Table Conferences for an all-India federation was formulated into the Government of India Act. The legislation provided for autonomous legislative bodies in the eleven provinces of British India, as well as the creation of a central Government which would represent the provinces and the princely states. It also stipulated that Muslim minorities would be protected. The following year, elections to the legislative bodies were held. The Congress Party was able to form governments in seven of the eleven provinces. The Muslim League was not in a position, however, to form a government in any province and coalition governments were therefore formed in the remaining provinces. Although the princely states represented only a quarter of the population, they were given over a third of the seats in the federal legislature. The viceroy, Lord Linlithgow, invited the rulers of the Indian princely states to join the federation as provinces of British India. Despite their earlier support for an all-India federation, however, they raised various objections and all refused to enter it.

The Government of India Act marked the beginning of the next stage in Britain's deliberations over how India should become self-governing. Amidst

3. The Gilgit Agency, 1930
(Source: Charles Chenevix-Trench, *The Frontier Scouts*, London, 1985)

the changing proposals, and the shifting attitude of the Congress Party and
Muslim League leaders, the idea of some sort of a federation remained a
constant feature. As the largest and most northerly princely state, strategically
located on the borders of China and the Soviet Union, the state of Jammu and
Kashmir could have played a key role in future negotiations. Hari Singh,
however, never seemed to have given the future of his state nor indeed the
sub-continent the consideration it deserved. At the end of August 1938 the
Kashmiri political leaders once more took to the streets to protest against
unemployment, high taxes, revenue demands and lack of medical facilities.
Muslims, Hindus, Sikhs made common cause and went to jail together. As
soon as they emerged from prison at the beginning of March 1939, they once
more reiterated their commitment to secularism. On 11 June 1939, the Muslim

Conference finally changed its name to the 'National Conference'. Abdullah's adherence to secularism brought him closer to the rising Congress Party leader, Jawaharlal Nehru, who promised a secular and socialist India.

Any movement towards self-government was, however, halted by Britain's – and consequently British India's – involvement in World War II. On 3rd September 1939, the viceroy, Lord Linlithgow, issued a proclamation that war had broken out between Britain and Germany and that there was a state of 'war emergency' in India. The divergent responses of the Congress Party and the Muslim League to the war demonstrated the growing rift between them. Congress politicians objected to their involvement in the war without prior consultation with their representatives and used the issue of their cooperation in order to bargain for immediate independence. Mohammad Ali Jinnah, leader of the Muslim League, used Muslim support of the war effort to demand representation in any decisions regarding the Muslims of India. As an expression of their dissatisfaction, the seven Congress ministries, which had formed governments after the 1936 elections in British India, resigned. In March 1940 Nehru condemned a war 'for imperialist ends' to which the Congress could not in any way be party.'[39]

Nehru's response to Britain's war effort coincided with a dramatic change in the Muslim League's strategy to secure the interests of the Muslims of the sub-continent. On 23 March 1940 the Muslim League adopted its 'Pakistan resolution' at Lahore, which declared 'that the areas in which the Muslims are numerically in a majority, as in the north-western and eastern zones of India, should be grouped to constitute "independent states" in which the constituent units shall be autonomous and sovereign.'[40] As President of the Muslim League, Mohammad Ali Jinnah, endorsed the resolution: 'To yoke together two such nations (as the Hindus and Muslims) under a single state, one as a numerical minority and the other as a majority, must lead to growing discontent.'

Although it was not clear how such a proposal would be formalised, the demand for a separate homeland for the Muslims of the sub-continent – on the basis that there were two nations – Muslims and Hindus – had its origin in a plan, first proposed by a student, Chaudhuri Rahmat Ali in Cambridge in 1933: that the Muslims living in Punjab, North-West Frontier Province (Afghan Province) Kashmir, Sindh and Balochistan, should be recognised as a distinct nation, PAKSTAN, later called 'Pakistan'. The scheme had been drawn up for the Muslim delegates of the Round Table Conference, but since it involved a massive transfer of people, it was dismissed by the delegates as 'a student's scheme' which was 'chimerical' and 'impractical'.[41] The inclusion of the predominantly Muslim state of Jammu and Kashmir, however, was an early indication that there was already a body of opinion which believed that the princely state should become part of Pakistan, if and when it could be achieved. After alternative avenues for a federation of British India and the princely states had been exhausted, and partition of the sub-continent took place, this opinion held fast.

As the war continued, both the Congress Party and the Muslim League continued to press for a plan for independence which would suit their varying objectives within a nominally united India. The entry of Japan into the war in 1941 and the threat of a Japanese invasion of the sub-continent did not inspire any of the political leaders to consider a compromise either with the British or amongst themselves. On 11 March 1942, four days after Rangoon fell to the Japanese, the British Prime Minister, Winston Churchill, announced that Sir Stafford Cripps, a member of the British war cabinet, would visit India with a 'draft declaration' on eventual independence after the war was over. Faced with the possibility, however, that Japan might be successful in invading India, there was little inclination amongst the political leaders to take Cripps' mission seriously. Churchill was also not inclined to give the political situation in India sufficient attention. The culmination of the Congress Party's civil disobedience movement was Gandhi's Quit India movement in August 1942 which led to the arrest of the main Congress Party leaders. By the end of 1943, India was comparatively calm and the acts of sabotage had decreased. The new viceroy, Field-Marshal Lord Wavell, who replaced Lord Linlithgow in October 1943, was committed to bringing the war to a successful conclusion against the Japanese. Politics initially had to come second; but, as British victory both in Europe and the Far East became assured, Wavell became increasingly drawn into the difficult task of working out how the sub-continent could become independent.

In the state of Jammu and Kashmir, Hari Singh, one of the two Indian representatives of the Imperial War Cabinet, lent assistance in World War II. In 1941 he went on a tour of the Middle East to meet the Kashmiri troops who were on active service there. Political activity in his state was not, however, in abeyance. Those Muslims who were discontented with Abdullah's pro-Congress stance, especially the non-Kashmiri speakers, became staunch supporters of the Muslim League. In 1941 Ghulam Abbas broke with Abdullah and joined with Mirwaiz Yusuf Shah in reviving the Muslim Conference, which eventually came out in support of the movement for Pakistan. In Jammu, the Muslims did not have the same majority status which they enjoyed in the valley. They were therefore liable to feel more threatened by the prospect of being governed by a Hindu-majority.

Sheikh Abdullah meanwhile busied himself with his plans for a 'New Kashmir' in what was one of the most advanced socialist programmes of its time. As Abdullah admitted, initially 'New Kashmir' was opposed by 'reactionary' elements from amongst both the Hindus and Muslims, but eventually the Indian National Congress Party approved the manifesto. Abdullah's own position as the most dominant of the Muslim leaders in the valley, as well as the strength of his friendship with Jawaharlal Nehru, who he is recorded as having first met in 1937, was a key factor in determining the future course of events. Had Abdullah ever developed any understanding with Mohammad Ali Jinnah, or had, for example, Ghulam Abbas or another political figure taken Abdullah's place as a popular leader, the future of Kashmir could have been very different.[42] But Abbas, born in Jullundur, was not a 'State Subject' and, since he came from Jammu, he did not speak Kashmiri. His appeal amongst the valley Kashmiris was therefore reduced. When Mohammad Ali Jinnah visited the valley of Kashmir in 1944 he also recognised the absence of a 'presentable' Kashmiri speaking leader. Attempts to find a leader who could challenge Sheikh Abdullah, including the suggestion that Ghulam Abbas learn Kashmiri, failed.

The stand which both the Congress Party and the Muslim League adopted towards the princely states was also an important factor in determining future events. Jawaharlal Nehru and the Congress Party had defined their position on the Indian states in August 1935: 'The Indian National Congress recognises that the people in the Indian states have an inherent right of Swaraj (independence) no less than the people of British India. It has accordingly declared itself in favour of establishment of representative responsible Government in the States.'[43] On the other hand, Jinnah and the Muslim League made it clear that they did not wish to interfere with the internal affairs of the princely states. Despite Rahmat Ali's 1933 description of Kashmir as forming part of Pakistan, Jinnah's main focus of attention remained with British India: 'We do not wish to interfere with the internal affairs of any State, for that is a matter primarily to be resolved between the rulers and the peoples of the States.'[44]

Once the war was over, the new British Labour Government under Prime Minister Clement Attlee, elected in March 1945, initiated further steps towards giving independence to British India. In March 1946 Sir Stafford Cripps returned to India, as part of a three-man team, in order to propose a new Cabinet Mission plan. The objective was to try and reach agreement on the establishment of a constituent assembly, which would draft the constitution of a self-governing but united India. The Cabinet Mission also proposed creating an interim government composed of Indian politicians, who would assume control of important departments of state. As the Congress Party and the Muslim League argued over acceptance of the Cabinet Mission plan (which they both finally rejected), Wavell moved ahead with the formation of the interim government. Initially Jinnah refused to join it because he was not permitted to nominate all the Muslim members of the government from the Muslim League. On 2 October 1946, the members of the new interim government were sworn into office without the Muslim League's participation. Nehru assumed control of the foreign affairs portfolio as well as becoming vice-president of the executive council. Sardar Patel took over the home department. When Jinnah finally agreed to participate in the interim government, these important ministries were already in the hands of the Congress Party. After the decision was taken to partition the sub-continent in 1946, the interim government, effectively controlled by the Congress Party, set up a States ministry. Its specific task was to encourage the princely states to join India or the new dominion of Pakistan either by acts of accession or 'standstill' agreements. In retrospect, that the Muslim League did not join the interim government at the outset meant that it lost the opportunity to attain parity with the Congress Party at 'the most important moment in the demission of British authority'.[45]

The announcement that full ruling powers would be returned to the rulers of the princely states left each of the 565 maharajas and nawabs with the responsibility of determining their own future. Only twenty were of sufficient size for their rulers to be in a position to make serious decisions about their future, of which one was the state of Jammu and Kashmir. Sheikh Abdullah objected to leaving the decision to the maharaja, who he maintained did not enjoy support from the majority of the people. Mirroring Gandhi's Quit India movement in 1942, Sheikh Abdullah launched a Quit Kashmir Movement, describing how 'the tyranny of the Dogras' had lacerated their souls. Abdullah's activities were, however, once more trying the patience of the authorities and when he attempted to visit Nehru in Delhi, he was arrested and put in prison. The prime minister, Ram Chandra Kak, placed the state under martial law. Other political activists, G.M.Sadiq, D.P.Dhar and Bakshi Ghulam Muhammad, escaped to Lahore, where they remained until after independence. Abdullah's Quit Kashmir movement had also come under criticism from his political opponents in the Muslim League, who charged that he had begun the agitation in order to boost his popularity, which he was losing because of his pro-India stance. In 1946, the leaders of the Muslim League were also taken into custody after Ghulam Abbas led a 'campaign of action' similar to Jinnah's in British India. Abbas and Abdullah were held in the same jail, where they discussed in night-long conversations the possibility of a reconciliation and resumption of the common struggle, which, as subsequent events showed, never materialised.

In a dramatic gesture, Nehru attempted to visit Kashmir in July 1946 with the intention of defending Abdullah at his trial. Although he was refused entry, he stood at the border for five hours until finally he was allowed in, only to be taken into protective custody, before being released. Karan Singh, the maharaja's son, believed that this episode marked a turning point in relations between his father's government and the future prime minister of India: instead of welcoming him and seeking his cooperation, they had arrested him! After the intercession of the viceroy, Lord Wavell, Nehru was subsequently permitted to enter the state and attend part of Abdullah's trial. The maharaja, however, refused to meet him on the grounds of ill health. In January 1947, even though the main political leaders of both parties remained in jail, Hari Singh called for fresh elections to the legislative assembly. The National Conference boycotted the elections, with the result that the Muslim Conference claimed victory. The National Conference, however, said that the low poll demonstrated the success of their boycott; the Muslim Conference attributed the low turnout because of the snows and claimed that the boycott was virtually ignored.

In the months preceding independence, Hari Singh appeared as a helpless figure caught up in a changing world, with which he was unable to keep pace. 'It has always seemed to me tragic that a man as intelligent as my father, and in many ways as constitutional and progressive, should have, in those last years, so grievously misjudged the political situation in the country,' writes Karan Singh. But, 'being a progressive ruler was one thing; coping with a once-in-a-millennium historical phenomenon was another.'[46] As Karan Singh also admits, his father was too much of a feudalist to be able to come to any real accommodation with the key protagonists in the changing order. He was also 'too much of a patriot to strike any sort of surreptitious deal' with the British. He was hostile to the Congress Party, dominated by Gandhi, Nehru and Patel, partly because of Nehru's close friendship with Abdullah. He was not able either to come to terms with the National Conference, because of the threat it posed to the Dogra dynasty. Although the Muslim League supported the rulers' right to determine the future of their states, Hari Singh opposed the communalism inherent in the League's two-nation theory. Thus, says Karan Singh, 'when the crucial moment came ... he found himself alone and friendless'.[47] Joining Pakistan would leave a substantial number of Hindus in Jammu as a minority, as well as Buddhists in Ladakh; joining India would be contrary to the advice given by the British that due consideration should be given to numerical majority and geographical contiguity. In retrospect, Karan Singh concluded that the only rational solution would have been to have initiated a peaceful partition of his state between India and Pakistan. 'But that would have needed clear political vision and careful planning over many years.'[48]

As ruler of the largest princely state, independence was also an attractive option. For this utopian dream, Karan Singh partly blamed the influence of a religious figure, Swami Sant Dev, who returned to Kashmir in 1946. The Swami encouraged the maharaja's feudal ambitions 'planting in my father's mind visions of an extended kingdom sweeping down to Lahore itself, where our ancestor Maharaja Gulab Singh and his brothers Raja Dhyan Singh and Raja Suchet Singh had played such a crucial role a century earlier.'[49] It also meant that when critical decisions had to be made, the maharaja did nothing. In hindsight, it also seems extraordinary how comparatively little influence the British assumed in assisting the maharaja with his decision. For over forty years, at the end of the 19th and the beginning of the 20th centuries, Britain had maintained virtual control over the state of Jammu and Kashmir. Yet, with the future peace and stability of the sub-continent hanging in the balance, the British government let the maharaja of Jammu and Kashmir pursue his destiny alone.

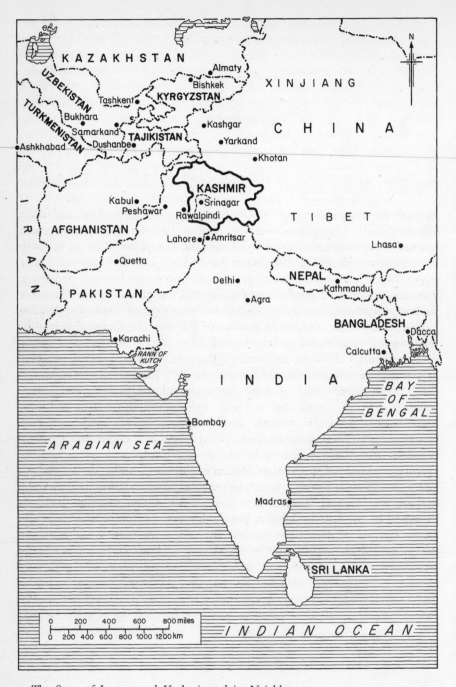

4. The State of Jammu and Kashmir and its Neighbours

CHAPTER 2

Independence

History seems sometimes to move with the infinite slowness of a glacier and sometimes to rush forward in a torrent. Lord Mountbatten[1]

By 1947 the independence of the sub-continent was assured. How and when still remained to be determined. On 20 February the British government announced 'its definite intention to take necessary steps to effect the transference of power to responsible Indian hands by a date not later than June 1948.' The last attempt to keep the sub-continent together as a federation had ended with the failure of the Cabinet Mission plan of 1946. Attempts to bring together the political leaders of the Congress Party and Muslim League were not successful. The concept of Pakistan, 'the dream, the chimera, the students' scheme', was to become reality.[2]

An indication of the shape which might constitute 'Pakistan' was provided by the viceroy, Field-Marshal Lord Wavell, in 1946. Known as the 'Breakdown Plan', his suggestion had been to give independence to the more homogeneous areas of central and southern India whilst maintaining a British presence in the Muslim majority areas in the north-west and north-east. Once agreement had been reached on final boundaries, the British would withdraw. Part of the inspiration behind the plan was to demonstrate how, by creating a country on the basis of Muslim majority areas only, Mohammad Ali Jinnah would be left with a 'husk', whereas he stood to gain much more by keeping the Muslims together in a loose union within a united India, as proposed by the Cabinet Mission plan.[3] Although the 'Breakdown' plan was finally rejected by the British government in January 1947, it had been the subject of serious consideration in the Cabinet in London, by the governors and in the viceroy's house, both before and after the failure of the Cabinet Mission plan. The significance of the plan in the context of future events is that, long before the British conceded that partition along communal lines was inevitable, there was already a plan in existence showing the geographical effect such a partition would have on the sub-continent.

In March 1947, Lord Wavell was replaced as viceroy by Rear-Admiral Lord Louis Mountbatten, whose brief from Prime Minister Attlee was 'to obtain a unitary government for British India and the Indian States, if possible.'[4] Soon after his arrival, Mountbatten made a gloomy assessment of trying to revive the Cabinet Mission plan: 'The scene here is one of unrelieved gloom . . . at this early stage I can see little common ground on which to build any agreed solution for the future of India.'[5] Although his initial discussions were not supposed to convey to the Indian political leaders that partition was inevitable, by the end of April, Mountbatten had concluded that unity was 'a very pious hope.'[6]

On 3 June the British government finally published a plan for the partition of the sub-continent. On 18 July the Indian Independence Act was passed, stating that independence would be effected on an earlier date than previously anticipated: 15 August 1947. As Mountbatten's press secretary was to note: 'Negotiations had been going on for five years; from the moment the leaders agreed to a plan, we had to get on with it.'[7] The sense of urgency was heightened by civil disturbances and riots between the communities, which were to reach frightening proportions in several areas, particularly in Punjab, which bordered the state of Jammu and Kashmir.

Lobbying for accession

Although the Cabinet Mission plan was rejected, the recommendations for the future of the 565 princely states, covering over two-fifths of the sub-continent, with a population of 99 million, became the basis for their future settlement. In a 'Memorandum on States' Treaties and Paramountcy' it was stated that the paramountcy which the princely states had enjoyed with the British Crown would lapse at independence because the existing treaty relations could not be transferred to any successor. The 'void' which would be created would have to be filled, either by a federal relationship or by 'particular political arrangements' with the successor government or governments, whereby the states would accede to one or other dominion.[8]

The state of Jammu and Kashmir had unique features not shared by other princely states. Ruled by a Hindu, with its large Muslim majority, it was geographically contiguous to both India and the future Pakistan. In view of a potential conflict of interest, there was 'pre-eminently a case for the same referendum treatment that the Frontier received,' writes W. H. Morris-Jones, constitutional adviser to Mountbatten. The North-West Frontier Province, with its strong Congress lobby, led by Khan Abdul Ghaffar Khan, opposed partition and favoured India. The decision was therefore put to the people in a referendum. (The Congress Party boycotted the referendum since the option of an independent 'Pashtunistan' was not included, and the Muslim League won an overwhelming majority.) A referendum in the state of Jammu and Kashmir would, says Morris-Jones, have been 'a carefully considered option – if only the States problem had been where it should have been in June, high on the Mountbatten agenda' – which it was not. By the time Mountbatten put forward the idea of a reference to the people in October, it was too late. 'He was no longer Viceroy and so no longer in a position to see it through as an integral part of the partition operation.'[9]

In hindsight, Sir Conrad Corfield, who was political adviser to the viceroy from 1945–47 also believed that, instead of listening to the advice of the Indian Political Department, Mountbatten preferred to take that of the Congress Party leaders. Corfield had suggested that if Hyderabad, second largest of the princely states, with its Hindu majority and Muslim ruler, and Kashmir, with its Hindu ruler and Muslim majority, were left to bargain after independence, India and Pakistan might well come to an agreement. 'The two cases balanced each other ... but Mountbatten did not listen to me ... Anything that I said carried no weight against the long-standing determination of Nehru to keep it [Kashmir] in India.'[10]

Although Jawaharlal Nehru's family had emigrated from the valley at the beginning of the eighteenth century, he had retained an emotional attachment to the land of his ancestors. This was reinforced by his friendship with Abdullah and the impending changes in the sub-continent. In the summer of 1947 Nehru planned to visit the valley in order to see Abdullah in prison. But, given the troubled situation, Mountbatten was reluctant for either him or Gandhi to go there and decided to take up a long-standing invitation from Hari Singh to visit Kashmir himself.

On 18 June the viceroy flew to Srinagar. He had with him a long note prepared by Nehru, which, on the basis of Sheikh Abdullah's popularity in the valley, made out a strong case for the state's accession to India:

> Of all the people's movements in the various States in India, the Kashmir National Conference was far the most widespread and popular . . . Kashmir has become during this past year an all-India question of great importance ... It is true that Sheikh Abdullah's long absence in prison has produced a certain confusion in people's minds as to what they should do. The National Conference has stood for and still stands for Kashmir joining the Constituent Assembly of India.

Nehru also pointed to the influence which the maharaja's prime minister, Ram Chandra Kak, had over him. Nehru held Kak responsible for the maharaja distancing himself from the National Conference and the possibility of joining the dominion of India. Most significantly, he made it clear to Mountbatten that what happened in Kashmir was:

> ... of the first importance to India as a whole not only because of the past year's occurrences there, which have drawn attention to it, but also because of the great strategic importance of that frontier State. There is every element present there for rapid and peaceful progress in co-operation with India.

He concluded by reaffirming Congress's deep interest in the matter and advising Mountbatten that, but for his other commitments, he would himself have been in Kashmir long ago.[11]

Although Pakistani accounts suggest that, from the outset, Mountbatten favoured Kashmir's accession to India, in view of his close association with Nehru, Mountbatten contended that he just wanted the maharaja to make up his mind. 'My chief concern was to persuade the Maharaja that he should decide which Dominion Kashmir should join, after consulting the wishes of his people and without undue pressure from either side, especially the Congress Leaders.'[12] He also brought the message from the Congress leaders that, if the maharaja were to decide in favour of Pakistan because of his Muslim majority population, they would not take it 'amiss'.[13]

During Mountbatten's short stay in Kashmir, the maharaja gave the viceroy very little opportunity to discuss the accession. As noted by his son, Karan Singh: 'Indecisive by nature, he merely played for time.'[14] Instead of taking advantage of Mountbatten's visit to discuss the future of the state, he sent Mountbatten on a fishing trip. Captain Dewan Singh, the maharaja's ADC, confirmed that Hari Singh had no intention of succumbing to any pressure: 'He told Mountbatten that he would consult with his people and meet with him the next day. The meeting was scheduled for 11 o'clock, but ten minutes before, the Viceroy was informed that the Maharaja was not feeling well. In fact the Maharaja did not want to meet Mountbatten again.'[15] On Mountbatten's return, his press secretary, Alan Campbell Johnson, noted that: 'Mountbatten had seen for himself the paralysis of Princely uncertainty.' The maharaja was 'politically very elusive'.[16]

Mountbatten believed, however, that he had succeeded in giving the maharaja some sound advice, which he hoped he would follow in due course. He suggested that the maharaja was not to join either of the constituent assemblies until the Pakistan Constituent Assembly had been set up and the situation was a bit clearer. He also advised that the maharaja should sign 'standstill' agreements with both India and Pakistan. Nehru was not pleased by the results. 'There was considerable disappointment at the lack of results of your visit,' he later wrote to the viceroy.[17]

When Lord Hastings Ismay, Mountbatten's chief of staff, visited Kashmir soon afterwards he received the same treatment as the viceroy: 'Each time that I tried to broach the question, the Maharaja changed the subject. Did I remember our polo match at Cheltenham in 1935? He had a colt which he thought might win the Indian Derby! Whenever I tried to talk serious business, he abruptly left me for one of his other guests.'[18] 'The Maharaja was in a Micawberish frame of mind, hoping for the best while continuing to do nothing,' observed former constitutional adviser V. P. Menon. 'Besides he was toying with the notion of an "independent Jammu & Kashmir"'.[19]

Despite the assurances given by Mountbatten to Hari Singh that the Congress leaders would not regard it as 'an unfriendly act',[20] if, given his Muslim majority population, he eventually acceded to Pakistan, it is clear that Nehru in particular had strong reasons for wanting the state of Jammu and Kashmir to accede to India. Furthermore, if the Muslim majority of the state of Jammu and Kashmir, under the popular leadership of Sheikh Abdullah, were to accede to India it would disprove the validity of Mohammad Ali Jinnah's two-nation theory.

Nehru was also supported by the formidable presence of Sardar Patel, who wrote to the maharaja on 3 July: 'I wish to assure you that the interest of Kashmir lies in joining the Indian Union without any delay. Its past history and traditions demand it, and all India looks up to you and expects you to take this decision.'[21] Sardar Patel's position in charge of the States Ministry in India, which he assumed on 5 July, gave him a unique platform from which to guide India's policy towards the states. He was to be assisted by V. P. Menon who already had intimate knowledge of the workings of the Government of India. Patel and Menon's influence persuaded Mountbatten to ensure adherence of the States before the lapse of British paramountcy, rather than leave them free to negotiate their future relationships with the successor states in what might potentially become turbulent conditions afterwards. Sardar Abdur Rab Nishtar and Mr Ikramullah were in charge of the States Ministry for Pakistan.

On 25 July, Mountbatten informed the Chamber of Princes that although their states would 'technically and legally' become independent, there were 'certain geographical compulsions' which could not be avoided. He therefore urged the princes to enter into 'standstill' agreements with the future authorities of India and Pakistan in order to make their own arrangements.[22] Although most of the states were too small to consider surviving on their own and geography determined their allegiance, three out of the 565 held back from taking any decision: Hyderabad, Junagadh and the state of Jammu and Kashmir.

When, at the end of July, Mountbatten heard that Nehru was once more planning to go to Kashmir he was not pleased: 'I called upon him as a matter of duty not to go running off to Kashmir until his new Government was firmly in the saddle and could spare his services.'[23] Mountbatten was obviously irritated by Nehru's insistence that he go to Kashmir and considered that a visit by Gandhi would be preferable, provided he did not make any inflammatory political speeches. In a confidential note to Colonel Wilfred Webb, the resident, Mountbatten had written: '[Nehru] is under very great strain and I consider that a visit by him to Kashmir at this moment could only produce a most explosive situation; whereas if His Highness can be persuaded to handle Gandhi tactfully, I believe there is a good chance that his visit could be passed off without any serious incident.'[24]

As Nehru persisted in attempting to visit Kashmir, Mountbatten continued to try and dissuade him. He noted that both the maharaja and his prime minister, Ram Chandra Kak, 'hate Nehru with a bitter hatred and I had visions of the Maharaja declaring adherence to Pakistan just before Nehru arrived and Kak provoking an incident which would end up by Nehru being arrested just about the time he should be taking over power from me in Delhi.' Mountbatten had also heard how, during a meeting with Patel, 'Nehru had broken down and wept, explaining that Kashmir meant more to him at the time than anything else.' After considerable correspondence between the

Congress leaders and the viceroy over whether Nehru or Gandhi would visit
Kashmir the issue was finally resolved by Sardar Patel, who believed that
neither should go but that in view of Pandit Nehru's great mental distress
if his mission in Kashmir were to remain unfulfilled, he agreed that one of
them must go. Mountbatten noted that Patel bluntly remarked: 'It is a choice
between two evils and I consider that Gandhiji's visit would be the lesser
evil.'[25]

The Congress leaders' interest in Kashmir evidently disturbed the future
leaders of Pakistan. The sub-continent was in the midst of a deep communal
and political crisis. Yet both Nehru and Gandhi had insisted on visiting
Kashmir. No Muslim leader visited the princely states of Hyderabad or
Junagadh, nor did they visit Kashmir. Nehru and Gandhi were both known
to be opposed to the maharaja making any declaration of independence. In
addition the princes of Patiala, Kapurthala, and Faridkot from east Punjab
visited Hari Singh in the summer, as well as the president of the Indian
National Congress, Acharya J. B. Kripalani. Why so many visitors, all of
whom must surely have had a vested interest in the advice they gave?

Gandhi finally left for Srinagar on 1 August. Muhammad Saraf was
amongst those who protested at his arrival in Baramula. 'The biggest, noisiest
demonstration was organised by me against Gandhi. Even some glass panes
of his car were broken by the demonstrators.' In the event, Gandhi's visit
passed off without any serious incident. But Saraf believed that during his
meeting with the maharaja and the maharani, he persuaded the maharaja to
accede to India.[26] 'Before his departure from Delhi the "Apostle of Truth"
announced that his tour was absolutely non-political,' writes Shahid Hamid,
private secretary to Field-Marshal Auchinleck. 'In reality it was to pressurise
the Maharaja to accede to India and to remove Kak.'[27]

The Muslim Conference in Srinagar, whose leaders remained in prison
after their 1946 agitation, was also perturbed by the potential impact of the
pro-India lobby in Kashmir. 'The trouble was that whereas the Congress said
that the people of the States will decide the future, the Muslim League was
continuing to stress that the rulers will decide,' says Mir Abdul Aziz.[28] In a
state like Hyderabad, ruled by the Muslim nizam there was a clear political
advantage in supporting the ruler, despite its location in the heart of India,
but with Jammu and Kashmir, the Muslim League was obliged to rely on the
wisdom of Hari Singh. 'I have no doubt that the Maharaja and the Kashmir
Government will give their closest attention and consideration to this matter
and realise the interests not only of the Ruler but also of his people,' Jinnah
had declared in July 1947. 'Wisdom demands that the feelings and sentiments
of the Muslims who form 80 per cent of the population should not be
ignored, much less hurt.'[29]

Unlike the Congress leaders, Jinnah had also endorsed the right of the
princely states to remain independent: 'If they wish to remain independent
and wish to negotiate or adjust any political or any other relationship such

as commercial or economic relations with Pakistan, we shall be glad to discuss with them.'[30] He was not alone in this view. Sir Walter Monckton, adviser to the government of Hyderabad, believed that provided the princely states were 'fairly treated' they had 'a sounder hope of survival than the brittle political structure of the Congress Party after they have attained independence.'[31]

The Boundary Commission

An extraordinary feature of the partition of the sub-continent, which was effected on the day of its independence from British rule, is that the details were not officially revealed in advance. Lord Ismay explained that, in his opinion, the announcement was 'likely to confuse and worsen an already dangerous situation.'[32] There were, however, enough areas of concern in the border districts to arouse the interest of Hindus, Muslims and Sikhs as to where exactly the partition would be effected.

The Partition Plan of 3 June 1947, established under the Indian Independence Act, envisaged two Boundary Commissions, consisting of four High Court judges each, two nominated by Congress and two by the Muslim League. The chairman was to hold the casting vote. The man entrusted with that post was a British lawyer, Sir Cyril Radcliffe, who arrived in India for the first time on 8 July 1947. The objective of what came to be known as the Radcliffe Award was to divide the provinces of Punjab in the west and Bengal in the east, leaving those Muslim majority areas in Pakistan and those with Hindu majorities in India. There was, however, a loose provision that 'other factors' should be taken into account, without specifying what they might be. Radcliffe had just five weeks to accomplish the task.

Since the state of Jammu and Kashmir adjoined British India, the partition of the sub-continent was relevant insofar as where the existing lines of communication would fall. Of the main routes by which Kashmir could be reached, two roads passed through areas which could be expected to be allocated to Pakistan: the first via Rawalpindi, Murree, Muzaffarabad, Baramula and thence to Srinagar – the route so treacherously undertaken in winter by Sher Singh, when he was governor of Kashmir in the 1840s; the other route went via Sialkot, Jammu and the Banihal pass. A third route, which was no more than a dirt track, existed via the district of Gurdaspur, which comprised the four tehsils of Shakargarh, Batala, Gurdaspur and Pathankot. A railway line from Amritsar passed through Gurdaspur tehsil and on to Pathankot. Another railway line went from Jullundur as far as Mukerian; from there the journey could be continued directly to Pathankot on another unsurfaced track via Bhangala by crossing the Beas river by ferry. From Pathankot the route carried on to Madophur, across the Ravi river to Kathua in the state of Jammu and Kashmir.

Under the 'notional' award provided in the first Schedule of the Indian

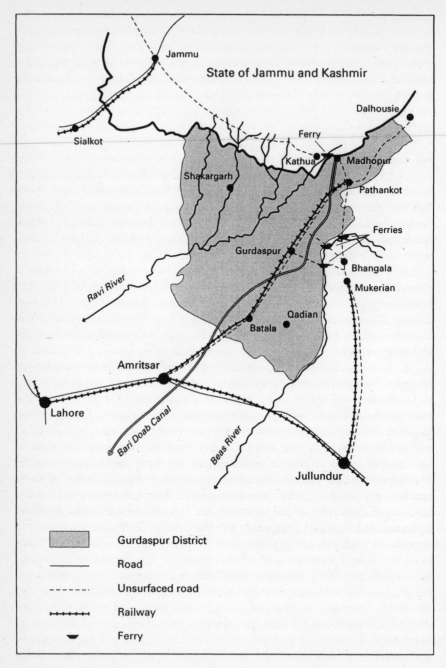

5. Gurdaspur District and Access to the State of Jammu and Kashmir
(Source: Royal Geographical Society Collection. Published under the direction of the
Surveyor-General of India, revised 1937)

Independence Act, all of the Gurdaspur district, with a 51.14 per cent Muslim majority had been assigned to Pakistan, which meant that all these routes would have fallen under the control of Pakistan. At his press conference on 4 June, in answer to a question regarding provisional and final demarcations, Mountbatten, however, suggested that the Boundary Commission would be unlikely 'to throw' the whole of the Gurdaspur district into the Muslim majority areas.[33] Of Gurdaspur district's four tehsils, one, Pathankot, was predominantly Hindu. Subsequently, the revised Mountbatten plan referred to the basis for partition by area rather than by district. The future Pakistanis soon became concerned by the prospect of a departure from the 'notional' award giving all of Gurdaspur district to Pakistan to one where part of Gurdaspur would be allocated to India. Chaudhri Muhammad Ali, one of the two joint secretaries on the Partition Council, suggested that it was 'highly improper' for Mountbatten to be commenting on the likely award. According to his account, his suspicions were confirmed when, upon instructions from Jinnah, he visited Mountbatten's chief of staff, Lord Ismay, on 9 August to talk about Gurdaspur. At first Ismay did not appear to understand Chaudhri Muhammad's concern. 'There was a map hanging in the room and I beckoned him to the map so that I could explain the position to him with its help. There was a pencil line drawn across the map of the Punjab.' The line followed the boundary along the Ravi river, which Jinnah had heard was to be drawn, allocating three of the four tehsils in Gurdaspur district to India. 'Ismay turned pale and asked in confusion who had been fooling with his map.'[34] Ismay, however, does not refer to this incident in his memoirs.

In the final award the three tehsils of Batala, Gurdaspur and Pathankot went to India. A memorandum prepared by the minister of state, which included Radcliffe's observations after he returned to England, reported that the reason for changing the 'notional' award regarding Gurdaspur was because 'the headwaters of the canals which irrigate the Amritsar District lie in the Gurdaspur District and it is important to keep as much as possible of these canals under one [i.e. Indian] administration.'[35] Wavell, however, had made a more significant political judgement in his plan, submitted to the secretary of state, Lord Pethick-Lawrence, in February 1946: 'Gurdaspur must go with Amritsar for geographical reasons and Amritsar being sacred city of Sikhs must stay out of Pakistan ... Fact that much of Lahore district is irrigated from upper Bari Doab canal with headworks in Gurdaspur district is awkward but there is no solution that avoids all such difficulties.' Wavell had also noted the problem this would create by leaving Qadian, the holy city of the Ahmadiyyas, in India, but the interests of the Sikhs were considered to be paramount. 'The greatest difficulty is position of Sikhs with their homelands and sacred places on both sides of the border. This problem is one which no version of Pakistan can solve.'[36] The Boundary Commission was supposed to be working in absolute secrecy and Radcliffe's award has always been presented as entirely original, even though in its final form, apart from the

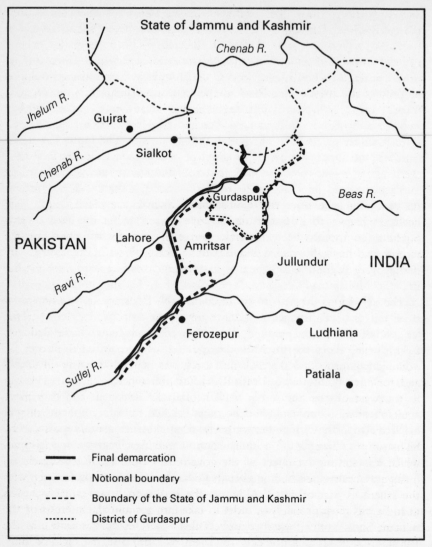

6. Partition Boundaries in the Punjab
(Source: Nicholas Mansbergh, (ed.) *The Transfer of Power*, 1942–47, Vol XII, London, (1983)

award of the Chittagong Hills in Bengal, which Wavell gave to India and Radcliffe awarded to Pakistan, the two plans are remarkably similar. Wavell, however, emphasised more strongly the British fear of upsetting the Sikhs as a key factor in determining the award of Gurdaspur to India.

It is also clear from correspondence emanating from the viceroy's house that the element of secrecy was selective. Mountbatten had chosen not to announce the partition plan until after independence in order not to 'mar' the celebrations, but this did not mean that advance information could not be given to the governors 'so that the best dispositions might be made of military forces and police.'[37] On 8 August Sir George Abell, Mountbatten's private secretary, who had also worked under Wavell and had been in London to present the 'Breakdown Plan' to the Cabinet in January 1947, wrote to Stuart Abbott, secretary to Sir Evan Jenkins, the governor of the Punjab, a 'top secret' letter: 'I enclose a map showing roughly the boundary which Sir Cyril Radcliffe proposes to demarcate in his award.'[38] Lord Ismay also asked for 'such advance information as could be given me of the award, so that the military and civil authorities directly concerned with law and order might make their plans, and if necessary redistribute their forces.' He did not address his request to the Boundary Commission 'with whose proceedings I had nothing whatever to do, but to the Viceroy's house.'[39] When this letter became public a few months later, it merely increased Pakistani suspicions that the viceroy and his staff were well aware of the disposition of the award. And if they were aware of it, might they also, for their own reasons, seek to alter it?

The suspicions created in the minds of the Pakistanis by the award of three tehsils of Gurdaspur to India were compounded by the issue of the 'salient' of the Ferozepur and Zira tehsils. In the map of the Radcliffe award, which Abell sent to Abbot, the salient, which protruded beyond the notional boundary into the Sikh heartland, was marked as part of Pakistan and, for once, did not accord with Radcliffe's preference for keeping Pakistan to the west of the Sutlej, but was theoretically designed to give a more equitable share of control over the canal headworks. A day after Abell sent his letter to Abbott, together with the map, the first serious massacre by Sikhs of prominent Muslim bureaucrats on the 'first Pakistan special' train which was shifting members of the government from Delhi to Karachi on 9 August occurred. Sometime after this date the boundary was finalised with the salient as part of India. Although the reason for its eventual inclusion in India was most probably in order to take into account the interests of the militant Sikhs rather than to deprive Pakistan of territory, sensitive as the Pakistanis were, it was not easy for them to rationalise the logic of draft awards which went in their favour, on the basis of Muslim majorities, only to be removed because of 'other factors.' 'It is very strange that other factors should have worked consistently in favour of India and against Pakistan,' commented Chaudhri Muhammad Ali.[40] Ironically, Wavell had not awarded the salient to Pakistan in the first place, probably because, as with the award of Gurdaspur, he was more concerned about the Sikhs.

The departure from the 'notional' award to Radcliffe's division of Gurdaspur between the two Dominions has created considerable bitterness, not only because of the loss of territory, but because of the growing realisation that India was thereby assured of access to the state of Jammu and Kashmir. Although the future of the princely states was a separate issue from the division of the Punjab and Bengal, for which purpose the Boundary Commission was instituted, Mountbatten himself had made the connection between Jammu and Kashmir and the award of the Boundary Commission. Kashmir, he said, 'was so placed geographically that it could join either Dominion, provided part of Gurdaspur were put into East Punjab by the Boundary Commission.'[41] V. P. Menon, whom Wavell had described as the 'mouthpiece' of Sardar Patel,[42] was thinking along the same lines: Kashmir 'does not lie in the bosom of Pakistan, and it can claim an exit to India, especially if a portion of the Gurdaspur district goes to East Punjab.'[43]

Had the whole of Gurdaspur District been awarded to Pakistan, according to Lord Birdwood, 'India could certainly never have fought a war in Kashmir.'[44] Birdwood maintained that even if only the three Muslim tehsils had gone to Pakistan 'the maintenance of Indian forces within Kashmir would still have presented a grave problem for the Indian commanders, for their railhead at Pathankot is fed through the middle of the Gurdaspur tehsil.' 'Batala and Gurdaspur to the south,' said Chaudhri Muhammad Ali 'would have blocked the way'.[45] The fourth route which passed through Hindu Pathankot tehsil, would have been much more difficult to traverse. Although it did provide geographical access, the railway at the time extended only as far as Mukerian and it required an extra ferry coming across the river Beas.

The Indian journalist, M. J. Akbar, interprets the award as a simple piece of political expediency on the part of Nehru. 'Could Kashmir remain safe unless India was able to defend it? Nehru could hardly take the risk. And so, during private meetings, he persuaded Mountbatten to leave this Gurdaspur link in Indian hands.'[46] This seems an over-simplification, given the other issues at stake, especially concern for the Sikhs. But in view of inadequate explanations and selective secrecy surrounding the Radcliffe award, the belief amongst Pakistanis that there was a conspiracy between Mountbatten and Nehru to deprive Pakistan of Gurdaspur has held fast. Mountbatten and his apologists repeatedly denied any prior knowledge of the award or any discussions with Sir Cyril Radcliffe. Christopher Beaumont, secretary to Radcliffe, asserts, however, that in the case of Ferozepur (although not over Gurdaspur) Radcliffe was persuaded to give the Ferozepur salient to India.[47] Alan Campbell-Johnson, however, maintains that Beaumont based this allegation on the proceedings of a meeting at which he was not present and about which he was not briefed.[48] When Professor Zaidi questioned Radcliffe in 1967, he said that he had destroyed his papers, in order 'to keep the validity of the award.'[49]

Stories of bad relations between Mountbatten and Mohammad Ali Jinnah also added fuel to the Pakistani argument that Mountbatten was not well disposed towards Pakistan and hence not willing to see Kashmir go to the new Dominion. 'He talked about mad, mad, mad Pakistan,' says Professor Zaidi.[50] As Morris-Jones relates, Mountbatten had assumed that he would continue as governor-general of the two dominions. 'When Jinnah, after long consideration, told him in July that the first governor-general of Pakistan would be Jinnah himself, the hope of a common Head of State was blasted and Mountbatten took it as a shattering blow to his own pride. As far as I can see from the records, that was the only moment in all the months of frustrating negotiations when the Viceroy lost his temper; on his own account he exploded in fury at Jinnah and stormed out of the room.'[51]

Pakistani apprehension about the intentions of both the Indians and the British arose from their long-standing feeling that neither Britain nor India wanted nor expected Pakistan to survive. They therefore wanted Kashmir in order to gain a strategic advantage over Pakistan and put pressure on Pakistan's north-eastern border. Possession of Kashmir would also give control of the headwaters of the important rivers which watered the plains of the Indus valley. 'The object of grabbing Kashmir was to encircle Pakistan militarily and strangle it economically,' writes Suhrawardy. 'India would have, through Gilgit, a common border with Afghanistan, then openly hostile to Pakistan and the only country in the world which opposed Pakistan's admission as member of the UN. Pakistan would get sandwiched and with the active support of India and Afghanistan, the Pukhtoonistan stunt backed by the Frontier Gandhi, Abdul Ghaffar Khan, would be used for military intervention.'[52] Anti-Pakistani feeling stemmed, believed Suhrawardy, from India's contention expressed in the Congress Resolution of 5 June 1947: 'Geography and mountains and the sea fashioned India as she is, and no human agency can change that shape or come in the way of her final destiny. 'The resolution went on to say that once 'present passions' had subsided 'the false doctrine of two nations will be discredited and discarded by all.'[53] Every move on the part of India was therefore interpreted by the future Pakistanis as being part of this long-term strategy.

Standstill?

In 1947, only the maharaja and a few close associates may have entertained the idea of remaining independent. Mountbatten was most unreceptive to this third possibility. In a long letter to the Earl of Listowel, dated 8 August, he wrote:

> The Indian Dominion, consisting nearly of three-quarters of India, and with its immense resources and its important strategic position in the Indian Ocean, is a Dominion which we cannot afford to estrange for the fate of the so-called independence of the States. I have no doubt that you will agree with me that we should leave no stone unturned to convince the Indian Dominion that although we had to agree to the plan of partition, we had no intention to leave it balkanised or to weaken it both internally and externally.

In addition, he did not want the reputation of Britain to suffer because the situation regarding the states was not fully resolved at independence:

If we leave the States without association with one or the other of the two Dominions, there will be plenty of justification for the allegations against us that while we unilaterally terminated all treaties and agreements, we took no steps for the safety and security of the States from either internal troubles or external aggression.[54]

But the maharaja's prime minister, Ram Chandra Kak, a Kashmiri Brahmin described by Karan Singh as 'the one man who had the intellectual capacity to make some coherent effort towards an acceptable settlement',[55] was also believed to be the main force behind the maharaja's reluctance to join India.[56] On the eve of independence, with obvious pressure from Delhi, the maharaja replaced his prime minister with a retired army officer. Mountbatten saw this as a sign that the main obstacle against accession to one or other dominion was now out of the way. He was pleased to note on 16 August, after the 'sacking' of Kak, that the maharaja now talks of holding a referendum to decide 'whether to join Pakistan or India, provided that the Boundary Commission give him land communication between Kashmir and India.' Mountbatten went on to observe with obvious, but misplaced, relief: 'it appears therefore as if this great problem of the States has been satisfactorily solved within the last three weeks of British rule.'[57]

Mountbatten was, however, precipitate in his analysis. When the subcontinent became independent from British rule on 14–15 August, for the first time since Yaqub Shah Chak submitted to Akbar in 1589, the state of Jammu and Kashmir was independent. It remained so for seventy-three days. On 12 August, in an exchange of telegrams, Hari Singh made a 'standstill' agreement with Pakistan. The objective was to ensure that those services which existed for trade, travel and communication would carry on in the same way as they had with British India. Pakistan therefore retained control of the rail and river links, which were used to float timber down the Jhelum river to the plains. India did not, however, sign a standstill agreement. V. P. Menon's explanation is revealing given the interest Congress had shown in Kashmir in the months preceding independence: 'We wanted to examine its implications. We left the State alone ... moreover, our hands were already full and if truth be told, I for one had simply no time to think of Kashmir.'[58] That India did not sign a standstill agreement with the state of Jammu and Kashmir has merely added to the suspicion amongst Pakistanis that the Indian government was already engaged in making its own arrangements for Kashmir's future and did not consider a standstill agreement to be a necessary part of those plans. The standstill agreement signed with Pakistan, says Abdul Suhrawardy, was really 'a camouflage to hide the real designs and lull Pakistan and her supporters into a false sleep of satisfaction.'[59]

In the state of Jammu and Kashmir there were staunch Muslim League supporters who believed they would become part of Pakistan at independence and when freedom came at midnight on 14 August they rejoiced. The Pakistani flag was hoisted on most of the post offices until the government of the maharaja ordered that they should be taken down. All pro-Pakistani newspapers were closed. Muhammad Saraf was in Baramula, where the flag remained flying until dusk: 'It was a spectacle to watch streams of people from all directions in the town and its suburbs swarming towards the Post Office in order to have a glimpse of the flag of their hopes and dreams.'[60] Those whose hopes were dashed at not becoming part of Pakistan set in train a sequence of events which was rooted in their past disappointment.

Revolt in Poonch

Of the 71,667 citizens of the state of Jammu and Kashmir who served in the British Indian forces during World War II, 60,402 were Muslims from the traditional recruiting ground of Poonch and Mirpur.[61] After the war, the maharaja, alarmed at the increasing agitation against his government, refused to accept them into the army. When they returned to their farms, they found 'not a land fit for heroes, but fresh taxes, more onerous than ever,' writes the British Quaker, Horace Alexander. 'If the Maharaja's government chastised the people of the Kashmir valley with whips, the Poonchis were chastised with scorpions'[62] Throughout his reign, Hari Singh had been working to regain control of Poonch. As a jagir of Gulab Singh's brother, Dhyan, although a fief of the maharaja, Poonch had retained a degree of autonomy. Friction between the maharaja and the Raja of Poonch had remained ever since Pratap's adoption of the raja in 1907 as his spiritual heir. After the raja's death in 1940, Hari Singh had succeeded in dispossessing his young son and bringing the administration of Poonch in line with the rest of the state of Jammu and Kashmir. This move was not welcomed by the local people. 'There was a tax on every hearth and every window,' writes Richard Symonds, a social worker with a group of British Quakers working in the Punjab: 'Every cow, buffalo and sheep was taxed, and even every wife.' An additional tax was introduced to pay for the cost of taxation. 'Dogra troops were billeted on the Poonchis to enforce the collection.'[63]

In the Spring of 1947, the Poonchis had mounted a 'no-tax' campaign. The maharaja responded by strengthening his garrisons in Poonch with Sikhs and Hindus. In July he ordered all Muslims in the district to hand over their weapons to the authorities. But, as communal tension spread, the Muslims were angered when the same weapons appeared in the hands of Hindus and Sikhs. They therefore sought fresh weapons from the tribes of the North-West Frontier who were well known for their manufacture of arms. This laid the basis for direct contact between the members of the Poonch resistance and the tribesmen who lived in the strip of mountainous 'tribal' territory bordering Pakistan and Afghanistan. In the belief that the maharaja had passed an order to massacre the Muslims, a thirty-two year-old Suddhan, Sardar Mohammed Ibrahim Khan, collected together the ex-soldiers amongst the Suddhans. 'We got arms from here and there and then we started fighting the Maharaja's army.' In about two months he says he had organised an army of about 50,000.[64]

The transfer of power by the British to the new Dominions of Pakistan and India on 14–15 August brought no respite to the troubled situation which the maharaja now faced as an independent ruler. Unrest in Poonch had turned into an organised revolt against the Dogras, which was reminiscent of the rebellion led by Shams-ud Din, governor of Poonch, in 1837. Amongst the activists was Sardar Abdul Qayum Khan, a landowner from Rawalakot:

> Unlike many other people who believed that the partition plan would be implemented with all sincerity of purpose, I thought that perhaps India would like to obtain Kashmir and that is why the armed revolt took place. Against the declared standstill agreement, the maharaja had started moving his troops along the river Jhelum. It was an unusual movement which had never happened before and I could see that it had a purpose of sealing off the border with Pakistan. In order to thwart that plan, we rose up in arms.[65]

Qayum Khan withdrew to the forests outside Rawalakot, from where the message of rebellion was spread throughout Poonch and south to Mirpur. The close links with their neighbours on the western side of the Jhelum river meant that the border was impossible to seal and the maharaja's government attributed the trouble in Poonch to infiltration from Pakistan. 'Intelligence reports from the frontier areas of Poonch and Mirpur as well as the Sialkot sector started coming in which spoke of large-scale massacre, loot and rape of our villagers by aggressive hordes from across the borders,' writes Karan Singh. 'I recall the grim atmosphere that began to engulf us as it gradually became clear that we were losing control of the outer areas.' He records how his father handed him some reports in order to translate them into Dogri for his mother. 'I still recall my embarrassment in dealing with the word "rape" for which I could find no acceptable equivalent.'[66]

The Pakistani government, however, believed the uprising in Poonch was a legitimate rebellion against the maharaja's rule, which was gaining increasing sympathy from the tribesmen of the North-West Frontier, who were also sympathetic to the troubles in the Punjab. On 23 September, George Cunningham, governor of the North-West Frontier Province noted: 'I have offers from practically every tribe along the Frontier to be allowed to go and kill Sikhs in eastern Punjab and I think I would only have to hold up my little finger to get a lashkar of 40,000 to 50,000.'[67]

Poonch was also undoubtedly affected by events in neighbouring Jammu. Whereas the valley of Kashmir was protected by its mountain ranges from the communal massacres which devastated so many families in the weeks following partition, Jammu had immediate contact with the plains of India and, as a result, was subject to the same communalist hatred which swept throughout the Punjab and Bengal. According to Pakistani sympathisers, whilst deliberating over accession, the maharaja was undertaking a systematic purge of Muslims. 'Certain it is that the Maharaja's government was using its Dogra troops to terrorise many Muslim villages in the neighbourhood of Jammu,' wrote Horace Alexander. 'Later in the year, I myself saw villages near Jammu that had been completely gutted.'[68]

Ian Stephens, editor of *The Statesman* (Calcutta), noted the situation in Jammu: 'Unlike every part of the state, Hindus and Sikhs slightly outnumbered Muslims, and within a period of about 11 weeks, starting in August, systematic savageries ... practically eliminated the entire Muslim element in the population, amounting to 500,000 people. About 200,000 just disappeared, remaining untraceable, having presumably been butchered or died from epidemic or exposure. The rest fled to West Punjab.'[69] There they reported that these atrocities had been perpetrated 'not only by uncontrolled bands of hooligans but also by organised units of the Maharaja's army and Police.'[70] In September, the outgoing chief of staff of the Jammu and Kashmir State Forces, Major-General Scott, had informed the maharaja that the situation was becoming difficult for his army to control on its own.

Manoeuvres

In the weeks following independence, despite the signature of the standstill agreement with Pakistan, political manoeuvring was taking place on all sides. Both Pakistan and India were actively trying to determine events so that Kashmir would accede to their respective Dominions. India retained the upper hand and despite the maharaja's dislike for Nehru, he communicated more regularly and amicably with the Indian leaders than with those in Pakistan. Although he had rejected Mountbatten's suggestion of retaining military links with either India or Pakistan, on 13 September he requested the Government of India for the loan of an Indian army officer to replace Major-General Scott as his commander-in-chief.

Prime Minister Nehru and Sardar Patel, who had become minister for Home Affairs, corresponded regularly in order to determine how Kashmir could be secured for India. 'One of the most interesting revelations of the Patel papers when they began to be published in 1971,' writes Alastair Lamb 'was the extent to which this powerful Congress politician had directly involved himself in all planning directed towards an eventual Indian acquisition of the State of Jammu and Kashmir.'[71]

Clear steps were being taken to improve communications with India, by telegraph, telephone, wireless and roads. On 27 September *The Pakistan Times* reported: 'the metalling of the road from Jammu to Kathua is also proceeding at top speed. The idea is to keep up some sort of communication between the State and the Indian Union, so that essential supplies and troops could be rushed to Kashmir without having to transport them through Pakistani territory.'[72] A boat bridge was also being constructed over the Ravi river near Pathankot, which would improve the access from Gurdaspur. In addition, there were reports that the Kashmir government was constructing an all weather road linking the valley of Kashmir with Jammu via Poonch instead of the Banihal road which was impassable in winter. In Pakistan it was widely believed that India was preparing to announce Kashmir's accession to India in the autumn. The Pakistani government alleged that India had violated the standstill agreement, because they had included Kashmir within the Indian postal system. As evidence, they produced a memorandum, dated 1 September 1947, signed by the director-general of Postal Telegraph, New Delhi, in which towns in the State of Jammu and Kashmir were listed as part of India.[73]

The Indian leaders were equally anxious about Pakistani moves. The armed raids from Pakistani territory into the state and disturbances in Poonch led the Indians to believe that there would be a full-scale Pakistani incursion before winter.: 'I understand that the Pakistan strategy is to infiltrate into Kashmir now and to take some big action as soon as Kashmir is more or less isolated because of the coming winter,' Nehru wrote to Patel on 27 September.[74] Nehru therefore suggested to Patel that the maharaja should 'make friends' with the National Conference, 'so that there might be this popular support against Pakistan.' Nehru had hoped that the maharaja could be persuaded to accede to India before any invasion took place and he realised that accession would only be more easily accepted if Abdullah, as a popular leader, were brought into the picture.

Two days after this letter, on 29 September, Abdullah, who had been in prison since his Quit Kashmir movement in 1946, was released from jail. His letter pledging allegiance to the maharaja was widely publicised. But he also repeated his pre-independence rhetoric: 'When I went into prison, I took a last look at undivided India. Today it has been broken into two fragments. We the people of Kashmir must now see to it that our long-cherished dream is fulfilled. The dream of freedom, welfare and progress.'[75] At the beginning of October Dwarkanath Kachru, the secretary of the All-India States Peoples' Conference, visited Srinagar with the objective of convincing Abdullah of the merits of joining India. He reported back to Nehru that 'Sheikh Abdullah and his close associates have decided for the Indian Union.' The decision, however, was not to be announced. The objective of the Kashmir National Conference 'is the attainment of people's sovereignty with the Maharaja enjoying a constitutional position.' This, explained Kachru:

> ... would be the main factor determining the position of the Conference in the matter of accession ... The threat to Kashmir is real and unless the Congress takes up a strong stand and forces the Maharaja to come to some agreement with the National Conference, Kashmir is doomed and there will be nothing to prevent the conquest of Kashmir by the Muslim League leaders and private armies.[76]

A copy of this report was passed on to Sardar Patel and he responded to Nehru: 'We are giving the Kashmir government as much assistance as possible within the limited resources available. There are all sorts of difficulties in our going all out to assist the State.'[77]

The Pakistani leaders were also actively trying to turn the situation in their favour, at the same time as being criticised by the Kashmiri government for the armed raids and a 'blockade' of the border. Immediately after Abdullah's release, he was visited by Dr Muhammad Din Taseer, a friend of Abdullah's and former principal of Sri Pratap College in Srinagar but now a Pakistani citizen. He was accompanied by Anwar-ul Haq, district magistrate, Rawalpindi, who was deputed to find out why essential supplies, including sugar, salt, petrol, kerosene, oil and cloth were being held up at Sialkot and Rawalpindi. The allegation from the Kashmiri side was that because they were not being transported into Kashmir, the Pakistanis were not honouring the terms of the standstill agreement and that it was tantamount to a blockade to force the state to accede to Pakistan.

The Pakistani government, however, maintained that this arose because of the troubled situation within Kashmir. Haq concluded that the lorry drivers were too frightened to make the journey because Sikhs and Hindus were attacking Muslims. After some investigation, the British High Commission concluded that there may have been obstructions which were overlooked, perhaps even encouraged, by some low grade officials.[78] But, from the Indian perspective, the allegations of the blockade were evidence of Pakistan's intended 'aggression' towards Kashmir and added fuel to the argument that an invasion was imminent.

While Anwar-ul Haq, was holding discussions with the concerned author-ities about the supplies, Taseer met with Sheikh Abdullah. 'When Taseer returned in the evening, he told me he had a very fruitful discussions with Sheikh Abdullah and he had agreed to meet Quaid-i Azam.' But the Sheikh was also playing for time. The Punjab was on fire. 'So I felt I had to be very careful about taking any decision concerning Kashmir,' he told Bilqees Taseer, recalling his earlier conversation with her husband in 1947. 'I also believed that any decision made had to be that of the Kashmiri people themselves, i.e. as regards joining Pakistan, because not merely those of the present generation would be affected by such a decision but also generations to follow.'[79] In his memoirs Abdullah noted: 'I firmly told him that the time to decide had not yet arrived. Both countries are caught in a vortex.'[80] He agreed, however, to meet Mohammad Ali Jinnah in Lahore after he had first visited Delhi.

In the meantime, Abdullah sent his 'trusted lieutenant', G. M. Sadiq back to Lahore with Dr Taseer for further discussions. Bakshi Ghulam Muhammad was already there. Ghulam Muhammad Sadiq was anxious to ensure accept-ance of the condition that no non-state subject would be allowed to purchase property in Kashmir (as was the case in pre-independence times). On the assumption that Kashmir would eventually go to Pakistan there were stories of wealthy Pakistani feudals making enquiries about buying land.

The Pakistani government was also pursuing diplomatic channels with the maharaja and his government. Liaquat Ali Khan, the prime minister of Pakistan, had sent a representative to Srinagar 'to try and lead the Kashmir Prime Minister towards accession to Pakistan. He said that for three or four days he was succeeding, but that then the new prime minister arrived and told him to clear out.'[81] The new prime minister, who had arrived in Srinagar on 15 October, when the state was 'on the chessboard of power politics', was Mehr Chand Mahajan.[82] An Indian judge, he had been one of the Hindu representatives on the Boundary Commission. In an exchange of telegrams, the Kashmir Government offered an impartial inquiry into the allegations made against Pakistan; otherwise, Prime Minister Mahajan stated that the Government of Kashmir would be obliged to ask for 'friendly assistance' from the state's other neighbour, India. The Pakistani government accepted the idea for an impartial inquiry, but on 18 October Mahajan sent another telegram to Mohammad Ali Jinnah again threatening to ask for 'friendly' assistance unless the Pakistanis acceded to their request to stop the alleged armed infiltration into Poonch, the blockade of the border, as well as continuing propaganda against the maharaja. This time, however, there was no mention of the impartial inquiry.

Jinnah responded to Mahajan's telegram, by sending a telegraphic message to Hari Singh deploring the 'tone and language' adopted by Mahajan. He also outlined numerous complaints against the maharaja's government. He noticed the more favourable treatment given to Sheikh Abdullah since his release at the end of September, and to the National Conference, compared with the Muslim Conference whose leaders, including Ghulam Abbas, remained in detention:

> The real aim of your Government's policy is to seek an opportunity to join the Indian Dominion through a coup d'état by securing the intervention and assistance of that Dominion ... I suggest that the way to smooth out the difficulties and adjust matters in a friendly way is for your Prime Minister to come to Karachi and discuss the developments that have taken place, instead of carrying on acrimonious and bitter telegrams and correspondence.[83]

At the same time Sardar Patel continued to correspond with the Kashmiri government. Mahajan had already requested arms and ammunition from India to deal with the growing unrest within the state. On 21 October, Patel once again encouraged Mahajan to enlist the support of Sheikh Abdullah: 'It is obvious that in your dealings with the external dangers and internal commotion with which you are faced, mere brute force is not enough ... It is my sincere and earnest advice to you to make a substantial gesture to win Sheikh Abdullah's support.'[84] Mahajan noted Patel's views but replied that 'the situation in the state at the present moment is such that one cannot get a single moment to think of politics.'[85] He urged Patel to send arms and ammunition at once to assist with the worsening situation which the Kashmiri government insisted was aided by Pakistan. 'No raids could take place if the Pakistani authorities wished to stop them.'[86]

As both India and Pakistan continued to court the old rulers of the state of Jammu and Kashmir and the new, such diplomatic initiatives were brought to an immediate halt when news was received that a large number of raiders from the tribal territory of Pakistan's North-West Frontier province had crossed the borders and were heading for Kashmir. G. M. Sadiq returned from Lahore to Delhi. According to Faiz Ahmed Faiz, chief editor of *The Pakistan Times* and an old friend of Sadiq's, when news of the tribal invasion reached Lahore, 'we could see that everything was lost.'[87] The 'jihad' of the tribesmen came in the wake of two months of nominal standstill, when, behind the scenes amidst a deteriorating law and order situation, India and Pakistan were both independently planning for the state of Jammu and Kashmir to accede to their respective dominions. 'There ended the opportunity of Kashmir's accession to Pakistan,' said Faiz. 'The rest is history.'[88]

other pro-Hindu organisations throughout India. In Delhi Nehru also had to contend with extremist elements anxious to derail his secular policy. Politics at the centre were also passionately nationalistic and Kashmir's separate status was tolerated, at best, on sufferance. In October 1951 orthodox Hindus launched the Jana Sangh, led by Shyama Prasad Mookerjee, which aimed at abrogating article 370 and fully integrating Jammu and Kashmir into the Indian Union. The Praja Parishad saw the National Conference not only as a Muslim communal party, but also as 'a cover for the extension of communist ideology'.[37]

In February 1952 there was violence in the streets of Jammu and curfew was imposed for seventy-two hours. Alarmed by the significance of the Delhi agreement, the Praja Parishad used the slogan: 'One President, one Constitution, One Flag'. They disliked the use of the distinctive titles, sadar-i-riyasat and prime minister, as opposed to those of governor and chief minister used by the other states. Claiming that they could not tolerate Jammu and Ladakh 'going to the winds'[38] the Parishad leaders accused Sheikh Abdullah of preventing the merger of the state of Jammu and Kashmir with the Indian Union. In November the Praja Parishad leader, Prem Nath Dogra, and one of his associates were detained by Abdullah. In February 1953 Dr Shyama Prasad Mookerjee wrote to Abdullah: 'You are developing a three-nation theory, the third being Kashmiris. These are dangerous symptoms.'[39] When Dr Mookerjee attempted to go to Jammu, he was arrested at the border. His death in detention, from a heart attack, fuelled suspicions of foul play. Right-wing elements never forgave the Sheikh for crushing their movement.

The Ladakhi people, of Tibetan origin, who lived in virtual isolation, had escaped the trauma of communal riots and massacres at the time of partition. During the war, when the raiders captured Kargil and threatened Leh, relations between the two communities of Buddhists and Muslims became tense, although their long tradition of goodwill enabled them to withstand the strain.[40] When Sheikh Abdullah took over as prime minister, he too recognised the spiritual qualities of Ladakh's Buddhist community. 'Kashmir has always been the cradle of love, peace, humanism and tolerance, which was created by Buddhism and which flourished in the valley for about a thousand years.'[41] Yet the Buddhists of Ladakh resented Abdullah's centralising tendencies. They neither wanted to join with Pakistan nor did they want to be governed by Srinagar.

The Ladakhis soon came to realise that Sheikh Abdullah had little knowledge or understanding of their way of life. Jawaharlal Nehru had himself realised that, in depending on Sheikh Abdullah as a political leader in Jammu and Kashmir, it might be difficult to keep together the multi-racial empire created by Gulab Singh in the previous century. In 1949 the Buddhist Association of Ladakh had sent a memorandum to Nehru suggesting that Ladakh be integrated with Jammu in some way, either to become an Indian state in its own right or as part of east Punjab totally separate from Sheikh Abdullah's administration in Kashmir. Although this plan was never put into practice, the Ladakhis remained restive under control from Srinagar. Before China's annexation of Tibet, the head Llama had suggested secession and union with Tibet; their spiritual allegiance was to the Dalai Llama in Lhasa, so too might be their political future. But after the communists took over Tibet in 1950, they lost the contact dating back seven centuries, which had influenced both their spiritual and cultural lives.

Abdullah's land reforms threatened the wealth of the Buddhist monasteries. In 1952 Kushak Bakula, the Abbot of Spituk Monastery, and regarded as the head Llama of Ladakh, declared that once power had been transferred from the maharaja to the National Conference 'the constitutional link, which tied us down to the state, was shattered and from that time we were morally and juridically free to choose our own course, independent of the rest of the state.'[42] There was still potential friction with the Muslim minority community in Kargil, who had traditionally controlled the Ladakhi economy, especially the supply of pashmina wool for weavers in Kashmir. Like Jammu, the people of Ladakh saw money poured into the valley at their expense. And, as Balraj Puri points out, 'the spectre of plebiscite' also haunted the people of Jammu and Ladakh. The fear of a pro-Pakistani verdict as well as the prevarication of the Kashmiri leaders over accession, made them suggest the possibility of a zonal plebiscite, which option Sheikh Abdullah refused to consider.[43]

The plebiscite and the United Nations

One of the reasons why Sardar Patel had impressed upon Hari Singh the need to absent himself from Srinagar for a 'few months' in 1949 was because of the 'complications arising from the plebiscite proposal then being actively pursued in the United Nations.'[44] UNCIP's visit to the sub-continent had laid the groundwork for demilitarisation and plebiscite, but as Joseph Korbel noted at the time, and their reports indicated, there was very little common ground other than the agreement in principle to hold a plebiscite. After their mission they recommended that the entire problem be turned over to one man, because the members of the commission were themselves divided. In 1949, General A. G. L. McNaughton, the Canadian president of the Security Council, was appointed as an 'informal mediator' in order to establish a plan for demilitarisation prior to the holding of a plebiscite. Although Pakistan agreed to his proposals, India did not. On 27 May 1950 the Australian jurist, Sir Owen Dixon, arrived in the sub-continent, as the one-man successor to UNCIP. Dixon's commitment in trying to resolve the problem was not lost on the Indians. Patel wrote to Nehru that Dixon was working to bring about an agreement on the question of demilitarisation. 'If we are not careful, we might land ourselves in difficulties because once demilitarisation is settled, a plebiscite would be, as it were, round the corner.'[45] Patel, however, did not live to see the outcome of the negotiations towards plebiscite. Regarded as the 'iron man' of the Indian government, who had so profoundly influenced India's policy towards the princely states, he died on 15 December 1950.

After three months of extensive discussions, Dixon made a number of suggestions, condemned by Nehru as an 'Alice in Wonderland business of vague proposals':[46] firstly, that there should be a zonal plebiscite region by region, and that the existing government should be replaced with an administrative body of UN officers; alternatively, that areas which would unquestionably vote for Pakistan or India would be allocated to the respective countries, with a plebiscite in the valley; that the state should be partitioned, with a plebiscite in the valley or, finally, that the country be divided along the ceasefire line. Yet again the question of demilitarisation was the sticking point, causing Dixon to conclude:

> I became convinced that India's agreement would never be obtained to demilitarise in any such form or to provisions governing the period of the plebiscite of any such character, which would in my opinion permit the plebiscite being conducted in conditions sufficiently guarding against intimidation and other forms of influence and abuse by which the freedom and fairness of the plebiscite might be imperilled.

Without such demilitarisation, the local 'Azad' and regular Pakistani forces were not prepared to withdraw from the territory they had retained. Dixon's final suggestion was to leave India and Pakistan to negotiate their own terms. 'So far the attitude of the parties has been to throw the whole responsibility upon the Security Council or its representatives of settling the dispute notwithstanding that except by agreement between them there was no means of settling it.' Dixon also noted the strange features of the problem:

> The parties have agreed that the fate of the state as a whole should be settled by a general plebiscite but over a considerable period of time, they have failed to agree on any of the preliminary measures which it was clearly necessary to take before it was possible to set up an organisation to take a plebiscite.[47]

The UN's decision to postpone further discussion of Kashmir unleashed a storm of protest in Pakistan.

The issue was briefly taken up by the Commonwealth, when, in January 1951, at a meeting of Commonwealth prime ministers, Robert Menzies, the Australian prime minister, suggested that Commonwealth troops should be stationed in Kashmir; that a joint Indo–Pakistani force should be stationed there, and to entitle the plebiscite administrator to raise local troops. Pakistan agreed to the suggestions, but India rejected them. In particular India was unhappy that Pakistan, whom India considered to be the aggressor, was placed on an equal footing. In March, the Security Council once again discussed Kashmir, and once more observed that India and Pakistan had accepted the resolutions of 13 August 1948 and 5 January 1949, affirming that the future of the state of Jammu and Kashmir was to be decided through 'the democratic method of a free and impartial plebiscite.'[48] The proposal, formulated by Britain and the United States, also suggested that in case of failure to reach agreement, arbitration might be considered. Pakistan accepted this recommendation, but Nehru responded by stating that he would not permit the fate of four million people to be decided by a third person. Korbel, who had continued to observe developments, was critical of India's stance: 'One could have expected that a country of such undisputed greatness led by a man of Nehru's stature and integrity would have reacted more favourably to such a valid, and under the Charter of the United Nations, the recommended technique of international co-operation.'[49]

When Dr Frank Graham, Dixon's successor as UN representative for India and Pakistan, visited the sub-continent in the Spring of 1951 he arrived in an atmosphere of extreme tension. Graham's brief once more was to try and effect demilitarisation, prior to the plebiscite. Yet again the two countries could not agree on the number of troops remaining in Kashmir. By the summer there was a significant concentration of Indian troops along the borders of western Pakistan and genuine concern that the two countries might again resort to war.

The Pakistani establishment was obviously also reviewing its policy regarding Kashmir. In January 1951 Ayub Khan took over as commander-in-chief of Pakistan's army. Two months later the newly appointed chief of general staff, Major-General Akbar Khan, 'hero' of the Kashmir war, was arrested with several others for plotting a 'coup'. Their alleged objective was to overthrow the government, replace it by a military dictatorship, favourable to Moscow instead of London and to move into Kashmir. Known as the Rawalpindi Conspiracy Case, the struggle for power between Akbar and Ayub was 'a tussle between two divergent perspectives on the Kashmir dispute within the Pakistani defence establishment,' writes Ayesha Jalal.[50] It also demonstrated that there was a body of opinion in Pakistan which believed that the Soviet Union might be a better ally than the British, who it was believed had failed to make good their promises of supplying arms and ammunition to Pakistan and consequently enabled India to achieve a *fait accompli* in Kashmir.[51]

In October 1951 Liaquat Ali Khan was assassinated by an unidentified gunman at a time when, speaking *ex tempore*, it was believed he was about to make a bid for support from the Muslim world.[52] Tension between India and Pakistan remained. Nehru's New Year message in 1952 warned of full scale war if Pakistan accidentally invaded Kashmir. Kashmir Day on 24 October 1952 was celebrated in an atmosphere of hostility towards the UN for its failure to solve the Kashmiri problem. And, as Korbel observed, the continuing uncertainty was matched by 'profound political changes in Kashmir which are not only dimming hope that an impartial plebiscite will be held' but also endangering peace and democracy. For a short while, there appeared to be a genuine dialogue between Nehru and Mohammad Ali Bogra, prime minister of Pakistan. In June 1953 they discussed Kashmir informally with Nehru in London, where they were both present for the coronation of Queen Elizabeth II. Nehru held talks with Bogra in Karachi. Soon afterwards Bogra visited Delhi and together they discussed the naming of a plebiscite administrator with the view to holding a plebiscite in the whole state. 'We have to choose a path which not only promises the greatest advantage but is dignified and in keeping with our general policy,' Nehru wrote to Bakshi Ghulam Muhammad on 18 August 1953.[53] But Pakistan's reluctance to consider a different nominee, other than the American Admiral Nimitz, whom India did not accept, stalled the whole proceedings. Such an opportunity never arose again. 'It is one of those ironies of history that just when India appeared to be willing to settle the Kashmir dispute, the prime minister of Pakistan allowed the opportunity to be frittered away,' writes Gowher Rizvi.[54]

The Western powers, most significantly the United States, were also reappraising their policy towards India and Pakistan. Initially, American liberals saw India 'in a romantic haze', writes Sam Burke. But the United States' failure, most demonstrably over Korea, to enlist India's support in the fight against communism and Nehru's commitment to a policy of 'non-alignment' finally alienated the US from India and brought them closer to Pakistan. 'To the Americans the main problem of the day was communism, to Nehru it was colonialism,' writes Burke. 'Americans viewed socialism as the road to communism; Nehru looked upon capitalism as the parent of imperialism and fascism.' Pakistan, however, took a different view of communism from that of India, which meant that the United States was prepared to look more favourably on Pakistan's position on Kashmir. This support was demonstrated in the UN, when both Britain and the United States voted for resolutions which were acceptable to Pakistan.

Pakistan's signature of a Mutual Defence Assistance Agreement with the United States in May 1954 and acceptance of American aid was regarded by India, as upsetting the sub-continental balance of power. Before the agreement was signed, Nehru had written to Mohammad Ali Bogra:

> If such an alliance takes place, Pakistan enters definitely into the region of the cold war. That means to us that the cold war has come to the very frontiers of India ... It must also be a matter of grave consequence to us, you will appreciate, if vast armies are built up in Pakistan with the aid of American money ... All our problems will have to be seen in a new light.[55]

As an Indian journalist was to observe, however, Pakistan's acceptance of Western support ensured its survival. 'India held the pistol at the head of Pakistan, until, in 1954, the American alliance delivered the country from the nightmare.'[56] In September Pakistan joined SEATO and the following year the Baghdad Pact (later called CENTO), whose other members were Turkey, Iran and the United Kingdom.

Initially, the Soviet Union abstained from voting when a resolution was passed regarding Kashmir in the Security Council and, through the Communist Party of India, was supportive of Kashmir's own nationalist stance. But, as relations deteriorated between the Soviet Union and its former allies in the Second World War, the Russians began to maintain that the British were using the Kashmir issue to keep control of both Dominions. In 1952 the Soviet representative at the Security Council said that the purpose of the United States and Britain was to convert Kashmir into a protectorate under the pretext of rendering assistance through the United Nations.[57] At the end of 1955 Nikolai Bulganin and Nikita Khrushchev stopped at Srinagar, where their visit marked a new phase in Indo–Soviet relations. They stated that the people of Kashmir had clearly already decided to join India. 'We are so near that if ever you call us from your mountain tops we will appear at your side,' said Khrushchev.[58]

Outside the forum of the UN, Chinese leaders had been evolving their own strategy towards the state of Jammu and Kashmir. In the early 1950s, like the Soviet Union, China maintained that the issue was being exploited by the UK and the US for their own 'imperialist' objectives, for which purpose they were using the UN. Even when the Soviet Union began to favour the Indian position, China remained neutral. Nehru, however, was interested in forming a special relationship with China. 'It was essential for the success of his programme of a resurgent Asia, from which western influence would have to be eliminated, that India and China, the two largest Asians, should march hand in hand,' writes Sam Burke.[59] In support of this objective, for reasons of 'realpolitik rather than morality,' Nehru was prepared to overlook Chinese actions in Tibet. China was, however, also moving towards confrontation with India because of disagreements over the demarcation of borders in the Aksai Chin area of Ladakh, which was one of three disputed areas along the 2,500 mile frontier. Unobserved by India, between 1956 and 1957 the Chinese had constructed a road in this inhospitable uninhabited north-eastern corner of Ladakh, rising to an altitude of 16,000 ft, which provided a direct link between Tibet and Chinese territory in Sinkiang province. By the time Indian patrols encountered Chinese vehicles using the road in 1958 their presence was already an accomplished fact. Nehru hoped to resolve any untoward border incidents by quiet diplomacy, but resentment amongst the Indian people at continued Chinese encroachments along the border was high.

In the late 1950s, as Indian and Chinese forces began to clash along their disputed frontier, Pakistan started a dialogue with China. In 1957, Po Yi-Po, chairman of the Chinese Economic Commission, arranged for a team of Chinese officials to visit the Hunza and Gilgit valley, which had long-standing contact with China because of the traditional Chinese relationship with the Mir of Hunza. Two centres were opened by Peking in Hunza and Gilgit for promoting 'good feeling' between China and Pakistan.[60] Zulfikar Ali Bhutto, who was Ayub Khan's minister for Fuel and Natural Resources 'recognised this simmering conflict between India and China as a major source of potential diplomatic advantage for Pakistan if properly exploited,' writes Stanley Wolpert.[61] In 1960 Bhutto became minister for Kashmiri Affairs. He led the Pakistani delegation to the UN and for the first time broke ranks with the established United States' position regarding China's membership of the UN. Instead of vetoing the proposal, Pakistan abstained. From India's perspective, writes Louis Hayes, the growing Sino–Pakistani co-operation constituted 'a vice, with Indian-held Kashmir in the middle'.[62] Discussions subsequently began to build a motorised road from Rawalpindi through the Khunjerab pass to China which would be visible proof of the growing link between the two countries.[63]

By the late 1950s, the United Nations had ceased to be a viable forum for the resolution of the Kashmiri dispute. In 1957, Dr Gunnar Jarring, the Swedish president of the Security Council, visited the sub-continent in order to assess the situation in Jammu and Kashmir. He stated that for the time being the present demarcation line must be respected and that the use of force to change the status quo must be excluded. The UN Security Council subsequently passed a resolution expressing its concern over 'the lack of progress towards a settlement of the dispute' shown by Jarring's report.[64] In 1962 Dr Graham returned again to the sub-continent. But the draft resolution, reminding the parties of the principles contained in their earlier resolutions calling for a plebiscite, was not adopted. For the first time, instead of abstaining, the Soviet Union voted against the resolution. 'It is now quite unrealistic to demand a plebiscite,' stated the Soviet representative 'just as, in the words of the representative of India, obviously no one would now demand a plebiscite in Texas, Ohio or any other state in the United States of America.'[65] But, even though the United Nations had failed to ensure that the plebiscite was held, the idea in principle of a referendum to ascertain the wishes of the people was handed down to a new generation of Kashmiris. That the plebiscite was agreed upon in a world body, such as the United Nations, meant that those Kashmiris who were opposed to union with India came to expect international support for what they perceived to be their right of self determination.

Azad or occupied Kashmir?

While India always refers to the part of the state under Pakistani administration as 'Pakistan-occupied Kashmir' or PoK, Pakistan refers to it as Azad Kashmir. Officially, the name used by Pakistan is 'the Azad government of the state of Jammu and Kashmir' which signifies that, in the opinion of Pakistan and the Azad Kashmiris, 'freedom' [i.e. from Indian control] should eventually extend to include the whole state. Technically, this narrow strip of mountainous land, covering some 5,134 square miles, is as much part of the

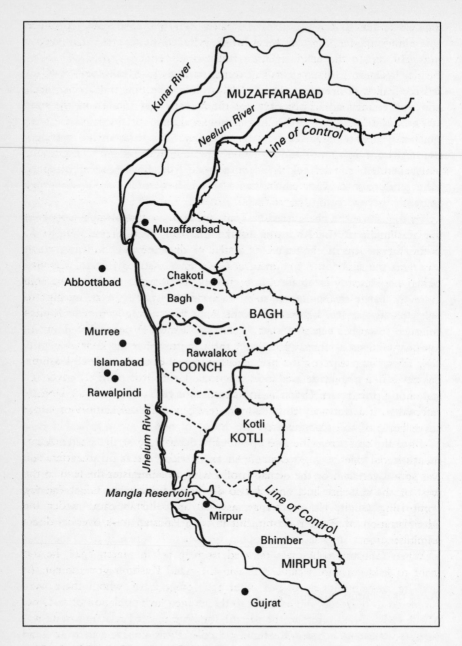

7. The Azad State of Jammu and Kashmir
(Source: *Azad Kashmir at a Glance*, Azad Government of Jammu and Kashmir, 1993)

state of Jammu and Kashmir as the valley, as is the approximately 27,000 square miles of the Northern Areas, which included the former Gilgit Agency and Baltistan. In the midst of the tribal invasion of 1947, on 24 October, the rebel Kashmiris had set up a government in exile. Sardar Ibrahim Khan was confirmed as president. The Azad Kashmir government described itself as a 'war' council whose objective was the liberation of the rest of the state of Jammu and Kashmir, as well as administration of that part of the state which was already under their control. A cabinet was formed with ministers appointed for Mirpur, Poonch, Kashmir valley, and Jammu. Despite the representation provided for the Kashmir valley, there was no one to speak for the valley. 'This reflected the fact that in the 1930s and 1940s the Valley Muslims had tended to support Sheikh Abdullah's National Conference Party,' writes Leo Rose.[66] The Muslims of Jammu, Poonch and Mirpur supported the Muslim Conference. But 'the government had practically nothing to do as the liberated territory was still in a state of disorder and confusion which was quite natural in the circumstances,' writes Muhammad Saraf, who had settled permanently in Pakistan once he realised that he would not be able to return to the Indian-administered side of the state.[67] In an attempt to assert its legality, on 3 November, the Azad Kashmir government leaders appealed to several heads of state, including Clement Attlee, Harry Truman, Joseph Stalin, and Chiang Kai-Shek, through the secretary-general of the UN, Trygve Lie, to recognise its formation. But the status of Azad Kashmir has never been legally defined in international terms. It is neither a sovereign state nor a province of Pakistan. In its resolution of 13 August 1948, UNCIP referred to it as territory to be 'administered by the local authorities under surveillance of the Commission'.

Once the ceasefire came into operation in January 1949, the Azad government's initial role of a government in exile, with its seat in Muzaffarabad, was soon overtaken by the demands of having to administer the land to the west of the ceasefire line, on a day to day basis. Initially the Gilgit Agency, comprising Gilgit, Hunza, Nagar, as well as Baltistan came under the administration of Azad Kashmir, but in 1949 Pakistan took over its direct administration.

When Ghulam Abbas was released from in jail in March 1948, he too went to Pakistan and became active in the Azad Kashmir government. At first he was appointed to look after the refugees, of whom there were estimated to be 200,000 in addition to the indigenous population of 700,000. Mir Abdul Aziz was just one of the thousands who fled. 'Actual warfare was going on. I came on foot, three hundred miles, I walked through snow. I lost all my toenails because of frost bite.'[68] Some refugees went to the main cities in Pakistan, most remained in Sialkot, Gujrat and Gujranwala. Others trekked back to their homes in Mehndar and Rajauri after the 1949 Ceasefire.

In 1950 an ordinance, 'Rules of Business of the Azad Kashmir Government,' was passed to serve as a basic law. Full executive and legislative powers were vested in the 'Supreme Head of State', which, in effect, was the Muslim Conference Party, which had the power to appoint the president, members of the Council of Ministers, as well as the chief justice and other judges of the Azad Kashmir High Court. The supreme head's absolute authority was, however, checked by the Ministry of Kashmir Affairs (MKA) of the Government of Pakistan, set up in 1948 and headed by a joint secretary. 'The Kashmiris, of course, were very skilful at exploiting and manipulating some of the poor, well meaning Joint Secretaries, but there were limits on how far this could be done,' writes Leo Rose.[69] Initially, the Muslim Conference was also subordinate to Pakistan's Muslim League. As the only political party in Azad Kashmir, the Muslim Conference, of which Ghulam Abbas remained president, was, observed Josef Korbel 'no more democratic than its opposite number, the National Conference.'[70] But relations between Ghulam Abbas and Sardar Ibrahim Khan were strained. As a Jammu Muslim, Abbas did not have any cultural affinity with Ibrahim, a Suddhan from Poonch. Although they attempted a compromise, while Ibrahim was president and Abbas was supreme head of the Azad Kashmir government, Azad Kashmir effectively had two parallel administrations running at the same time. Disagreements, however, between Ibrahim and Abbas continued until eventually Ibrahim was dismissed as president in May 1950. The reaction in Poonch amongst the independent-minded Suddhan community was defiant, with the result that in the early 1950s the Azad government was not able to function in large areas of Poonch.

Under the terms of the agreement, Pakistan was to retain control of defence, foreign policy, negotiations with the UNCIP, as well as publicity in foreign countries and in Pakistan, co-ordination of arrangements for the refugees, publicity regarding the plebiscite and all activities within Pakistan regarding Kashmir, such as transport and procurement of food. The Azad Kashmir government retained control of the administration, local publicity, development of economic resources within its territory, as well as the daily running of the state. The Muslim Conference was allotted specific functions, which related to the organisation of publicity and political activities in the entire state of Jammu and Kashmir, as well as organisational work for the plebiscite. Its objective remained the unification of the state of Jammu and Kashmir and unification with Pakistan. Unlike the National Conference, its leaders did not raise the objective of independence. When Ian Stephens, the British journalist and former editor of *The Statesman*, visited Muzaffarabad in 1953 he noted the strange paradox, that although the government of Sheikh Abdullah in Srinagar may have been politically stronger, the Azad Kashmir government had more trained Muslim officials, many of whom had come from Srinagar in 1947.[71]

In the early years, the Azad Kashmiris continued to press for firmer action from the Pakistani government to assist their development. One of the poorest areas of the former princely state, with the exception of the area around Muzaffarabad and the more fertile region around Mirpur, extending north from the Punjab plains, there was no land reform comparable to the reforms enacted by Sheikh Abdullah in the valley. Although the old feudal system was abolished, living conditions were only just bearable. There was a desperate need for schools, hospitals, doctors and nurses. In May 1954 Ibrahim protested against bribery, corruption and embezzlement, as well as accusing the minister of Kashmiri Affairs in Pakistan of proposing 'to colonise' Azad Kashmir.

Partly because of its truncated nature and its general poverty, Azad Kashmir remained an adjunct to Pakistani politics, at times used as a launching pad for initiatives into the valley, at others, a poor relation, which, because of Pakistan's claim to the whole of the state of Jammu and Kashmir, the Pakistani government never found itself in a position to acknowledge as a province of Pakistan. At the same time, Azad Kashmir remained dependent on Pakistan for its economic survival. The Azad Kashmiris were as much waiting for the plebiscite as their counterparts in the valley in order to resolve their status, which the Pakistani government was obviously anxious to ensure would go in favour of accession to Pakistan, if and when the plebiscite were held. But, while they waited, Azad Kashmir become a semi-autonomous unit in its own right. 'This new-born baby,' writes Muhammad Saraf, who later became chief justice of the Azad Kashmir High Court 'whom so many of the leading politicians were afraid to own at the time of its birth, has, over the years, got transformed into a huge structure, with all the paraphernalia of a modern State, from a flag down to town committees.'[72] And so long as 'Azad Jammu and Kashmir' existed, an alternative formula other than integration within the Indian Union presented itself to the Kashmiris across the ceasefire line. Although at times critical of Azad Kashmir, Sheikh Abdullah had kept in touch with its leaders. 'There can be no doubt,' writes Alastair Lamb 'that the prospect of a deal between Sheikh Abdullah and Azad Kashmir for what might be called an "internal settlement" of the Kashmir question caused great anxiety in New Delhi; and it was certainly a contributing factor in Sheikh Abdullah's downfall in 1953.'[73]

Abdullah under arrest

By 1953 Nehru and Abdullah had grown apart. Suspicions about Abdullah's true commitment to India had festered. Abdullah had also become dis-illusioned with India's secularism. Although he remained opposed to the two-nation theory, contrary to his earlier expectations, Pakistan was proving viable and there were some useful comparisons to be made. His speech in Jammu in 1952 pointed to specific areas of dissatisfaction: 'I had told my people that their interests were safe in India, but educated unemployed Muslims look towards Pakistan, because, while their Hindu compatriots find avenues in India open for them, the Muslims are debarred from getting

Government service.'[74] He also objected to discrimination against Muslims in the central departments as well. 'Muslims were almost entirely debarred from working in postal services. Instead of striving for secularism, the officers of this department did just the opposite.'[75]

Despite the Sheikh's earlier allegations that Pakistan was the aggressor against the state in 1947, he began to talk about India and Pakistan in the same terms. His meeting with Adlai Stevenson in May 1953 in Srinagar was viewed with alarm. As reported by the *Manchester Guardian*, Stevenson had stated that the best status for Kashmir could be independence both from India and Pakistan.[76] Although the Americans denied any interference in Kashmir's affairs, the Indian government believed that the US preference for an independent Kashmir was encouraging Abdullah to think likewise. On 13 July 1953, the anniversary of 'martyr's day' following the arrest of Abdul Qadir in 1931, Abdullah stated that it was not necessary for Jammu and Kashmir to become an appendage of either India or Pakistan.[77] In addition, there were also allegations that Abdullah was running a one-party state. Even the land reforms could be side-stepped by those with influence, who used the names of family members to increase their holdings. By 1953 the government had to admit that the co-operatives, which had been set up to help the peasants, had collapsed because of corruption and poor administration.

On 8 August, Sheikh Abdullah was dismissed as prime minister after five years in office and put under arrest. Abdullah's sense of indignation at his dismissal is clear from his memoirs, written many years after the event: 'How did a patriot, praised by Jawaharlal Nehru and Mahatma Gandhi for his straightforwardness, turn into an enemy of the country?'[78] Abdullah's procrastination in confirming the Instrument of Accession was not, however, serving India's objective of consolidating its hold on Kashmir. 'From a position of clearly endorsing the Accession to India, he had over the last few months moved into an entirely different posture,' writes Karan Singh who, as sadar-i-riyasat, signed the letter of dismissal.[79] Although Nehru knew of Abdullah's impending dismissal, he appears to have deliberately distanced himself from the precise circumstances, leaving it to the 'men on the spot' who knew best.[80]

Sheikh Abdullah's role as prime minister of Kashmir from 1948–53 has come under scrutiny ever since. Was Abdullah still the secular nationalist who had been let down by India's own ambitions to integrate Kashmir as part of India? Or was he charting his own course for Kashmir in order to retain the autonomy promised by the Instrument of Accession and enshrined in Article 370 in order to safeguard the interests of his fellow Kashmiris? Or was he working towards the independence of Jammu and Kashmir, as Nehru came to believe? 'I really cannot explain his new attitude except on the uncharitable assumption that he has lost grip of his mind,' Nehru wrote.[81] Such a remark, however, says Nehru's biographer, Sarvepalli Gopal, demonstrates the 'total failure of communication' between the two men who had worked so closely for over twenty years. B. N. Mullik, the Indian Intelligence Bureau chief, was probably more accurate in assessing that Abdullah was looking for a semi-independent status. India would protect him while he would benefit economically from the tourist industry and other sources of Kashmiri wealth, free from interference from what he had come to regard as the Hindu-dominated government in New Delhi.[82]

Abdullah's thinking at that time was also assessed in *The Times* of London:

> The Sheikh has made it clear that he is as much opposed to the domination of India as to subjugation by Pakistan. He claims sovereign authority for the Kashmir Constituent Assembly, without limitation by the Constitution of India, and this stand has a strong appeal to Kashmiris on both sides of the Ceasefire line and if his movement of purely Kashmiri nationalism was to gain ground, it might well oblige India, Pakistan and the United Nations to modify their view about what ought to be done next.[83]

Ian Stephens met Abdullah just before his arrest. He described the Sheikh as 'a Kashmiri patriot: full of zeal to improve his countrymen's plight; preoccupied with the Vale, the centre and motive of his whole political life; little concerned with the rest of the sub-continent's affairs.' Stephens, whose sympathies lay with Pakistan, went on to note that: 'it emerged from what he said that he did not at first take the idea of Pakistan seriously, nor expect her, when eventually created, to survive. Many others, better placed misjudged likewise.'[84]

Abdullah's downfall was only made possible by the support given to Delhi by some of the Sheikh's most trusted associates, G. M. Sadiq and Bakshi Ghulam Muhammad, who had been with Abdullah since the 1930s. Bakshi, from a poor family, with little education, had risen to prominence as Abdullah's right hand man. But in the post-independence years he had begun to make his own way. From 1948 to 1950 he had developed a special relationship with Sardar Patel and Karan Singh, which meant that, when the time came, he acquiesced in the Sheikh's dismissal. Only Mirza Afzal Beg was not prepared to go along with the plan. In the early hours of the morning on 9 August, Bakshi was sworn in as chief minister. Sheikh Abdullah did not return to political office until 1975 after an absence of twenty-two years, by which time he was seventy years old.

Bakshi the builder

'No one, except perhaps he himself in his secret thoughts,' writes Bilqees Taseer, 'could have dreamt then that the time would come when he, an eighth class pass student, would rise to such heights that he would intrigue to topple the Lion of Kashmir in 1953 and take his place for a reign of ten years of dictatorship and corruption.'[85] The outcry at Sheikh Abdullah's arrest was not sufficient to destabilise Bakshi's new government. The right wing was content because of his moves against the Praja Parishad movement; the leftists had been alarmed at Abdullah's meetings with US politicians. Even the Communist Party of India, which had initially given its support to Abdullah, had become disenchanted. The Pakistanis, however, reacted angrily at Abdullah's dismissal, despite their earlier criticism of the Sheikh's pro-India stance. Karachi went on strike and the Government of Pakistan announced the cancellation of their August independence day celebrations.[86]

Bakshi, however, had a substantial package to offer the people of Kashmir, which included salary rises for all government servants and workers. Known as Bakshi the Builder, he also managed to secure funds for economic development, building and road construction. From 1947 to 1953 the Indian government had invested 100 million dollars in the state and built 500 primary schools. During Bakshi's tenure they undertook the construction of a one and a half-mile long tunnel under the Banihal pass.[87] Still bitter at his dismissal, Sheikh Abdullah later described how 'lavish amounts of money were distributed by India to appease the Kashmiri Muslims'. He complained that Bakshi was distributing 'largesse' to his supporters, as well as 'filling his own coffers'.[88] Abdullah did, however, concede that some positive developments took place while Bakshi was in office: for the first time a medical college and a regional engineering college were set up. From primary to university level, education was made free. Kashmiris were economically better off in the 1960s – especially when compared with those in Azad Kashmir or as they had been in the days of the maharaja.

Part of Bakshi's brief was to finalise the details of Kashmir's accession to India. In 1954 the Constituent Assembly formally ratified the accession of the state of Jammu and Kashmir, which was intended to legitimise the Instrument of Accession, signed by Hari Singh in 1947. This measure was also meant to end all discussion of a plebiscite. On 13 April 1954 the customs barrier between Kashmir and the rest of India was lifted. President Rajendra Prasad made the first official visit by a president of India to the state of Jammu and Kashmir. Still under arrest, Sheikh Abdullah watched anxiously as the Constituent Assembly set about framing a constitution for the state of Jammu and Kashmir. His request to attend the session was refused. He therefore argued that the Constituent Assembly was not in a position to ratify the Instrument of Accession, since, without him and his supporters, it no longer represented the will of the people.

On 26 January 1957 the state of Jammu and Kashmir approved its own Constitution, modelled along the lines of the Indian Constitution; Abdullah described the introduction of the Constitution as a direct repudiation of the Indian commitment to a plebiscite under United Nations supervision. His protests and those of the United Nations Security Council, however, went unheeded. The next step was elections for a legislative assembly. Throughout this period the Constituent Assembly also functioned as a state legislature. In March 1957 elections were held and Bakshi was elected as prime minister with a majority of sixty-eight seats. The elections caused a split in the National Conference – G. M. Sadiq led a breakaway group, which included D. P. Dhar and Mir Qasim, to launch the Democratic National Conference. On 9 August 1955, two years after Sheikh Abdullah's dismissal, Mir Afzal Beg had also launched the All Jammu and Kashmir Plebiscite Front. Each year, 9 August, was observed as a 'black day' by Front activists.

After over four years in prison, Abdullah was released in January 1958. Soon afterwards he issued a statement to the press, in which he began to talk once more about the plebiscite and the right of self-determination for the people of the state. 'Expression of the will of the people through a plebiscite is the one formula which has been agreed upon by the parties concerned, and in a mass of disagreements about details, this common denominator has held the field so far.'[89] He also stated that Bakshi could 'shout from the top of the Banihal pass' that Kashmir's accession to India was 'final and irrevocable' but his government was composed of 'goondas, opportunists and thieves.'[90] The Indian authorities regarded his provocative statements as the result of contacts with Pakistan, by whom they alleged he was being financed. After only four months of freedom, Sheikh Abdullah was arrested in April and detained again for six more years.

This time the charge brought against him, along with twenty-five other co-defendants, including Mirza Afzal Beg, was of conspiracy. Abdullah's re-arrest created an angry reaction in Pakistan, where the leading Kashmiri activists, Muhammad Saraf, Sardar Qayum Khan, Ghulam Abbas decided to launch a Kashmir Liberation Movement (KLM) by crossing the ceasefire line. Their slogan was 'Kashmir Chalo' – 'Let's go to Kashmir'. But the Pakistani government, headed by President Iskander Mirza, did not wish to provoke India by supporting the attempt to cross the ceasefire line. Hundreds of activists were arrested in Azad Kashmir, including Ghulam Abbas. Muhammad Saraf pointed to the irony that Abbas, who had championed the cause of Kashmir's accession to Pakistan was in a Pakistani jail, while his old colleague, Sheikh Abdullah, who had supported Kashmir's accession to India, was under detention in India. With considerable optimism, Saraf believed that had the Pakistani government permitted them to cross the ceasefire line, it would have attracted world-wide attention, which would have 'brought home not only to the leaders of India, but also to those of the world, the urgency of solving the Kashmir issue in accordance with justice.'[91]

During Abdullah's conspiracy trial the prosecution examined 229 witnesses and exhibited nearly 300 documents. Abdullah continued to protest his innocence whilst looking at the larger interests of the people of Kashmir. 'It is a small matter as to what happens to me,' he said in a court appearance in 1961. 'But it is no small matter that the people of Jammu and Kashmir suffer poverty humiliation and degradation ... My voice may be stifled behind the prison walls, but it will continue to echo and ring for all times to come.'[92] Although he had raised the issue of plebiscite and self-determination again,

Abdullah did not, however, renounce his allegiance to India. 'My comrades [in jail] felt that we could not continue to hitch our wagon to a country in which we were treated so badly. I told them that we were wedded to certain ideals, so long as India propagated those we could not snap our ties.'[93] On 25 January 1962, the special magistrate committed all the accused to the Court of Sessions for trial, which dragged on for another two years.

Bakshi's government was not popular. Although he allowed the nominal existence of other political parties, their leaders were arrested indiscriminately and public meetings were banned. The 'Peace' Brigade was used to victimise opponents of the government. Foreign journalists were not welcome in the state. Stephen Harper, a reporter for the *Daily Express* wrote:

> I had scarcely arrived in Srinagar, the capital, last week when a mob swarmed around my car. They shouted "Murder him – we don't want British reporters here!" Car doors and canopy were ripped off. Hands grabbed and tore at my clothes. Little baskets of charcoal – carried around for heat were poured over me and burned my face.[94]

Political dissent was crushed. 'The common man, under Bakshi's tyrannical rule, was denied even basic civil liberties,' noted Mir Qasim, a former associate, but now a political opponent. 'The government agents forced hot potatoes into the mouths of their opponents, put heavy stones on their chest; and branded them with red hot irons.'[95] Various newspapers critical of the government were banned, including the *Voice of Kashmir*, edited by Prem Nath Bazaz, who had moved to Delhi. The elections in 1962 were so evidently rigged, that Jawaharlal Nehru commented: 'In fact, it would strengthen your position much more if you lost a few seats to bona fide opponents.' All that could be said of Baskhi's government was that the people had more freedom than under the maharaja. 'It is true that political liberty does not exist there in the same measure as in the rest of India. At the same time, there is much more of it than there used to be.'[96]

'So far as the economic and social life of the Kashmiris is concerned,' wrote Prem Nath Bazaz, who visited the valley in the early 1960s, 'I have no doubt that they are grateful to India for the little progress they have made … but political persecution and suppression of free opinion coupled with harassment by the goonda element is, besides making them sullen and resentful, neutralising the good effects of the benevolent attitude of the Union government.' He also believed that the accession issue had not gone away. 'To make Kashmir's accession to India everlasting, it is essential that the Kashmiris should feel convinced that economically as well as politically they will enjoy freedom by remaining as part of the great Indian nation.' He also noted that whereas Sheikh Abdullah guarded Kashmir's autonomy, 'to curry favour with the Indian public opinion' Bakshi Ghulam Muhammad 'made inroads into it.' With some foresight to the future deterioration of relations he concluded: 'Before long when India wakes up, as it must some day, in the near future, if not today, it may be too late. No liberalisation of policy may be able to repair the damage."[97] On 3 October 1963 Bakshi was one of many cabinet ministers and chief ministers who agreed to resign under the terms of the plan put forward by K. Kamaraj, the chief minister of Madras, who suggested that he and some other chief ministers might resign in order to do party work. Bakshi Ghulam Muhammad was replaced by Khwaja Shamsuddin. Subsequently, a one-man commission, under Mr Justice Ayyangar, enquired into charges of corruption and misuse of power by Bakshi. Initially 77 charges were brought against him, of which 38 were referred to the commission. Ayyangar ruled that fifteen were proved.

The ten-year period of Bakshi Ghulam Muhammad's rule is noted for the steady erosion of the special status with which Kashmir had begun its relationship with India. Some of the changes appeared to be cosmetic, but they increased suspicions amongst Kashmiris that the state of Jammu and Kashmir was being made to conform with the other states in India. Shortly before his resignation, Bakshi Ghulam Muhammad had announced that the head of the Kashmir state would, in future, be called chief minister rather than prime minister, which would conform with the other states of the Indian Union and that the sadar-i-riyasat would be known as the governor. The jurisdiction of the Supreme Court and the Election Commission of India was also extended. Throughout most of this period, Sheikh Abdullah was in prison, but his influence and that of his supporters kept alive not only the issue of the plebiscite but also of Kashmir's 'special status'.

Diplomacy and War

The talks between India and Pakistan resemble badminton. The arrangement was to talk a few days first in Pakistan, now a few days in India. The thing is to get the shuttle back in the other court. John Kenneth Galbraith[1]

India's basic advantage lay in the fact that she was already in occupation of what she wanted. If Pakistan wished to change the status of the disputed territory, it was for her to do something about it and risk seeming belligerent. Outsiders are prone to treat the maintenance of the status quo as peace and its disturbance by either side, even for good reasons, a move toward war. Sam Burke[2]

Throughout the 1960s the Kashmiri issue continued to cause concern at an international level. In October 1962 the unresolved dispute between India and China over their Himalayan border erupted when the Chinese overran Indian outposts and moved troops into the North-East Frontier Area (N-EFA) and Ladakh. Although the immediate crisis between India and China ended when, on 21 November, the Chinese declared a unilateral ceasefire, the Indians, who had shown themselves particularly ill-equipped for such high altitude fighting, still felt vulnerable over their long-term security. Nehru, who had earlier shunned military assistance as signifying 'practically becoming aligned to that country', was now prepared to accept it. In a much quoted passage, he admitted that through his policy of non-alignment: 'We were getting out of touch with reality in the modern world and we were living in an atmosphere of our own creation.'[3] He was even prepared to talk in terms of a tacit air defence pact with the United States in case the Chinese resumed their offensive.[4] In return, however, the Indian government was obliged to submit to political pressure from Western countries for talks with Pakistan regarding a resolution of the Kashmir issue.

Endless talks

At the end of November 1962 both Britain and the United States sent missions to New Delhi, led respectively by Duncan Sandys, the secretary of state for Commonwealth Relations, and Averell Harriman, the assistant secretary of state for Far Eastern Affairs in order to determine what military help India might need. The Americans and British were also anxious to reassure Pakistan regarding the extent of any military assistance to India. In a statement on 20 November President John Kennedy said: 'In providing military assistance to India, we are mindful of our alliance with Pakistan. All of our aid to India is for the purpose of defeating Chinese communist subversion.'[5] The Anglo–American team also wanted to initiate bilateral talks between India and Pakistan to help them resolve their differences, in order to present a united front against the threat from communist China.

Pakistan, under President Ayub Khan, who had assumed power in a military coup, ousting Iskander Mirza in 1958, was, however, not convinced that such solidarity would work to Pakistan's advantage. Not only did the Pakistanis mistrust the Indians, but they were angered that India, which had so consistently pursued a policy of 'non-alignment' should receive weapons from the West, which the Pakistanis had been permitted only after joining the two Western military alliances, CENTO and SEATO; in addition, Pakistan had been obliged to allow the Americans to install surveillance equipment on Pakistani soil, which had displeased the Soviets and potentially impaired Pakistan's relations with the Russians. The grant of military equipment appeared to have put India on the same level as Pakistan, who was supposed to be America's 'most favoured ally'.

The Indian government also reacted less positively to the talks because the Pakistani government was already engaged in its own separate negotiations with the Chinese to demarcate the common boundary between China and northern Kashmir. Even before the Sino–Indian war, Krishna Menon, the Indian defence minister, had stated in the UN Security Council in June 1962 that any agreement was in 'total violation of any rights of authority Pakistan may possess, for Pakistan has no sovereignty over the state; it is not Pakistan's to trade away or to negotiate about.'[6]

Sandys and Harriman were, however, able to use the Indians' desperate need for weapons to persuade Nehru to meet Ayub in order to try and resolve the Kashmir problem. 'Dependent on the United States and Britain for military assistance, India could not refuse to talk to Pakistan,' writes Nehru's biographer, Sarvepalli Gopal.[7] Lord Mountbatten was once more back in Delhi with Sandys in order to prepare the ground for the talks. By this time, according to Philip Ziegler, Mountbatten believed that the only solution was for Kashmir to be independent and demilitarised. 'When Nehru pleaded how dangerous any change of the present balance in Kashmir might be for the large Muslim minority in India, Mountbatten replied that he was never one to stir up sleeping dogs unnecessarily, but that this dog was already awake and barking.'[8] Nehru's cabinet ministers were unreceptive to the proposal. In their joint statement, issued on 29 November, announcing the talks, Ayub Khan and Jawaharlal Nehru merely announced that a renewed effort should be made to resolve outstanding differences between the two countries on Kashmir and other related matters.

The first round of talks over Jammu and Kashmir between India and Pakistan was held at the end of December 1962. During this, and subsequent meetings various proposals were put forward. Whereas India suggested the ceasefire line should become the international boundary, with a few minor realignments around Poonch, the Pakistanis wanted to draw the boundary far to the east, giving themselves the whole state with the exception of south-eastern Jammu. Out of a total area of over 84,000 square miles India was to be left with less than 3,000 square miles.

After the second round of talks came the official signing of the Sino–Pakistan Border Agreement, which soured an already tense atmosphere. Zulfikar Ali Bhutto, who had taken over as foreign minister in January 1963 after the death of Muhammed Ali Bogra, went to Beijing to meet with his Chinese counterpart, Chen Yi, for the ceremony on 2 March 1963. Although the Pakistanis claimed to have gained 750 square miles of land, the Indians believed they had ceded 2,700 square miles of what they regarded as 'Indian' (because it was Kashmiri) territory.[9] The Pakistanis countered the allegation, stating that the agreement was provisional pending a proper boundary treaty once the Kashmiri dispute had been resolved. China's agreement to the negotiations was interpreted as public acceptance of Pakistan's position that the status of Jammu and Kashmir had not yet been finalised.

Another of Pakistan's proposals, supported by Britain, was to inter-nationalise the valley so that Indian troops could be withdrawn and replaced by forces of other countries; after six months the wishes of the people were to be ascertained. This was, however, writes Gopal 'a suggestion which even the Americans saw to be impractical, as it played into the hands of the Chinese, who would work on any Asian and African powers concerned.'[10] Sir Morrice James, the British high commissioner in Pakistan, believed 'the right course would be for India and Pakistan each to accept that the other should have a substantial position in the Vale, and the Indian government could not be expected to give up Ladakh.' The proposal was designed 'to permit clearly defined arrangements for sovereignty, political freedom, the free movement of people, the development of tourism, and economic development.'[11] Initially, this solution was favoured by President Kennedy, who urged the Indian government to make such proposals 'which will be proof positive to the Pakistanis that you genuinely seek a settlement by signalling a willingness to give Pakistan a substantial position in the Vale.'[12] In April 1963 Walt Rostow was sent by President Kennedy to India and Pakistan to assess the prospects for agreement between the two countries. But he did not find 'a driving determination to settle the quarrel' on either the Indian or the Pakistani side.[13]

After six rounds of talks, which were held intermittently until May 1963, and in which Bhutto and Swaran Singh, the Indian foreign minister, were the principal negotiators, a joint communiqué was issued which stated that with regret no agreement could be reached on a settlement of the Kashmir dispute. Whereas during the talks the two sides had discussed the possibility of partitioning the state, in their public statements this suggestion was rejected.[14] The Indian government proposed that both countries should seek only peaceful methods to settle their differences and that neither should seek to alter the status quo in Kashmir. Bhutto did not endorse the 'no war' declaration but gave the assurance that Pakistan did believe in peaceful methods. 'To have promoted the 1962–3 Indo-Pakistan talks and seen them fail, had thus served the useful purpose of showing that further efforts of the kind would not succeed,' commented Sir Morrice James.[15]

From the Indians' point of view, due to their vulnerability over China, the 1962–63 talks were one of the rare occasions when they were obliged to depart from their established position over Kashmir: that discussion in someway implied that the status of Jammu and Kashmir was in doubt. The Pakistanis mistakenly hoped that Britain and the United States would withhold the promised weapons to India in return for a more favourable outcome for Pakistan over Kashmir, but it is unlikely that Nehru would have yielded to such a threat. By 1962 possession of the best part of Kashmir was both politically and psychologically too important, particularly when the Indian public were still reacting to their army's defeat by the Chinese.[16]

After the talks Nehru went to Srinagar where he noted how China's attack on India had given the Pakistanis an opportunity to revive the Kashmir issue. But, he said: 'Pakistan is mistaken if it thinks it can intimidate us because we are facing this threat from the Chinese.' The new relationship between China and Pakistan meant, however, that the Pakistanis also felt inclined to speak from a position of strength: 'Attack from India on Pakistan today is no longer confined to the security and territorial integrity of Pakistan,' said Zulfikar Ali Bhutto in Pakistan's National Assembly in July 1963. 'An attack by India on Pakistan involves the territorial integrity and security of the largest state in Asia.[17] He also made the dramatic statement: 'Kashmir is to Pakistan what Berlin is to the West' and warned that, since the conflict threatened peace and security of the world, 'it was an issue hanging heavily on the conscience of mankind.'[18]

Amongst the Kashmiris watching as Pakistan and India discussed their future were those who were discontented with the status quo, but not yet in a strong enough position to do anything about it. One of this older generation of activists was Amanullah Khan. Born in Astor near Gilgit and educated in Srinagar, he and some colleagues reacted to the discussion on the partition of Kashmir by forming an organisation called the Kashmir Independence Committee. 'We suggested that if there has got to be some sort of deviation from plebiscite, from the right of self-determination, it should not be the division of Kashmir, it should be the independence of the whole state.'[19] The talks failed and the Committee was later disbanded. But, says Amanullah Khan, it was the first time the Kashmiri nationalists in exile in Pakistan began to think seriously about independence.

In October 1963 the Government of Pakistan once more referred the question of Kashmir to the Security Council and, in the Spring of 1964, the issue was debated for the 110th time in fifteen years. On his way to New

York, Bhutto announced that Pakistan was prepared to discuss the issue a thousand times in order to see that it was settled 'in an honourable manner'.[20] But, in view of the Soviet veto, there was little the United Nations could do. The president of the Security Council expressed the concern of all the members that 'two great countries which have everything to gain from re-establishing good relations with each other and whose present disputes, particularly that centring upon Jammu and Kashmir, should be settled amicably in the interest of world peace.'[21]

Politics in the vale

In mid-winter, on a freezing cold night in late December 1963, an event of extraordinary significance had occurred in the valley. The most sacred Muslim relic in Kashmir, the strand of hair from the beard of the Prophet, the Mo-i Muqaddas, was stolen from the mosque at Hazratbal. Word of the theft spread throughout the city and thousands marched through the streets of Srinagar, demanding that the thieves should be caught and punished. A 'Sacred Hair Action Committee' was set up by the outraged Kashmiris, which temporarily united pro and anti-Abdullah factions. The Sheikh's son, Farooq, and Mirwaiz Maulvi Farooq, jointly protested at the theft.

Chief Minister Shamsuddin was slow in taking the initiative, and Nehru dispatched his Intelligence Bureau chief, B. N. Mullik, to take steps to recover the relic. While he set about the delicate task of locating it, the anger of the people spread into the countryside. In order to diffuse fears of communal strife, on 4 January Karan Singh arrived in Srinagar and visited Hazratbal. He organised prayers in the temples for the return of the sacred relic. Later that evening the mosque was cleared of policemen and officials. It has never been revealed who stole the holy relic, but Mullik succeeded in tracking down the thieves and arranging for the relic to be returned quietly to the mosque that evening.

From the Pakistani perspective, the tremendous Islamic fervour which manifested itself throughout the state over the missing relic seemed to be a sure sign that all was not well with the so-called secularism espoused by the current rulers of Kashmir. Muslim disturbances in Srinagar were accompanied by protests from Hindus at the theft of holy objects from temples in Jammu. As unrest increased, the government crushed the demonstrations by force, killing several people. As a reaction there were riots against Hindus in East Pakistan, which in turn resulted in communal outbreaks in some towns in India. The tense atmosphere was only relieved when, at the beginning of February 1964, a panel of holy men examined the relic and judged that it was the original.

Soon after the return of the sacred relic, Shamsuddin was replaced as chief minister by Ghulam Muhammad Sadiq. The atmosphere in the valley changed considerably. Prem Nath Bazaz described an 'altogether different political climate'. People were able to express their political views freely, hooliganism was dying down and corruption decreased.[22] At the same time Bazaz felt that it was necessary to maintain the momentum of liberalisation. 'I found that after restoring the civil liberties of the Kashmiris, the Sadiq government was inclined to rest on its oars, thinking that the people should remain beholden for what had already been done for them.'[23]

The accession issue, however, was still unresolved in people's minds. In addition, Abdullah's conspiracy case had dragged on for nearly six years and his continuing detention was proving embarrassing to the Government of India. 'Sheikh Abdullah on Trial but India in the Dock' was just one of many newspaper headlines at the time.[24] On 8 April 1964 Abdullah was honourably acquitted and released from Jammu Central jail. 'Falsehood has a rotten core. Their vile accusations were fully exposed before the public and the case became a joke,' wrote Abdullah.[25] He immediately went on the offensive: 'We have to win hearts and if we fail in this regard we cannot be ruled by force,' he said two days after his release.[26] But the Indian government continued to maintain that the accession of the state of Jammu and Kashmir to India was 'full final and complete.'[27] 'Whatever be the grandiose delusions and dreams Abdullah now nourishes, New Delhi must leave him and his supporters in no doubt that accession is an accomplished fact and that only some of the processes of integration remain to be completed,' stated an editorial in the Indian Express.'[28] 'Sheikh Abdullah is now a demagogue at large, and he is plainly engaged in secessionist political activity,' said The Times of India, Bombay.[29]

At the highest level, however, the ailing prime minister of India, Jawaharlal Nehru, was no longer prepared to share these misgivings about his old friend. 'His attitude to Abdullah at this time was a blend of guilt at having allowed him to have been kept so long in detention and of concern at the consequences of his activities,' writes Sarvepalli Gopal.[30] After his release, Abdullah went to stay with Nehru in Delhi:

> Panditji expressed his deep anguish and sorrow at the past incidents. I also became very emotional and told him that I was glad to have convinced him that I was not disloyal to him personally or to India . . . I implored him to take the initiative in resolving the Kashmir problem. Panditji agreed and asked me to visit Pakistan and try to persuade the President, Ayub Khan, to enter into negotiations with his Indian counterpart.[31]

For the first and last time in his life, Sheikh Abdullah went to Pakistan. Before he left he issued a press statement: 'We are faced with an alarming situation. If we fail to remedy it our future generations will never pardon us . . . The Kashmiri problem is a long-standing bone of contention.'[32]

When Abdullah arrived in Rawalpindi, he received an enthusiastic welcome from a crowd estimated to be half a million. 'There was much excitement in Pakistan about the first ever visit of Sheikh Abdullah – the Lion of Kashmir,' writes Altaf Gauhar, Ayub Khan's minister for information. 'His critics preferred to call him the "leopard of Kashmir" who had finally changed his spots. What was India's game in allowing Sheikh Abdullah to visit Pakistan?'[33] According to Gauhar, the official view was that Sheikh Abdullah should be given a warm but not effusive welcome and an elaborate programme was drawn up 'so that he could see for himself the progress Pakistan had made since independence.'[34]

Although the personal rapport between the Kashmiri leader and the Pakistani president was good, Ayub Khan was obliged to reject Abdullah's suggestion of a confederation. 'Any kind of confederal arrangement would undo the partition and place the Hindu majority in a dominant and decisive position in respect of confederal subjects, i.e. foreign affairs, defence and finance.'[35] Abdullah later said that the idea of confederation was only one proposal among many and that the purpose of his visit was specifically so that both parties 'should abstain from rigid attitudes and sympathetically consider each other's viewpoint.'[36] At a press conference, he declared that a solution of the Kashmiri problem must satisfy the wishes of the Kashmiri people and depended on friendship between India and Pakistan. He also stated that it must not give either side a sense of defeat.[37] Ayub Khan agreed to consider any solution which met Pakistan's minimum conditions. He also accepted the invitation to come to Delhi to meet Nehru in the middle of June.

The day the news of the proposed meeting was announced was 27 May. Sheikh Abdullah left for Muzaffarabad. But his visit was cut short by the sudden news that Jawaharlal Nehru, aged seventy-four, had died. In one of those mysteries of history, the Indian prime minister left unfinished whatever he might have been able to do for Kashmir in the last days of his life. Bhutto travelled with Abdullah to Delhi for Nehru's funeral, and discussed Kashmir with the Sheikh, who, according to Stanley Wolpert's account, advised Bhutto to hold to requesting a plebiscite for the entire state whilst suggesting that partition below the Chenab river might be a realistic solution. Bhutto was apparently 'elated' by the Sheikh's 'flexibility', since during his talks with Ayub, Abdullah had insisted that partition was not possible.[38] But further proposed talks did not materialise. According to Abdullah, Nehru's successor, Lal Bahadur Shastri, was keen to finish Nehru's work, but 'he did not have the strength to bring his colleagues round to his viewpoint.'[39] Furthermore, the Indian government was continuing to pass measures designed to strengthen Kashmir's links with India.

The Presidential Order passed by the Indian government on 21 December 1964 enabling the president to govern the state of Jammu and Kashmir directly was bitterly resented by opponents of India's increasing control. So too was the announcement on 9 January 1965 that the local National Conference party would be dissolved and that the Indian National Congress party was to establish a branch in Kashmir. 15 January 1965 was observed as a Protest Day.

In February 1965 Abdullah decided 'to fulfil the tenets of Islam which have been ordained for all Muslims – the performance of Haj.'[40] He and a small party which included his wife and Mirza Afzal Beg, planned to visit some other Islamic countries, as well as Britain and France. In Algiers, Abdullah met Chou en-Lai, China's prime minister and, according to his memoirs, they discussed China's agreement with Pakistan over the northern frontier of Gilgit. The Chinese premier stated: 'At present, Gilgit is under the control of Pakistan and, therefore, we entered into an agreement stipulating that the agreement shall remain valid only as long as Gilgit is under the control of Pakistan.' Abdullah says that he sent a summary of his conversation to the Indian ambassador to China, but news of Chou en-Lai's invitation to Abdullah to visit China upset the Indian authorities. Abdullah had also written an article in a US quarterly magazine in which he suggested that India, Pakistan and the Kashmiris should find a solution which would concede to the Kashmiris 'the substance of their demand for self-determination but with honour and fairness to both Pakistan and India.'[41] When he returned to India in May 1965 Abdullah was arrested. He was interned in Tamil Nadu at Otacamund, 2,000 miles away from Kashmir. Afzal Beg was imprisoned in Delhi. Begum Abdullah was also interned in Delhi. Protests in the valley against the arrests were crushed. 'A vilification campaign was started against us under a well-planned conspiracy with a view to distorting our image and creating a psychological environment in which harsh measures may be used against us.'[42]

In Pakistan Ayub Khan was coming under increasing domestic pressure to take some initiative over Kashmir. During the July Presidential campaign, when he was opposed by Mohammad Ali Jinnah's sister, Fatima, Ayub had stressed his role as the defender of Kashmir. He was also being pressed by the 'Azad' Kashmiris, who claimed to have a force of 20,000 trained men in order to mount an Algerian-type struggle to liberate their 'brothers'. On the military front, time was also running out. In April 1963 the Indian defence ministry had announced that the strength of the army would be doubled. The following September, the Indian government gave further details of the expansion of the Navy, Army and Air Force, made possible by the assistance of the UK, the USA and the USSR.[43]

Armed conflict

Internationally, Pakistan was beginning to emerge from its political dependence on the United States. Ayub Khan's successful visit to China in March 1965 had considerably enhanced his domestic standing. 'The people felt elevated by the knowledge that China had become Pakistan's friend and ally against India,' writes Altaf Gauhar.[44] When President Johnson cancelled Ayub Khan's scheduled visit to the United States,[45] Ayub Khan at once accepted an invitation by the Russians to visit the Soviet Union, making the first ever visit by a Pakistani head of government to Moscow. According to Gauhar, who accompanied the president, Ayub Khan had a frank conversation with Prime Minister Alexei Kosygin about Kashmir. He pointed out that by using the veto, the Soviet Union was 'bailing India out' in the UN Security Council. The Soviets were upset at the recent U2 episode when an American espionage plane, launched from the Badaber base in Pakistan, had been shot down over Soviet territory. What began, however, as a cool exchange of views was, according to Gauhar, described by Kosygin at the end of their meetings as 'a turning point which will lead to further exchanges of views and to big decisions in the interest of our two countries.'[46] A trade treaty was signed as well as a credit agreement on oil prospecting. But while Ayub Khan was still in Moscow he received a cable from Islamabad indicating the movement of Indian troops into the disputed territory of the Rann of Kutch.

Distant from Kashmir, the Rann of Kutch affair preceded the outbreak of formal hostilities between India and Pakistan in their second war over Kashmir in September 1965. This tract of land, equivalent in size to the valley of Kashmir, separates Sindh in Pakistan from Kutch in India. Inhabited mainly by flamingos and wild donkeys, during the monsoon it is flooded; at other times of the year it is dry and desolate (which is the meaning of the word 'rann') Ever since partition, Pakistan had been contesting the boundary between Sindh and Kutch. In the spring of 1965 a clash between border patrols escalated into fighting between the regular armies. When Indian forces withdrew, leaving behind them 40 miles of marshland, the Pakistanis were jubilant. A ceasefire was mediated in the name of the British prime minister, Harold Wilson, facilitated by the two British high commissioners in Islamabad and Delhi, Morrice James and John Freeman. Agreement was finally reached on 30 June 1965, which provided for arbitration. A year later Pakistan was awarded the northern half of the Rann. 'The Pakistanis thus gained more by accepting Western mediation between India and themselves than they would have achieved alone,' writes Morrice James.[47] The significance of this affair is that it undoubtedly encouraged the Pakistanis in their assessment that the Indian army, still suffering from the after-effects of its defeat by the Chinese, and not yet bolstered by its planned expansion, was inferior to their own.

The conclusion which Morrice James believes President Ayub Khan, Zulfikar Ali Bhutto and Aziz Ahmed, Ayub's expert on Indian affairs, drew from the Rann of Kutch affair was as follows: if the Kashmir dispute could be reactivated by stirring up a rebellion in the Indian-held section, a critical situation would arise which would be sufficient to oblige the western countries to intervene. India might then be pressurised to submit the dispute to mediation, which if successful might lead to a more favourable solution to Pakistan than the status quo. They also deduced that after the Rann of Kutch affair the morale of the Indians was low.[48] 'For all his realism and prudence,' writes Altaf Gauhar, 'Ayub's judgement did get impaired by the Rann of Kutch in one respect. His old prejudice that the "Hindu has no stomach for a fight" turned into belief, if not a military doctrine, which had the decisive effect on the course of events."[49] Viewed from across the ceasefire line, the valley of Kashmir appeared ripe for revolt. The theft of the holy relic from Hazratbal in 1963 had demonstrated the intense Islamic feeling amongst the Muslims of the valley.

The headquarters for what came to be known as 'Operation Gibraltar' were based at Murree under Major General Akhtar Hussain Malik. Malik was in command of several task forces, named after famous generals drawn from Muslim history: Tariq, Qasim, Khalid, Salahuddin, Ghaznavi, and Nusrat, which would advance across the ceasefire line into Kashmir and attack specific targets. The initiative, however, was not without risk. The Indian army was three times the size that of Pakistan and there was no guarantee that India would not invade Pakistan across the international frontier. In addition, writes Major-General Shahid Hamid, 'the Army was not trained or ready for the offensive; some 25 per cent of the men were on leave. There was little time to make up for this deficiency in our planning and the crisis created a series of isolated battles.'[50]

The objective was for Salahuddin force to assemble in Srinagar on 8 August; the next day – the 12th anniversary of Sheikh Abdullah's arrest in August 1953 – supporters of the Plebiscite Front had planned to hold a strike against Abdullah's recent arrest. The Pakistani strategists therefore believed that the discontented population would support their invasion. After seizing the radio station and Srinagar airport, a Revolutionary Council would issue a declaration of 'Liberation', proclaiming it was the only legitimate government of Jammu and Kashmir. In an additional operation, known as Grand Slam, lines of communication were to be attacked in the Poonch/Nowshera district; possession of Akhnur Bridge across the Chenab river would isolate the state of Jammu and Kashmir from the rest of India, trapping the Indian army in the state as well as the forces facing the Chinese in Ladakh.

No contact, however, appears to have been made in advance with the Muslim political leadership in the valley. Contrary to Pakistani intelligence information, the valley was not ripe for revolt. 'Pakistani commandos, armed to the teeth, would appear as liberators in the middle of the night only to create panic and terror,' writes Altaf Gauhar.[51] On 5 August, a shepherd boy reported to the police the presence of some 'strangers' in Tanmarg who had offered bribes in return for information. He led the police directly to Salahuddin's base camp. 'Pakistan at this stage had little mass support in the valley and that is why this ingenious plan failed to take off,' writes the Indian Major-General Afsir Karim. 'In fact no one was quite sure what was going on. Pakistan kept denying its "involvement" at the top of its voice and called it a local uprising - but there was no local uprising.'[52] Kashmiri anger demonstrated over the missing sacred relic did not, at this stage, mean that the people were prepared to throw their lot in with the Pakistanis and fight

India. With the exception of Ghaznavi, the forces were not able to make any impact on the Indian positions.

The Indian prime minister, Lal Bahadur Shastri, was also under pressure from his military advisers to take decisive action. On 16 August a crowd of over 100,000 marched on the Indian parliament in Delhi to demonstrate against any weakness over the state of Jammu and Kashmir.[53] The Indian counter-offensive was more far-reaching than the Pakistanis had anticipated. For ostensibly defensive reasons, in order to close the points of entry from the infiltrators, they attacked Pakistani positions in the Kargil sector, as well as in Tithwal and Uri-Poonch. Their operation against the Haji Pir Pass on 28 August left the Pakistani forces dangerously exposed.

Despite the setback to Operation Gibraltar, of which Ayub Khan appears to have been unaware, General Muhammed Musa, the commander-in-chief, was 'urging Bhutto to obtain Ayub's approval' to launch Operation Grand Slam.[54] Musa had been appointed by Ayub, writes Major-General Shahid Hamid, 'though quite aware of his limitations. His chief virtue was that he would never challenge his leader's authority or position. On the other hand, Musa played it safe, and always toed the line.'[55] On 29 August President Ayub Khan sent Musa a 'top secret' order 'to take such action that will defreeze the Kashmir problem, weaken India's resolve and bring her to a conference table without provoking a general war.'[56] Under Malik's leadership, Operation Grand Slam was launched on 31 August. The objective was to move in from Bhimber and cut off Indian lines of communication along the Pathankot road from Jammu to Srinagar via the Banihal pass, much as was planned in 1947. Once Pakistani forces reached Akhnur, they had only to take the bridge across the Chenab river in order to reach the city of Jammu. 'At this point, someone's prayers worked,' writes the Indian journalist M. J. Akbar. 'An inexplicable change of command took place.'[57] Hussain Malik was replaced by Major-General Agha Mohammad Yahya Khan.

Gauhar describes the details of Grand Slam as still being shrouded 'in a haze of confusion, indecision and loss of communication.'[58] The operation was based on the assumption that the Indian forces were exposed, but they had in fact been building up their defences and the Pakistani troops were not able to make the swift breakthrough they had envisaged. Furthermore, the Pakistanis had crossed a small section of the international frontier between Sialkot and Jammu, which was an open provocation for the Indian forces to extend the war. Although the view both in India and even amongst 'sensible army officers' in Pakistan was that Malik's sudden replacement led to the failure of Grand Slam, Gauhar maintains that Malik had already lost all credibility after Gibraltar. 'The truth is that General Malik was a broken man because he knew better than anyone else that his mission had failed.'[59] Once Ayub Khan was aware of the failure of Operation Gibraltar and realised how vulnerable the Pakistani forces were, the task of winding up the operation was given to Major-General Mohammad Yahya Khan.

In addition, the assessment, supported both by Bhutto and Aziz Ahmed, that the Indians were in no position to attack across the international frontier was also disproved. At first light on 6 September two columns of the Indian army marched towards Lahore which lay only fourteen miles from the international border. 'Astonishingly the Pakistanis were taken by surprise,' records Morrice James. 'Their troops had not been alerted and were asleep in their barracks. Some of them left with their weapons for the front line in their pyjamas for want of time to put on battle-dress.'[60] A third column crossed into West Punjab towards Sialkot, north-east of Lahore. The Indian air force also bombed Pakistani air bases. The sub-continent was set for all-out war. Both Britain and the United States, who were the main suppliers of weapons to both sides, announced a halt in military aid until peace was restored. During the war, Russia continued to supply military equipment to India, but remained ostensibly neutral. Muslim countries, with the exception of Malaysia, promised assistance and moral support to Pakistan. The Arab summit conference commended the principle of self-determination and requested India and Pakistan to settle their differences according to the UN resolutions.[61]

Once again the United Nations was drawn into trying to bring about a ceasefire. On the basis of information provided by the UN Military Observer Group, which had been monitoring the ceasefire line for the past sixteen years, Secretary-General U Thant repeatedly appealed to the governments of India and Pakistan to return to their original positions along the ceasefire line. On 4 and 6 September the Security Council had adopted resolutions calling for a ceasefire and on 9 September U Thant visited first Pakistan and then India in an attempt to get the two sides to stop fighting. When Morrice James met Ayub Khan on 7 September he found him 'visibly depressed', saying that the ceasefire 'must be a purposeful one that would open the door to a settlement of the Kashmir dispute.'[62] India refused to negotiate and Pakistan was running out of ammunition. With the capture of Khem Karan, an Indian village across the border, the Pakistani counter-offensive against Amritsar looked as if it might temporarily succeed. But on 11 September India opened the floodgates of its dams trapping nearly 100 Pakistani tanks and Khem Karan, became, according to Gauhar, 'a graveyard of Pakistani tanks ... for Pakistan the war was over'.[63]

Before finally being drawn to the negotiating table, Ayub Khan turned to the Chinese. On 4 September the Chinese foreign minister, Chen Yi, had met Bhutto in Karachi and supported Pakistan's 'just action' in repelling the Indian 'armed provocation' in Kashmir.[64] Further statements in support of Pakistan followed, warning against Indian intrusion into Chinese territory. On 16 September the Chinese issued an ultimatum accusing India of building up military works on the boundary of the Chinese-Sikkim frontier. Unless these were dismantled and the Indians agreed to refrain from further raids, they were warned that they would have to face the consequences.[65] The

British and Americans viewed the entry of China into the diplomatic war of words with increasing alarm and as a potential prelude to intervention and the escalation of the war. The British prime minister, Harold Wilson, issued a statement promising the assistance of both the United States and United Kingdom to India if the Chinese intervened in the war.[66]

How close this intervention could have become is related by Altaf Gauhar, who describes Ayub Khan's secret visit to Beijing on the night of 19 September, when he met Prime Minister Chou en-Lai. According to Ayub's verbatim account to Gauhar, the Chinese premier gave the Pakistani president an offer of unconditional support on the understanding that Pakistan realised it would have to be prepared for a long war in which some cities like Lahore might be lost. Ayub Khan was not prepared to undertake a protracted war and returned to Pakistan as secretly as he had come, without taking up the Chinese offer.[67] Moreover, he knew that the Army and Air Force were opposed to prolonging the conflict. As Shahid Hamid noted: 'All planning was based on a short, sharp encounter and ammunition and reserves were organised accordingly.'[68] Subsequently, the Chinese backed down on their aggressive stance towards India. The precise nature of India's alleged 'military installations' on the border was never established.

On 20 September, the UN Security Council passed a strongly worded resolution, for the first time in its history, 'demanding' that a ceasefire should take effect in two days. Bhutto flew to New York to address the Security Council on the night of 22 September. Pakistan's official position was still not conciliatory towards India and, in a speech, whose rhetoric was thrilling to the Pakistanis back home, he warned that Pakistan would wage a war for 'a thousand years, a war of defence.'[69] But the opportunity for Pakistan to fulfil its declared objectives had now passed.

The ceasefire came into force at midday on 23 September on the understanding given to Ayub Khan, by both the British and Americans, that they would do their best to settle the political problem between India and Pakistan which had caused the current conflict.[70]

Tashkent

Once the ceasefire was put into effect an uneasy truce prevailed. Neither the United States, preoccupied with Vietnam, nor Britain was in a position to pressurise India to negotiate a settlement over Kashmir which would be favourable to Pakistan. India was certainly not going to give up through diplomacy what Pakistan had failed to secure in war. Swaran Singh, the Indian foreign minister, had declared in the General Assembly that Kashmir was an integral part of India and that its future was not negotiable.[71] Bhutto's veiled threats in the General Assembly and the Security Council that Pakistan would have to withdraw from the UN unless the ceasefire was made conditional on a resolution of the plebiscite issue went unheeded.

In January 1966 Indian and Pakistani delegations met in Tashkent where the Soviet prime minister, Alexei Kosygin, acted as unofficial mediator. Ayub and Shastri accepted a declaration in which both countries reaffirmed their commitment to solving their disputes through peaceful means. They also agreed to revert to their positions prior to 5 August 1965. Within hours of the close of the negotiations, on 10 January 1966, Shastri died of a heart attack. He was succeeded as prime minister by Jawaharlal Nehru's daughter, Indira Gandhi. Ayub Khan returned to Islamabad having accepted a return to the status quo which was far removed from Pakistan's declared war aims. While the Tashkent declaration noted the existence of the Kashmir dispute, it effectively put the issue into cold storage.

In Pakistan the controlled press did not allow criticism of Tashkent and 'continued to beat the patriotic drum as if the war with India was still going on,' writes Morrice James.[72] The 'spirit of Tashkent' was taken to symbolic extremes with the banning of the popular – but anti-Russian – James Bond film, 'From Russia with Love'.[73] But there was discontent beneath the surface. Those who had been led to believe that Pakistan was poised for victory, could not understand the necessity of the ceasefire. In early 1966 there were student riots in the colleges and universities. In Lahore the police opened fire on a group of demonstrators and two students were killed. Once the true significance of the ceasefire and Tashkent were apparent the people reacted against their president. 'The feeling of let-down and frustration was particularly strong amongst the people who lived in the areas of the Punjab around Lahore and Sialkot, where over the years many Kashmiris had settled,' writes Morrice James. 'For them Ayub had betrayed the nation and had inexcusably lost face before the Indians.'[74]

What is significant about the 1965 war from a Pakistani perspective is that, despite its failure to achieve its objectives, undoubtedly based on wrong assessments and policy decisions, the belief that the incursion was morally justifiable prevailed both in the rhetoric of the politicians, especially Zulfikar Ali Bhutto, and in subsequent recollections of the war. Pakistan's war dead are still referred to as 'martyrs' to the cause of freedom. When Bhutto was accused of adventurism and aggression, he replied: 'If support to the struggling people of Jammu and Kashmir constituted aggression against India, then all those countries like China, Indonesia, and others who unstintedly supported the cause of the Kashmiris were committing aggression against India.'[75] This conviction, so evident in 1965, was incompatible with the Indian position that by launching an invasion into the valley, the Pakistanis were effectively attacking India.

The war which Bhutto so enthusiastically supported had failed, but he emerged as the most popular politician in Pakistan precisely because he had pursued a much more vigorous – and therefore domestically more popular – line against India. He had also skilfully managed to disassociate himself from a regime which was becoming unpopular, and he succeeded in sweeping

the political ground from beneath Ayub Khan's feet in a movement which had mass appeal.[76] In 1967 he formed his own political party, the Pakistan Peoples Party, which had a radical programme of socialist reform. In 1968, Ayub was replaced by General Yahya Khan, Malik's successor in operation 'Grand Slam'. His mandate was to hold elections and return the country to civilian rule. The issue of Kashmir was temporarily set aside as domestic politics in East and West Pakistan held centre stage.

Valley reaction

Although there had been no large scale uprising of the Kashmiris of the valley to coincide with Pakistan's invasion in 1965, there was evidence of the beginnings of political dissent amongst the younger Kashmiris, which meant the movement for plebiscite and self-determination would, as the older pro-Pakistan activists hoped, be carried on to the next generation. 'The greatest headache of the politically alert sections of my generation was how to get the new generation – our children – involved in the struggle for the State's accession to Pakistan,' writes Muhammad Saraf. Most were young children, some not even born in 1947, and many of their politically active parents, like Ghulam Abbas, Muhammad Saraf, and others had opted for Pakistan. In addition, under the influence of Sheikh Abdullah, although they might not be happy with the erosion of their 'special status', large sections of the population still supported accession to secular India and no longer looked to acceding to Pakistan under military dictatorship: 'In my estimation martial law had badly affected the liberation movement,' says Justice Abdul Majeed Mallick. 'The liberation movement primarily rested on the principle of the right of self-determination. When the first martial law was enforced in 1958, the Indian government snubbed Pakistan by saying "when you don't have fundamental rights in Pakistan, how can you have them in Kashmir?"'[77]

However, when Selig Harrison toured Kashmir in July, he reported that he found the people were solidly hostile to Indian rule and that it was only the presence of twelve Indian army brigades which kept the movement for self-determination contained.[78] Despite its adherence to a secular platform, Muslims believed that some elements inside the state, supported by the pro-Hindu Jana Sangh (which had merged with the Praja Parishad), wanted to reduce the majority Muslim preponderance by forcing them to leave. In the late 1960s fires in Muslim areas left many Muslim families homeless; activists hostile to the Indian government regarded the occurrence of these fires with suspicion as part of a plan to make Kashmir into a majority Hindu state. Ever sensitive of the incursion of outsiders into the state, they objected to 'citizenship' certificates being awarded to non-Muslims who had settled in the valley. In October 1969 a bill making evacuee property available to non-Muslim refugees was adopted by the Srinagar assembly. With the opening of a University in Srinagar in 1948, however, and free education, a new generation of educated graduates emerged. Since there was virtually no industry in Kashmir, large numbers remained unemployed.

G. M. Sadiq, the chief minister, was becoming increasingly aware of the problem of the educated unemployed. In 1968 he met Prime Minister Indira Gandhi to explain the rising discontent in the state. In the presence of Inder Gujral, he told her: 'India spends millions on Kashmir but very little in Kashmir. If I were to tell you that the law and order situation requires one more division of the army, you would send it, without the blink of an eye, but if I ask you to set up two factories, you will tell me twenty reasons why it cannot be done and therefore what do our youth do?' Gujral subsequently acted as convener for a Committee of Ministers of State to deal with Kashmir:

> But I confess with a great deal of regret and dismay, that our achievements were very marginal. We succeeded in setting up two factories, but we were unable to make any dent on unemployment. Some progress was made in agriculture, but that was not much of an achievement because agriculture and fruits were growing in any case. Most of the concessions which were given were utilised by the industries more in the Jammu area, but hardly anything in Kashmir. The major failure is that we should have concentrated more on public sector investment. Apart from the merits and demerits, public sector investment encourages the private sector. And since in Kashmir disquiet was there all the time, for one reason or the other the private sector was very reluctant to invest.[79]

Nevertheless Dharma Vira, a civil servant, recalled how much better off the Kashmiris were in this period compared with their conditions under the maharaja. 'Then I saw people coming in large numbers, in tatters, saying: "God give us food". But today the standard of living has changed. It is Indian money that has produced that change.'[80] He attributed the current distress of the Kashmiri people to the greed of their leaders.

Algeria's successful struggle against France and the Vietnamese resistance against the United States, were beginning, however, to show the Kashmiri nationalists in exile in Pakistan that there might, after all, be a way to change the status quo. In 1965 Amanullah Khan, Maqbool Butt, and several others had joined together to form a political party in Azad Kashmir. 'One day they came to my house to discuss not only the formation of the party but also sought my participation,' recalls Muhammad Saraf.[81] 'We could not agree because I insisted that the Party should have, as its political goal, the State's accession to Pakistan.' The party was to be called the Plebiscite Front (as distinct from the Plebiscite Front formed in the valley). The armed wing, which gained greater notoriety, was called the Jammu and Kashmir National Liberation Front (NLF). 'We said there can't be freedom unless we shed our own blood as well as that of the enemy,' said Amanullah Khan.[82] As Butt later recounted: 'Interestingly, Amanullah Khan and several others in my group had seen eye to eye with my proposal favouring an Algerian type struggle to free Kashmiris from Indian occupation.'[83] Butt, who had first come to Pakistan in 1958, crossed back secretly to the valley in June 1966. For four months he trained local workers for sabotage and set up secret cells.

In September 1966 Butt clashed with the Indian army during an exchange of fire in Kunial village, near his hometown of Handwara; a co-worker was killed as well as an Indian army officer. As the group captain of what was called the 'OID' (Operations against Indian Domination) Butt and several others were charged with sabotage and murder. Detained in the women's jail in Srinagar, Butt defended his actions in the armed struggle:

> I could not reconcile to the new political set-up brought about in Kashmir after Sheikh Abdullah's dismissal and arrest in 1953. The Sheikh's successor, Bakshi Ghulam Muhammad, had, much against the wishes of the average Kashmiri, added some more laws to the armoury of repression. Any citizen could be detained in prison for five years at a stroke and Bakshi's government was under no obligation to inform the detainee about the grounds of detention. The helpless victim could be rearrested after release and detained for another term of five years.[84]

Butt and another activist were sentenced to death in September 1968, but, before the sentence was carried out, they escaped from the jail and fled across the ceasefire line to Azad Kashmir. 'It created a sensation and electrified the people who rejoiced on their brilliant escape,' writes Saraf. 'Can there be any better proof of Kashmiris' innate hatred against India than the fact that for one month they were sheltered, transported and guided by their people and safely entered Azad Kashmir in January 1969?'[85]

Sheikh Abdullah had been released from jail in 1968. In support of his release, Jai Prakash Narain, Nehru's old socialist friend and co-worker of the freedom movement had written to Mrs Gandhi in 1966:

> We profess democracy, but rule by force in Kashmir ... the problem exists not because Pakistan wants to grab Kashmir, but because there is deep and widespread political discontent among the people ... Whatever be the solution, it has to be found within the limitations of accession. It is here that Sheikh's role may become decisive. Why do I plead for Sheikh's release? Because that may give us the only chance we have of solving the Kashmir problem.[86]

After his release, Abdullah revived his association with Prem Nath Bazaz who had frequently visited him in jail. They participated in two conventions, held in 1968 and 1970, to ascertain peoples views on Kashmir. In his inaugural speech, Jai Prakash Narain stressed that no government in India could accept a solution to the Kashmir problem which placed Kashmir outside the Union. He also encouraged the Kashmiri leaders to enter into a dialogue with the Indian government. In the June 1970 Convention, the Sheikh again stressed the need for freedom and self-determination of the Kashmiri people. When Ved Bhasin, editor of the *Kashmir Times*, pointed out the Kashmiri leadership's *volte face*, Abdullah countered with the assertion that it was not he who had gone back on his commitment, but Nehru, who had kept him in prison and failed to honour the commitments he had made to the Security Council.[87]

After 1970 the security situation in the valley deteriorated. Although protests and demonstrations were common, a new phenomenon of systematic violence had emerged. The Indian authorities blamed the frequent acts of sabotage on a group known as Al Fatah, which supposedly was working in the interests of Pakistan. But neither its membership nor real allegiance was clear. In January 1971 an Indian airlines plane, 'Ganga', en route from Srinagar to New Delhi, was hijacked by two Kashmiri youths armed with a hand grenade (subsequently discovered to be made of wood) and a pistol. The plane was diverted safely to Lahore, the twenty-six passengers were allowed to leave and it was subsequently blown up. The hijacking created tremendous euphoria in Pakistan, where disappointment over the failure of the 1965 war still lingered. Crowds numbering hundreds of thousands gathered at Lahore airport. Maqbool Butt came into the limelight by meeting the hijackers and claiming responsibility for the hijacking. The two Kashmiris were at first treated like heroes, but later, under pressure from India, they were arrested by the Pakistani authorities. Subsequently, Pakistan argued that the hijacking was a 'sting' operation planned by Indian intelligence.[88] A direct consequence was the Indian ban of overflights between West and East Pakistan, which strained relations between the two wings prior to the outbreak of war later in the year.

Maqbool Butt's dealings with the hijackers were regarded as a demonstration of his commitment to the Kashmir freedom struggle and no proceedings were taken against him in Pakistan or Azad Kashmir. But when he returned again to the valley in the 1976, he was caught and imprisoned for the murder of a bank clerk. This time he did not manage to escape and was kept in prison. After Butt's re-arrest, Amanullah Khan moved to England. 'We changed the name of the National Liberation Front, because I could not run an organisation in England which had a constitution which had armed struggle as an objective.' The organisation was changed to Jammu and Kashmir Liberation Front (JKLF), and for ten years Amanullah Khan operated out of Birmingham. 'I used to shuttle between London, New York, Paris, Amsterdam, Berlin, just projecting Kashmir at an international level. That used to pinch the Indians a lot.'[89]

War and Simla

In 1971 President Yahya Khan held the promised elections in East and West Pakistan, but their outcome was traumatic. The overall victory by the Awami League in East Pakistan, led by Sheikh Mujib-ur Rahman, was challenged by Bhutto and his Peoples Party, who had won a majority in the West. Bhutto suggested handing over power to the majority parties of both wings. But after the breakdown of negotiations, Sheikh Mujib began to call for an independent country for the Bengalis, Bangladesh. 'An eager India interfered,' writes M. J. Akbar.[90] Relations had been deteriorating steadily between India and Pakistan throughout 1971, and the third war between the two countries led to the break-up of Pakistan as created in 1947. The Pakistani army's severe repression of the secessionist movement caused a reaction in India. 'Humanitarian feelings were the main motivating force behind this outcry,' writes Indira Gandhi's biographer, Inder Malhotra, 'but many Indians also saw in the heart-rending situation an opportunity to cut Pakistan down to size.'[91] Indira Gandhi's role in the creation of Bangladesh is a matter of pride for Indian citizens and hatred for Pakistanis, who still hold India responsible for the dismemberment of their country. On 16 December 1971, in what was a humiliating defeat for Pakistan, the Pakistani army surrendered to India at Dacca race course. India retained 94,000 prisoners of war, mainly Pakistani soldiers. The Indians had also occupied about 5,000 square miles of Pakistani territory in Sindh, including that part of the Rann of Kutch which they had lost to Pakistan as a result of the 1965 arbitration. 'The Indian government's attitude after the war,' says former Indian foreign secretary, J. N. Dixit, 'disproved the theory of those who still believed that India was opposed to the existence of Pakistan. Had India wanted to dismember Pakistan completely, the army could have marched straight on to Rawalpindi.'[92] Although the war was not extended to Jammu and Kashmir, it remained a stumbling block to complete normalisation of relations. In an open letter to President Richard Nixon, Indira Gandhi wrote: 'We do want lasting peace with Pakistan. But will Pakistan give up its ceaseless yet powerless agitation of the last 24 years over Kashmir?'[93]

At the end of June 1972, Indira Gandhi met Zulfikar Ali Bhutto, who had become Pakistan's new president, at Simla.[94] As the Indian White Paper on the war acknowledged, Pakistan was 'economically shattered and psychologically bruised while India was feeling the euphoria of triumph.'[95] It appeared that Indira Gandhi could have achieved any political objective she wanted. Most of the Simla agreement related to restoring peace between the two countries in the aftermath of war. The clause relating to Jammu and Kashmir in the Simla agreement is inconclusive:

> In Jammu and Kashmir, the line of control resulting from the cease-fire of December 17, 1971 shall be respected by both sides without prejudice to the recognised position of either side. Neither side shall seek to alter it unilaterally, irrespective of mutual differences and legal interpretation. Both sides further undertake to refrain from threat or the use of force in violation of this line.

Both governments further agreed to meet again 'at a mutually convenient time in the future' to discuss further the modalities of '... a final settlement of Jammu and Kashmir and the resumption of diplomatic relations.'[96] Noticeable by its absence from the clause relating to Kashmir was any mention of plebiscite.

T. N. Kaul, who was part of the Indian delegation at the plenary meeting at Simla, recorded his conversation with Zulfikar Ali Bhutto:

> At Tashkent, when you were Foreign Minister, you said that Kashmir is the root cause of all our differences. Today, you, the President, have the opportunity of reaching a final settlement of the Kashmir question peacefully and bilaterally. Will you do it?" He smiled and replied. "You are correct, Mr Kaul, about what I said at Tashkent. But there I did not represent a defeated country while today I do; if I accept any settlement of Kashmir here I shall be accused by my people of having given in to pressure."[97]

The Indians, however, gained the impression from their discussions with Bhutto that once he returned home he would prepare the ground for an eventual settlement.

The Pakistanis were in no position to press for any favours and Bhutto's political opponents alleged that he had in fact secretly agreed to the status quo as a permanent solution. When he was on trial for conspiracy to murder in 1978, what he called the 'canard' of the secret clause was raised. 'If the Simla agreement had contained a secret clause about Kashmir, it would have been revealed long ago,' he responded.[98] He also stated that there was no legal difference, as some commentators were suggesting, in changing the name of the ceasefire line into the line of control: 'The ceasefire line is a line of control and the line of control is a ceasefire line. They are interchangeable terms.'[99]

Yet still the idea persisted of a secret resolution of the dispute. In April 1995 a former secretary of Mrs Gandhi, P. N. Dhar wrote in *The Times of India* that Bhutto had agreed that the ceasefire line should become the international border.

> Bhutto agreed not only to change the ceasefire line into a line of control, for which he had earlier proposed the term 'line of peace', but also agreed that the line would be gradually endowed with the 'characteristics of an international border' ... An important feature of the proposal was that neither country was gaining or losing territory on account of the war. It also did not involve any transfer of population from one side to the other. Kashmiris as an ethnic community were left undivided on the Indian side. The line of control was, therefore, an ethnic and linguistic frontier. In fact, in 1947, at the time of the partition, it was also an ideological frontier, being the limit of the political influence of Sheikh Mohammad Abdullah and his National Conference party.[100]

J. N. Dixit, who was also present at Simla, concurred with Dhar. The idea of converting the ceasefire line into a line of control and subsequently an international border was 'conceptualised in such a manner that it would have resulted in the Jammu and Kashmir dispute being resolved.'[101] Muhammad Saraf believes that Bhutto convinced Mrs Gandhi that it was not possible to solve all the problems between India and Pakistan at once: 'Bhutto was a very clever man. He said to Mrs Gandhi, "You keep your options open, and

I will keep mine open more. They named the ceasefire line the line of control but that made no difference.' Saraf also believes that the Indians did not want to see another military dictatorship in Pakistan, which might have arisen had Bhutto been forced to settle Kashmir. 'It was preferable to have Mr Bhutto and make a compromise.'[102]

Most of those directly involved at Simla have died. P. N. Haksar, the chief negotiator, aged 82 in 1995, took pride in recalling the part he played in drafting the clause relating to Kashmir. 'It is too simplistic to say that Bhutto reneged on any promises he had made on Kashmir. The idea was to try and restore mutual trust and confidence in order to put Indo–Pakistani relations on a durable basis of peace.' Step-by-step all differences were to be resolved and Kashmir was part of this procedure. He also countered the suggestion, as had Bhutto, that by changing the name of the ceasefire line to the line of control (sometimes also called the 'line of actual control') this was a de facto recognition that it was equivalent to an international border. 'The ceasefire was imposed by the UN, which was a multilateral organisation; the line of control demonstrated the new bilateralism of the relationship.' Haksar believed, however, that the Pakistani army would not let go of its power, which prevented the bilateral relationship from developing.[103]

Commentators in India today also believe that Indira Gandhi lost the opportunity of her political career to settle the Kashmir issue once and for all. 'Even more outrageously than at Tashkent, the advantage gained by the Indian army was lost by its civilian masters,' writes Ajit Bhattacharjea 'India's iron lady and her advisers let the opportunity slip ... An official spokesman fended off criticism by asserting that it would not be correct to doubt Bhutto's bona fides. India would have to pay heavily for yielding to flattery.'[104] Rather than the two leaders entering into a secret agreement, it is much more likely that Bhutto managed to convince Indira Gandhi that he could not survive politically the announcement of a settlement of Kashmir as well as the severance of Pakistan's eastern wing. 'Mrs Gandhi felt that Mr Bhutto wanted to open a new chapter and a period of reconciliation and friendship will start. She went along some way to help Mr Bhutto's political standing in Pakistan,' says Girish Saxena, who was present in Simla as a member of RAW, India's Research and Analysis Wing. No further negotiations over Kashmir ever took place while he was alive. But, says Saxena, 'although Mr Bhutto made noises, he never did anything significant on the diplomatic front to unsettle Simla or to disturb the arrangements on the line of control. He did not proceed further to cement the outcome of the agreement and what was decided; he kept the whole thing fluid.'[105]

From his base in the United Kingdom, Amanullah Khan noted Bhutto's speech to the National Assembly after his return from Simla:

They said to me: 'settle Kashmir if you want (sic) prisoners of war.' I said 'I cannot'. They said 'at least settle the principles.' If I settle the principles it means settlement, that is what I told them, because there is only one principle and that is self-determination ... If the people of Jammu and Kashmir want their independence, if they want to be liberated from the Hindu yoke, if they want to be a free people in fraternity and friendship and comradeship with Pakistan, they will have to give the lead and we will be with them. Even if the Simla agreement is broken, even if we jeopardise all our relations with India, I tell you, Sir, on the floor of this House with solemn commitment of the people of Pakistan that if tomorrow the people of Kashmir start a freedom movement, if tomorrow Sheikh Abdullah, or [Mirwaiz] Farooq or others, start a people's movement, we will be with them, no matter what the consequences.[106]

Subsequently, without any further commitments other than those expressed in the agreement, Bhutto secured the release of the prisoners of war and the 5,139 square miles of territory.

Despite Bhutto's rhetoric, from what Farooq Abdullah heard during his visit to Pakistan in 1974,[107] he also concluded that the Kashmir issue was resolved. 'The entire bureaucracy of Pakistan and Bhutto's secretary himself told me that a final solution has been arrived at; there can be nothing more. What we (the Pakistanis) have got (in Kashmir) we are keeping, what they have got they are keeping, and that is how it is.'[108] Farooq Abdullah also said that this information was confirmed to him in conversations he had with D. P. Dhar. 'Bhutto had made it abundantly clear to Mrs Gandhi that the line of actual control will become the border; that over the years he would be able to convince his people what is India's is India's and what is ours is ours.'[109] Stanley Wolpert argues that Bhutto never meant to close off the Pakistani claim to Kashmir. 'He had needed the agreement primarily to prove to the rest of the world – doubting London, as well as sceptical Washington and Moscow – that Pakistan remained in the "great game".'[110] The absence of any formal declaration one way or the other left the situation subject to change, depending on the political circumstances in India, Pakistan and within the state of Jammu and Kashmir. Besides, as the Kashmiris on both sides of the line of control were to observe, the Simla agreement had been negotiated without their participation.

Within Azad Kashmir, in addition to his support for the Kashmiris across the line of control, Bhutto is remembered as the first Pakistani leader to introduce reforms and investment. 'It was not until the 1970s and Zulfikar Ali Bhutto that the Pakistani government began to take an interest in us,' said an Azad Kashmir government official in 1994. 'Money was poured in and our conditions improved.'[111] Until then the economy was at subsistence level. In 1947 there were 256 metalled and fair-weather roads. By 1977 these had been increased to 939. In 1947 there were no hospitals and only six high schools. By 1977, there were eleven hospitals and 136 high schools.[112] During his 1974 visit to Muzaffarabad, however, Farooq Abdullah remarked on his return to India, that the best way to assure the Kashmiris in the valley that they were better off under India, was for them to visit AJK and see how poor the region was.[113]

Until the 1970s, Azad Jammu and Kashmir operated under the basic democracy system first introduced by Ayub Khan in 1960 and amended in 1964 and 1968 to accommodate the demands both of the local Azad Kashmiris and the refugee committee, who wanted greater representation. But although the local councils had limited powers, their funds were scarce and they remained dependent on Pakistan. The 1970 Azad Kashmir Government Act, passed under President Yahya Khan, instituted a presidential system of government, which, in theory, provided for a fully democratic system. When Bhutto framed the 1973 Constitution in Pakistan, which substituted a parliamentary system of government for the presidential one, the same system was also introduced for Azad Kashmir. As in Pakistan, the prime minister was the chief executive and the president a titular head. Nonetheless, the Azad Kashmir Council in Islamabad continued to exercise considerable jurisdiction over the affairs of Azad Kashmir. What was most significant, however, was that although Azad Kashmir remained administratively apart from the rest of Pakistan, according to Leo Rose, who made a detailed study of Azad Kashmir politics in 1989, this was the first time Pakistan 'assumed a direct and open institutional role in the governance of Azad Kashmir' in the wake of the Simla agreement. In fact, Rose interprets the Simla agreement as 'a first step in the actual accession of Azad Kashmir into Pakistan, in form as well as fact.'[114]

The Kashmir accord

Bhutto's vocal support of the Kashmiris' right of self-determination could not hide the fact that Pakistan's position over any further initiatives in Kashmir was greatly weakened. The failure of the 1965 war, which Bhutto had blamed on Ayub, and Pakistan's defeat and the emergence of independent Bangladesh in 1971 left those Kashmiris who would have preferred the state to be joined to Pakistan with little hope for the future. G. M. Sadiq had died in office in the middle of the 1971 war. He was replaced as chief minister by a former colleague, Syed Mir Qasim, president of the Jammu and Kashmir Congress Party formed in 1965 out of the former National Conference.

Sheikh Abdullah had wanted to participate in the forthcoming elections in the state but, in January 1971, the Plebiscite Front had been banned and Abdullah was externed from the state. The Indian government still associated the Front with the activities of the terrorist group Al Fatah. Abdullah was scathing over the ban: 'Over a million politically conscious members of the outlawed Plebiscite Front were conveniently removed from the field to clear the path for a walk-over for the Congress. The door of democratic processes have thus been banged on the real representatives of the people'[115] In the absence of any serious opposition, when elections were held in March 1972 Mir Qasim won with a comfortable majority. The Jamaat-i Islami, with its pro-Pakistani leanings, won five seats and the Jana Sangh won three. Mirwaiz

Maulvi Farooq, who had founded his own Awami Action Committee in 1964, alleged rigging and manipulation. Mir Qasim protested at the time that the elections were 'the freest and fairest'[116] but in his memoirs he put the exclusion of the Plebiscite Front and Abdullah in the context of a proposal to hold talks with Sheikh Abdullah in order to try and resolve the ongoing conflict between New Delhi and the Kashmir state: 'If the elections were free and fair, the victory of the [Plebiscite] Front was a foregone conclusion. And, as a victorious party, the Front would certainly talk from a position of strength that would irritate Mrs Gandhi who might give up her wish to negotiate with Sheikh Abdullah. That in turn would lead to a confrontation between the centre and the Jammu and Kashmir government.'[117]

After the elections Mir Qasim began to relax a number of restrictions on his opponents. In April 1972 Begum Abdullah was allowed to return to the state, political prisoners were released and, in June, the externment order on Sheikh Abdullah was lifted as well as those on Mirza Afzal Beg and G. M. Shah. The ban on the Plebiscite Front was also lifted, which once more gave Sheikh Abdullah a political platform. Referring to the recently signed Simla agreement, he stated that neither India nor Pakistan could discuss the fate of the state of Jammu and Kashmir without the participation of the Kashmiris. Whilst noting Bhutto's remarks on self-determination, he nonetheless pointed to the absence of any comment on the situation in Azad Kashmir, where the people might also like the same right of self-determination. He had also begun to shift emphasis by pressing for greater autonomy within the Indian Union rather than drawing attention to the unheld plebiscite. 'There is no quarrel with the Government of India over accession; it is over the structure of internal autonomy. One must not forget that it was we who brought Kashmir into India; otherwise Kashmir could never have become part of India.'[118] When Zulfikar Ali Bhutto once more called for the self-determination of the Kashmiri people, Abdullah spoke against any intervention in the internal affairs of the state. In a series of negotiations, which lasted for over a year, Indira Gandhi chose to capitalise on Abdullah's more favourable stance towards India.

In his memoirs, Abdullah justifies his agreement to what came to be known as 'the Kashmir accord': 'We only wanted Article 370 to be maintained in its original form ... Our readiness to come to the negotiating table did not imply a change in our objectives but a change in our strategy.'[119] Abdullah wanted the clock to be put back to pre-1953 before his dismissal by Nehru, but Mrs Gandhi did not make many concessions. There were to be no fresh elections; Abdullah was to be elected chief minister by Congress. 'Forgetting my past experiences I agreed to co-operate with the Congress, but soon regretted my decision.'[120]

Details of the six-point accord were announced by Mrs Gandhi in the Indian Parliament on 24 February 1975. 'Mrs Indira Gandhi was at her best that day,' writes M. J. Akbar. Her recognition of Abdullah's status as the leader of secular Kashmir, 'was Indira Gandhi's finest achievement. She did not put the clock back. But she picked it up and wound it again; and it was because of her that Kashmir saw a wonderful decade of freedom and peace. There was great joy in the nation at the news.'[121] Although Kashmir's special status, enshrined in article 370 of the Indian Constitution was retained, the state was termed 'a constituent unit of the Union of India.' The Indian government was able 'to make laws relating to the prevention of activities directed towards disclaiming, questioning or disrupting the sovereignty and territorial integrity of India or bringing about cession of a part of the territory of India from the Union or causing insult to the Indian national flag, the Indian national anthem and the Constitution.'[122] This effectively gave India control in the areas which mattered most. There was to be no return to the pre-1953 status. The titles of sadar-i-riyasat and prime minister, evidence of Kashmir's special status, were not to be re-utilised. Instead, as with all other states they were to remain as governor and chief minister. Commentators at the time believed that the issue of plebiscite and self-determination could now be laid to rest. The accession of the state of Jammu and Kashmir by the autocratic maharaja in 1947 had been confirmed by Sheikh Abdullah, a popular leader, who nearly thirty years after the accession, still commanded majority support in the state. From an Indian standpoint, the movement for self-determination virtually came to an end with the 1975 accord.[123]

Pakistan was less than happy with the accord. Tension had once more increased between India and Pakistan after India's first nuclear explosion in May 1974, resulting in a steady determination on behalf of Pakistan's leaders to acquire nuclear capability. In June the Pakistani politicians intensified their cry for a liberated Kashmir in protest at the ongoing negotiations prior to the conclusion of the Kashmir accord. When the accord was announced it was termed a 'sell-out' and Zulfikar Ali Bhutto called for a strike throughout Pakistan on 28 February 1975. Bhutto also stated that the accord had violated the terms of Simla and the UN requirements for a plebiscite. The Chinese government also voiced its disapproval.

Within the state of Jammu and Kashmir, Mirwaiz Maulvi Farooq believed that Abdullah had relinquished the Kashmiris' right of self-determination. Throughout 1974 there had been clashes between his Awami Action Committee and the Plebiscite Front. The Jana Sangh in Jammu and Delhi protested against the accord. As always opposed to the special treatment meted out to the valley in preference to Jammu, Jana Sangh supporters wanted article 370 to be abrogated and the whole state included in the Indian Union, like all the other states. Abdullah, however, was not going to be the pliant tool, which perhaps the Indian government hoped he would be in his old age. In April 1975 he talked about a merger with Azad Kashmir.[124] Although both he and Mirza Afzal Beg had assumed power as independent candidates in staged by-elections under the auspices of the Congress Party, they rejected the suggestion of a formal alliance with the Congress Party. M. J. Akbar attributes this to personal rivalries between the outgoing chief minister, Mir Qasim, and Muhammad Mufti Sayeed, a prominent Congress minister. When they both realised that there was to be no place for them or their relatives in a coalition government, they dissuaded Abdullah from contemplating the idea.[125] Akbar, however, does not provide any documentary evidence for this assertion. Mir Qasim took up a more prestigious position in Mrs Gandhi's cabinet and committed himself to working for Congress–National Conference co-operation.[126]

For the first two years of Abdullah's administration, only he and Beg were officially in the government. Although the National Conference, which had lain dormant for so many years, was revived out of what remained of the Plebiscite Front, it was not represented in the legislative assembly, which was controlled by the Congress. Abdullah therefore made use of his own family to support him – his wife, Begum Abdullah, his two sons, Farooq and Tariq, and his son-in-law, Ghulam Muhammad Shah. This led to allegations of corruption and nepotism. Prem Nath Bazaz, who remained, as ever, a critical commentator on events, described Sheikh Abdullah's new administration as 'democracy through intimidation and terror.'[127] The visual high-point of Abdullah's return to power was reached in October 1975, when Indira Gandhi, by now ruling India under Emergency powers, visited Srinagar. Her progress on Dal lake by boat, propelled by turbaned oarsmen was reminiscent of the visits of the Mughal emperors. People lined the banks and cheered. Her presence in Srinagar was, however, a powerful reminder to the people of Kashmir's reinforced links with the government at New Delhi, led by a prime minister who had curtailed civil liberties throughout India, muzzled the press and arrested her political opponents.

In March 1977 Mrs Gandhi lost the general election to the Janata party in India. The two year Emergency had greatly reduced her popularity. 'When it became obvious that the Janata Party would form the government at the Centre, the leaders of the State Congress party conspired to capture power in Kashmir,' writes Abdullah. 'A petition was submitted to the Governor declaring that they had lost confidence in me.'[128] Moraji Desai, the new prime minister, dissolved the state assembly and called for fresh elections, which gave Sheikh Abdullah the opportunity of re-establishing his political credentials in his own right. P. S. Verma comments that these 1977 elections were 'relatively free from the vices of rigging and other related irregularities' and attributes this to the fact that the Congress Party was out of power in Delhi and Janata was still in its infancy. Thus no official patronage from Delhi was forthcoming. The Sheikh, still the National Conference's biggest asset, suffered a severe heart attack in 1977. He was not able to campaign extensively and his candidates had to rely on his taped speeches. Rumours persisted that he had already died, so when he appeared lying on a stretcher and raised his right hand to show that he was alive, the crowds cheered. His statements referring to the Kashmiris as a *qaum* (nation) were not lost on the people. Maulvi Farooq, who had consistently adopted a pro-Pakistani stance, lost credibility amongst his traditional sympathisers, by campaigning for the Janata party, as did the Jamaat-i Islami.

Abdullah was also not beyond playing the Pakistani card to his advantage in order to gain support. There was in addition a theatrical side to the campaigning. Mirza Afzal Beg used to carry a lump of Pakistani rock salt (as opposed to Indian sea salt) in his pocket wrapped in a green handkerchief. As his speech reached its climax, he would take out the salt with a dramatic gesture and exhibit it to his audience, 'indicating thereby that if his party won, Pakistan would not be far away.'[129] The National Conference contested all 75 seats and won 47, of which 39 were in the valley. The Jamaat-i Islami won only one seat compared with the five it had won in 1972. At the age of 72, Abdullah once more braced himself to meet the challenge of the future.

Confident of his new mandate, the Sheikh once more began to speak out assertively and relations with the ruling Janata party in Delhi became strained. On 23 May 1977 Abdullah threatened to secede from the Union unless the people were accorded their place of honour in terms of the safeguards guaranteed to them under Article 370 of the Constitution and he warned of an 'explosive situation'. When Mrs Gandhi returned to power in 1980, Abdullah continued to make provocative declarations about Kashmiris not being the slaves of either India or Pakistan. But it is doubtful that at this stage in his life, his rhetoric was designed to do anything more than assure Kashmiris of the importance of their Kashmiriyat – their cultural identity – without envisaging any significant change to the now established status quo.

At the same time, Abdullah was confronted by new problems in the state, whose political character had changed since he was last in power in the early 1950s. Opposition to the Kashmir accord continued and a new educated class was being drawn into the political arena. 'Our education taught us that the accord is not the resolution of the Kashmir dispute' said a Kashmiri journalist, who was editing a daily newspaper in Srinagar in 1975.[130] 'Our youth awoke and realised that we can't any longer be the slaves of India.' 'We Muslims feel we have been deprived of something,' said Ali, a carpet dealer, in 1981. 'We haven't been allowed to join India or Pakistan of our own free will. Rather we have been forced to be with India.'[131] Kashmir still depended on tourism and despite economic progress there was no real industry in which middle class Kashmiris could feel they had a stake. Increasingly, the Kashmiri youth moved not towards communism or socialism, but back to the fundamentals of their respective religions. Muslims, Hindus, Sikhs, Buddhists were all reasserting their cultural and religious identity which was in total contradiction to the secularism which the Indian government had espoused since independence. Although Sheikh Abdullah made some attempt to accommodate the regional sentiments in the state by granting a small degree of autonomy to the component parts of Jammu, Ladakh and the valley, the numerical superiority of the valley meant that its voice was predominant. Abdullah's political opponents also criticised his government for discrimination and lack of performance.[132]

Within the valley, some of the young Muslims were attracted to the schools run by the Jamaat-i Islami, who gained inspiration from the growing fundamentalist movement, which had affected Muslim countries of the Middle East. Some young Kashmiris also joined the Jamaat-i Tulba, a youth organisation set up by the Jamaat-i Islami. In 1975 Sheikh Abdullah had ordered the closure of the Jamaat schools. He later banned a convention of the Jamaat-i Tulba planned to be held in Srinagar in 1981. The Sheikh's reaction to the Muslim influence in the schools of the Jamaat demonstrated his concern, but the Jamaat-i Islami had only won one seat in the 1977 elections and did not appear to be a significant political force. Neither he nor anyone else could have predicted the growth in support for the Islamic movement, which came in later years, especially after the Iranian revolution in February 1979. This resurgence could not have been more dramatically demonstrated by the Afghan resistance to the Soviet invasion of Afghanistan in 1979: 'A small nation with a small population, with limited resources and weapons rose in revolt against the Soviet onslaught in Afghanistan, to the extent that the Soviet Union ultimately disintegrated into fragments,' says Azam Inquilabi, a teacher in Srinagar at this time. 'Out of that five Muslim states emerged as independent states. So we got inspired, if they could offer tough resistance to a super power in the east, we too could fight India.'[133]

CHAPTER 6

Bravado and Despair

History has seen such times, when the crime was committed by a moment, but the punishment was suffered by centuries. Sheikh Abdullah, 1981[1]

It is a thin line between bravado and despair. Farooq Abdullah, 1989[2]

The decade of the 1980s began peacefully for the valley of Kashmir. Its fame as an idyllic place for a holiday attracted foreigners from far and wide, who brought in welcome currency and left laden with traditional Kashmiri handicrafts. Sheikh Abdullah's charismatic presence as chief minister was in marked contrast to the personalities of those who had preceded him. His accord with Indira Gandhi in 1975 and his subsequent electoral victory in 1977 meant that the government of New Delhi was temporarily restrained from controlling Kashmiri affairs from the centre. Pakistan, under the military dictatorship of General Muhammad Zia-ul Haq since 1977, after the overthrow of Zulfikar Ali Bhutto,[3] was preoccupied with the war in Afghanistan. It did not appear that Zia's Kashmiri policy would be much different from that of Zulfikar Ali Bhutto. Pakistan's options were to be kept open.

Under the surface, however, disaffection was present. Sheikh Abdullah was not popular in Jammu or in Ladakh and the Islamic groups, which had opposed the accord, were gaining support in the valley. As the Sheikh's health began to fail and, in 1981, he settled the succession on his son, Farooq, a new era of violence began.

Crown of thorns

Farooq Abdullah, unlike his father, had not been schooled in the politics of the freedom movement. He had spent most of his adult life in Britain, where he had trained as a doctor. In a ceremony which dazzled the people, who had assembled in Iqbal Park in Srinagar, on 21 August 1981, Sheikh Abdullah appointed his untested progeny as president of the National Conference:

> This crown that I am placing on your head is made of thorns. My first wish is that you will never betray the hopes of your *qaum* [nation]. You are young, Dr Farooq Abdullah, young enough to face the challenges of life, and I pray that God gives you the courage to fulfil your responsibilities to these people whom I have nurtured with such pride, and to whom I have given the best years of my life.[4]

Farooq's words of response were greeted with a roar of approval: 'I will give my life before I play with the honour of this community.' But as Indian journalist Tavleen Singh observes: 'He was his father's son but not his father and he was not capable of taking them seriously except then, on that tumultuous day, for that moment, when the event and the overwhelming response of the people made him seem like a bigger man.'[5]

Although Sheikh Abdullah was able to hand over the office, he could not pass on the experience to his son. As subsequent events were to show, his rise to power came too easily. 'In happier times,' writes Ajit Bhattacharjea 'Farooq Abdullah could have proved an ideal leader for Kashmir. Tall, handsome, engaging, and forthright, he attracted crowds easily, making them believe that he would lead them out of the uncertainty, intrigue and corruption that darkened the last days of his father.' But he was also impulsive, gullible, easy-going and a novice in administration and politics.'[6] 'He liked the attention, the fun that went with power, and he liked the atmosphere of a feudal court that surrounded his father,' says Tavleen Singh. 'He was also both surprised and delighted by the adulation of the people and the society hostesses in Delhi.'[7]

For the time being, however, Kashmir's future seemed assured. Secession appeared no longer to be an issue and there were not many Kashmiris talking about the plebiscite. The tourists continued to come. Hotels were opened along the Boulevard facing Dal lake. Food grain and fruit production increased, as well as income from Kashmir's world famous handicrafts. 'Kashmir's economic boom gave it an atmosphere of permanent festivity, forcing the opposition politicians, who continued to remain suspicious, to keep their pessimism to themselves. Sheikh Abdullah was too powerful, too popular to touch.'[8]

On 8 September 1982 the 'Lion of Kashmir' died. After his death even those who had opposed the Sheikh politically praised his conviction. Shahnawaz Khan Niazi, an old friend who migrated to Pakistan, describes what he believed Sheikh Abdullah represented for a large majority of the people.

> Sheikh Abdullah was a total idealist and his only interest was the best deal he could get for Kashmir and his Kashmiris. His often repeated statement to me was that destiny had played an important role, that circumstances were such that they did not permit him to come to an understanding with Pakistan. Every small opportunity he got to make a point or establish the separate identity of the Kashmiris he took.[9]

For those who were able to see through the shifts from India to Pakistan to independence and back again, of all their leaders, Sheikh Abdullah best personified the spirit of Kashmiriyat. At times, safeguarding Kashmiriyat meant independence; at others, when Delhi was prepared to loosen the reins of control, it meant autonomy within the Indian Union. Since Kashmiriyat included both Muslims and Hindus, he had opted for the secularism of India, which Jawaharlal Nehru had promised in his early speeches.

Yet critics, such as Sardar Abdul Qayum Khan, who had risen from being a 'mujahid' of the 1947 war to become first president and later prime minister of Azad Jammu and Kashmir, believe that Sheikh Abdullah was a 'stooge' of the Indian government. 'He had no *locus standi*; he was a nonentity. He was a quisling boosted by the power of the Indian Congress Party.'[10] Qayum condemned Abdullah's accord with Indira Gandhi in 1975 as 'getting power through the back door' and had little sympathy with an old man who, perhaps, after so many years wanted peace. Amanullah Khan acknowledged the Sheikh's contribution in the early years of the independence struggle against the Dogras. But in later years he held the Sheikh 'mainly responsible for the trials and tribulations of the Kashmiris. He trusted in Nehru far more than he should have done.'[11]

At Sheikh Abdullah's funeral all the shades of dissatisfaction and disappointment in him were forgotten. 'The grief, as the cortege passed,' writes Tavleen Singh, 'burst out like an uncontrollable wave. The salutation – our lion – was on everyone's lips. People wept, they chanted dirges and mouthed melancholy slogans ... for that day the man Kashmir remembered was not the Sheikh who had been chief minister for five years but the man who, for nearly thirty years, had symbolised Kashmir's identity.'[12] There is a certain irony in the present day that his marble tomb overlooking Dal lake, close to the Hazratbal mosque, is protected by Indian soldiers against desecration by the sons of those Kashmiris whose cause he had championed.

The Sheikh's legacy

Once Sheikh Abdullah was gone, in a climate of renewed assertion of religious identity, it was impossible to prevent the rise of communalist tendencies. During the period following his death, mistakes were made both by the state government and in Delhi, which changed the course of events and renewed the demand not so much for Kashmiriyat or union with Pakistan, but for *azadi*, freedom – for the people of the valley from what they perceived to be not secular, but Hindu-dominated, India.

Famed as the 'disco' chief minister, who enjoyed riding around Srinagar on his motor bicycle, the first problem which Farooq Abdullah inherited from his father was the Jammu and Kashmir Grant of Permit for Resettlement bill. Before his death the Sheikh had put forward a bill which enabled anyone who was a citizen of Kashmir before 14 May 1954 or a descendant to return to Kashmir, provided he swore allegiance both to the Indian and Kashmiri constitutions. As a refugee from the valley, Mir Abdul Aziz, a Muslim Conference supporter and political opponent of Abdullah's since the 1930s, believed it was 'the only good thing Sheikh Abdullah did.' In Delhi the bill, which had been passed by the legislative assembly, but still required assent from the governor to become law, aroused fears that Pakistani sympathisers and agents could cross the border and create trouble in the valley. Yet Abdullah was obliged to follow through a measure introduced by his father. He was also aware of the sensitivities of many of the Hindus and Sikhs in Jammu, who had been settled on the land of many of the Muslims who had left.

The Government of India was dissatisfied that an issue concerning citizenship, which it regarded as within its domain, was being dealt with in the state. 'What Abdullah did to save his skin and please his Indian masters was that he referred it to the Supreme Court of India for advice. So it has been kept in cold storage without any action,' says Mir Abdul Aziz.[13] He compared the situation with that of the many Indians and Pakistanis who have been to the UK in time of political strife, but, who are not prevented from returning to their respective countries when they want to do so. Farooq Abdullah, however, was already beginning to realise the need to balance the needs of Kashmiris with the demands of the government in Delhi.

In domestic affairs, however, Farooq Abdullah did not demonstrate the same caution. His attempts to eradicate corruption were greeted enthusiastically by the people. But, asks, M. J. Akbar, 'was it totally wise to drop all the "stalwarts" of his father's ministry after publicly calling them corrupt?'[14] His brother-in-law, G. M. Shah, married to his sister Khalida, was just one stalwart who was not included in the chief minister's cabinet. Abdullah scheduled elections for June 1983 in order to obtain an endorsement from the people. Indira Gandhi, however, wished to establish her Congress(I) Party[15] standing in the valley and requested an alliance between the Congress and the National Conference. 'They thought probably I would be a mere puppet and would go the way they wanted me to go.'[16] Abdullah refused the alliance, believing that the people of Kashmir would resent it. Instead, he offered to put up weak candidates in a few constituencies in order to allow Congress to win some seats. Mrs Gandhi did not accept this proposal and exponents of her subsequent actions believe that she never forgave Abdullah.

Tavleen Singh, who was covering the elections for the Indian press, witnessed the extraordinary interest the prime minister took in the campaign. 'Mrs Gandhi seemed to be staking her own *izzat* [honour] on winning. After whirlwind tours of Jammu, she descended on the valley with all the pomp and paraphernalia that accompanies prime ministers on such visits.'[17] During her interviews in the valley, Tavleen Singh asked whether the plebiscite was an issue. 'Almost everywhere the answer was an emphatic no. People said that the past was dead and they were participating in this election as Indians.'[18] Farooq Abdullah was popular, but the people were really voting in his father's memory.

The politics of the campaign between the National Conference and the Congress Party led to animosity on both sides. 'The electioneering set a new record in viciousness which often degenerated into "downright vulgarity",' writes Indira Gandhi's biographer, Inder Malhotra.[19] Abdullah reached an agreement with Mirwaiz Maulvi Farooq, whose uncle's feud with the Sheikh in 1932, had caused a lasting split amongst the Muslims. 'The pro-Pakistani *bakra* [goat][20] lay with the Abdullah lion arousing suspicions in Delhi,' writes M. J. Akbar.[21] In Jammu, the Hindus feared that the more numerous Muslims of the valley were, once more, uniting against them on the basis of religion. Abdullah also made the mistake of bowing to pressure from his family to include some Shah supporters amongst the candidates he fielded, whose reputations were questionable.[22] So too was their loyalty to Abdullah. Despite mistaken predictions by Indira Gandhi's advisers and some sections of the press that she would defeat Abdullah, the National Conference won forty-six seats out of seventy-five. Congress won only two seats in the valley. In Jammu, where the Congress Party had campaigned vigorously, it obtained twenty-four seats. Both the right wing Bharatiya Janata Party (BJP), favouring Hindu interests, and the Jamaat-i Islami, promoting those of the Muslims, failed to win any seats.[23] Tavleen Singh describes the 1983 elections as the first 'real' elections and that it seemed the Kashmir issue was over.[24]

Almost as soon as the election results were announced, the Congress began to campaign against Farooq Abdullah, alleging that the elections had been rigged. But, as Tavleen Singh noted, 'in that summer of 1983 there was no turmoil in the valley despite Congress attempts to create it. The Congress had an important ally in the national press and in retrospect I would go so far as to say that the press was the main reason why the alienation of Kashmir began.'[25] With the advice of her kitchen cabinet, which Singh describes as more like 'a mediaeval court in which nearly every decision was taken personally by Mrs Gandhi,' the Prime Minister of India set about subverting the elected government of Kashmir.[26] 'Indira seemed determined not to let him rule in peace because the abusive election campaign and Farooq's victory had made her angrier with him than ever before,' writes Malhotra.[27]

Abdullah also played into Mrs Gandhi's hand. Instead of confining himself to the politics of Jammu and Kashmir, he entered the national stage by discussing regional autonomy with the leaders of Andhra Pradesh, Karnataka, West Bengal and Tamil Nadu, in preparation for the launching of an anti-Congress alliance in the 1984 general elections. He also met with the Akali Dal in the Punjab, where a violent separatist movement amongst the Sikhs was ultimately to cost Indira Gandhi her life. In October 1983 he hosted a three-day opposition conclave in Srinagar involving fifty-nine state leaders from seventeen different regional parties. 'All this was anathema to Indira Gandhi,' writes Ajit Bhattacharjea. 'Always insecure, she now felt gravely threatened.'[28]

Mrs Gandhi did not appreciate Abdullah's independent line, reminiscent of tactics so often employed by his father. The Sheikh, however, had never challenged the Congress Party outside Kashmir as was clearly Farooq Abdullah's intention. Gandhi gave a clear warning that what she termed 'anti-national' – i.e. pro-regional autonomy – sentiments would not be tolerated. Over the next few months she set about destabilising those states which were exhibiting such tendencies. 'The hook-or-crook methods used to

try and break the governments of Karnataka, Andhra and Kashmir,' writes
M. J. Akbar 'were a blot on the very concept of a federation. Farooq
Abdullah, for his sins, was at the top of the hit list.'[29]

Part of the strategy was to depict Farooq Abdullah as being 'soft' on
Pakistan. In October 1983 much was made of a cricket match held in Srinagar
between India and the West Indies. The Indian team was booed by the
assembled crowd, and supporters of the Jamaat-i Islami waved their green
party flags, which resembled, but were not identical to the Pakistani flag. 'For
Delhi, this was heaven-sent material for propaganda. The Pakistani flag was
fluttering freely in Farooq's reign,' writes M. J. Akbar.[30] On 28 October Mufti
Muhammad Sayeed, the Congress leader in Kashmir, announced that Farooq
had lost his hold on the administration. A crowd in Jammu protested against
the failure of the government. Throughout the valley, small demonstrations,
clearly orchestrated by the Congress, led to arrests. Farooq's self-defence fell
on deaf ears.

'At this point, there was no Pakistani hand visible in the valley at all,'
writes Tavleen Singh, 'but charges of Pakistani involvement were openly
bandied about by Congress leaders.'[31] The kidnapping in February 1984 of
Ravindra Mahtre, the assistant high commissioner in Britain, provided another
opportunity to implicate Abdullah. The kidnappers requested a £1 million
ransom and the release of several prisoners held in India, including Maqbool
Butt, who was awaiting execution in Tihar jail after India's re-introduction of
the death penalty. The Kashmir Liberation Army (KLA), believed to be
associated with Amanullah Khan's JKLF, was held responsible for the
kidnapping and subsequent murder of Mahtre. Farooq Abdullah's alleged
connection with the kidnapping was that he had met Amanullah Khan in
1974 when, at the request of his father, during the discussions prior to the
1975 accord he had visited Muzaffarabad; this visit, nearly ten years earlier,
was now given a sinister interpretation to add fuel to the argument that
Farooq Abdullah could not be trusted. When Butt, described by Ajit
Bhattacharjea as 'a colourful double agent used both by India and Pakistan',[32]
was executed on 11 February a strike was held in Srinagar and some other
towns of the valley to mourn his death, which again demonstrated to New
Delhi the potentially subversive leanings of the state of Jammu and Kashmir.

Farooq Abdullah also had enemies within the state. Ghulam Muhammad
Shah had never accepted his brother-in-law's ascent to the top position. A
long time political supporter of the Sheikh, he had regarded himself as the
natural successor. As relations between the two deteriorated, in October
Farooq expelled G. M. Shah from the National Conference; Shah retaliated
with the formation of the Awami National Conference Party. 'The air became
filled with rumours of dirty deals and vast quantities of money being spent
on National Conference malcontents to persuade them to join G. M. Shah's
breakaway faction.'[33] A willing conspirator in the plan to topple Farooq,
Shah brought together thirteen discontented members of the legislative

assembly, including those of his supporters to whom Farooq had given seats. Combined with the twenty-six seats won by the Congress, they could claim a simple majority in the legislative assembly. Braj Kumar Nehru the governor and cousin of the prime minister, could have been ideally placed to acquiesce in a drawing-room dismissal of Farooq. Yet, despite provocation by Abdullah's high-handed style of government, Nehru insisted that the dissident members establish their majority in the legislative assembly. In early 1984 he was asked to resign and was later transferred to Gujerat. The new governor was Shri Jagmohan, a bureaucrat, who had stood by Indira Gandhi during the 1975–77 Emergency.

At the beginning of June, Mrs Gandhi's Operation Blue Star in the Punjab was put into action with the storming of the Golden Temple against the Sikh extremists of the Akali Dal led by Sant Jarnail Singh Bhindranwale. In the aftermath, Punjab was in turmoil. Yet with supreme confidence the plan for Farooq's dismissal was put into action. Soon after Blue Star, Gandhi visited Ladakh. On her return she summoned several newspaper editors, including Inder Malhotra. 'She made no secret of her conviction that Farooq's continuance as chief minister of Kashmir was bad for the state and the country. This shook most of us. After what had happened in Punjab it was hardly prudent to embark on a clash course in Kashmir.'[34]

On the national stage, because of his meeting earlier in the year with Bhindranwale, Farooq was charged with secretly supporting the Sikh separatists and of permitting them to train in the state of Jammu and Kashmir. Vehement denials from Farooq and members of his government could not silence the uproar in Delhi which reached a crescendo at the end of June. On 28 June, Governor Jagmohan received a letter signed by the thirteen members of the Kashmir legislative assembly, stating that they had withdrawn their support from the government of Farooq Abdullah. Delhi now had sufficient ammunition against Farooq and, what he later called Operation New Star, was put into action. G. M. Shah and his supporters were summoned to the governor's residence in the Raj Bhavan in Srinagar in the early hours of the morning on 2 July. In an operation which Jagmohan claimed was totally unplanned, yet took place with clockwork precision, Farooq was ousted and later replaced by his brother-in-law. 'With unaccustomed speed,' writes Ajit Bhattacharjea 'a contingent of the Madhya Pradesh armed police landed in Srinagar early next morning, suggesting that they had been alerted a day or more earlier.'[35] The army was also standing by. Jagmohan carried through his role as Mrs Gandhi's 'hatchet man'[36] with conviction. 'I was very anxious to prevent violence in the streets. Kashmir crowds are easily excitable. They soon get hysterical. It is immaterial whether they support or denounce a particular cause.'[37]

Jagmohan informed Farooq that he had 'lost the confidence' of the majority of the members of the legislative assembly. Tavleen Singh, who was covering the story, describes the deposed chief minister as reacting 'with the emotionalism of a schoolboy rather than the maturity of a politician.'[38] In an indignant document entitled 'My Dismissal' Farooq later pointed to the blatant compliance of Jagmohan:

> He was a direct party to the conspiracy but various trappings were given a dramatic touch to make it appear a natural political event ... The Governor's action in dismissing my government was invalid in law. The Raj Bhavan was not the place to test my majority that day; it should have been tested on the floor of the House.[39]

Farooq also pointed to Congress attempts to 'play up' his alleged links with the JKLF and gave the background to his visit to Muzaffarabad in 1974 when he was still living in England. 'Since negotiations were going on between Sheikh Abdullah and Mrs Gandhi for a probable accord, they wanted the feelings of the people of Pakistan-occupied Kashmir to be known first hand and to be conveyed to my father by me.' He also denied the accusations that he was in any way linked with pro-Pakistani organisations. 'As far as pro-Pakistan elements are concerned, they have been there all along since 1947. They did not appear all of a sudden during my regime or because of me.'[40]

Unfortunately for Abdullah, his plausible defence served only to set the record straight on paper. With the weight of Delhi behind Abdullah's brother-in-law, and contrary to Jagmohan's own preference for Governor's rule to be imposed first, G. M. Shah was appointed chief minister. In retrospect, had Farooq been more adept at convincing Delhi of his loyalty to India before, rather than after the event, had the power seekers in his party been less easy to exploit, had Indira Gandhi been less insecure and had she worked through the National Conference, as Nehru had done, rather than insist on a Congress presence in the valley, Farooq may have been able to maintain a workable relationship with the centre at the same time as focusing his attention on material improvements for the people of Kashmir. The fact that the prime minister of India was willing and able to set Abdullah aside for what essentially were personal reasons demonstrated the lack of regard she and the government of Delhi had for Kashmir's so-called special status. As Mir Qasim wrote: 'Mr Jagmohan's unconstitutional act was another nail in the coffin of the Kashmiri's faith in Indian democracy and law.'[41] 'The clock has been put back thirty years,' said Tavleen Singh. 'Kashmir has been reminded that no matter how much it feels that it belongs to the mainstream of India, no matter how often its chief minister asserts that he is Indian, it will always be special, always be suspect.'[42]

Farooq's dismissal touched off a wave of protest. Shah's government was unpopular from the outset. His past record as a minister under Sheikh Abdullah was 'far from savoury,' writes Inder Malhotra 'and even his best friends were not willing to vouch for his probity.' Under his chief ministership, the government sank 'to the lowest depths of corruption and capriciousness.' Why then did Mrs Gandhi allow him to be installed? 'The more one explores this question the more convinced one is that she was virtually blinded by her intense dislike of Farooq.' As Malhotra writes, 'According to Arun Nehru, a cousin of Rajiv Gandhi and a member of Mrs Gandhi's 'kitchen cabinet', 'Indira *puphi* (aunt) asked us to get rid of Farooq at all costs and we did.' The installation of G. M. Shah appears to have been so that Farooq's dismissal seemed to have been instigated by the Kashmiris and not New Delhi.[43]

All thirteen defectors were sworn in as cabinet ministers, which meant Shah was in no position to gain further supporters from amongst the National Conference by offering them places in his cabinet. 'The government made money like there was no tomorrow and given the uncertainty of the situation there may well not have been,' says Tavleen Singh.[44]

Mrs Gandhi's assassination in October 1984 by her Sikh bodyguards in revenge for Operation Bluestar removed the architect of Farooq's dismissal. But the memory of betrayal remained, not necessarily because of what happened to Farooq Abdullah personally, but because of what his dismissal signified for Kashmir. Apologists on behalf of the Indian government, like Jagmohan, have argued long and earnestly in support of their actions. But no amount of self-justification can hide the fact that Abdullah's drawing-room dismissal merely confirmed what Kashmiris had long suspected: that despite their 'special status', no leader could remain in power in Srinagar if he did not have the support of Delhi. This lesson was not lost on Farooq Abdullah. When he returned to power in 1987 it was at the head of a Conference–Congress alliance.

Rajiv Gandhi, who became prime minister after his mother's assassination, made it a policy to attempt to accommodate regional forces, not only in Kashmir, but also in the Punjab and Assam. Despite the role he may have played in Farooq's dismissal, their personal relationship was better than that between Farooq and Mrs Gandhi. After less than two years in office, G. M. Shah was dismissed on 7 March 1986 in the wake of severe communal riots which the state government had been unable to control. The army was called out and people were advised to remain indoors for fear of getting shot. Indefinite curfew had been imposed, which gave G. M. Shah the name 'Gul-e Curfew' (the Curfew flower). After Shah's dismissal, Jagmohan took advantage of Kashmir's 'special status' by assuming exclusive power, a privilege reserved under Article 370 for an elected sadar-i riyasat, not a nominated governor:

> I feel the burden of the challenges. But I am a bit elated too. I have an opportunity to show the nobler, the purer, the more radiant face of power. I can now demonstrate how government can function in a poor and developing country, how a person, inspired by a higher purpose can serve as a model administrator, how domination of the elites can be done away with.[45]

He took steps to clean-up both the administration and the city of Srinagar. Muslims, however, found that they were being excluded from key jobs and that there was a general onslaught on Muslim culture and identity, both through the educational curriculum and socially. They objected to the prevalence of alcohol readily available in numerous bars in Srinagar. The Muslim political parties had called for peaceful strikes (*hartals*) in the valley to challenge the power of Delhi. Many were arrested. Azam Inquilabi, general secretary of the Mahaz-i Azadi (Independence Front) was detained in 1985 and his services as a teacher were terminated for his alleged involvement in 'subversive' activities. Shabir Ahmed Shah was also arrested. A veteran activist who had begun his political career in 1968 at the age of fourteen when he was arrested for demanding the right to self-determination he was now leader of the People's League.

Instead of ordering fresh elections in the state of Jammu and Kashmir, Rajiv Gandhi insisted on a Conference-Congress alliance. This time Abdullah, who had spurned the alliance with Mrs Gandhi five years earlier, agreed to it. He seemed to have realised that Kashmir would never be able to prosper unless it had the open backing of Delhi. After six months of discussions, in November 1986, Rajiv reappointed Farooq as chief minister in an interim National Conference–Congress coalition government. The election was scheduled for the following year. But Abdullah was already beginning to pay the price for bowing to Delhi. 'Overnight, Farooq was transformed from hero to traitor in the Kashmiri mind,' writes Tavleen Singh. 'People could not understand how a man who had been treated the way he had by Delhi, and especially by the Gandhi family, could now be crawling to them for accords and alliances.'[46] He 'was charged with betraying his father's fifty-year legacy of pride,' says M. J. Akbar. 'It created a vacuum where the National Conference had existed, and extremists stepped into that vacuum. Kashmiriyat had become vulnerable to the votaries of violence and Muslim hegemony, both injuring Kashmir and perverting Kashmiriyat.'[47] Later Farooq Abdullah admitted that the 1986 accord was his most serious political mistake.

Rise of MUF and militancy

Amongst those who entered the political vacuum were the collection of political parties which organised themselves in September 1986 to form the Muslim United Front to contest the election. Under the dominance of Sheikh Abdullah the National Conference had retained its secular character. But the party was now split between Abdullah's supporters and those of G. M. Shah, and, with Jagmohan demonstrating a decidedly pro-Hindu bias within the administration, MUF had considerable appeal.

A key component of MUF, led by Maulvi Abbas Ansari, was the Jamaat-i Islami; founded in 1942, the party had first fielded candidates in the 1972 elections and again in 1977, but its main impact was felt not in politics but, as Sheikh Abdullah had realised, in the mosques and schools.[48] Delhi analysts believed that the Jamaat's strength lay in 'funds from abroad' and overlooked the genuine appeal which the party was beginning to have. At least ten other smaller Islamic parties joined MUF. In addition, Abdul Gani Lone's People's Conference and G. M. Shah's Awami National Conference held discussions with MUF. Maulvi Farooq's Awami Action Committee also expressed solidarity with MUF. Although subsequently they argued amongst each other, the potential combination of so many opposition parties presented the first real challenge the National Conference had faced since it had returned to active politics after Sheikh Abdullah's 1975 accord.

MUF's election manifesto stressed the need for a solution to all outstanding issues according to the Simla agreement. It also assured the voters that it would work for Islamic unity and against political interference from the centre. As the candidates, dressed in white robes, were presented to the people at Iqbal Park on 4 March, slogans were raised: 'The struggle for freedom is at hand and what do we want in the Assembly; the law of the Quran.'[49] Farooq Abdullah became unnecessarily alarmed by MUF's electoral strength. Before the election, several MUF leaders were arrested as well as a number of election agents.

When the election was held on 23 March 1987, there was nearly 75 per cent participation, the highest ever recorded in the state, with nearly 80 per cent overall voting in the valley.[50] The Conference–Congress alliance claimed sixty-six seats; Congress won five out of the six seats in the valley which their candidates had contested. *The Times of India* described the victory of the alliance as 'heartening from a non-partisan point of view.'[51] MUF had expected to win ten out of the forty-four seats they had contested, but they won only four. Even so, Balraj Puri commented that the election results reflected 'a phenomenal increase in the strength of fundamentalist forces in the Kashmir valley.'[52] The Bharatiya Janata Party (BJP) secured two seats of the twenty-nine seats it contested. Although this was an insignificant number, the subsequent rise of the BJP in India gave a new impetus to Hindu communalism, which aroused suspicions amongst the Muslims of Kashmir regarding their status within secular India.

Despite national jubilation at the Conference-Congress victory, there were widespread charges of rigging. 'Votes were cast in favour of the Muslim United Front, but the results were declared in favour of the National Conference,' says Mir Abdul Aziz, who was observing events from Pakistan. To this day, Farooq Abdullah denies all charges of rigging. 'My own law minister lost his seat. If there had been rigging would I not have ensured that he retained his seat?'[53] His critics however maintain that Abdullah did panic; if his law minister did not win, it was because he was one of the candidates Abdullah did not want to win. 'The rigging was blatant,' writes Tavleen Singh. 'In the constituency of Handwara, for instance, Abdul Gani Lone's traditional bastion, as soon as counting began on 26 March, Lone's counting agents were thrown out of the counting station by the police.'[54]

The Muslim United Front supporters were angered at their lack of electoral success. 'That manipulation of the election disappointed the Kashmiris,' says Mir Abdul Aziz. 'They said that "we were trying to change the political framework by democratic and peaceful methods, but we have failed in this. Therefore we should take up the gun." That was one of the reasons for the militancy. The people of Kashmir got disgusted and disappointed and disillusioned.'[55] Educated but unemployed, their grievances were fuelled by events both within and outside the valley. They were also the ones who considered themselves economically deprived because they were neither part of the bureaucracy nor the elite. Alienated youth found a ready outlet for their frustration in one or other of the politico-religious organisations. At the same time the broader MUF alliance fell apart. The People's Conference and Awami National Conference did not adhere to the Jamaat's emphasis on promoting a 'theocratic state'. Jamaat supporters were also beginning to call for self-determination of the people of Kashmir. 'The Jamaat's accent was on secession,' said Abdul Gani Lone, leader of the People's Conference. 'We are looking for economic justice and a better deal from India.'[56]

The armed insurgency which gathered momentum after the 1987 election caught the rest of the world unawares. To most onlookers, Kashmir was a tourist spot, a place for rest and relaxation after a hot and exhausting trip through the hotter plains of India. Despite the political discontent at the outcome of the election, in 1987 it remained ostensibly calm. One of the conditions of the Rajiv–Farooq accord was a massive programme of state spending and initially Farooq appeared confident that, because of the accord, he would receive all the assistance he needed. But the promised package of Rs 1,000 crores was never received.[57]

Unwittingly, an impetus to the activities of the exiled Kashmiri nationalists in Pakistan was given by the deportation of Amanullah Khan from England. He had been arrested in England in September 1985 over a year after the murder of Mahtre, the Indian deputy high commissioner in 1984. The charge brought against him was possession of some illegal chemicals which the prosecution alleged could be turned into explosives. Khan protested that they were insecticides for his back garden. He was acquitted in September 1986 but was deported three months later despite appeals to the home secretary, Douglas Hurd, from several Labour members of parliament. Khan maintains that he and a Sikh extremist were traded off in return for India's purchase of some British helicopters.[58] The agreement for the purchase of the twenty-one Westland helicopters was announced on 24 December 1985 after three years of discussion. As the defence correspondent of *The Times* observed, the order was delayed for a year 'because of Indian resentment that the British government did not do more to restrain the activities of members of the Sikh community in Britain after the assassination of Mrs Gandhi.'[59]

Amanullah Khan took refuge in Pakistan from where he began to direct operations across the line of control. He had realised that, in order for his movement to gain momentum, he had to attract support from the valley. Four young Kashmiris were recruited and brought to Azad Kashmir. Known as the 'Haji' group, their names were Ashfaq Majid Wani, Sheikh Abdul Hamid, Javed Ahmed Mir and Muhammad Yasin Malik.[60] Malik's disaffection arose from the violence of his childhood:

> As a young boy of ten years old I remember while I was wandering on the roads of Srinagar city, sudden panic gripped the streets, people were running here and there for shelter and armed men in uniform were attacking the people, catching hold of just anybody on the roads and taking them into custody or beating them. I was terrorised.[61]

In May 1987 the first major act of violence was perpetrated against Farooq Abdullah when his motorcade was attacked on the way to the mosque.[62] Throughout the year sniper attacks became more common and, according to Tavleen Singh, there was evidence of increasing arms in the valley 'some time in that summer of 1987, once the bitterness of the stolen election had sunk in.'[63] Farooq Abdullah's domestic standing was further diminished by his attempt to locate some of the government departments permanently in either Jammu or Srinagar instead of shuttling them back and forward in winter and summer. His suggestion caused an outburst in Jammu, where the people went on strike in protest. Regional groups began calling for a separate state for the Jammu region. On 14 November 1987 the order was rescinded. Jammu rejoiced, but the valley was discontented. A strike was observed which paralysed life in the towns. The Bar Association was in the forefront of the agitation. Their associates believed that Abdullah had surrendered to Jammu and they demanded that Srinagar be made the permanent capital of the state. Although the agitation died down after about a week, Abdullah's critics protested that he had instigated the move in order to gain support for the National Conference from amongst the Kashmiri Muslims after the loss of popularity during the elections earlier in the year.

Throughout 1988 there were continuing disturbances which disrupted daily life with such frequency that Jagmohan, who was still the governor, made a detailed note of them in his diary.[64] In June, there were demonstrations in Srinagar against the sudden rise in the cost of electricity. The price increase annoyed people because supplies of electricity were at best erratic, but the government's response was unsympathetic. For the first time in over twenty-five years of activism, Amanullah Khan was able to talk convincingly about 'an armed struggle' in the valley. There were two bomb blasts which just missed the Central Telegraph office in Srinagar and the television station. In September there was an attack on the director-general of police, Ali Mohammed Watali. The JKLF claimed their first martyr, Ajaz Dar, who was killed during police firing. Although the early acts of sabotage did not cause much damage, they were a warning of what was to come. Resistance factions, whose adherents were called militants, proliferated under an array of names.

The JKLF, however, was singled out by the Indian authorities as being mainly responsible for the upsurge in internal disorder.

Anti-Indian feeling within the valley was mirrored by a surge of support for Pakistan. On 11 April 1988, young Muslims in Srinagar had forced shopkeepers to keep their shops shut in sympathy with all those who had been killed in an ammunition dump at Ojhri in Pakistan. The camp had been used as a depot for arms destined for the Afghan rebels. Mirwaiz Maulvi Farooq sent a condolence telegram to General Zia for the loss of life. Prayers were said in the Jama mosque.

A mourning procession was taken out in the streets of Srinagar which raised pro-Pakistani slogans, burnt buses and clashed with the police. The Gandhi Memorial College was ransacked. Hindu sympathisers were critical of the government, but for different reasons. The BJP accused the government of failure to take action against the protesters in time. The Panthers Party, formed in 1982, representing the Rajput community in Jammu, demanded Farooq Abdullah's resignation.

As India prepared to celebrate forty-one years of independence, anti-India slogans were raised in the valley. Pro-Pakistani supporters celebrated Pakistan's independence day on 14 August, but India's independence on 15 August was called a 'black day'. Two days later, on 17 August, General Zia-ul Haq was killed in a plane crash at Bahawalpur in Pakistan. His death was mourned in the valley, which led to disturbances. Eight people were reported to have been shot dead and at least thirteen wounded. Trouble between the Shias and Sunnis led to increased violence. 'An impression was created that the Shias in Pakistan felt happy at the death of President Zia-ul Haq. Some Shias in the valley were also accused of raising anti-Pak and anti-Zia slogans,' states P. S. Verma.[65] On 27 October – the anniversary of India's airlift into Srinagar in 1947 – there was a complete strike on what the protesters were now calling 'occupation day'. Whereas in 1947 the Pakistanis were deemed the invaders whilst the Indians were greeted as the liberators, by 1988 in the minds of the militants, the roles had been psychologically reversed.

The revenge factor

Pakistan could not fail to be aware of events in the valley. 'It was a tempting scenario,' writes Ajit Bhattacharjea, 'another chance to make up for the failures of 1947 and 1965, coupled with the desire to take revenge for the loss of Bangladesh in 1971, in which Indian infiltrators had played a role.'[66] Indian commentators maintain that as early as 1982, almost immediately after Sheikh Abdullah's death, General Zia had instigated a plan to train Kashmiri youth to launch an 'armed crusade' in the valley. But it did not meet with much success and it was not until the mid 1980s that the plan was again revived.[67] General Zia's official stand towards India on Kashmir was openly conciliatory. 'Pakistan's point of view is: let us talk. You can claim the whole of Kashmir,' he said in an interview with Indian journalist Rajendra Sareen in 1983. 'But maybe there is a *via media*. So let us talk at least. We are not in favour of resorting to force. But we are not in favour of being browbeaten by the Indian point of view that since there is a line of control, there is therefore no issue involved.'[68]

The perception, however, of Pakistan's early involvement in the growing militancy was fuelled by the Indian government's own propaganda machinery. K. Subramanyam, one of India's top defence specialists maintained that 'Operation Topac', named after Topac Amin, an Inca Prince who fought a non-conventional war against Spanish rule in eighteenth-century Uruguay, was established in Pakistan in April 1988 in order to nurture an indigenous insurgency. Widely publicised in the Indian Defence Review of July 1989, including reports of alleged instructions from General Zia to his army officers, Topac was denied by the Pakistani authorities. They countered that it was invented by the Research and Analysis Wing (RAW) of the Government of India, as a hypothetical exercise, a fact which Subramanyam later acknowledged.[69]

Such 'hypothetical' exercises did not help to improve the strained relations between the two countries. In the mid-1980s, the threat of war loomed with clashes between Indian and Pakistani forces on the Siachen glacier, one of the most northerly points of the state of Jammu and Kashmir, where, due to its 20,000 ft altitude, the line of control had never been clearly defined. Discussions in January 1986 between the two defence secretaries helped to diffuse the situation but sporadic fighting continued throughout 1987. In 1988 the Indian government introduced high altitude helicopters which gave their forces a strategic advantage.

The new administration of Benazir Bhutto, who had been elected prime minister of Pakistan in elections following General Zia's death in 1988, attempted to demonstrate concern over the deteriorating Indo-Pakistani relationship. Her meeting with Rajiv Gandhi in Islamabad soon after she became prime minister in December 1988 was widely seen as an opportunity for members of the new post-partition generation to resolve their differences. In early 1989 top-level talks were instituted. Two agreements were signed whereby the two leaders agreed not to bomb each other's nuclear installations and that they would respect the 1972 Simla accord signed by their parents. But Gandhi and Bhutto were both subject to their own domestic pressures, which did not give them the necessary latitude for any constructive policy reassessments. For Benazir Bhutto détente with India meant that her political opponents, of whom Nawaz Sharif, leader of the IJI (Islami Jamhoori Ittehad) was the most vociferous, alleged that she was pro-India in order to discredit her government at home. Rajiv Gandhi likewise faced difficulties over rapprochement with Bhutto at a time when Pakistan was being widely condemned in India for supporting the Sikh separatist movement. In August 1989, Bhutto, who had demanded that Indian troops should withdraw from

Siachen, demonstrated Pakistan's continuing interest in the region by making a personal visit to the glacier; given its immense altitude, the struggle for Siachen was perhaps symbolic, but the tensions between the two countries remained.

As the law and order situation deteriorated in the valley, Indian analysts continued to assert that the trouble was instigated by Pakistan. They argued that Pakistan's ISI - the Inter-Services Intelligence - which had been set up by General Zia-ul Haq and was known to have played a leading role in the war in Afghanistan, was also active in Kashmir. The alleged 'foreign hand' was, however, also a convenient scapegoat which prevented the Indian government from seeing the internal trauma within the valley. The grievances amongst the Kashmiris, which had been allowed to fester, the steady erosion of the 'special status' promised to the state of Jammu and Kashmir in 1947, the neglect of the people by their leaders, were clearly India's responsibility. Tavleen Singh believes that Kashmir would not have become an issue 'if the valley had not exploded on its own thanks to Delhi's misguided policies.' Over a period of time, 'the LOC would have been accepted as the border and we could have one day forgotten the dispute altogether.'[70] Instead, as the decade of the 1980s drew to a close, the valley of Kashmir became 'the explosive situation' of which Sheikh Abdullah had so often warned.

CHAPTER 7

Vale of Tears

I will put it bluntly. Independence is out. And they have to come to terms with it. They must realise it. But having said that, everything else is open. Girish Saxena.[1]

As the insurgency in the valley gained momentum, the acts of sabotage increased in frequency and intensity. The police and security forces reacted violently, often at the expense of innocent civilians who were caught in the crossfire. Every youth in Kashmir came to be regarded as a potential militant. Reports of human rights abuses began to hit the headlines world-wide. Stories emerged of torture, rape and indiscriminate killing. Although the insurgents seemed to have no long-term strategy, they appeared to hope that the repression of the Indian authorities in the valley would attract international attention which would take note of what they believed to be their 'just cause' and oblige the Indian government to relinquish control of the valley.

Farooq Abdullah was being side-lined as a political force by the Muslim parties, nearly all of whom developed a militant wing, and the continuing bomb attacks gave ample proof of the extent to which their supporters were armed. Amongst several direct assaults, Neel Kanth Ganju, the retired sessions judge who had passed the sentence of death on Maqbool Butt, was fired upon. Firing across the line of control was occurring regularly and a dawn to dusk curfew was imposed in all the border districts. Oblivious of the time-bomb which was about to explode in the valley, holidaymakers flocked to spend their summer on a houseboat or trekking in the foothills of the Himalayas. It was estimated that in 1989 a record number of nearly 80,000 foreign tourists visited Kashmir in what effectively became the valley's last tourist season.

The insurgency begins

While peace was 'breaking out' after the downfall of the communist regimes in Eastern Europe, 1989 marked the real beginning of the insurgency. A strike was called for India's Republic Day on 26 January. It was the first of many *hartals* in 1989, which took up one-third of the year's working days.[2] Severe riots in Jammu between Sikhs and Hindus led to unruly mobs roaming the city while the police 'acted merely as passive spectators.'[3] The fifth anniversary of Maqbool Butt's execution on 11 February was the occasion for another strike. Two days later there was a massive anti-Indian demonstration against Salman Rushdie's *Satanic Verses*, which lasted nearly a week, even though the government had banned the book. The whole of Srinagar went on strike. When five people were reportedly killed in police firing, the strike spread to other towns in the valley. In March there was violence between Muslims and Hindus in Rajauri. And throughout 1989 there was sporadic violence between Muslims and Buddhists in Ladakh. The Buddhists, ever conscious of the dominance of the valley Muslims, raised slogans like 'Save Ladakh, Free Ladakh from Kashmir.'[4]

On 12 July 1989 Jagmohan relinquished his position as governor after five years in office. In his memoirs he describes how since 1988 he had been sending 'warning signals' to New Delhi about the 'gathering storm'. 'All these clear and pointed warnings were, unfortunately, ignored.'[5] Jagmohan was replaced by a retired general, K. V. Krishna Rao. A former chief of army staff, Rao had considerable expertise in counter-insurgency, but none in politics. Farooq Abdullah was criticised by his political opponents for being unable to control the situation. 'The last symbol of secular Kashmiriyat remained a lightweight,' writes Bhattacharjea, 'given to helicopter sorties over the stricken valley; to elitist projects to attract tourists, while basic facilities were ignored.'[6] Enforced *bandhs* and *hartals*, attacks on government offices, bridges, buses, murder of police informers and intelligence officers all contributed to the increasing paralysis of the government.

Part of the militants' strategy was to intimidate National Conference activists in order to oblige them to disassociate themselves from the party, ultimately leading to a complete breakdown of the political process. On 21 August, Mohammed Yusuf Halwai, a National Conference leader was killed near his home in downtown Srinagar; shopkeepers downed their shutters 'in fear, confusion and mild disapproval'.[7] A placard on Halwai's body identified the JKLF as responsible for his death. The government was clearly being outmanoeuvred by the militants in 'the battle for hearts and minds' to which Farooq Abdullah repeatedly referred. 'They remain faceless and underground and yet control Kashmir,' wrote Tavleen Singh on 27 August 1989. 'This is the most frightening aspect of the current political situation in this troubled valley. All of last week shops remained closed in Srinagar without anyone being sure why except that there had been orders from "them".'[8]

Despite its waning popularity, the National Conference still managed to organise a rally on the anniversary of Sheikh Abdullah's death on 8 September. But the militants called for a strike which was observed in Srinagar and other towns throughout the valley. Effigies of the Sheikh were burnt. A week later, the first Kashmiri Pandit was murdered, the BJP leader, Tikka Lal Taploo, who was also an advocate of the High Court. Then Neel Kanth Ganju, who had escaped the earlier attack, was shot dead in broad daylight on 4 November. The Hindus, who for centuries had lived in harmony with the

Muslims, began to fear for their lives. There was a blackout on 14 November, Nehru's birthday, and on 5 December, Sheikh Abdullah's birthday.

Farooq Abdullah's response to the insurgency was described by Balraj Puri as more 'a sense of bravado rather than maturity'.[9] Stringent measures were adopted whether the protests were because of religious sentiments, pro-Pakistani feeling, economic grievances or civil liberties. Abdullah also attributed the alienation not so much to the 'rigged' 1987 elections, but to the failure of the government in Delhi to fulfil its promise to give the funds which were agreed at the time of Farooq's accord with Rajiv. 'We were unable to create jobs, to stop corruption. We were unable to provide factories and power generating stations. At each stage we were not given the help which we envisaged when we joined hands with the Congress.'[10] Too many Kashmiri youth were unemployed; a problem which Farooq understood but could not remedy. 'What can I do? There are 3,000 engineers looking for jobs even after we gave jobs to 2,000 in the last two years.' Nearly 10,000 graduates were unemployed. Amongst those with school leaving qualifications, unemployment was around 40,000 to 50,000. Allegations of corruption in the admissions procedure also alienated the people: 'Bright students could not get admission into colleges in the 1980s unless they paid bribes to politicians,' stated a lecturer at the University of Kashmir. 'This led to a loss of faith in the system and eventually the revolt.'[11] Individual students also corroborated this statement.

By 1989, a number of significant militant groups had begun to operate throughout the valley, mainly centred on the towns of Srinagar, Anantnag, Baramula and Sopore.[12] Their objective was either complete independence or unification with Pakistan. The Jammu and Kashmir Liberation Front, led within the valley by the core 'Haji' group, was the most prominent. True to its earlier objectives, its supporters were fighting for an independent state of Jammu and Kashmir as it existed in 1947. Several of the Muslim political parties, who had been components of MUF, had formed militant wings. The militant group, Al Barq, had links with Abdul Gani Lone's People's Conference. Al Fateh, led by Zain-ul Abdeen, a former contestant in the 1987 elections, was the armed wing of one faction of Shabir Shah's People's League. Both parties had also come out in support of the independence movement. Another armed faction of the Peoples' League was Al Jehad. Additional groups aimed at the formation of a 'theocratic' state. On a less significant level, the Allah Tigers had demonstrated that their main concern was closing video shops and beauty salons because they were 'unislamic'. In the early days of the insurgency, the Hizb-ul Mujaheddin, based in Sopore and regarded as the militant wing of the Jamaat-i Islami, did not have widespread support within the valley. The official Hizb-ul Mujaheddin objective was reunification with Pakistan. The Harkat-ul Ansar was also not yet part of mainstream militancy. Smaller groups believed to favour Pakistan were Hizbullah, Al-Umar Mujaheddin, Lashkar-i Toiba, Ikhwan-ul Mujaheddin,

Hizb-ul Momineen, Tehrik-ul Mujaheddin, as well as other numerous splinter groups.

Azam Inquilabi had transformed his Mahaz-i Azadi (Independence Front) into Operation Balakote. His objective was to create a united front between the rival groups to fight for the liberation of Kashmir from Indian rule. 'India and Pakistan must recognise our right to self-determination so that the two parts of Jammu and Kashmir be allowed to annex with each other. Then the people must be able to decide whether they want to remain free or join with Pakistan. We want to be able to determine our political future for ourselves.'[13] At the outset, the divisions between the groups remained below the surface; when one group called for a strike, the others complied.

Many of the militants were the disappointed political workers and traditional opponents of the National Conference in the 1987 elections. Young men aged between sixteen and twenty-five, they came from the towns of Srinagar, Anantnag, Pulwama, Kupwara and Baramula. Unlike their forbears who had campaigned for education and political rights in the 1930s, the majority were well-educated – doctors, engineers, teachers, policemen – who had become alienated by Indian government policies in New Delhi and lack of job opportunities. Their grievances were as much economic as political. Older militants, like Amanullah Khan of the JKLF, Ahsan Dar of Hizb-ul Mujaheddin and Azam Inquilabi of Operation Balakote, provided the motivation and historical context in which the struggle was being waged: 'We kept struggling for a peaceful resolution of the dispute, but failed,' said Inquilabi, 'so this young generation has opted for active resistance and it has gained momentum and it will continue to gain momentum come what may.'[14]

At the beginning of December 1989, Rajiv Gandhi lost the general election in India to his former finance minister, V. P. Singh. Although Kashmir was not an election issue, the new prime minister chose to try and win some support in the troubled state by appointing a Kashmiri Muslim, Mufti Muhammed Sayeed as India's first Muslim home minister, a position once held by Sardar Patel. Six days after he took office, on 8 December 1989, the JKLF made headline news with the kidnapping of the home minister's twenty-three-year-old daughter, Dr Rubaiya Sayeed, an intern at the Lalded Memorial Women's Hospital in Srinagar.

The kidnappers demanded the release of five militants, including JKLF leader, Sheikh Hamid, and the brother of Maqbool Butt, in return for her freedom. Farooq Abdullah, who was abroad at the time, returned to face mounting panic in the state. Journalists and bureaucrats became involved in the negotiations to free Rubaiya. Although the kidnapping of a young unmarried woman was giving the militants adverse publicity, the government at New Delhi was not prepared to risk any harm coming to the hostage and on 13 December the militants were freed; two hours later, Rubaiya Sayeed was also released unharmed. The released militants were taken out in a triumphant procession. Jubilant crowds rejoiced and danced in the streets of

Srinagar. The perceived weakness of V. P. Singh's government in negotiating with the militants raised their morale considerably. In an interview with *India Today* Mufti Muhammed Sayeed attributed the current alienation of the people to 'the mishandling of the situation by the previous [centre and state] governments ... the 1987 Assembly elections were rigged and the people lost faith in democratic institutions.'[15]

The frequent strikes through the year, targeted assassinations, bomb blasts and attacks on government property, culminating in the JKLF kidnapping, all contributed to the impression of increasing disorder. 'I was in the valley in late 1989,' recalled Dr Muzaffar Shah, president of the Kashmir Action Committee in Pakistan and a refugee from Baramula. 'I saw the whole thing simmering, about to burst; there was no administration. It had failed to stop the people coming on the streets; they took out demonstrations and called for strikes. Then the whole place burst open like a dam in 1990.'[16]

The return of Jagmohan

After the kidnapping of Rubaiya Saeed, New Delhi adopted a tougher approach. Shri Jagmohan was sent back to Kashmir as governor in place of General Krishna Rao, who had been in office for just over six months. 'The tragic irony of the situation was that I, who had been persistently pointing out that poisonous seeds were being planted, had to come back to face a thick and thorny harvest.'[17] Farooq Abdullah immediately resigned on the grounds that he could not co-operate with 'a man who hates the guts of the Muslims.'[18] As a supporter of the Indian Union, Abdullah shared none of his father's pretensions towards independence, and had no sympathy with the demands of the militants, whom he at times referred to as 'misguided youth'. But the accord with Rajiv Gandhi, the 1987 elections, alleged corruption of his government and subsequent inability to control the situation had all lost him popular support. Farooq, however, was also feeling injured: 'Someone told him after he resigned,' reported M. J. Akbar, 'that the people of Kashmir were unhappy with him. "Well," he replied, "I am unhappy with them too."'[19]

Jagmohan compared the administration, of which he was once more in charge, to 'a sprawling but lifeless octopus ... Frenzied chaos and savage anarchy gripped the valley'.[20] His return to full control of events in Kashmir on 19 January 1990 marked the beginning of a new intensity both in New Delhi's dealings with the Kashmiris and their response. His appointment was probably 'the worst mistake the central government could have made at the time,' writes Tavleen Singh. 'But there was nobody in V. P. Singh's newly-elected government who could have told him this.'[21] His government depended heavily on the extremist BJP whose supporters wanted to abrogate article 370 and integrate Kashmir within the Indian Union. The attempt to find a political solution to Kashmir's problem was put aside in favour of a policy of repression.

On the night of 19 January an intensive house-to-house search was carried out in an area where militants were believed to be hiding. Three hundred people were arrested, most of whom were later released.[22] Jagmohan claimed that the search had been ordered, before he resigned, by Abdullah whom he accused of abandoning the valley. The former chief minister denied this. The reaction from the people was unprecedented. 'The whole city was out. I was sleeping – it was midnight. I heard people on the road shouting pro-Pakistani slogans and Islamic slogans – "Allah o Akbar", "What do we want? We want freedom!"' recalls Haseeb, a Kashmiri medical student.[23]

The next day, as Jagmohan was sworn in as governor with the promise that he would treat the state like a 'nursing orderly' a large demonstration assembled in the streets of Srinagar to protest against the search the night before. In response, paramilitary troops gathered on either side of the Gawakadal bridge over the Jhelum river. When the unarmed crowd reached the bridge it was fired on from both sides of the river. The shooting has been called the worst massacre in Kashmiri history. Over a hundred people died, some from gunshot wounds, others because, in fear, they jumped into the river and drowned.[24] Farooq Ahmed, a mechanical engineer who was watching the demonstration, was wounded. Presumed dead, he was put into a lorry filled with bodies, until he was finally rescued by Kashmiri police and taken to hospital. 'I was fortunate, my back was just touched. Six bullets ... but my head was safe, I was conscious also. I saw the bridge was completely full of dead bodies ... there was chaos, people running here and there.'[25]

Whereas the Indian press played the incident down, the foreign press reported the massacre and its repercussions to the world. 'Thousands of Muslims, chanting "Indian dogs go home," "We want freedom" and "Long live Islam" marched through Srinagar and other towns, despite police "shoot-on-sight" orders,' reported the *Daily Telegraph*.[26] As a result, foreign correspondents were banned from the valley. A curfew was imposed indefinitely. Several other towns were put under curfew. Jagmohan stated that he had no information about bodies floating in the Jhelum river and failed to mention the incident in his memoirs. No public enquiry was ordered afterwards. 'With this incident,' writes Balraj Puri, 'militancy entered a new phase. It was no longer a fight between the militants and the security forces. It gradually assumed the form of a total insurgency of the entire population.'[27]

However, even as the insurgency was gaining in intensity in Kashmir, Indian television 'went overboard with live coverage of the mass movements against authoritarianism in East Europe and Central Asia, inanely oblivious of the tremendous impact each visual of a woman kissing the Quran and taunting a soldier was having on Kashmir,' writes M. J. Akbar.[28] In defiance of what came to be called 'crackdown' by the authorities, the people continued to come out on the streets: 'There were loudspeakers in the mosques, encouraging people to come out. Everyday, all day people were shouting slogans,' recalls Haseeb. '*Azadi, Azadi* ... Allah-o Akbar – Freedom, Freedom,

God is Great' was broadcast from the minarets. With extraordinary optimism, the people believed they had won their struggle almost before it had begun. 'Even I was thinking within ten days, India will have to vacate Kashmir.'[29] Teachers, doctors, lawyers, civil servants, students all came out on the streets in protest. For the first time the Indian flag was not hoisted to celebrate India's Republic Day on 26 January, which was observed as a 'black day'. Those journalists already in Srinagar remained confined to their hotel rooms; their curfew passes were withdrawn; telephone and telex lines were cut.

Pakistan seemed to be taken unawares by events in the valley. 'Islamabad was as surprised as New Delhi by the sudden, dramatic outburst of sentiment for *azadi*,' writes Edward Desmond, the *Time* magazine correspondent.[30] Given the past history of Indo–Pakistani relations over Kashmir, the Pakistani government was bound to repeat its demand of the past decades: the Kashmiris should be allowed their right to self-determination under the terms of the United Nations resolutions. Benazir Bhutto made an assertive speech in Azad Kashmir pledging Pakistan's moral and diplomatic support to the 'freedom fighters'. Talks in January 1990 between Inder Gujral, the Indian foreign minister, and Sahibzada Yaqub Khan, the Pakistani foreign minister, did not reduce the continuing tension between the two countries. 'Yaqub Sahib came with a very hard message,' said Inder Gujral. The Indian foreign minister described his Pakistani counterpart as 'almost challenging the Indian state's authority on Kashmir, saying that nothing in the past was binding on them and the Simla agreement was not relevant.'[31] The Indian government also talked of the need to be psychologically prepared for war, claiming that 10,000 Kashmiri youth had gone to Pakistan to undergo training.[32] But, writes, Indian journalist Tavleen Singh, 'the moral support became military support only after thousands of Kashmiris had taken to the streets to demand *azadi*.'[33]

Jagmohan withstood what he termed the 'propaganda missiles' emanating from Pakistan. 'I persuaded myself that I had a national obligation to discharge. With all the frozen turbulence in my mind with all the millstones round my neck, and with my back badly wounded by the stabs from the rear, I proceeded ahead.'[34] Restrictions on the press, however, prevented genuine information from getting through to the valley. With the exception of foreign radio, the Kashmiris were obliged to rely on press releases issued from Jagmohan's office in Raj Bhavan. The same stories appeared in different newspapers with the same content under different by-lines.

On 13 February Lassa Kaul, the local director of Indian television, Doodarshan, was murdered by militants in Srinagar on his way home. Jagmohan explained the murder on the grounds that Kaul had incurred 'the wrath of the terrorists by showing on television programmes which they termed unislamic and forming part of what was labelled as cultural aggression by India.' The militants blamed the administration for pressurising Kaul into broadcasting pro-Indian government material, 'thus indirectly bringing about his death'.[35] The next day, employees of Doordashan resigned on the grounds that Jagmohan had ruined the credibility of the official media. 'The media,' says Ved Bhasin, editor of the *Kashmir Times* based in Jammu, 'was caught in the crossfire between the militants and the military.'[36] The pressure from both sides to slant stories or omit information meant that journalists found it impossible to function.[37]

When Jagmohan dissolved the State legislative assembly on 19 February he dispensed with the only avenue for political expression other than the mosque. He explained his actions to the home minister, Mufti Muhammed Sayeed: 'Without dissolution there was no moral legitimacy for the use of force on an extensive scale. Nor was it possible for me and the advisers to secure the obedience of our orders from local officials, who were constantly being fed with the impression that Dr Farooq Abdullah and his colleagues were coming back after the role of "butcher" has been played by the Governor.'[38] With the backing of Delhi, Jagmohan's strategy was to militarise the state. The local police were bolstered by a federal paramilitary unit, the Central Reserve Police Force (CRPF); their harsh methods were resented by the local police who temporarily went on strike. 'Unofficial estimates have it that nearly a lakh [100,000] of army, paramilitary and police personnel have been deployed in Kashmir in the past six weeks. If this is not war, what is it?' asked journalist, Shiraz Sidhva after a visit to the valley in February 1990. 'That the people are with the militants is quite clear. In the one month since the new administration has taken over, not one single militant has been captured.'[39]

At the end of February an estimated 400,000 Kashmiris marched on the offices of the United Nations Military Observer Group to hand in petitions demanding the implementation of the UN resolutions. It was reported as the largest demonstration the Kashmir valley has seen.[40] But the UN officials were obliged to point out that their presence in the valley was only to monitor the line of control. Nearly every day a procession of lawyers, women, teachers, doctors marched through the streets of Srinagar. On 1 March more than forty people were killed in police firing when a massive crowd, estimated at one million took to the streets. The continuing curfew led to severe shortages of food, medicines and other essential items. The hospitals were becoming so full of the victims of the insurgency that the name of the Bone and Joint hospital in Srinagar was changed to the Hospital for Bullet and Bomb Blast injuries.[41]

Driven by his own sense of personal mission, Jagmohan saw the insurgency as a movement, abetted by Pakistan, which had to be brutally crushed, even if it meant targeting virtually the entire population.

> Obviously, I could not walk barefoot in the valley full of scorpions – the valley wherein inner and outer forces of terrorism had conspired to subvert the Union and to seize power ... I must equip myself to face all eventualities. I could leave nothing to chance. A slight slip or error would mean a Tienamen Square or a Blue Star or a formal declaration of a new theocratic state with all its international embarrassment ...[42]

Farooq Abdullah accused the governor of unleashing a reign of terror on the people.

The government of New Delhi took some remedial steps to control the effects of the repression by appointing George Fernandes as minister for Kashmir who was well known both in India and in the rest of the world for his concern for human rights. Jagmohan regarded Fernandes's approach as impractical and he took an unsympathetic view of his interviews with 'unresponsive elements in the subversives' camp'. Fernandes, he said, 'gave no consideration to the fact that as long as the pro-Pakistani elements, intoxicated by past successes, had faith in their guns and bombs, no worthwhile political process could be initiated and those who responded to it, were most likely to be eliminated.'[43] Fernandes, however, believed in dialogue. 'I know these people. I have met with them – quite a few of them before they became militants, and many of them thereafter. One has to interact with them to get a sense of the kind of alienation that these young people have experienced.'[44]

The flight of the Hindus

In a mass exodus, at the beginning of March, about 140,000 Hindus[45] left the valley for refugee camps outside Jammu. The more affluent took up residence in their second homes in Delhi, but the vast majority were housed in squalid tents in over fifty camps on the outskirts of both Jammu and Delhi. Their story is as familiar as any the world over. Displaced from their homes because of a war over which they had no control, they too seemed to be caught in the crossfire – used as propaganda material by the Indian government to demonstrate that not only Muslims were suffering during the insurgency. 'In the wake of terrorism, we left the valley. We are living in a miserable condition' said Jawaharlal, who used to be a teacher in Kupwara, a small town near the line of control. 'We used to live in peace. The Kashmiri Muslims are our brethren. We have been living with them for centuries together; we shared their joy and sorrow. But the gun culture forced us to leave.' Living in unhygienic conditions, with insufficient food, Jawaharlal believed that the human rights of Hindus have also been violated. 'The Kashmiri Pandits are in a minority. Our rights must be safeguarded in the hands of the Muslim majority in the valley. We have left our hearths and homes. Our civil liberties have been curtailed. Only if the majority community invites us to go back, then can we return to the valley; otherwise it is out of bounds for us.'[46] Dr Pamposh Ganju of the Indo–European Kashmir forum says that since 1990 over 6,000 Hindus have died in the camps, because of poor conditions, compared with 1,500 Kashmiri Pandits who were killed during the early months of the insurgency.[47] (Indian government figures for murdered Hindus number less than 200 in 1989/90.)

There was and still is, however, a widespread feeling that the departure of the Hindus was not necessary and that Jagmohan, who had a reputation for being anti-Muslim dating back to the days of the Emergency, attempted to give the Kashmiri problem a communal profile by facilitating their departure in government transport. It was an allegation he strongly refuted:

> What can you say of a Committee which comes out with a proposition that it is not the fearsome environment, it is not the brutalised landscape, it is not the ruthless Kalashnikov of the marauders, it is not the bomb explosions and fires, it is not the threatening telephonic calls, it is not the hysterical exhortations for "Jihad" from hundreds of loudspeakers fitted on the mosques ... but the inducements of the trucks that have impelled the Kashmiris to abandon their homes and hearths in the cool and crisp Valley and to move to the hot and inhospitable camps of Jammu?[48]

After their flight, there were numerous reports of Muslim neighbours and friends looking after the houses of the Hindus. 'The property, houses, orchards owned by the Pandits have not been damaged in the last one year,' stated George Fernandes in October 1990.[49] Furthermore, says Balraj Puri, only 'a thorough independent enquiry ... can show whether this exodus of Pandits, the largest in their long history, was entirely unavoidable.'[50] Their departure meant that the militant groups, like the JKLF, who maintained that their objectives for the state included all the occupants of the former princely state, could no longer claim to represent the Hindus, who were drawn to the extremist· Hindu parties, the BJP and Shiv Sena.

Two eminent jurists, V. M. Tarkunde, in his eighties, and Rachinder Sachar, as well as the educationalist, Amrik Singh, and Balraj Puri, toured Kashmir in March and April 1990. They condemned both militants and Jagmohan for the deteriorating situation in the valley: 'The fact is that the whole Muslim population of the Kashmir valley is wholly alienated from India and due to the highly repressive policy pursued by the administration in recent months, especially since the advent of Shri Jagmohan in January 1990, their alienation has now turned into bitterness and anger.' Their report also condemned the militants for their tactics following the kidnapping and murder in April of the vice-chancellor of Kashmir University, Mushir-ul Haq, his secretary, Abdul Ghani, and the general manager of the Hindustan Machine Tools watch factory, H. L. Khera: 'The militants are strengthening the repressive machinery of the state by their activities and are providing a semblance of justification to the government to assume more and more arbitrary powers.'[51] In a sense, this was their strategy: the greater the repression by the Indian government, the more support the militants hoped to gain amongst the people, and consequently, the more international pressure could be brought to bear. But with foreign correspondents banned from the valley and top political activists under arrest, there was no dialogue to modify the stand taken either by the government or the militants.

Death of the Mirwaiz

Since his days of opposition to Sheikh Abdullah, arising out of his uncle Yusuf's feud in the 1930s, Mirwaiz Maulvi Farooq had been known for his pro-Pakistani sentiments. The Farooq-Farooq alliance with Abdullah in 1983 marked a short-lived shift in attitude; as Farooq Abdullah's own position was marginalised with the rise of the Muslim parties, Mirwaiz Farooq assumed the role of a respected elder, someone who, in the present crisis, both the government and the militants could approach. As chief preacher at the Jama Masjid in Srinagar, his religious influence was considerable. On 21 May he was shot dead at his home. Militants blamed Indian agents; the government of New Delhi blamed the militants, but not convincingly enough so no one believed them. His death shocked both groups. His teenage son, Omar, blamed 'those elements who were working against the interests of the Kashmiri movement' for his death.[52] Supporters of the state's accession to India observed how his reputation changed overnight with his death. 'Till he was shot dead ... he was considered a traitor and a secessionist,' writes Tavleen Singh. 'No sooner was he dead than he came to be instantly revered as a martyr and a moderate.'[53]

The repercussions after his death did even more damage to the government. During his funeral procession, as the crowd passed Islamia College, where the 69th battalion of the CRPF was quartered, some officers opened fire; the government claimed that it did so in retaliation for an attack on the security forces by a section of the crowd. Officially, the government acknowledged twenty-seven dead, but unofficial sources claimed as many as 100 died, possibly more.[54] The Mirwaiz's coffin was also pierced with bullets. Outrage at the murder turned into hysteria against the government.

When interviewed by the Punjab Human Rights Organisation, Satish Jacob, one of the BBC's correspondents in Delhi, described the militant groups as not being 'a wee bit sad about Maulvi's death. Not to the extent they pretended to be. All the show of sorrow is spurious.' In his opinion, the murder was carried out by the Hizb-ul Mujaheddin because Maulvi Farooq was a supporter of the JKLF On the basis of his own information, Jacob also said that the security forces were wholly at fault in firing on the funeral procession and that there was no evidence that there was any provocation prior to the firing or any one from the crowd fired. He estimated that forty-seven people died.[55]

The valley under Jagmohan was a closed war zone. When the Punjab Human Rights Organisation investigated Maulvi Farooq's death, they described 'a complete iron curtain' separating the Kashmir valley from the outside world. 'The regime of the curfew is all pervading. There are severe restrictions on outsider Indians seeking to enter the valley.'[56] In retrospect, it is surprising that the Indian government did not appreciate earlier the adverse effect of crushing the insurgency so indiscriminately. Although

Jagmohan's tenure as governor lasted less than five months, during this period, the alienation of the valley against the Indian government became almost total.

By the time he left Kashmir, Jagmohan's thinking had none of the qualities of the promised nursing orderly:

> Every Muslim in Kashmir is a militant today. All of them are for secession from India. I am scuttling Srinagar Doordarshan's programmes because every one there is a militant ... The situation is so explosive that I can't go out of this Raj Bhavan. But I know what's going on, minute by minute. The bullet is the only solution for Kashmir. Unless the militants are fully wiped out, normalcy can't return to the valley.[57]

Ashok Jaitley, a respected civil servant, who worked under Jagmohan, saw things differently: 'What Jagmohan did in five months they (the militants) could not have achieved in five years.'[58]

Saxena steps in

After Mirwaiz Farooq's death, Jagmohan was replaced as governor by Girish 'Gary' Saxena. He had spent seventeen years with RAW, India's intelligence agency, Research and Analysis Wing. On his assumption of office, he received a memorandum form ten senior civil servants, which included the signature of Ashok Jaitley. In their report, they attempted to give Saxena a realistic picture of the alienation of the valley due to mishandling by the authorities. Although Saxena is generally regarded as being more benign in his approach than Jagmohan, Tavleen Singh believes he was just more subtle. 'The last thing the new governor wanted to hear were any home truths about Kashmir.'[59] He did not adopt Jagmohan's overtly repressive tactics, but he was equally committed to crushing the insurgency through force.

Increasing reliance was placed on the border security forces to combat the insurgency, but, as Saxena later admitted, they were young boys not trained for the sort of duties they were called to discharge.

> Border security forces are trained to guard the borders, patrol and guard pickets, they are not trained for urban terrorism and guerrilla warfare. So they had to learn many things the hard way. A person can act in haste or in panic. This is more likely in a small outfit led by a junior officer. Suddenly he is subjected to machine gun fire or a rocket attack, there is a feeling that he or his party might be over run ... Because of a proxy war being conducted from across the border and sponsoring of terrorist violence on a large scale, it was at times difficult to ensure targeted measured responses by the security forces. There were occasions when there was overreaction or even wrongdoing.[60]

Like many Indians officials, Saxena firmly believed that Pakistan was waging its own 'proxy war' in Kashmir, not only by supporting the militants by giving them arms but also by allowing them to train in their territory. In

February 1990, Indian intelligence had disclosed over 46 camps throughout Azad Kashmir, which they described as 'safe houses' where militants were given weapons and explosives training.[61] In June 1990 *Financial Times* journalist, David Housego travelled throughout Azad Kashmir and was shown Jamaat-i Islami refugee camps which were:

> ... quite unlike the official camps of the local Azad Kashmir government where you see the familiar miseries of refugee life ... In the Jamaat camps, there are no women, children or older men. They are all young men coming from different towns and villages in the Valley ... their morale is high. They say that they are well looked after...they describe themselves as refugees. But stickers on the wall proclaim they are members of the Hizb-ul Mujaheddin.[62]

The Pakistani and the Azad Kashmir governments denied that they were giving any material support to the militants. But the activities of the Jamaat-i Islami and other militant sympathisers were obviously not restricted. 'There are no training camps in Pakistan, of course, but insofar as Azad Kashmir is concerned, this is part and parcel of the State of Jammu and Kashmir,' says Azam Inquilabi.[63] 'We can establish military training camps there and we have been doing it.' Justice Tarkunde assessed the training camps in the context of the Kashmiris political struggle against the government of India:

> It is very likely that Pakistan has provided military training and arms to the militants in Kashmir. But it is not responsible for the disaffection of the people of the valley from the government of India. The cause of the Kashmir debacle is the initial denial of the right of self-determination and the subsequent anti-democratic policies pursued by the Indian government.[64]

In March 1990, John Kelly, assistant secretary of state for Near Eastern and South Asian Affairs told a House Foreign Affairs subcommittee: 'We are concerned at the recent flare-up of tensions between India and Pakistan over Kashmir ... the United States thinks the best framework for a resolution of this dispute can be found in the 1972 Simla agreement.'[65] With the weakening of the Indo–Russian relationship following the collapse of the Soviet Union, as Indian commentators observed the United States was also aware of the significant opportunities for developing stronger ties with India. Indian military purchases from the United States increased from $56,000 in 1987 to $56 million in 1990.[66] Pakistan was, however, facing difficulties with its relationship with the United States because of its nuclear programme. In October 1990, under the terms of the Pressler Amendment, American military supplies were cut off. At the same time, Nawaz Sharif, who replaced Benazir Bhutto as prime minister after her dismissal in August 1990, was coming under domestic criticism for his Kashmiri policy. Amongst some circles in Pakistan it was believed that, regardless of statements to the contrary, the US was favouring an independent Kashmir in order to be able to use it as a base for American strategic objectives and that, by not taking a tough enough stand on Kashmir, Nawaz was acceding to this objective. 'The scenario which the West is trying to create here goes something like this,' said Mian Zahid Sarfraz, a former political colleague of Nawaz Sharif:

> If Kashmir can't be buried on Indian terms, then it should become an independent country rather than a part of Pakistan through a plebiscite as originally envisaged. But if Kashmir becomes independent or is given some such status, it will at best be a landlocked domain, an international protectorate doomed to remain under Indian control forever ... By accepting this US vision, Nawaz has forsaken national security.[67]

It was clear, however, that despite a certain ambivalence in Nawaz Sharif's statements, Pakistan's long-standing commitment to resolving the Kashmir issue on the basis of the UN resolutions, meant that the policy shift required to accommodate the 'third option' of an independent Kashmir was in fact not acceptable.

Repression and retaliation

For the Kashmiris, the familiar pattern of attacks by militants on specific targets, reprisals by the government, cordon and search operations to flush out militants and find weapons and the call by the militants for strikes, had become part of their daily life, with very little dialogue in between. Human rights organisations, although restricted in their access, condemned the violations of human rights. In 1991 Asia Watch stated that the government forces 'have also systematically violated international human rights law by using lethal force against peaceful demonstrators.'[68] Kashmir would disappear from the international news for a few weeks or months only to reappear again when a journalist reported on some fearful event.

Although Saxena encouraged the security forces to use restraint on the grounds that excesses won recruits to militancy, stories of brutality by the security forces continued to emerge, especially in rural areas, where control from the top was not so effective. There was also very little check on security forces' operations. The Armed Forces (Jammu and Kashmir) Special Ordinance, introduced in July 1990, provided the security forces with extraordinary powers to shoot and kill, search and arrest without a warrant, all under immunity from prosecution 'in respect of anything done or purported to be done in exercise of power conferred by this Act.' Soon after its introduction, the security forces were reported as going on 'a binge' of arson, burning shops and houses in retaliation for a recent ambush by the militants.[69]

One of the most serious allegations of excess which Governor Saxena faced happened in the small town of Kunan Poshpura. In February 1991 there were reports of fifty-three women being gang-raped, while the men were kept outside in the freezing cold or locked in houses and interrogated. 'What happened in Kunan Poshpura is seen as the greatest single atrocity by security forces,' wrote Christopher Thomas in *The Times*.[70] The soldiers were identified as members of the 4th Rajput rifles. Three separate inquiries concluded that the evidence of the women was inconsistent and, on the basis of these inquiries, the Indian government asserted that the episode was 'a massive hoax orchestrated by terrorist groups, their mentors and sympathisers in Kashmir and abroad.'[71] The mission of the International Commission of Jurists which visited Kashmir in 1993, however, concluded that 'while mass rape at Kunan Poshpura may not have been proved beyond doubt, there are very substantial grounds for believing that it took place.'[72] 'Indian security forces tied up and shot seven men and boys, all members of the same Kashmiri Muslim family in this remote village at the weekend, in what seems to have been a calculated act of brutality to deter villagers from helping Kashmiri separatists,' wrote David Housego from Malangam in the Kashmir valley in April 1991. 'The apparently cold-blooded reprisals by the BSF against villagers they believed to be shielding militants or weapons is further evidence of breakdown in discipline among Indian forces in Kashmir.'[73]

In June 1991, Tony Allen-Mills reported how the inhabitants of Kulgam were subjected to indiscriminate firing in the streets in reprisal for a rocket attack on BSF barracks, when two soldiers were slightly injured:

> Abdul Hamid Wazi, a baker's assistant, saw soldiers pouring gunpowder on the outside walls of his house. They fired a shot and set the place alight. The thatched roof collapsed on him. Wazi jumped through the flames, badly burning his leg and face. By the time the soldiers' wrath was spent, twenty-eight shops and two houses had been torched, there were bullet holes in the mosque and several women claimed to have been raped.[74]

In 1991 Tim McGirk of *The Independent* generously assessed the combined strength of the main militant groups at 45,000 armed and trained fighters. Indian army and paramilitary were initially estimated to be 150,000.[75] Over time, these figures fluctuated both in reality and perception. The belief that 'half a million Indian troops' were stationed in Kashmir became an established fact in the opinion of all opposition groups. The Indian government maintained there were less militants and definitely less military.

After the JKLFs early successes, its leaders found that the Hizb-ul Mujaheddin was finding more support in Pakistan at their expense. Amanullah Khan complained that his recruits were being coerced to join the Hizb and other groups. In December 1991 at a press conference in Islamabad, Khan regretted that the pro-Pakistani Hizb was killing JKLF workers. The JKLF also accused pro-Pakistani supporters of providing clues to the Indian security forces regarding the JKLF hideouts, which made them easier to catch. In 1992 Amanullah Khan made such a publicised attempt to cross the line of control; in order to demonstrate that the JKLF did not recognise the line dividing 'the motherland of Kashmir.'[76] His first attempt, on 11 February 1992 – the eighth anniversary of Maqbool Butt's execution – was stopped by the

Pakistani authorities and twelve of the marchers were killed. Before Amanullah could make another attempt on 30 March, he was detained with 500 supporters. A third attempt in October also failed. Although thwarted in his objective, the publicity involved did boost his support and demonstrated that the JKLF was prepared to pursue its independent objectives in the face of opposition from the Pakistani government.

'The JKLF staged a comeback,' writes Balraj Puri 'and the slogan of *azadi* returned to the valley at the expense of pro-Pakistani sentiments.' Puri believes at this stage the Kashmiris began to shed many of their illusions about Pakistani support for their movement: 'If this process of disillusionment was not complete, it was due to the central government's failure to appreciate the basic aspirations of the Kashmiris and the repressive acts of the Indian security forces.'[77]

The government in New Delhi was undergoing its own convulsions. After less than two years in office, V. P. Singh was replaced as prime minister following elections in June 1991. His successor was Narasimha Rao, the new leader of the Congress Party after the assassination of Rajiv Gandhi in May. Although the BJP no longer wielded the same influence on Kashmiri policy, Hindu communalism remained a factor during this period. It reached alarming proportions at the end of December 1992 with the destruction by Hindu extremists of the mosque at Ayodha in Uttar Pradesh, south of Nepal. 'After Ayodha,' commented one Kashmiri activist, 'we did not understand why the Muslims in India did not do like us and rise up against the Indian government.'

Under Saxena, the Indian government also worked to improve its intelligence gathering operation and counter-insurgency measures in the valley. Those militants who could not withstand torture under interrogation, were 'turned' and used as 'Cats' [Concealed Apprehension Tactics] to identify fellow militants. 'Operation Tiger,' launched in August 1992 was the first in a series of security forces operations code named 'Shiva', 'Eagle', 'Cobra'. Their aim was to suppress the various militant groups through a 'catch and kill' policy. One of the towns to suffer most at the hands of the security forces was Sopore. On 6 January 1993, at least forty-three people were killed and a whole section of central Sopore was burnt to the ground. It was considered to be the largest reprisal attack by the security forces during the insurgency. 'The incident marked a watershed, forcing state and central government forces to acknowledge for the first time that the BSF forces responsible had retaliated against the town's civilian population after two of their forces were injured and subsequently died in a militant attack.' According to Asia Watch, witnesses reported seeing the BSF soldiers pour gasoline on to rags, set them alight and toss them on to houses and shops. Witnesses also stated that the BSF prevented fire fighters from putting out the blaze.[78]

Every so often during the Indian government's war against the insurgents, as with Mirwaiz Maulvi Farooq, a well known person was killed which attracted more attention and generally caused more embarrassment to the Indian government. Even the death of a militant could be the occasion for a huge funeral procession, which of itself was a manifestation of anti-government feeling. On 18 February 1993 Dr Farooq Ashai, chief orthopaedic surgeon at the Bone and Joint hospital in central Srinagar, was killed while returning home in his car with his wife and daughter. A respected doctor, his death caused an outcry. His widow, Dr Farida Ashai, recounted how the only shooting which took place were the three shots fired at their car. 'It was a deliberate killing. Instead of reaching home, he reached the graveyard.'[79] Although the government maintained that there was cross-firing, his family believed he was killed because of his known association with foreign journalists and human rights representatives. He also acted as a spokesman for injured civilians in Kashmir. 'Because he was an expert in bullet injuries, so he was also frequently sought out by militants.'[80] His students later erected a monument in his memory outside the hospital to their beloved teacher '... eminent surgeon, efficient intellect, humanist patriot fell to the bullets of security forces.'

Governor Saxena maintained that because there had been cross firing, the incident was not deliberate. 'It is very unlikely that anyone could have had an inkling that this car was carrying Dr Ashai. So there was no motivation and this incident shook us all up because he was a highly respected law-abiding man.'[81] But the perception persisted that the security forces had once more taken the law into their own hands.

In March another renowned doctor, Dr Abdul Ahad Guru, a heart surgeon, was shot in Srinagar. A known sympathiser of the JKLF, dubbed by Jagmohan as one of 'the unresponsive elements in the subversives' camp', it was suggested he had been shot by members of the Hizb-ul Mujaheddin. He had, however, been under surveillance from the government and both militant groups believed his death was caused by the security forces, although this was denied by the government. Once again there was anger that no enquiry took place. During his funeral procession, a large crowd assembled. 'There were 5 to 6,000 people but the BSF had cordoned off the area to the Martyrs graveyard and said that only a hundred people will go,' said a relative.[82] In the encounter which followed, the police opened fire and Dr Guru's brother-in-law, Ashiq Hussain, one of the pallbearers, was shot in the head and died instantly. 'Although the evidence does not indicate that the police targeted Hussain, it is evident from the testimony and photographs that they fired directly into the crowd,' stated Asia Watch.[83]

In February 1993 over thirty political parties had grouped together to form an umbrella organisation known as the All Parties Hurriyat (Freedom) Conference (APHC). Maulvi Farooq's teenage son, Omar, as the 'least objectionable leader to each of the factions of the Hurriyat',[84] became its chairman. The seasoned political element behind the APHC was provided by Syed Ali Shah Gilani of the Jamaat-i Islami, Abdul Gani Lone of the People's

Conference, Maulvi Abbas Ansari of the Liberation Council, and Professor Abdul Ghani Bhat of the Muslim Conference, all of whom were under arrest throughout most of this period. Proud of his achievement in bringing together so many disparate groups, Omar Farooq had also taken on his father's position as Mirwaiz of the Jama Masjid. Although the various components differed over whether they wanted independence or unification of the state with Pakistan, they had one common objective: that the people should be given the right to choose. It was the long-standing plea for self-determination and a plebiscite. But this time, the Kashmiris insisted that the third option of independence should not be excluded. Since the UN resolutions provide for a plebiscite to choose only between India and Pakistan, Omar Farooq suggested that 'a more equitable solution might be found in tripartite talks.'[85] The Hurriyat Conference gave the militants a united political platform through which they could voice their grievances, but their demands did not permit them to consider a solution which lay within the existing framework of the Indian Union.

Mindful of the harmful effects of censorship, practised during Jagmohan's days, Saxena lifted restrictions on the press: 'Right through my time in Kashmir, everyone was allowed in, all the press correspondents, journalists, TV teams, BBC, *Time*, *Newsweek*, German TV – you name it and they were there. I must have personally met over a hundred foreign journalists. Access to the valley was not denied. Even diplomats were able to meet top militants.' Only Amnesty International was persistently forbidden access. Saxena put this down to Pakistan's role. 'Any organisation like Amnesty, which has a tremendous international flavour will be exploited by Pakistan as a weapon for internationalising the issue.' He also maintained that the militants would use the presence of Amnesty to bring about a confrontation. 'I did not want the old phenomenon of hundreds of thousands of people marching in the streets.'[86]

During his three years as governor, Saxena was confident that the security situation 'qualitatively improved tremendously. 1990 and 1991 witnessed our efforts to contain militancy on the ground and that phase was over by early 1992, when the JKLF march also fizzled out on 11 February. Fear of the gun is still there, the militants still have significant striking capability. They can attack security forces at times, they can hit at soft targets'. Saxena also stressed that during his governorship, the lines of communication for a political dialogue with the militant outfits and the 'misguided youth' were kept open. Efforts were made through these channels to make them give up violence and join mainstream politics. The policy was never to settle the whole thing by force or political issues by guns.[87]

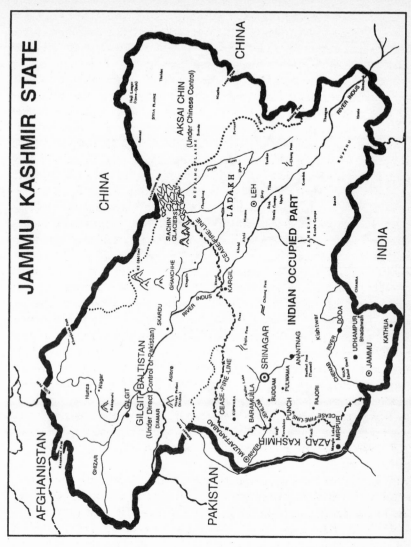

JAMMU KASHMIR STATE

CHINA

CHINA

AKSAI CHIN
(Under Chinese Control)

SIACHEN GLACIERS

K2 (8611m)

GHANCHHE

LADAKH

⊙ LEH

SKARDU

GILGIT BALTISTAN
(Under Direct Control of Pakistan)

RIVER INDUS

KARGIL

DIAMAR

Astore

Hunza

Nagar

GHIZAR

AFGHANISTAN

SRINAGAR ⊙

INDIAN OCCUPIED PART

DODA

KISHTWAR

UDHAMPUR
Bhadarwah

JAMMU ⊙

KATHUA

INDIA

RIVER INDUS

CEASE-FIRE-LINE

BARAMULLA

KUPWARA

BUDGAM

PULWAMA

ANANTNAG

PUNCH

RAJORI

CEASE-FIRE-LINE

AZAD KASHMIR

MUZAFFARABAD ⊙

MIRPUR

PAKISTAN

8. An Independent State of Jammu and Kashmir? (Source: Jammu and Kashmir Liberation Front)

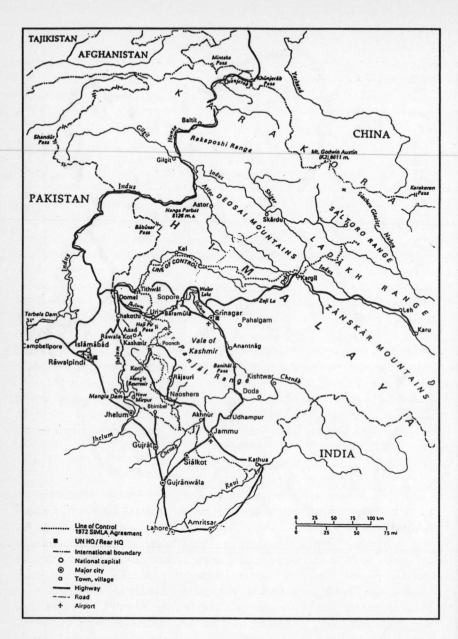

9. Jammu and Kashmir Today
(Source: United Nations Cartographic Section, 1994)

CHAPTER 8

Hearts and Minds

You can't just form a government and ignore that somehow you have to win their hearts again. Farooq Abdullah[1]

We should think about the hearts of the people, not the heads of government. Mirwaiz Omar Farooq[2]

By 1993 the Government of India was confident that the mass movement in the valley against India was weakening. There were no more large-scale demonstrations in the streets. People appeared to want their lives to return to normal. The problem remained how this was to be achieved. No political leader prepared to voice the demands of the Kashmiri activists and militants would be acceptable to Delhi; any leader of whom Delhi approved would be rejected by the militants. And, although the militancy had decreased in and around Srinagar, militants continued to operate throughout the countryside and were still capable of mounting serious attacks on the security forces. Pending a political settlement, the valley remained under siege. In addition, human rights groups, British MPs, US Congressmen and other international observers were beginning to look more critically than ever at events in the valley of Kashmir since the insurgency began.

Normalisation?

In March 1993 Girish Saxena was recalled and replaced by retired General Krishna Rao for a second term of office. 'That sent a mixed message to the people of the Kashmir valley,' stated the Srinagar correspondent of the *Economist*. 'As governor of the state in 1989, he bears some responsibility for the drift towards Kashmiri militancy during that time. On the other hand, General Rao's background as a professional soldier should help instil more discipline among the security forces.'[3] In July 1993, Rajesh Pilot, minister of state for internal security, reiterated that the government would respect human rights in its efforts to curb the 'separatist' movement in Jammu and Kashmir. The Indian government also permitted a team of international jurists to visit Kashmir during the summer.[4] In October the government set up the National Human Rights Commission under the Protection of Human Rights Act, 1993. But, according to Amnesty International, whose observers were still not allowed into the valley, its efficacy was reduced by the fact that it was

163

not empowered to enquire into complaints of human rights violations by the army and paramilitary forces. 'All it can do when faced with complaints of this nature is to call for official reports from the government, effectively functioning as a 'post box' of official views.'[5]

In October 1993 the mosque at Hazratbal once more attracted international attention. Since the spring, the militants had been parading openly in the streets nearby. They were happy to talk to journalists and show off their weapons. 'I saw militant leaders, both JKLF and Hizb-ul Mujaheddin being escorted by armed bodyguards in public,' recalls one western journalist. 'I had several interviews with leaders in the open air. The area was completely controlled by the militants. There were no security forces around.'[6] By the autumn, the Indian government decided to take action. Azam Inquilabi, whose Operation Balakote militants were also at Hazratbal, said that the intention of the Indian army was to destroy the mosque:

> They wanted to humiliate the religious sentiments of the Kashmiris, to the extent that, once the shrine would have been demolished through shelling, they would then tell the Kashmiris "you see even after having this shrine demolished, Pakistani forces could not intervene. So they do not express solidarity with you struggling people. They are leaving you in the lurch; so this is hypocrisy of the Muslim world, therefore why should you fight for the Muslim world and you should reconcile yourselves to the situation as it was in 1989."[7]

Pakistan condemned the Indian action in surrounding the mosque as sacrilege and onlookers, both domestic and foreign, feared the outcome would be similar to the storming of the Golden Temple in Amritsar when the Indian army moved against Sikh militants in 1984.

M. N. Sabharwal, the director-general of the Jammu and Kashmir Police, had a different story to tell:

> A religious place which had been very dear to the Kashmiris was used by the militants, not only as a hideout but as an interrogation centre. We also had reason to believe that the locks where the holy relic is kept, were being tampered with by the militants. This was done to malign the security forces. So the security forces moved in to save the relic.[8]

The area was cordoned off, leaving about a hundred militants and some civilians inside the mosque. Negotiations took place and after thirty-two days, the militants surrendered. Both sides prided themselves on the outcome. 'The militants did not let the Indians fire a bullet on the shrine,' says Inquilabi. The Indian authorities took credit for the care and restraint used by the security forces at Hazratbal. 'Food was sent in, so that neither the militants nor civilians starved,' says Sabharwal.

The image of Indian restraint was, however, undermined by the actions of the border security forces in Bijbihara when they shot at least thirty-seven unarmed demonstrators who were protesting against the siege of Hazratbal. Fourteen BSF members were held responsible. According to the Indian government, a Magisterial Inquiry and a Staff Court Inquiry were undertaken. The SCOI blamed four security force personnel for excessive use of force, while the Magisterial Inquiry indicted twelve people.[9] The magistrate also concluded that the shootings were unprovoked.[10]

In order to prevent the militants occupying the mosque again, the Indian government posted security forces in bunkers around Hazratbal. The Kashmiris objected to the mosque being 'fortified' by Indian troops. A year later Yasin Malik said that he put forward 'a daring initiative to lift the siege – I proposed to go for a fast until death and so there would be only two options for the Government of India – either they should concede our death or they should remove their bunkers.' His suggestion, however, led to a temporary rift with the Hurriyat Conference. 'Their response was negative. They gave a statement that the fast was unislamic.'[11]

International concern over Kashmir reached a high point in February 1994 when the Pakistani prime minister, Benazir Bhutto, who had returned to office in October 1993, raised the issue in the United Nations Commission for Human Rights in Geneva. The situation in Kashmir was intolerable, she said, as was the world's silence. Despite its repression, India had failed to impose its will on the indomitable people of Jammu and Kashmir. Defending the Indian government's position, the finance minister, Dr Manmohan Singh, said that the prime minister of Pakistan had given a wholly erroneous view of the situation. Farooq Abdullah also defended India by once again condemning Pakistan for training and arming the militants.[12] Although Pakistan's resolution against India did not gain enough support and had to be withdrawn due to pressure from China and Iran, the fact that other countries were alerted to the human rights situation in Kashmir boosted the morale of the Kashmiri activists. It also surprised the Government of India. 'Indian policy makers were jolted by the new Pakistani aggressiveness that could only be attributed to a growing belief in Islamabad that this Indian government was weak, focused exclusively on the economy and distracted from national security concerns,' reported Shekhar Gupta in *India Today*.[13]

Soon afterwards, Narasimha Rao, who called the Geneva resolution 'a tendentious ruse to secure other ends in Jammu and Kashmir,'[14] set up a cabinet committee to oversee Kashmiri policy with a view to starting a political dialogue. There was, writes Shekhar Gupta, 'a realisation that "Kashmir had been totally messed up by us" and any solution would have to be found in the Valley.'[15] Political process and normalisation became the key phrases of the Indian government's discussions on Jammu and Kashmir in order to hold elections to Jammu and Kashmir's state legislative assembly dissolved by Jagmohan in February 1990. Invitations were extended to Delhi-based ambassadors to visit Kashmir as well as those from the Organisation of Islamic Countries. Still out of the question, however, was any dialogue with Pakistan on an area which the Indian government continued to maintain was an integral part of India.

The militants' response to such initiatives was negative. The murder in March 1994 of Wali Mohammed Yattoo, a National Conference leader and former speaker of the Jammu & Kashmir legislative assembly, was taken to be a warning against attempts to introduce an unwanted political process in the valley. The government, however, pressed on with its initiative. Rajesh Pilot talked about 'rehabilitation'[16] of the Kashmiri youth; Karan Singh returned to the limelight by calling for a Kashmir Affairs ministry to be set up in order to begin 'a process of reconciliation'.[17] At India's independence day celebrations on 15 August 1994, Prime Minister Narasimha Rao formally announced that a political process would be initiated for the normalisation of affairs in the valley. In order to commence its dialogue, the government released some of the top political activists, including Shabir Shah, who had been in jail intermittently for nearly twenty years, as well as Syed Ali Shah Gilani and Abdul Gani Lone; 276 detainees were also released. Yasin Malik, under arrest since August 1990, had been released on bail in May 1994. At the end of October, however, the militants further attempted to derail the election process by stealing the electoral rolls for Srinagar from a government building and setting them on fire 'sending up in smoke the Indian government's latest attempts to bring peace to troubled Kashmir' wrote Tim McGirk in *The Independent*.'[18]

Given the hostility of the militants to the proposal to hold elections, it was not clear how elections could be a practical option when there appeared to be no obvious contestants. 'Firstly, they don't have the right kind of infrastructure; there is no support for manning polling booths or acting as returning officers,' said Haroon Joshi, an Indian journalist based in Srinagar in 1995. 'Normally it is the task of the government employees but they don't want to do it; secondly, who will vote? and thirdly, whoever contests, what will happen to their family and friends?' Even if the polls were phased, holding them for one week in Jammu, a second week in Kashmir, and then in Ladakh, approximately 10,000 people (3,000 polling stations with three to a polling booth) would be needed to man the polls in the valley. 'But even if they were to find these officials by bringing them in from Jammu,' said Joshi 'there is still no strategy for getting people to stand.'[19]

When election speculation was at its height during the spring of 1995, one by one the members of the All Parties Hurriyat Conference said they would not participate. 'The Indian government has thrust this election process on us because they want to convey to the external world that they believe in the democratic system,' said Yasin Malik. He felt so strongly about the proposed elections that he threatened to immolate himself:

> I am not doing this act against India. If the world conscience will come forward, they can stop the Indian government in this so-called election process. If they do not come forward then I will do this act against the world conscience; then I will be convinced that there is no one who can listen to the voice of the oppressed people.[20]

Shabir Shah, believed to be one of the few leaders who could be a unifying force throughout the state, said that he would not take part in the elections. 'We have no trust in Delhi. They have eroded our rights since 1953 and therefore we don't believe they will return them.'[21] Abdul Gani Lone was prepared to consider elections only as part of a process which would determine the future of the state:

> This is neither part of India nor part of Pakistan nor is it independent yet. The future disposition is to be settled through free and fair elections ... When we talk about our right of self-determination, no restrictions can be put on our choice. There are not two choices, the third option of independence is also there.'[22]

Professor Abdul Ghani of the Muslim Conference described the Indian government's attempt to hold elections as 'political prattle as opposed to political initiative.' As a supporter of accession to Pakistan, Ghani continued to reject the idea of independence. 'A small landlocked nation, surrounded by powerful neighbours could not survive.'[23]

'The Hurriyat conference has only one goal: that India should vacate Kashmir,' says Mian Abdul Qayum, president of the Srinagar Bar Association and member of the Hurriyat.[24] The Indian government, however, continued to woo the political leaders, pointing out that until they participated in elections, they could not speak on behalf of the people. 'Let those who claim to represent the people, demonstrate their support in the elections, without the use of the gun,' said Governor Krishna Rao in April 1995.[25]

Despite assertions that elections could be held any time in 1995, the political impasse remained. Even Farooq Abdullah, who is committed to finding a solution within secular India, placed stringent conditions on his participation. 'We demand a return to autonomy as it existed before 1953 and a substantial economic package which must be announced formally in the Indian Parliament.'[26] Yet his association with the Government of India had lost him support in the valley. Although he appeared confident that his cadres were ready to contest an election, provided their terms were accepted, the possibility of a National Conference electoral victory was seen as a step back to 1987 when the recent troubles began.

In November 1995 the Government of India once more demonstrated its commitment to the political process by sending election agents to Srinagar with the object of holding elections in December. This time a return to the status of Kashmir at the time of the 1975 accord between Sheikh Abdullah and Indira Gandhi was promised. Yet again the political parties, represented by the Hurriyat, indicated that they would not be willing to participate in an election process within the framework of the Indian constitution. 'Their idea of elections is just to create a government, a chief minister, an administration and then stop,' said Omar Farooq. 'While our stand is that elections cannot be a substitute for self-determination. If elections were a solution to the problem, we have already had eight or nine elections. But still the basic issue is unresolved.' He also believed that India's pledge to hold elections was for the benefit of the international community. 'India realises that they cannot make a dramatic change with elections, but they want to impress upon the international community that they are doing something and divert attention from the main issue of self-determination.'[27] Once more the December election date was postponed.

Mind of the military

Until a political process, acceptable to all protagonists, could be initiated, the Indian government remained dependent upon the armed forces to control the insurgency in the valley of Kashmir. Their adjustment to a guerrilla war has not been easy. 'The man in uniform has been trained to fight an identifiable enemy,' said Brigadier Arjun Ray in 1995:

> The aim of a soldier is to kill, or capture; win or lose he must apply maximum force because of military considerations. But in Kashmir overnight he has to do a flip-flop. There is no enemy with whom he can identify. It is his own people who have taken up arms against him. Therefore, although you can win militarily, you can lose the war.[28]

The soldiers have also paid for their presence. According to military sources, the Indian army has suffered a proportionately high casualty rate. Coming from distant parts of India, they have no historical knowledge and little sympathy for the militants. Young soldiers have also suffered the trauma of war and hypertension is common. 'Troops have to stand in bunkers, constantly on vigil. One minute of negligence and it can be all over.'[29] On 29 March 1994 one of the more serious attacks against the military took place. An explosion at Badami Bagh cantonment outside Srinagar killed Major General E. W. Fernandes, who was to take over as director-general, Military Intelligence, and thirteen army men. Ten others were wounded. 'This incident is horrendous. Nobody will buy the line that it was an accident,' an army officer stated after the explosion.[30] The Jamiat-ul Mujaheddin, one of the smaller militant groups, claimed responsibility for the blast as well as a series of smaller bomb blasts on government vehicles following the expiry of a deadline for the removal of Indian troops still stationed around the Hazratbal mosque.

Opponents of India's military occupation of the valley of Kashmir continue to maintain that 600,000 troops are stationed throughout the state in what is the highest troops to civilian population density ratio in any region in the world.[31] This figure is taken to include over half of the 33 divisions of the regular army, border security forces (100,000) and Jammu and Kashmir Police (30,000). Indian authorities say this is a gross exaggeration. 'It is known that our army is just over 1 million. How we would possibly have half our army in Kashmir and leave our borders exposed elsewhere?' asked one army officer. But he was predictably evasive about how many troops were there.

Other sources suggest 'around 100,000 personnel of the paramilitary border security forces and 30,000 men of Kashmir's state police force,' with five divisions of the army.[32] A 'crack' corps of Rashtriya (National) Rifles (RR) was also brought into the valley to deal specifically with counter-insurgency.

Throughout the insurgency, the government has remained extremely sensitive about the behaviour of the security forces in Kashmir. Initially there was tremendous reluctance to acknowledge or publicise any of the alleged excesses, indiscriminate killing or arbitrary disappearances noted by the human rights groups for fear of humiliating and hence possibly demoralising the soldiers. But, as the insurgency continued, the Indian government came to realise that any abuses by the security forces created further alienation amongst the people and it was therefore important, for both international and domestic opinion, to pay greater attention to the behaviour of the soldiers. 'Nodal cells have been set up in the Army and in each of the paramilitary forces to monitor cases of delinquencies. Fortnightly reviews are being held at a senior level in the Ministry of Home Affairs with the representatives of the Army and the para-military forces.'[33] As noted by the report of the International Commission of Jurists after their visit in August 1993, 'the Army has become increasingly conscious of the need to improve its image, and has placed greater emphasis on human rights education with various "do's and don'ts". The jurists, however, also noted that the authorities had been 'tardy in instituting proceedings against governmental personnel who commit abuses against the people and have created an aura of impunity surrounding officials who violate human rights.' In conclusion, they stated:

> The Indian Government is genuinely anxious to improve its human rights record in Kashmir. Breaches of human rights are not in its interest ... There is, however, a long way still to go to overcome indiscipline and misconduct of the security forces, particularly the BSF, the persistent and regular use of torture in interrogation and the practice of extra-judicial execution.[34]

Since the insurgency began, torture of militants and suspected militants has been a feature of Indian counter-insurgency tactics as a means of extracting information, coercing confessions and punishment. According to Amnesty International, 'the brutality of torture in Jammu and Kashmir defies belief. It has left people mutilated and disabled for life. The severity of torture meted out by the Indian security forces in Jammu and Kashmir is the main reason for the appalling number of deaths in custody.'[35]

The torture has included electric shocks, beatings, and the use of a heavy roller on leg muscles, which can result in extensive muscle damage, leading to acute renal failure. Other forms of inhuman treatment on various parts of the body, including sexual molestation have also been reported. According to one victim, quoted by Amnesty, 'You always know in advance about the "current" because they send in the barber to shave you from head to foot. This is supposed to facilitate the flow of electricity. After he finishes shaving you, he hands you a cup of water to drink and then they attach the electrodes.'[36] Other common methods, described by the US Human Rights Agency, Asia Watch, include suspension by the hands or feet, stretching the legs apart and burning the skin with a clothes iron or other heated object. Victims have also been kicked and stamped on by security forces wearing spiked boots.[37]

In 1995, sixty-three interrogation centres where torture has been carried out were believed to exist in Jammu and Kashmir, mostly run by the BSF and the CRPF. Army camps, hotels and other buildings have been taken over by the security forces as detention centres. One BSF centre was located in one of the maharaja's old guest houses overlooking Dal lake and the mountains. With faded wallpaper, worn carpets and stags' antlers on the walls, the luxuries of the past intruded inappropriately on the brutality of the present. Whereas an officer on duty admitted to the necessity of giving 'a few slaps' to captured militants to make them reveal where they have hidden their weapons, gruesome photographs of mutilated bodies are part of any press kit given to concerned journalists by human rights activists and militant sympathisers.

In its December 1993 report, Amnesty produced information about disappearances in Kashmir. In its response, the Indian government answered many of the allegations contained in Amnesty's report and supplied details on some of those listed as missing. 'The Government of India has never claimed that anything goes in the name of terrorism by way of complete freedom or immunity to the police and security forces.' Despite a dialogue initiated between the Indian government and Amnesty in 1992, the government continues to mistrust Amnesty's motivation. 'We do not look for kudos from Amnesty but equally we ask – is this an inquiry or an inquisition?'[38] Another report by Amnesty in January 1995 regarding 705 people who, since 1990, had died in custody as a result of torture, shooting, or medical neglect, produced yet another rebuttal from the Indian government. Amnesty, however, described their response as 'evasive and misleading. Complacently, the government refuses to recognise that there is an urgent need to take decisive action to put an end to the appalling human rights violations in Jammu and Kashmir.'[39]

In its reports Amnesty has also condemned the 'deliberate and arbitrary killings, torture and hostage-taking,' carried out by the militants, but the organisation maintains that 'however provocative' their abuses were, they could not justify excesses by the security forces. 'Such practices clearly contravene international human rights standards which the Indian government is bound to uphold.'[40]

Legal redress?

The nature of the legislation in force in the state of Jammu and Kashmir, which was described by the International Commission of Jurists as 'draconian', has given the military extensive powers without redress. According to

Amnesty, court orders to protect detainees are routinely flouted. Despite promises of inquiries into custodial deaths, official investigations are rare. When they have taken place, the evidence is not made public, which diminishes the credibility of government findings. 'It also makes a mockery of its expressed intention to eradicate human rights violations.'[41]

The Jammu and Kashmir Public Safety Act (1978) permits people to be detained for up to two years on vaguely defined grounds to prevent them acting 'in any manner prejudicial ... to the security of the state and the maintenance of public order.'[42] Detention without charge is possible for up to one year in the case of a threat to public order and for up to two years when there is a threat to the security of the state. The order must be communicated to the arrested person not later than five days after the arrest. In 1990 the act was amended in order to exempt the authorities from informing the detainee the reason for his arrest. In its report, the ICJ concluded that the law has led to 'hardships among those arrested under its scope. Its highly discretionary tone undermines efforts to discover the whereabouts of arrested persons and the quest for habeas corpus.'[43]

The Terrorist and Disruptive Activities (Prevention) Act 1987 (TADA) prohibited not only terrorist acts but also broadly defined 'disruptive' activities. In force until 1995, the act established special courts to try those arrested. The term 'disruptive activities' is defined as including:

> any action, whether by act or by speech or through any other media or in any other manner, which questions, disrupts ... the sovereignty or territorial integrity of India, or which is intended to bring about or supports any claim for the cession of any part of India or the secession of any part of India from the Union.[44]

As the international jurists pointed out, the definition of 'disruptive activities' is 'a blatant contravention of the right to freedom of speech.' The two 'designated courts' were in Srinagar and Jammu, but the operations of the Srinagar court were temporarily suspended. Speedy hearing of bail applications was therefore impeded because of the necessity to go to the court at Jammu.

The discretionary nature of the Armed Forces (Jammu & Kashmir) Special Powers Act, introduced by Saxena in 1990, which gave the governor or the government in New Delhi the authority to declare all or part of the state a 'disturbed area' and to use the armed forces to assist the civil power, meant that the military could be used 'to suppress legitimate political activity' and, according to the ICJ, could not possibly be justified. Since the military had the power to shoot and kill, 'this involves a potential infringement of the right to life.'[45] Additional laws have been either introduced or revived 'with negative impact on human rights'. In February 1992 Presidential rule was extended, which dispensed with any obligation on the government to revert to an elected government. When this time period elapsed, a further amendment to the Constitution was passed.

The cumulative effect of such legislation is that the government has been able to act with relative impunity in the state of Jammu and Kashmir. Since the judicial system is 'almost dysfunctional'[46] there are long delays in court proceedings. 'The judiciary here in the state of Jammu and Kashmir has almost become irrelevant,' said Mian Abdul Qayum, president of the Srinagar Bar Association, in 1994. 'if they pass any kind of an order, those orders are not obeyed by anybody. Right now there are some 5,000 habeas corpus petitions pertaining to the people who are detained under preventive laws, pending in the High Court Srinagar and nobody is going to hear them.'[47] According to the Indian authorities, the state government has responded to '99 per cent' of all such petitions 'despite the tremendous strain under which the whole legal and administrative system has been put by the continuing violence and terrorism.'[48]

Mind of the militant

In the opinion of the Indian government the real culprits have always been the militants, whom they hold responsible for terrorising the people of Kashmir into open hostility against India and committing numerous extra-judicial executions, amongst whom they list Mirwaiz Maulvi Farooq, Professor Mushir-ul Haq, the vice chancellor of Kashmir University, Dr A. A. Guru, Maulana Masoodi, aged eighty-seven, a contemporary and colleague of Sheikh Abdullah who was shot in December 1990 allegedly for the part he played in the state of Jammu and Kashmir's accession to India. Through the efforts of the military, however, the insurgency has now been 'capped and brought down to acceptable levels,' said Brigadier Arjun Ray in 1995.[49] 'More and more people are coming to realise the futility of the gun,' said M. N. Sabharwal.[50] In 1995, the Indian government noted that the level of violence had declined still further except during the months of May, October and November, when announcements were made about elections.[51]

The Indian government also believed that militancy did not enjoy the popular support it had in the early 1900s. 'The militants lost some of their original élan,' says Balraj Puri, 'due to a number of reasons: a continuous proliferation of groups, confusion and division in their ranks, regarding their ultimate objective, and Pakistan's changing policy towards different groups of militants.'[52] Government analyses estimated that no more than 6,000 militants were operating throughout the valley, which made the ratio of their own troops to militants extremely high. Indian authorities also alleged that young men have been abducted against their will to become militants. In August 1993 The Times of India reported how Indian forces had intercepted a large group of 'Kashmiri youth' who were being taken to Azad Kashmir at gun point by members of the Al Jehad militant group and that they had been promised sums ranging from Rs 2000 to Rs 10,000.[53]

In contrast to Jagmohan's assessment of the militants, General Krishna

Rao had adopted a conciliatory approach: 'We do not consider militants as enemies, but as our own kith and kin, although they have allowed themselves to be misled. The Government takes responsibility to rehabilitate them in an appropriate manner, provided they return to the path of sanity.'[54] The Indian government assessed the life expectancy of a militant at two years, after which time they either get killed or lose their enthusiasm for the fight. Militants who surrender are provided with a rudimentary rehabilitation programme and sometimes a change of identity.

Like the security forces, the militants have been subject to allegations of excesses, mainly intimidation and extortion as well as their indiscriminate attacks on those suspected of sympathising with the Indian government. 'The lady next door was approached one night by militants and asked for money,' recalled a student in 1995; 'in the old days, she would have asked them in and given them food. This time she refused and shut the door in their face. So they pushed the door in and shot her.'[55] 'The militants would come to your door and ask for money or a son to fight. If you didn't have the money, then you would have to give up a son,' says a local Kashmiri. 'In 1993 the militants asked for 5 lakhs,' said one businessman in 1995, 'last year it was 3 lakhs; this year I am expecting them to ask for 1 lakh.'[56] Rich houseboat owners and carpet dealers have been targeted for money. They have also been afraid to speak out about loss of business because of the insurgency: 'They say to us: "You complain you are losing money, and we are losing our lives."'[57] Journalists were threatened by the militants for writing reports interpreted as favourable to the Government of India's position. In September 1995, a parcel bomb was sent to Yusuf Jameel, the BBC and Reuters correspondent in Srinagar. A photographer in his office opened the parcel and died in the explosion.

In June 1994 the JKLF admitted that atrocities committed by the militants had alienated the people and stated that strict action would be taken against 'erring elements' in the movement.[58] The most serious incident of a communal nature was the murder of sixteen male Hindus who were taken off a bus in Kishtwar on their way to Jammu on 14 August 1993 and shot. Both the JKLF and Hizb condemned the action. The murder of the vice-chancellor of Kashmir University in 1990 was described by activists as the work of 'renegades' amongst the numerous fringe groups which are operative.

Reports of rape by militants also tarnished their image. 'While it is not clear that militant leaders have explicitly sanctioned such abuses,' states Asia Watch, 'there is little indication that the militants have done anything to stop their forces from committing rape. Some incidents of rape by militants appear to have been motivated by the fact that the victims or their families are accused of being informers.'[59] In 1994 former Governor Saxena rather surprisingly claimed that: 'For every allegation of rape by security persons, there will be a hundred by militants.'[60] In the early days of the insurgency, attacks were made on women for not adhering to the prescribed dress code, the wearing of the *burqah*. The Daughters of the Nation, an orthodox women's group, was particularly active in issuing threats and some women had to be hospitalised because acid was sprayed on their exposed faces. Due to adverse publicity, by the middle 1990s this had stopped and, especially in Srinagar, women no longer felt obliged to wear the veil.

Allegations of corruption and drug dealing have also been levelled against some militants, in what the authorities call the 'criminalisation' of the movement, as well as against military and government officials. 'There is a nexus,' said Farooq Abdullah in 1995 'between the militants, the paramilitary forces and some sections of the government, who have enjoyed absolute power and corruption that no government has ever enjoyed.'[61] There are allegations that militants and government officials split development funds; also that security forces not only sell back captured weapons but will allow border crossings at a price.[62] 'Many of the orchards in Kashmir, owned by the Hindus, who fled, have now been divided between the top militants. They are changing the deeds and so it will be impossible to trace their original owners.'[63] The government maintains that the main incentive of many militants is money rather than political conviction. Yet despite such allegations, the militants still seek and obtain refuge amongst the people. 'How else do you think they are surviving?' asked Mirwaiz Omar Farooq in 1995, who insisted that the militancy was still widely supported by the people.[64]

By 1993 the JKLF appeared to have lost its military ascendancy to the Hizb-ul Mujaheddin, although politically, the organisation claimed to have retained 85 per cent of the people's support. When Yasin Malik was released from jail in May 1994, he renounced the armed struggle and made an offer of political negotiations. 'We offered a unilateral ceasefire and offered to negotiate with all concerned powers – Pakistan, India and the Kashmiris – we believe all should be given equal status.' According to Malik, a message came through from the Government of India that negotiation would be possible, but only between the Government of India and the Kashmiri people, because they did not recognise Pakistan as a party to the talks. Malik disagreed on the grounds that Pakistan was a party to the dispute because nearly one-third of the state lies under its control. He was also adamant that the third option of independence must be offered to the people of Jammu and Kashmir in order for a permanent solution to be reached. 'Until they put the third option of independence into the UN resolution, it will be unacceptable to the people of Jammu and Kashmir.'[65]

From his earlier days as one of the core 'Haji' group, reportedly involved in the kidnapping of Rubaiya Sayeed in December 1989, Malik now describes Mahatma Gandhi and his principles of non-violence as one of his motivating forces. This has led him to reaffirm the JKLF's secular nature, based on traditional Kashmiriyat, which includes Hindus. But his non-violent approach caused a rift with Amanullah Khan, who has continued to operate as chairman of the JKLF *in absentia* from Rawalpindi and Muzaffarabad.

'Unfortunately our organisation is practically divided into two groups. Our basic difference was Yasin Malik's offer of a unilateral ceasefire, without informing us,' said Amanullah Khan.[66] At the end of 1995, Amanullah Khan removed Yasin Malik as president of the JKLF; in return Yasin Malik expelled Armanullah Khan as chairman. Shabir Ahmed Siddiqi, who was released from jail in the summer of 1995,[67] temporarily took over leadership of Amanullah's faction. Relations, however, were further complicated by Pakistan's recognition of Yasin Malik as the leader of the JKLF rather than Amanullah Khan, although Amanullah remains based in Pakistan.

Other militant groups have also been reassessing their position. In 1995, Azam Inquilabi of Operation Balakote left his base in Azad Kashmir and returned to Srinagar, where he declared himself in favour of working towards a 'political situation.' The Hizb-ul Mujaheddin, whose active strength was assessed by the Indian authorities at around 2,500 in 1995, was able to gain its ascendancy militarily in the middle 1990s because of support from Jamaat sympathisers based in Pakistan. It dominates smaller pro-Pakistani groups and, through the Jamaat-i Islami, it also has a strong hold on the Hurriyat Conference. In the early days, Ahsan Dar, leader of Hizb, maintained that their strategy of making the country impassable for Indian security forces would eventually confine the army to their camps, where the militants would be able to attack them. But the strategy failed. (Ahsan Dar, who left the Hizb to form the Muslim Mujaheddin, was later arrested.) The militants are also split between commitment to Pakistan and an undefined belief in freedom. A young militant stated that he wanted *azadi* and the decision on whether to join Pakistan would be taken by the elders; rather surprisingly, his mentor, in his mid-40s, affirmed that *azadi* meant freedom from both India and Pakistan.[68] The Harkat-ul Ansar operated alongside the Hizb. Al Barq and Al Jehad remained active in the Doda, Poonch and Rajauri areas.

Personal disagreements and rivalries clearly reduced the efficacy of the militants. But, said Omar Farooq, 'in a movement like this there are ups and downs. There was a time when there were many inter-group clashes but if you study the situation now the graph has really come down. The differences have been resolved.' Omar Farooq believed that India's repressive tactics and counter-insurgency measures still remained a factor in uniting the people against India. The government, however, detected a split in the leadership of the APHC which it believed had broadly divided between two factions – one including Yasin Malik, Abdul Gani Lone and Syed Ali Shah Gilani, and the other Omar Farooq, Abdul Ghani, Maulvi Abbas Ansari, with tacit support from Shabir Shah.[69]

In 1996 the Indian government opened a dialogue with four former militants including two from the Hizb-ul Mujaheddin as well as Baba Badr, a former chief of the Muslim Janbaz, and Bilal Lodhi, former leader of Al Barq, in an attempt to create an alternative political base to the Hurriyat. The militants were also being challenged by a former folk singer, Kukka Parrey, who, with the support of the Indian government, assembled a group of over 1,000 fighters whose objective was the 'liberation' of part of the valley from control by the militants. Activists denied that Parrey had any standing amongst the Kashmiris. Even the four dissident militants insisted that the Government of India should recognise that Kashmir is a historical and political problem.

On account of the war in Afghanistan and the plentiful weapons supplied to the Afghans, there has been an apparently inexhaustible supply of weapons for the Kashmiri militants. 'The US supplied the weapons to fight the war in Afghanistan against the Soviets,' said one Kashmiri, saddened by the gun culture prevalent in the valley, 'but they never returned to take the weapons away and now they are in the valley.' M. N. Sabharwal said that before the insurgency there were no Kalashnikov rifles in the valley. Now, however, there are quantities of weapons ranging from AK rifles, universal machine guns, Chinese pistols, snipers, rocket launchers and grenades. Just how many was indicated by government figures for those weapons captured between 1989 and 1995. These included 13,427 AK 47s, 750 rocket launchers, 1682 rockets, 54 light machine guns, 735 general purpose machine guns.[70] On average the government claimed to recover 4,000 weapons a year of varying sophistication. In 1995 it retrieved 587 bombs compared with 300 in 1994.[71] The Kashmiris were, however, less well armed than the Afghans. To the obvious relief of the Indian security forces in 1995, there were no reports of the militants being able to bring in stingers. Nor had they, as yet, brought their struggle to the streets of Delhi, Calcutta or Bombay, where urban terrorism would have a greater impact on the lives of the Indian people and consequently the Indian government. Strangely, amongst the unsympathetic pro-government analysts, the belief persisted that the Kashmiris, despite all their guns, were not good fighters: 'In Kashmir, you talk of paper-thin almonds, paper-thin walnuts – well, we also talk of paper-thin militants.'[72]

The proxy war

Throughout the insurgency the Indian authorities continued to point to the 'foreign hand' in Kashmir, without which they believe the insurgency would never have gained momentum nor have been able to sustain itself. 'Pakistan took a firm and bold decision to meddle,' stated former governor Saxena in 1994.

> This time they pulled out all the stops and went about creating trouble in a big way, training thousands of youths, giving huge quantities of arms to them, and not bothering so much as they earlier did about the threshold of India's tolerance, with the result that this environment acquired the proportions of a widespread terrorist movement and armed insurgency, which was conducted at the initiative of Pakistan by youth trained in Pakistan.[73]

The tactics the militants used to disrupt the government were considered to be similar to those used by Pakistanis sent into the valley in 1965: bomb blasts, cutting lines of communication, attacks on patrols and police.

Although the Government of Pakistan's denials that its support was anything other than moral and diplomatic (and genuine uncertainty about Pakistan's actions before 1990), it was the common perception in India that Pakistan, through the ISI, supplied material and financial support without which the movement would have been easier for the Indian army to suppress. 'Pakistan is unlikely to drop its covert support,' wrote *Time* correspondent, Edward Desmond, 'the Kashmir issue is central to the nationalistic and Islamic identity of Pakistan ... the burden of assisting the rebels is light.'[74] 'On a scale of one to ten, if we were committed in Bangladesh up to ten, then the same is true for Pakistan's commitment in Kashmir,' said a Delhi-based Indian journalist in 1995.'[75] In support of this assertion, the Indian government quoted a February 1993 report by the US House of Representatives 'Task Force on Terrorism and Unconventional Warfare' which claimed that Pakistan 'began expanding its operation to sponsor and promote separatism and terrorism primarily in Kashmir, as a strategic long-term programme,' an allegation which the Government of Pakistan denies.[76]

Despite Indian attempts to seal the border, which it is impossible for a Western journalist to reach from the Indian side, the 500 mile line of control has remained open. In 1995 the prime minister of Azad Kashmir, Sardar Abdul Qayum Khan, also admitted that, from their side, the border is not sealed. 'We don't mind the boys coming in and going back.'[77] Militants and refugees take what they call the 'natural' route to cross from one side to the other. When the ICJ visited the area in 1993 they concluded that, despite Pakistani denials and the sensitivity of the issue, the presence of many representatives of militant groups in Azad Kashmir 'pointed to an affinity with operations in neighbouring Jammu and Kashmir.' The international jurists also considered that the provision of any military assistance would be in breach of obligations accepted by Pakistan under the Simla agreement and that therefore Pakistan should 'discontinue any support of a military nature' (including the provision of finance for military purposes).'[78] It was, however, evident that the Jamaat-i Islami, and hence the Hizb, still had a considerable presence both in Azad Kashmir and in Pakistan. In November 1995 a BBC documentary programme showed evidence of camps supported by the Jamaat, where fighters were trained and openly professed their intention of going to fight a holy war in Kashmir.[79] And some sympathisers believe rightly so: 'After 1945 the world has shrunk. No one can give me one instance in the world in any liberation movement – in any country – which has started without a foreign base,' stated Muhammad Saraf. He also pointed to the genuine grievances of the local Kashmiris: 'You don't give people money and weapons and they just start dying. The question you have to ask is what made them prepared to start dying?'[80] Amongst some activists there was also a view that the Pakistani army should intervene overtly, not in order to claim the land for itself but in the same way the Indian army intervened in East Pakistan in 1971 to help the Bengalis.

In 1995, Omar Farooq took a pragmatic view. 'The issue of Pakistan giving support or not does not present a problem for us. The United States gave support to Afghanistan; they were not asked to explain why they were supporting the Afghans. So if Pakistan supports the Kashmiris on whatever grounds, it doesn't matter. You see ours is a totally indigenous movement and it is the Kashmiris who are getting killed.' Farooq included in his analysis the support from Azad Kashmir. 'If they are helping us, no one should be concerned because, historically, they belong to the state of Jammu and Kashmir and they have a duty towards their people, who are occupied.'[81] Yasin Malik, however, is opposed to 'any kind of foreign presence in Kashmir, whether it is Pakistani or Indian foreign mercenaries.'[82]

Amongst the fighters who have crossed the line of control from Azad Kashmir and Pakistan are those who fought in Afghanistan. Their presence in the insurgency is facilitated by what is also a porous border in the tribal territory which divides Pakistan and Afghanistan and their numbers are believed to have increased after the fall of the Najibullah regime in Afghanistan in 1992.[83] The Kashmiris maintain that the Afghans, belonging mostly to the Harkat-ul Ansar, came to support their struggle as Muslims after the help the Kashmiris gave during the Afghans' own jihad against the Soviet Union. Between 1990 and 1995, the Indian government identified 297 'foreign mercenaries' arrested or killed of which 213 were from Pakistan or Azad Kashmir, and 84 from Afghanistan.[84] In addition, the Indian government maintained that there were smaller numbers of Sudanese, Egyptians, Lebanese who became attached to rival groups. Invariably, the reality of the insurgency in Kashmir did not match their expectations: 'When I first came I thought it was for holy war, but then I heard about the struggle for power within the militant groups,' said Sheikh Jamaluddin, a nineteen year-old from Gardez in Afghanistan, who was captured by the security forces on the outskirts of Srinagar in 1993.[85]

The foreign presence in Kashmir became publicised when, in March 1995, Master Gul, a former shopkeeper from Pakistan's North-West Frontier, occupied the mosque at Charar-e Sharif about twenty-five miles from Srinagar which is revered for its association with Nund Rishi, the patron saint of the valley. Gul had trained during the war in Afghanistan and amongst his followers were what the Indian government referred to as about seventy 'mercenaries'. The militants claimed to have liberated the area from the Indian security forces, but the Indians responded by cordoning off the area as they had done at Hazratbal. This time, however, the mosque was destroyed by fire, which the militants blamed on the security forces, who in turn blamed the militants for starting it. Krishna Rao expressed 'grief and anguish' over the destruction of the shrine.[86] Security was increased to deter protests within the valley. Although over forty people were killed, Master Gul escaped to Pakistan, from where he continued to preach a holy war.[87] The presence of foreigners however, also had its repercussions amongst the local Kashmiris. 'They have been rather overbearing, they feel they've come to do a job and should be obeyed. They don't have any official position but they tend to bully,' said one Kashmiri militant.

Pakistan's official stand has been to highlight the abuse of human rights on the international stage and point to the alienation of the Kashmiris of the valley from Indian rule while putting the issue in its historical context and referring back to the UN resolutions. Obviously aware that self-determination is invariably interpreted by the valley Kashmiris as independence from India and Pakistan, in 1994, Pakistani foreign secretary Nazimuddin Sheikh maintained that it was putting the cart before the horse to talk about independence at this stage. 'It requires a measure of sagacity to avoid entering a debate on this issue before India has granted the right of self-determination to the Kashmiri people.'[88]

'Free' Kashmir and the Northern Areas

The insurgency has also affected the lives of the Azad Kashmiris, who are still waiting for their own constitutional position to be finalised. Wholehearted support for accession to Pakistan has now been tempered, for some, with their own dreams of independence. But whereas those in the valley have believed that it is within their reach, there is far less conviction amongst the Azad Kashmiris that life will ever be much different. If there were to be a change, in 1994 Prime Minister Sardar Qayum expressed his solidarity with the valley. 'We accept in final terms the leadership from the valley. They are the people who are suffering, and there should be no dispute over power sharing'.[89] In November 1995, Mirwaiz Omar Farooq met Sardar Qayum in New York. 'He agreed,' said Omar Farooq 'that the All Parties Hurriyat Conference should represent them as well at the international level.'[90]

Traditionally, Azad Kashmiris have been sympathetic to the Kashmiris of the valley where many still have relatives. A 'liberation cell' has been operating in Muzaffarabad since 1987, which retains close links both with the AJK government in Muzaffarabad and Islamabad. Its representatives guide foreigners through the political issues at stake as well as the refugee camps which have been set up to accommodate those who fled from the border towns of Kupwara, Handwara and Baramula in the early years of the insurgency. 'We eat and are clothed,' said one refugee from Ambore camp outside Muzaffarabad, 'but everything gets distasteful when we remember our brothers and sisters in occupied Kashmir.'[91] 'We notice the need for women to have psychiatric help,' said Nayyar Malik, who has worked as a voluntary social worker in the camps. 'They have seen such terrible things and they need to talk.'[92] A radio station has also been operating since 1960. It was initially set up to publicise the development activities of the Azad Jammu and Kashmir government. But, said Masood Kashfi, the station director, 'it was not possible to keep our eye shut on the situation in Occupied Kashmir, therefore, a fair proportion of its broadcast was reserved for broadcasting programmes on the subjects of freedom movement, freedom history and other relevant topics.' After the insurgency began in 1989, Azad Kashmir Radio changed its programme schedules to eliminate the 'entertaining aspects' and concentrate on 'inspiring' programmes related to the freedom struggle, which also includes relaying some programmes from Radio Pakistan. The stand of the Government of Pakistan on the Kashmir issue is projected and the reaction of the people on both sides of the control line is depicted in a fair and balanced way,' said Kashfi. He believed that the Azad Kashmir radio is so popular in 'occupied Kashmir' that the Indian government imposed a ban on listening to the station and 'was making her best efforts to jam the transmission.'[93]

The influx of Kashmiris from the valley in recent years also created some friction between Kashmiri speakers from the valley, and those from Poonch and Rawalakot district. 'I am often told I am not a Kashmiri, because I don't speak Kashmiri,' said a Suddhan from Poonch whose father and grandfather were politically active in the 1940s. 'But politically I am Kashmiri because I belong to the state of Jammu and Kashmir.'[94] The Poonchis today still stress their historical legacy of independence. Many Azad Kashmiris are also far less concerned about independence than the absence of a proper status within Pakistan, enabling them to have access to the same funds, political rights and development aid granted to the other provinces. At the same time, the government is beholden to Islamabad. 'You see I have to keep in step; and to keep in step you cannot do things what you really wish to do at times, and so you have to cater to the situation,' said Prime Minister Sardar Qayum in 1994.[95]

Resentment has also been expressed by the Azad Kashmiris against their 'brethren' in Pakistan and the Muslim world for not doing enough over the years to help the cause of the Kashmiris of the valley. Those who would prefer to see the whole of the state of Jammu and Kashmir independent are as much opposed to Pakistan's 'occupation' of Azad Kashmir as they are with the Indian position in the valley. 'We are not satisfied with the de facto situation of Pakistan in Azad Kashmir,' said Azam Inquilabi in 1994. 'They have their forces there, they have a control there, we are tolerating this situation only to some extent.'[96] 'The reason we have not started a military movement there [in PoK]' said Yasin Malik, 'is because, so far as Pakistan is concerned, it is their official stand to accept the right of self-determination for the people of Jammu and Kashmir.'[97]

Although geographically distant, the fate of the Northern Areas, with a population of less than a million, remains directly affected by the current situation in Jammu and Kashmir. Despite the rebellion which took place in October/November 1947, the Northern Areas have never been integrated into Pakistan. 'I was seven when I fought for Pakistan,' said Raja Nisar Wali, member of the Northern Areas Motahida Mahaz (joint platform), formed to press for political representation. 'Now I am fifty-seven and going grey and still I am struggling to be part of Pakistan.'[98] In 1975 Zulfikar Ali Bhutto abolished the old landholdings and kingdoms of Hunza and Nagar and re-organised the whole area into five administrative districts. 'He introduced far-reaching reforms,' said Wazir Firman Ali, who grew up in Skardu under 'the Dogra slavery' and later worked for fifteen years as a government servant in the Northern Areas. 'If Bhutto had lived, I think the Northern Areas would have become the fifth province, but under General Zia's military dictatorship, the Northern Areas became the 'fifth zone' – zone E – and he did nothing for them.'

The JKLF in particular made attempts to establish its representatives in Gilgit and Baltistan in order to foster the independence movement, but the people have little political affiliation with the valley and are generally believed to favour full integration with Pakistan. 'The first choice would be integration with Pakistan and a provincial arrangement,' said Wazir Firman Ali, 'secondly, a set up similar to Azad Kashmir and thirdly, integration with Azad Jammu and Kashmir.'[99] In March 1993 the High Court of Azad Jammu and Kashmir declared that the Northern Areas were part of Azad Kashmir and ordered their administration to be returned to the government of Azad Kashmir. But the Shia population, who predominate in the Northern Areas, were reluctant to amalgamate with Sunni-dominated Azad Kashmir. The decision of the High Court was quashed on appeal in the Supreme Court.[100]

The Pakistani government has attempted to satisfy the lack of constitutional representation by a package of reforms. The government, however, has held back from formally integrating the Northern Areas within Pakistan lest such an action would jeopardise the Pakistani demand for the whole issue to be resolved under the terms of the UN resolutions. No attempt appears to have been made to make use of the British assessment in 1941 that the Gilgit Agency and related territories were considered only to be under the suzerainty of the state of Jammu and Kashmir and not part of it. Therefore, despite Pakistan's support of the Kashmiris' right to self-determination, it is not in the government's interest to support the demand for the 'third option' of independence of the entire state as it existed in 1947, which would include the Northern Areas. Gilgit and Hunza, which provide access to China through the Khunjerab pass along the Karakoram highway, opened in 1978, are as important to Pakistan strategically as they were to the British in the days of empire. Pending a final resolution of the Jammu and Kashmir dispute, the Northern Areas remain administered by Pakistan, although not part of it. 'We have many suspension bridges in the Northern Areas, and our constitutional position is also in suspension,' stated one local government official in 1995.

Civilians under siege

The losers in the insurgency against the Indian government are the Kashmiris. In 1995, the city of Srinagar was dusty and dirty, with uncollected rubbish dumped on the roadside for dogs and cows to forage through. The streets were full of potholes. The charred remains of once revered buildings, such as the library next to the mosque at Hazratbal, were a visual reminder of past battles. Dal lake was thick and stagnant with weeds. The lives of the Kashmiris have been convulsed by bomb attacks, reprisals, crossfiring and curfew. Their homes have been raided and sometimes destroyed because of frequent security operations. Sopore was still half-gutted by fire. 'I used to be frightened when the army came, but now I am used to it,' said a young girl from Sopore. 'The searching totally destroys our houses. They scatter our belongings and break things.'[101]

Since 1989, the Kashmiris have lived in fear of the gun, whether it is that of the militants or the Indian security forces. Their sons, as militants, suspected militants or sympathisers, have been arrested, tortured, killed or just disappeared. 'In practice any young Muslim man living within a village, rural area or part of town noted for activities of any of the pro-independence or pro-Pakistan groups can become a suspect and a target for the large-scale and frequently brutal search operations,' stated Amnesty in 1993.[102] Extra-judicial executions of militants have often been publicised as death in 'an encounter.'

Nearly every Kashmiri has a sad tale to tell of a family member who has been picked up by the security forces on suspicion of being a militant. Dr Rashid is one of thousands who suffered personal loss:

> My brother was twenty-five years old. He was running a cosmetics shop. The BSF came and took him. In front of my father and family, he was killed. Someone had pointed him out as being a militant. He was not armed and in the news that evening they gave that there was an encounter, when there was no encounter at all.

Not long afterwards Dr Rashid's younger brother was also shot for being a suspected militant. Then he heard the news about his cousin's son:

> He was eighteen years old – he was a student. He was captured; I went to the police station and asked to see him because I had heard he had got some bullet injuries. They told me to wait and they would see where he was. For two hours I waited there. Then they brought his dead body. The report said he was running away and then they shot him. If he was running away he would have had bullet wounds on the back. But he had two bullet injuries at 2cm distance just on his heart in front.[103]

For the majority of the people, the ill-effects of living under siege have been tremendous. Although there have been no floods and the harvests have been good, no one has yet been able to evaluate the trauma of events on their lives since 1989. Children have frequently been unable to go to school and the standard of education has declined. Since 1950, the number of schools had increased ten times, but many schools have been burnt by 'renegade' militants who the Kashmiri activists believe are working against their cause.

Schools in rural areas have been occupied by the security forces, who have also installed themselves in university campuses. Official figures maintain that the schools functioned for ninety-three days in 1993–94 and 140 days in 1994–95 and primary education in general has regressed.[104] In higher education, Kashmiris had made great advances, but the general disruption of the insurgency has once more reduced the level of education and general lawlessness prevails. Militancy for a number of Kashmiri youth has become a way of life. Young fighters show off their weapons and use their guns to resolve personal disputes. Older Kashmiri Muslims, who have known the valley at peace, regret the insurgency because they believe it has ruined the lives of so many without bringing about any political gains.

Medical facilities are insufficient and the hospitals are unhygienic. The doctors are overworked and many have fled. Some have been taken at gun point to treat injured militants and then returned. In 1995 the Bone and Joint Hospital had only three senior medical staff, besides nine registrars and six consultants. Immunisation programmes for children have fallen behind. In 1995 it was estimated that there were twenty times the number of psychiatric cases than in 1989.[105] Unofficial statistics estimate that 40,000 people died between 1988 and 1995, although the government put the figure at about 13,500.[106] Of this number, less than half were militants. Amnesty bases its figures on police and hospital sources and assessed the number as in excess of 17,000. 'But we also believe there are several thousand more for whom we have no statistics,' said a representative of Amnesty in 1995.[107] The martyrs' graveyard in Srinagar is full of fresh graves with weeping mothers and onlookers standing by. The mausoleum to Maqbool Butt, who remains buried within the confines of Tihar jail in Delhi, is a painful reminder that the man who inspired so many in their fight for *azadi* has died long ago.

Injury or death in crossfiring between militants and security forces has also taken a heavy toll. In 1994 M. N. Sabharwal, the director-general of Police in Srinagar admitted that at least 1,500 civilians had been killed in the crossfire, with many more injured. Just one of those casualties lay in a ward of the Bone and Joint Hospital in April 1994. He had been out shopping with his wife on his motorcycle. When firing began in a crowded street, soldiers shouted at them to get off their motorcycle and lie face down on the ground. Both he and his wife received bullet wounds. At first he thought they had been fired at on purpose, but then he realised that they were mere civilians caught in the crossfire. He was crying as he related his story: 'My Mrs is in the ladies hospital. I am here. What have we done to deserve this?' His own injury, close to his heart, was so serious that the doctor had only permitted him to be interviewed on the understanding that I did not tell him that his wife had already died. 'The shock,' warned the doctor 'might kill him.'[108]

By the beginning of 1996 the tremendous euphoria which lifted people's spirits in the early days of the movement had gone. The civilians of the valley were war weary. But the people's desire for their lives to return to normal, is tempered by a persistent rejection of a return to the status quo. 'Yes, they want peace,' said Omar Farooq, 'but at what cost?' Too much suffering has taken place for the clock to be put back. Despite all the disruption of the past years, taxi drivers, houseboat owners, shopkeepers still talk of independence, without being any closer to realising how it can be achieved. 'They demand *azadi* but it is a concept which has not been choreographed,' said Brigadier Arjun Ray.[109] *Azadi* means different things to different people. For some it is independence of the entire state; for those inhabitants of the valley it is preservation of their unique culture – Kashmiriyat – which includes both the Hindus and Muslims. For others, influenced by the Islamic resurgence, it means the creation of a theocratic state. 'It is not a geographical concept but an emotional one,' said Ashok Jaitley, 'the freedom to be themselves, with dignity and self-respect, wherever they can get it.'[110]

Farooq Abdullah, who prefers to talk about autonomy within the Indian union, describes *azadi* as a bitter pill which has been covered with a sweetness:

People would like to see *azadi* but they don't see the consequences of that *azadi*. If we become independent, how are we going to sustain ourselves, where does the money come from? Where is it possible for us to develop? We are landlocked with powerful neighbours of China and Pakistan. If we get independence and India quits, I am sure Pakistan will march in overnight and take over. The people say we want *azadi*, without telling us what *azadi* will hold for us.[111]

Neither the Buddhists of Ladakh nor the Hindus of Jammu share the objectives of the Muslim Kashmiris of the valley. Their main concern has been to press for autonomy against dominance from the more populous valley. 'Both feel the fruits of development have not reached them; most of the money has been spent on the valley,' said Ram Mahan Rao, adviser to the government of Jammu and Kashmir in 1995. 'A problem in our country is that we have a blanket which is too short. If it covers the head, then it is not able to cover the feet.'[112] Indian officials point out that there are eight linguistic and cultural districts in the Indian-administered state of Jammu and Kashmir, and Kashmiri is only one of them. The implication is that although in the valley Kashmiris may be numerically superior, their objectives cannot determine the future of the entire state.

In Ladakh, the troubles between Muslims of the Kargil district and Buddhists which erupted in 1989 have now subsided. 'There is little chance of the Hurriyat Conference gaining a standing in Ladakh,' said Ladakhi politician Pinto Narboo.[113] The object of the Ladakh Autonomous Hill Development Council has been to further the objectives of the sparse population of Buddhist Ladakhis of the Leh area. But the valley Kashmiris have interpreted this as a move, backed by the Indian government, to divide the state on communal lines. However, even the Muslims of Jammu, who are not Kashmiri speaking, do not necessarily support the demands of the valley Kashmiri Muslims. 'The Jammu Muslims stand for the status quo and we support accession and integration,' said a Muslim Congress leader from Jammu in 1995. 'One-fifth of the total population of J & K state are Gujars, who do not speak Kashmiri; the Kashmiris have nothing in common with these people, other than a shared religion.'[114] Omar Farooq, however, maintains that in Jammu, the districts of Rajauri, Doda, Kishtwar, Poonch are not so wholeheartedly behind the Indian government as the politicians in New Delhi like to maintain and in 1996 the APHC planned to open an office in Jammu. 'We have been very democratic in our approach. We have said that all these regions, Gilgit, Baltistan too, should have a proper representation.' Mistrust, however, remains between Muslims and the displaced Kashmiri Pandits, some of whom are now demanding a separate homeland in the valley for the 700,000 Pandits living in different parts of India.

All communities have suffered during the insurgency. For those Kashmiri Muslims of the valley who so enthusiastically supported the demand for *azadi*, on the understanding that they had been promised a plebiscite in order to determine their future, the sense of betrayal is perhaps greatest. The repression of the 1990s, the indiscriminate and unnecessary killings have merely added fuel to their anger. Time and again I heard people say: 'How could we ever accept the Indian government again, after what the military did to our people?'

Kidnapping tourists

Since the conflict began in earnest in 1989, kidnapping civilians has been part of militant strategy. As with the kidnapping of Rubaiya Sayeed, the objective has generally been to keep them as hostages, pending the release of detained colleagues or to pressurise rival militant organisations. Several hundred Kashmiri civilians have also been kidnapped during the insurgency in order to extort money from their families. According to the Indian government, in 1995 430 people were kidnapped of which nearly half were killed, compared with the previous year, when 315 people were kidnapped, of which less than a quarter were killed.[115] But only on rare occasions were foreigners taken hostage.

As a result, with the exception of 1990, the Government of India, with its own sense of bravado and its international image in mind, liked to maintain that the valley was not closed to tourism and that tourists were welcome. Those who visited the valley in the 1990s have often been surprised to find that, provided they remained on their houseboats, they were not troubled by the insurgency and were able to enjoy their holiday. 'I was a bit alarmed when I arrived at the airport will all the military, but once I got on the houseboat I felt all right,' said Stephen Humphrey, an accountant from

Birmingham, who visited Kashmir in April 1994.[116] Robert Shadforth of Top Deck bus tours has taken tourists to Kashmir, as part of a tour from Nepal to London, twice a year, with the exception of 1990. Sylvain Soudain takes select parties of Europeans heli-skiing. Their main problem was not the insurgency but the government-run Centaur hotel on the outskirts of Srinagar which lacked basic facilities and hygiene.

The record numbers of nearly 80,000 foreign tourists who visited the valley in 1989 were reduced to about 9,000 in 1995. Isolated incidents of kidnapping foreigners who were either working in Kashmir or had come as tourists, as well as the rape of a Canadian girl in October 1990 by two army officers, acted as an obvious deterrent. So too the militarisation of the valley and the paradox of enjoying a holiday, while the local people were subjected to crackdowns and crossfiring. The lack of tourists, of course, meant that the business of the local Kashmiris suffered accordingly: houseboat owners, the Hanjis, who, for generations have managed the houseboats, the shikara wallahs, taxi drivers, tonga drivers, hotel owners, and those who depended on selling their handicrafts to visiting tourists, all lost what was the only avenue of income open to them. 'This houseboat which used to be so popular is now nearly gone,' said Iqbal Chapra, founder president of the Houseboat Owners Association.[117] 'We pray for peace in our valley and then the tourists will come,' said Muhammed Kotru, president of the Houseboat Owners Association in 1994.[118] Only the privileged few have been able to continue to export and sell carpets, handicrafts and embroidery throughout India and abroad. A Kashmiri Pandit who fled from the valley maintains that some Muslim Kashmiris are now better off because they no longer have to go through the Hindus as middlemen.

In 1994 the attention of the Western media was focused on the valley because two men, one of whom was the son of former *Financial Times* journalist David Housego, were kidnapped. The Housego family were on holiday in Kashmir to celebrate Jenny Housego's fiftieth birthday. On 6 June, when they reached the village of Aru, after three days in the mountains near Pahalgam, they were held up and robbed of money, watches and clothing. They were taken to a hotel where they met another couple David and Cathy Mackie who were also being held at gun point. They too had been trekking in the mountains. The militants took the Housegos' son, Kim, 16, and David Mackie, 36, leaving the Housego parents and Cathy Mackie to negotiate through a series of intermediaries for their release. After their release seventeen days later, Mackie made some revealing comments about the militants: 'They had heard on the BBC that I had a bad knee and next morning provided me with a stick and detailed one of the party to stay close to me. I was allowed to walk at my own pace.'[119] 'They made sure we had the best places by the camp fire,' said Kim Housego. 'They listened to the BBC Urdu service and translated for us.'[120] Harkat-ul Ansar were held responsible for the kidnapping, which was believed to have been a mistake.

By the following year the incident had almost been forgotten. As the winter snows melted, small numbers of tourists, who had either not heard about the troubles or were not sufficiently disturbed by them, arrived in the valley. Martha Fichtinger, an Austrian women, who visited Kashmir in April 1995, said that she did not find travelling on her own in Kashmir any more daunting than previous trips to South America and had heard very little about the insurgency.[121] Sam Valani, a Ugandan Asian and his family, now living in Canada, had always wanted to come to Kashmir but thought it was too dangerous. 'But when an Indian airline official in Delhi told us that it was possible, we cancelled our trip to Udaipur and Jaipur and came to Kashmir instead.'[122] Gary Lazzarini, a shoe shop owner, and Philip Peters, a construction engineer from London, spent sixteen days in Kashmir with the intention of going skiing in once fashionable Gulmarg. Finding that the slopes were virtually closed, they stayed on a houseboat whose owner's only request was for them to send him some flies and lines for trout fishing when they returned to England. 'Everyone had something to say about the troubles going on. They didn't seem very optimistic and were more interested in getting their lives back to normal. But they were worried about human rights.'[123] A South African couple preferred to stay at Ahdoo's hotel in central Srinagar, because they felt trapped on the houseboats. In 1995, Ahdoo's was still the only hotel which remained open; the lights sometimes failed, the telephones generally worked, and the food was just bearable. The manager of Ahdoo's was delighted with the presence of the South African couple: 'These are the first tourists we have had. Otherwise it has been just journalists who come to report on the insurgency.'[124]

In July 1995 the hopes of those who were trying to say the valley was safe for tourism were once more dashed. Six foreigners were kidnapped and held by what was referred to as a 'little known' militant group, Al Faran, believed to be a radical wing of Harkat-ul Ansar. The tourists had also been trekking in Pahalgam and were apprehended in three separate incidents. One tourist, John Childs, escaped within days of being kidnapped. The others were Donald Hutchings, an American, Paul Wells and Keith Mangan, both British, Dirk Hasert, a German and a Norwegian, Hans Christian Ostro. The kidnappers demanded the release of twenty-one militants held by the Indian authorities, mostly belonging to Harkat-ul Ansar. Unless the militants were released, the kidnappers threatened to kill the hostages. On 17 July a hand-written statement was received by the news agencies in Srinagar: 'The Indian government is not showing any interest in securing the release of the hostages. The international community, particularly those who have appealed to us [to release the foreigners] should pressurise India to stop human rights violations in Kashmir and accept our demands immediately.'[125] The group's objective in taking the tourists was regarded as another variation on the persistent theme of the insurgency: the involvement of the international community in the 'just' cause of the Kashmiris.

Despite the release of the militants in 1989 after Dr Rubaiya Sayeed's kidnapping and the numerous other incidents where bargains had been made, the Indian government publicly refused to consider an exchange. 'There is no question of releasing any militant [in exchange for the five abducted tourists]', stated the home secretary, K. Padmanabhaiah, in the first of many refusals.[126] While the Indian authorities tried to contact Al Faran, deadlines for the killing of the hostages came and went. The JKLF condemned the kidnapping, as did Omar Farooq, who claimed the APHC had tried but failed to get in touch with the Al Faran militants. Pakistan also condemned the kidnapping and some commentators even believed that the incident was an elaborate ploy by Indian intelligence to discredit the Kashmiri movement and, indirectly, Pakistan. 'Although Pakistan has undoubtedly not got anything to do with this kidnapping, their overall support of the insurgency would make them responsible,' commented a Western analyst who believes Pakistan has supplied weapons to the insurgents. 'In the same way, if you give a child a gun and leave him in a room with his siblings and he shoots them, you are responsible for their murder.'

On 13 August, the decapitated body of Hans Christian Ostro was found by the roadside. By murdering a foreigner, the kidnappers succeeded in attracting world-wide publicity, but for the wrong reasons. The action was condemned by both the political and other militant groups. A one-day strike throughout the valley was intended to show that the Kashmiris disassociated themselves from the murder, which Omar Farooq called an act of terrorism. Because of the potential publicity damage to their movement, he and many others were sceptical about the group's origins and their motivation. 'Who are these people who come into existence at a time when we are trying to gain support for our movement day and night? I do not believe that they are in anyway committed to the Kashmiris' struggle.'[127] In December 1995 three members of the Al Faran group were captured by Indian security forces. They confirmed that the hostages were still alive, but no information was given regarding their release. By 1996 it was feared they were dead.

The diametrically opposed viewpoints of Pakistan and India on the kidnapping demonstrated how far apart they still were over what takes place in Kashmir. On the one hand, the Indian government was convinced the group were foreign mercenaries, aided and abetted by Pakistan. On the other, Pakistanis believed that they were agents of the Indian government, paid to discredit the Kashmiris' struggle for self-determination and, by association, Pakistan. In the midst of these conflicting views, the Kashmiri people were, as ever, caught in their verbal crossfire. The valley, surrounded by the magnificent Himalayan mountains, whose beauty has, for centuries, attracted visitors from far and wide, was still the home of tragedy.

CHAPTER 9

Conflict or Consensus?

Recalling ... that an environment of peace and security is in the supreme national interest of both sides and the resolution of all outstanding issues, including Jammu and Kashmir, is essential for this purpose... *Lahore declaration*, 21 February 1999.

A decade after thousands of Kashmiris took to the streets to demand *azadi* there was still no clarity on how they could achieve their objective, when neither Pakistan nor India was prepared to contemplate *azadi* as meaning independence. Even so, commentators and observers continued to analyse the Kashmiris' demand for self-determination in order to see what the consequences might be if a plebiscite were held. Firstly, would it be fair on all the inhabitants to hold a unitary plebiscite where the voice of the majority might prevail at the expense of the minority? Or should there be a regional plebiscite which would let ethnic groups decide according to their regions, even though this would inevitably formalise the partition of the state?

Secondly, if, on the basis of a majority vote, the inhabitants of the entire former princely state chose to become independent, how could one possibly prise the Northern Areas and Azad Kashmir away from Pakistan, and Ladakh and Jammu away from India? Or if there were a regional vote, and only the valley chose independence, how could it survive? Furthermore, how could the Government of Pakistan continue to insist that the Kashmiris be given the right to determine their future and then permit them only the option to choose between India or Pakistan? Would, in reality, India and Pakistan concede anything at all? What could be the basis for a consensus or would the conflict continue?

World opinion

Throughout their struggle, the Kashmiri activists regretted the unwillingness of the rest of the world to assist them in what they perceived to be a 'just' cause. They believed that their inability to attract material international support was in contrast to that given to the Afghans throughout the 1980s during their struggle against the Soviet Union; the Kashmiris were also conscious of the sub-continent's past history, in which Britain played its own imperial role. At the height of the insurgency, their optimistic belief that they had only to create enough trouble in the valley to attract international support did not materialise. 'No country was willing to risk its entire agenda with New Delhi over the Kashmir cause,' wrote *Time* correspondent Edward Desmond in 1995 'especially when it was clear that New Delhi had no intention of backing down.'[1]

In the early years of the insurgency, British Members of Parliament, Euro MPs, US Congressmen, human rights activists all played a part in listening to the grievances of the Kashmiris. Once they had lodged their complaints and written their reports, however, there was very little action they could take. International opinion was as much concerned about Pakistan's own alleged role in 'exporting terrorism' and its potential nuclear capability, as it was about events in what India persistently termed an integral part of its territory. In the face of a movement which demanded independence, Pakistan – which opposed that independence – was also losing credibility as the self-appointed spokesman for Kashmiri interests. Moreover, as western business interests in India increased, so did the willingness of their governments to take provocative action over Kashmir diminish. Kashmir also appeared remote, an issue, which did not have the same immediacy as Bosnia, Northern Ireland, the Middle East or, in the late 1990s, Kosovo.

The toughest international criticism, which India faced, was in the early 1990s over violations of human rights. When, however, foreign observers took up the refrain of plebiscite and self-determination, as recommended by the United Nations resolutions, the commentators found themselves on less secure ground. Not only did the UN resolutions omit the choice of the 'third option' of independence for the Kashmiri people, but, to call for the implementation of the resolutions would also unearth all the old reasons why the plebiscite was never held. In the Indian armoury of excuses was the fact that Pakistan had never vacated that part of the state of Jammu and Kashmir, which it occupied in the Northern Areas and Azad Kashmir and which was a prerequisite for holding a plebiscite. Moreover, one of the strongest arguments put forward by the Indian government was that if the state of Jammu and Kashmir left the Indian Union, other disaffected parts of the country might also wish to secede, and no member of the international community wanted to see the sub-continent destabilised.

The Kashmiris who challenged Indian rule, however, also believed that it was the moral duty of the international community to support their cause because successive resolutions, unanimously adopted by the members of the Security Council, called for the settlement of the dispute by the means of a free and impartial plebiscite under the auspices of an international body, the United Nations. They also considered that it was essential for the 'third option' to be included in the UN resolutions. 'The people should be given free choice to accede to India, Pakistan or to become independent,' said Yasin Malik in 1995. 'And whatever the people decide, we will accept this democratic decision wholeheartedly, because we believe in the democratic process.'[2] The

Kashmiri activists refuted India's suggestion that if Kashmir seceded it would lead to the break-up of India. Nor did they believe that, with over 100 million Muslims already living in India, India had to retain Kashmir for the sake of its 'secular' image.

After its early diplomatic initiatives in the 1950s and 1960s the United States kept aloof from the Kashmiri issue. The 1972 Simla agreement between India and Pakistan had also lulled the international community into thinking that it need not concern itself with what was now termed a 'bilateral' issue. In the 1990s, however, without the weight of the Soviet Union to balance power in the region, the United States took more interest in an issue which, in 1993, James Woolsey, head of the CIA, assessed as posing 'perhaps the most probable prospect for the future use of weapons of mass destruction, including nuclear weapons.'[3] The prospect of a war between India and Pakistan over rival claims to the Siachen glacier, where their troops clashed intermittently ever since Indian troops had been airlifted onto the glacier in 1984, was chilling indeed. The fear of such a local dispute spreading into a greater conflict was fundamental to the shift in emphasis of US foreign policy in the mid-1990s. 'We felt it was time to get out our Kashmir file, dust it off and see what could be done,' stated a State Department official in 1995.[4]

As the US administration involved itself in the issue, so its officials began to appreciate the sensitivities felt by both the Indian and Pakistani governments. When, in October 1993, Robin Raphel, assistant secretary of state on South Asian Affairs, commented that the US still regarded the status of Jammu and Kashmir as a 'disputed territory and that means we do not recognise the Instrument of Accession as meaning that Kashmir is for evermore an integral part of India', her remarks were rejected by New Delhi.[5] In April 1994, when U.S. deputy secretary of state, Strobe Talbott, visited New Delhi and Islamabad, both countries reacted nervously at any perceived favouritism towards the other. 'The US has good relations with India and with Pakistan,' Talbott declared at his press conference in New Delhi.'[6] British foreign secretary, Douglas Hurd's remarks that the UN resolutions no longer had the same relevance upset the Pakistanis during his visit to Islamabad at the end of 1994. When Robin Cook, as shadow foreign secretary in 1995, addressed a meeting organised by Indians at Wembley in the UK and stated that Kashmir was a part of India, there was an outcry from the Pakistanis and Kashmiris of Mirpuri origin. Cook was obliged to clarify his remarks by emphasising that his statement was meant to reflect the situation on the ground rather than the legal situation; subsequent political lobbying on behalf of the Kashmiris also led to the passing of a strongly worded resolution on Kashmir at Labour's annual conference in October 1995, drawn up by its National Executive Committee.

> Britain must accept its responsibility as the former imperial power in a dispute that dates from the arrangements for independence and recognise that it is under an obligation to seek a solution that is based on our commitment to

peace, democracy, human rights and mutual tolerance. ... Labour in government will be prepared to use its close relationship with India and Pakistan to provide good offices to assist in a negotiated solution to this tragic dispute.

Western inability to pressurise the Indian government to modify its stand was not only interpreted as a lack of its basic resolve but also led to considerable anti-western feeling. 'The West has absolute double standards,' said Abdul Suhrawardy, one of the early generation of 'freedom fighters', in 1994. 'They have no morality. They talk of democracy, they talk of human rights but these are just hypocritical slogans.'[7] Kashmiri sympathisers pointed to examples where the western powers were prepared to intervene forcefully, such as in Kuwait in 1990, where their interests were obviously at stake or as in Kosovo in 1999, which was in the heart of Europe. Nonetheless, in view of the Indian government's refusal to grant any concessions to the Kashmiri activists, and their own realisation that the militants would not be able to defeat the Indian army, they continued to recognise that their best hope lay in involving the international community in their 'just' cause.

Political change

1996 saw a renewed effort on the part of the Indian government to 'normalise' the situation in the valley. Its strategy was the same as in previous years: a combined attempt to suppress the militants at the same time as winning over the local people with the objective of holding elections to the state of Jammu and Kashmir's legislative assembly. As in the past, stories of human rights abuses against civilians continued to tarnish the Indian government's assertion that it was only targeting militants. On 27 March 1996, Jalil Andrabi, a prominent Kashmiri human rights lawyer was found tortured and shot to death in Srinagar. According to his wife, who was with him at the time of his 'disappearance', Andrabi was detained while driving home by soldiers from the Rashtriya Rifles. Although the Indian government denied that any members of the RR were responsible, as with the shooting of Dr Farooq Ashai in 1993, his death was widely condemned by international commentators and human rights groups.[8]

Domestic politics in India, however, temporarily posed a question mark over the future direction of the government's Kashmiri policy. After five years in office, Narasimha Rao was defeated in the May general election. In the state of Jammu and Kashmir, the election of its six representatives to the Lok Sabha – the first to be held since 1989 – was contested under heavy security in three stages: in Jammu and Ladakh, Baramula and Anantnag, Srinagar and Udamphur. An additional 50–60,000 troops were reportedly brought into the state. Since the APHC and National Conference had refused to participate, the only contestants for the state's six constituencies were from the BJP, Congress (I) or independents. The APHC boycott was accompanied by threats from the militants against election officials and voters.[9] Pro-government commentators enthused over the results. 'The overwhelming voters' participation in the Lok Sabha elections in Kashmir nailed the persistent propaganda made in Pakistan that the poll in the State would either not be held or would be rigged,' wrote Dev P. Kumar.[10] International press coverage, however, suggested that there were numerous incidents where voters had been forced to the poll at gunpoint.[11]

In the Lok Sabha, no political party emerged with a clear majority; for fourteen days, a BJP government coalition attempted to form a government but failed to show that it had majority support and had to step down. Even though the BJP was not successful in forming a government on this occasion, that it nearly did so was an indication of its growing strength. In the 1989 elections it had gained only two seats; in 1996 it had increased its support to 202 including its allies. H. D. Deve Gowda, a relatively unknown politician, finally succeeded in bringing together enough support to form a United Front coalition government: the first of its kind at a national level.

In Jammu and Kashmir, the UF government moved forward with elections to the state's legislative assembly – a feat which, a year earlier, had seemed impossible and which was all the more pressing because President's rule in Jammu and Kashmir was due to expire on 16 July 1996. Governor Rao felt confident that the poll would go ahead because 'the message had gone home that the Government can weather all challenges.'[12] The APHC, however, once more stood firm in its refusal to contest and attempted to encourage a boycott of the poll. The Indian government's efforts to involve the majority of the people in the political process also received a set back when government employees went on strike in the valley, in protest against the dismissal of 22 colleagues for allegedly having links with the militants. This time, however, after a certain amount of prevarication, Farooq Abdullah and his National Conference agreed to participate and elections were finally scheduled for September. His manifesto was for 'maximum autonomy' and a substantial economic package, neither of which his more critical observers believed he would ever achieve. Abdullah defended his *volte face* on the grounds that it was better to be doing something rather than nothing. 'Either you allow the situation to drift and have no public involvement or you take up the challenge and see how best you can change it.'[13] Although the turnout was low and there were reports of APHC supporters being harrassed, Farooq Abdullah's re-election as chief minister was hailed as turning a page in the 'nightmarish chapter in Kashmir's recent history'.[14] The Indian *Statesman* newspaper added a note of caution: 'The margin and sweep of his victory must convince him that the vote is not a vote so much for his demand for greater autonomy but in the hope that he will find a way out of the present mess.'[15] For the first time since the worst days of January 1990, the Indian government could congratulate itself on a return to civilian government in Jammu and Kashmir.

In Pakistan, the election was condemned as 'a sham' by Prime Minister
Benazir Bhutto, who immediately requested the UN to convene a multilateral
conference (involving India, Pakistan, the five members of the Security
Council as well as Germany and Japan) to resolve the Kashmir issue and
establish a regional security system in South Asia. The elections which had
been held in Azad Jammu and Kashmir in June were similarly criticised by the
Indian press. In what Sumantra Bose described as 'a manipulated farce', Sardar
Qayum Khan was replaced as prime minister by a Pakistan Peoples Party
member, Sultan Mehmood. Pro-independence parties were banned from
participating in the AJK elections because their candidates refused to sign
affidavits swearing their allegiance to Pakistan.[16]

The Prime Minister of Pakistan was, however, also facing her own political
troubles. At the beginning of November, President Farooq Leghari dismissed
Benazir Bhutto as prime minister on allegations of corruption, mal-
administration and extra-judicial killings in Karachi. Once more a caretaker
government was instituted in Pakistan, pending fresh elections in February
1997.

Anniversary celebrations

The significance of 1997 was not lost on either India or Pakistan as the
opportunity for a major media initiative to portray their respective countries to
the outside world as progressive and democratic in the 50th year of their
independence. 1997 was also characterised by a change of Prime Minister in
Pakistan, India and Britain, which provided the opportunity for a fresh
approach over 'oustanding issues' between India and Pakistan and a new
policy initiative in Britain.

In February 1997 Nawaz Sharif was re-elected prime minister of Pakistan
with a clear majority in the National Assembly. He immediately sent a message
to the prime minister of India to resume talks, which would be the first talks at
prime ministerial level since Benazir Bhutto met Rajiv Gandhi in 1989. In
March, discussions were held between the foreign secretaries in New Delhi. 'All
issues' were on the agenda. A month later the foreign ministers met in New
Delhi and confirmed their commitment to holding bilateral talks. At the same
time, the Indian government demonstrated its toughened stance towards
compromise with Pakistan over the state of Jammu and Kashmir. When
Farooq Abdullah suggested that the LOC should be formalised as the
international frontier between India and Pakistan, his remarks were attacked by
the right-wing Indian nationalists in an acrimonious debate in the Lok Sabha as
well as by the Kashmiri political activists. Defence minister, Mulayam Singh
Yadav, stated that the Indian government was determined to regain Azad
Jammu and Kashmir which was also an 'integral' part of the Indian Union.[17]
The storm of protest regarding AJK was in marked contrast to the tacit
acceptance of the LOC as the end point of Indian influence after Simla in 1972.

By the time the prime ministers of India and Pakistan met at the South Asian Association for Regional Cooperation (SAARC) summit in the Maldives in May, Deve Gowda had been replaced as prime minister by his 77 year old foreign minister, Inder Kumar Gujral. As prime minister, Gujral evolved what became known as the 'Gujral doctrine': a friendlier approach to India's neighbours, easing tensions in South Asia and improving relations with Pakistan. At their meeting in the Maldives, Gujral and Sharif announced a plan to constitute joint 'working groups' to consider all outstanding issues. When the foreign secretaries met again in June in Islamabad, 'with the objective of promoting a friendly and harmonious relationship,' they agreed to the formation of eight groups which would consider all major issues, including Kashmir.[18] At their meeting in New Delhi in September, there was, however, no agreement on any issue, except the commitment to hold another round of talks. When the Prime Ministers met again at the UN General Assembly in New York at the end of September, they agreed to take action to end border skirmishes in Kashmir, but nothing more.

Privately, some Pakistanis expressed the wish that, from his position of strength in the National Assembly, Nawaz Sharif would officially sanction the status quo in Jammu and Kashmir on the understanding that Pakistan would be better off without the Kashmir issue continuing to burden both its economy and its emotional development.[19] In the months which followed, however, Nawaz Sharif took no such initiative and was soon absorbed into the traditional rhetoric about the Kashmiris' right of self-determination without being able to move the debate forward by defining how it could be achieved in view of India's persistent statements that the state of Jammu and Kashmir was an integral part of the Indian Union and Pakistan's own refusal to consider the third option of independence.

The election of a Labour government in Britain in early May also renewed the focus of the Kashmiri diaspora on the issue and encouraged them to think that Britain would now be in a position to involve itself more openly in a possible resolution. The adoption of the NEC resolution in 1995 meant that it had become part of Labour's election manifesto and official policy. The admission that Labour considered the Kashmir issue to be part of the 'unfinished business of partition' was interpreted as an official commitment by the British government to take a more pro-active stance over Kashmir. The 'third party' interference of Britain was, however, rejected by the Indian government. Indian coolness towards Britain's influence as a world power was openly expressed by Gujral during Indian independence celebrations in August. 'Britain ceased to be a major power in the middle-Forties. It was an exhausted nation, a nation that lost a great deal in the war. The Americans were a rising power and Churchill and the others who followed him thought it better to piggyback.'[20]

Relations between Britain and India were further soured when, as foreign secretary, Robin Cook accompanied the Queen to Pakistan and India on her

State visit to the sub-continent in October 1997. While in Pakistan, Cook held the customary meetings with his opposite numbers in the Pakistani foreign ministry. He also held a meeting with Nawaz Sharif during which he assured the Pakistani prime minister of Britain's 'good offices' over Kashmir. It was, he believed, an inocuous remark in keeping with comments about Kashmir previously made by former prime minister, John Major. When the Pakistani press, acting on a briefing from the Pakistani Ministry of Foreign Affairs, reported that Cook had offered his services as a meditator in the Kashmir dispute, the Indians were incensed. That Cook had returned to the UK for the weekend meant that he was unable to counteract the growing storm in India. 'Reports that British foreign secretary, Robin Cook, had offered to mediate in India and Pakistan in their dispute over Kashmir – a matter India considers an internal affair – inflamed the Indian press,' reported CNN.[21] 'Cook spoils the broth, wants finger in the Kashmir pie,' commented the *Indian Express*.[22] On his arrival in India, Cook immediately denied that he had given 'any statement, interview or press conference on Kashmir while in Pakistan'.[23] According to his biographer, Cook believed that the only way he could have avoided mentioning Kashmir at all during his visit to Pakistan was not to have met Nawaz Sharif, which was 'not an option'.[24] The damage to the British government's credentials of professed impartiality was, however, tremendous. Prime Minister Gujral yet again made it clear that the Indian government did not want any third party mediation in the Kashmir issue.

Kashmiri political activists, however, used the independence celebrations as an excuse to demonstrate their defiance against Indian rule. Pakistani flags were raised from electricity poles and houses at several sites in Srinagar as well as in the towns of Anantnag, Baramula and Kupwara.[25] The flags were quickly removed by Indian troops. India's Republic Day, 26 January 1998, was hailed by the Kashmiri diaspora across the world as a 'Black Day'. Protest rallies were also held in Islamabad and in towns throughout Azad Kashmir. Yet again the demand was for a UN sponsored referendum in the region. The non-violent protests were marred, however, by the shooting of 23 Kashmiri Pandits, including five women and two children, on the eve of the Republic Day celebrations. Once again the APHC was put on the defensive. 'It is a dastardly act,' stated Shabir Shah. 'The killings have been committed by criminals. I condemn it. It's a game plan to alienate Hindus from us.'[26]

Continuing Militancy

Western media interest in the militancy was sustained by the blackout on the fate of the four western hostages, kidnapped in 1995. Since their disappearance and following the murder of the Norwegian, Hans Christian Ostro, in August 1995, there had been regular contact between Al Faran and the Indian authorities, who coordinated with the British High Commission, the US, German and Norwegain embassies. A particular concern was that

Indian operations against the militants in the valley should not target areas in which Al Faran might be holding the hostages, lest a military strike jeopardise their security. In mid-December 1995 a member of the group had telephoned Sir Nicholas Fenn, the British High Commissioner in India, following earlier conversations with Fenn's deputy, Hilary Synnott. The caller asked for direct talks with the High Commissioner in the hope of securing money. Fenn stressed 'the value of magnaminity' and also explained why the four govern-ments could not pay ransom.[27] He agreed, however, to receive the caller in New Delhi a few days later. The appointment was not kept.[28]

This appears to be the last contact anyone had with the group, although, at the time, none of the embassies involved 'had reason to believe that the hostages were dead and efforts continued to secure their release'. [29] Over the next three years, their relatives and friends returned regularly to both Pakistan and India in an attempt to follow up any leads on possible sightings. None materialised. It is now widely believed that the hostages were in fact killed some time in December 1995. In early December, Indian security forces operating against militants in the area had killed a number of Al Faran members, including one of its operational leaders, Hamid al-Turki. In 1998 Sean Langan, reporting for the BBC, travelled deep into the valley to Pahalgam, where the hostages were kidnapped, towards Kishtwar area to try and locate a militant who, he believed, was 'the last known member of Al Faran' in order to question him about the fate of the hostages. When, after numerous false starts, Langan finally reached the village, where the militant was reported to be hiding, to his great disappointment, he found, without any further explanation, that the militant had been killed only hours before his arrival.

After the 1995 kidnapping, foreigners were warned not to travel to the valley, and especially not to venture out of Srinagar to go trekking in the mountains. Tourism therefore remained well below its pre-insurgency peak. Yet, as the memory of the kidnapping faded, holidaymakers began once again to visit the valley. 'Tourists are coming back' said Farooq Abdullah enthusi-astically at the end of 1998. 'This year we had 150,000 visitors to the Amarnath caves. The cinema has re-opened; we are opening a new five-star hotel for tourists.'[30]

When Alexander Evans, a research student, returned to the valley in 1997 for the first time in four years he noticed the reduction in tension. He was also unnerved by the silence. 'A while later it occured to me: no shooting. Evidently things had changed, if only in Srinagar itself.'[31] Danny Summers, who visited the valley in June 1998, felt more intimidated by the Indian soldiers with their guns than he did by the unseen militants.[32] M. J. Gohel, Chief Executive of the South Asia Secretariat, a London-based 'conflict-resolution' organisation, who visited Jammu and Kashmir on a private visit in August 1998, found that there was 'a distinct atmosphere of normalcy' in Srinagar: 'Young couples were boating on Dal lake until very late in the evening, hotels had re-opened, the houseboats were doing business again, the streets were full of people, including foreign tourists. Amongst many Kashmiris he detected 'relief tinged with the fear that the peace would be shattered at some point.'[33] Lord Avebury, who made his first visit to the valley of Kashmir in November 1998, found 'deep concern over the continuing loss of life in Kashmir, including political assassinations and sectarian massacres. These have engendered an atmosphere of intimidation, in which it is difficult for people to express themselves freely.'[34] According to journalist, Jonathan Harley, 'life in the summer capital is improving.' But he believed that what the Indian officials called 'normalcy' was more accurately described as 'adaptability'.[35] As *The Economist* pointed out in its May 1999 survey: 'Normality is relative. Sringar still looks like a city dumped inside a maximum-security prison, with guns poking through piles of sandbags on nearly every corner.'[36]

A decade after the insurgency began, people still suffered from anxiety and depression. Women continued to weep for their sons who had 'disappeared'. As Amnesty International stated, those who 'disappeared' in the custody of the state 'are at risk of further human rights violations ... away from the scrutiny of lawyers, family members and human rights monitors, the "disappeared" are likely to be tortured or killed with impunity.'[37] In 1999 the state of Jammu and Kashmir was still subject to laws which allowed the security forces to shoot suspects and destroy property. When they abused their powers, there was still no effective legal redress.[38] Based on investigations at the end of 1998, the Human Rights Watch report concluded that both India and Pakistan were to blame for human rights violations and that the repression and abuse had kept the conflict in Kashmir alive. Of those targeted by militants, more than 300 civilians were killed between 1997 and mid-1999. The report also accused the Indian army and security forces of employing brutal tactics, including summary executions, disappearances, torture and rape.[39] The Kashmiri Pandits also remained a casualty of the insurgency. With the exception of the rich who had managed to escape to their houses in Delhi, those who were confined in the refugee camps outside Jammu were becoming increasingly despondent. 'They would like to return to their homes, businesses and farms but these have been either destroyed or taken over by Muslim Kashmiris,' said M. J. Gohel, who visited the camps in August 1998. 'No one seems to be concerned about their human rights.'[40]

A key feature of the Indian government's successful operations against the militants was its counter-insurgency measures. In 1993 a 'unified command' was set up to co-ordinate army and paramilitary forces in the valley. The Indian government also adopted its own 'psychological' strategy, which was intended to counteract the Pakistani and Kashmiri public relations initiatives. Part of its strategy was to improve the image of the Indian security forces in the valley, with the provision of free medical aid to the people, free filmshows of some of the latest Bollywood films and a greater policy of 'transparency' insofar as allegations of human rights abuses were concerned. Most significantly, the campaign included support to pro-Indian militant groups, by using former 'rehabilitated' militants to guide the security forces in operations against the militants and by using intelligence agents as operatives within active militant groups.

The most well-known of the counter-insurgent militant groups was that led by the former folk singer, Kukka Parrey, who operated under the name Mohammed Yousuf alias Jamsheed Shirazi. Leader of Ikhwan-ul Muslimoon, a splinter group of Ikwan-ul Muslimeen, at the height of counter-insurgency operations in the valley in the middle 1990s, the group succeeded in restricting the activities of the Hizb-ul Mujaheddin. Numerous Jamaat activists were eliminated together with Hizb militants. Ikhwan-ul Muslimoon also targeted the media and is believed to have been responsible for the bomb blast in September 1995 at the BBC offices in Srinagar, when photographer, Mushtaq Ali, was killed. Other counter-insurgency groups included the Muslim Liberation Army, operating around Kupwara, the Muslim Mujaheddin, founded by Ahsan Dar (who was under arrest and whose group had gone over to counter-insurgency), Al-Ikhwan, Indian Al Barq and Taliban, a Gujar militant group, which operated in the Kangan area in Srinagar, where Gujars predominate. The BSF succeeded in creating the Kashmir Liberation Jehad force out of former 'surrendered' militants. Its main occupation involved leading the security forces in operations against militants in Srinagar. In military terms, these groups operated effectively throughout the middle-90s. According to Indian army sources, Bandipur was cleared of Hizb militants because of the activities of counter-insurgency groups. Ikhwan-ul Muslimoon successfully counteracted the activities of the Ikhwan-ul Muslimeen in Baramula.[41] Contrary to the Indian government's attempts to portray them as a reflection of a spontaneous reaction amongst the people to militancy, their activities were undoubtedly sponsored by the government. Despite their military successes, the counter-insurgents did not encourage pro-Indian sentiment amongst the people; consequently their usefulness was limited in the Indian government's overall strategy of normalisation.

Allegations of human rights abuses and extortion also tarnished their image. In 1996, APHC members, who were attempting to gain support for their boycott of the 1996 state elections, were reported as being targeted by the Ikhwan-ul Muslimoon. Amnesty also noted that many of them had 'reportedly been lured, persuaded or subjected to ill-treatment in custody or other forms of pressure to joining the side of the government.'[42] That many of them were reported to be Gujars, who had not traditionally supported the militancy, reflected the dynamics of an insurgency which, in reality, had not engendered widespread support from amongst the non-Kashmiri speakers of the valley. By the late 1990s, the usefulness of the counter-insurgents was being undermined by their own behaviour. In October 1997, Director-General of Police, Gurbachan Jagat, reported: 'Continued services of the surrendered militants was proving to be counter-productive in view of reports of excesses during the operations.' Both the government in New Delhi and the state government therefore sought to 'rehabilitate' them into the security forces, especially the CRPF and the BSF. Some were also appointed as Special Police Officers (SPOs) in the state police. It appeared, however, that some rehabilitated 'renegades' still engaged in 'freelance' criminal activities.[43]

Although the idea of an insurgency which had the mass support of all the Kashmiris had receded compared with the early 1990s, militants continued to carry out numerous acts of sabotage, increasingly with 'high-tech gadgets', operating from bases both in the valley and the Doda district of Jammu. 'Security forces recently recovered a lethal device – two remote control Aerodynamic Modules with a powerful engine,' reported Iftikhar Gilani of *The Kashmir Times* in January 1999.[44] Although Farooq Abdullah talked of militants who had 'gone straight', he also recognised that others still needed 'to be rehabilitated'. Reports of encounters and the death or capture of militants appeared regularly in both the Indian and Pakistani press. In January 1999, a Union home ministry report submitted to Prime Minister Vajpayee demonstrated that, contrary to the view being propagated by Abdullah, the law and order situation in the state was actually deteriorating. During 1997 the report documented 186 security personnel killed; in 1998 the figures had increased to 234. In keeping with militant strategy not to target civilians but security forces and the police, civilian deaths had decreased from 938 in 1997 to 833 in 1996. The Indian government also had to recognise that, despite its pro-active policy against the militants, they were less successful in eliminating them in 1998 than in the previous year. Government figures noted 950 militants killed in 1998 compared with 1,075 in 1997.[45]

As in the past, in addition to the attacks on Indian security forces, members of the National Conference were also liable to be targeted by the militants. In Feburary 1998 Farooq Abdullah survived an assassination attempt when an 'improvised explosive device' was planted at a meeting he was addressing in Gandarbal. In September 1998, another National Conference activist, Ghulam Nabi Rather, was shot at his home on the outskirts of Srinagar. Militant activity against the National Conference demonstrated that, contrary to the state government's assurances of 'normalcy' it was not 'roses all the way for the people in general and the party cadre in particular.'[46] In May 1999 Abdul Ahad Kar, a member of the state legislative assembly was shot dead in Langate, in northern Kashmir.

In the late 1990s, of the groups which continued to predominate, Lashkar-i Toiba (the army of the pure), Harkat-ul Ansar and Hizb-ul Mujaheddin, established in 1989, had the most adherents. The United Jihad Council, led by Syed Salahuddin, was an umbrella organisation for fourteen smaller groups, operating out of Muzaffarabad, which included Al Badar and Tehrik-i Jihad. In November 1997 Harkat-ul Ansar was declared a terrorist organisation by the United States on the grounds that it had links with Al Faran and that many Al Faran members, including Hamid al-Turki, were ex-Harkat members. In order to avoid US restrictions on travel and funding, it immediately renamed itself, Harkat-ul Mujaheddin. Based in Muzaffarabad, it was believed to have a core group of about 300 militants operating in 1999, who were Pakistanis, Kashmiris as well as Afghans and Arabs who had fought in the Afghan war.[47]

The continuing presence of militant activity was used by both Pakistan and India to lend weight to their respective propaganda. Whereas the Pakistanis described the militants as indigenous freedom fighters of the valley, the Indian government continued to point to 'trans-border crossings' and the omni-present 'foreign hand' without which it maintained the militancy would have no standing. That militants were more vociferously preaching jihad – a holy war – added to the belief shared not only by Indians but also by western observers that there were far less Kashmiri militants and that they had indeed come from the more orthodox ideological training ground of Afghanistan or Pakistan, especially the *madrasssas* which had trained the young students who had formed the Taliban in Afghanistan. Reports that the Saudi dissident, Osama bin Laden had been training militants to fight a holy war appeared entirely credible.[48] When, in August 1998, the United States attacked the camp where Osama was allegedly training fighters near Khost in Afghanistan, some of those killed were identified as Kashmiris militants.[49] Nonetheless, the Indian government chose not to make a distinction between those who might be 'indigenous' Kashmiris but had gone elsewhere to get trained and those who were genuinely foreign and could be classified as 'mercenaries'.

The Hizb-ul Mujaheddin was still regarded as the group which had the most indigenous support. For this reason, the Indian government noticeably downplayed its activities compared with those of the Harkat or Lashkar-i Toiba, which were believed to have many more 'foreign' adherents.[50] As with the objectives of the political activists, differences remained regarding their ultimate objective: independence or Pakistan. Inevitably those groups who derived support from Pakistan, were more vocal in expressing their desire ultimately to join Pakistan. It was also evident that, throughout the insurgency, Pakistani patronage had been a key variable in determining how the various groups developed and sustained themselves. In addition to support from within Pakistan, donations came from sympathisers in Islamic countries.

Political options

Increasingly the trend of many of the political parties, who had come together under the umbrella of the All Parties Hurriyat Conference, was to dissassociate themselves from militancy. Political activists in the valley of Kashmir realised that acts of violence and sabotage including the kidnapping of the western hostages and murder of one of them in 1995 had not helped their movement. 'It is portrayed as a terrorist and Islamic fundamentalist movement, while that is not the case. We want the Kashmiri Pandits to return,' said Omar Farooq in 1995. 'We feel that the battle has to be fought on political grounds. We know that the gun cannot really be the answer to the problem It introduced the Kashmiri issue at the international level, by bringing it out of cold storage into the limelight, but now it is the job of the political leaders to work for the movement.'[51] Moderates within the movement also recognised the damage done by continuing militancy which could get into the hands of extremists such as had happened in Afghanistan.

Each year the APHC traditionally honoured 'martyrs day' – 13 July – in memory not only of those who had died in the Abdul Qadir incident, which marked the beginning of the movement of protest against the autocracy of the maharaja in 1931, but also in memory of those who had died fighting the Indian security forces. As the APHC struggled to assert itself as an alternative political force to the state government, the message was clear: the Hurriyat Conference and not the government of Farooq Abdullah was the heir to the nationalist movement of the 1930s and the unfinished mission of the 'martyrs'.[52] Unlike the agitation against the maharaja which became a secular movement against his despotism, the APHC was moving increasingly towards expressing a demand for *azadi* which was not shared by the religious minorities. Attempts to broaden its base of support to Ladakh and Jammu were not successful; although Shabir Shah, who had joined the APHC in the hopes of forging 'a positive unity' after his release from prison in 1995, made several visits to various regions of the state, the APHC still appeared as a valley-based organisation which was not representative of either Ladakh, Jammu or the displaced Pandits.

Prominent activists were also becoming disillusioned by the inability of the APHC to put an end to clashes between the militant organisations. After returning to the valley in January 1995, having renounced militancy, Azam Inquilabi charged the APHC with having 'taken the people and the whole movement for granted'. In a speech in the Jama Masjid marking his return to political activity, he stated that the APHC had failed to deliver *azadi* to Kashmiris and that its leadership must 'seek counsel and consent of the historical forces which have been working in this movement for the past thirty years.'[53] Those 'historical forces' were personified in Inquilabi's own contribution and that of many of his colleagues in the decades preceding the insurgency. His experience also pre-dated the more communal Islamic character of the movement.

The Hurriyat was also undergoing a period of internal change in its hierarchy. In 1997, after four years as head of the APHC, Omar Farooq was replaced by Syed Ali Shah Gilani, leader of the Jamaat-i Islami. Although Omar Farooq's resignation as chairman after four years was treated as a normal transition of power from one office holder to another, there were unconfirmed reports that there had been an internal wrangle after Farooq had offered unconditional talks to the Indian government (which was, however, denied).[54] The Jamaat was itself no longer presenting a unified front. Although the Jamaat's support of its militant wing, the Hizb-ul Mujaheddin, had greatly contributed to the Hizb's early successes and especially its ascendancy over the militant members of the JKLF, in the middle 1990s, the moderates of the party began to disassociate themselves from militancy. They believed militancy had altered the religious direction of the party and the murder of the religious leader, Qazi Nissar, in Anantnag in 1997, led to demonstrations both against the Jammat leadership and 'Pakistani-sponsored' militancy. In a surprise move, on 23 October 1997, a number of leaders from Kulgam publicly denounced terrorism and vowed to eliminate militancy. In an interview on the same day, the new Ameer, Ghulam Mohammed Butt, called for a negotiated settlement of the crisis in Jammu and Kashmir. 'Our party should be read and seen through its message and the programme, and not through the propaganda of vested interests.' Butt's statement was interpreted as a direct challenge to the influence of Gilani, who traditionally dictated militant and political policy.[55] Gilani was also criticised for allegedly siphoning of millions of dollars of foreign donations intended to rebuild the mosque at Charar-e Sharif. Other Hurriyat leaders were also criticised for alleged corruption. Yet, contrary to the moderates' changed stance, Jamaat activists continued to maintain that the Jamaat was still directing the militancy.

Shabir Shah had also begun to question the Hurriyat's efficacy. In July 1996 he was 'suspended' from the APHC by the executive council for the independent stance he had adopted in conducting private discussions. His disillusionment with their achievements stemmed from the fact that the APHC had not been willing to adopt his 8-point programme for reform, submitted in December 1994, which he believed was necessary to re-energise the struggle. In May 1998, he announced the formation of a new party, the Jammu Kashmir Democratic Freedom Party; his slogan for the party: 'Nations are built from the bottom up,' reflected his belief that only with representative support at grass roots level could the movement strengthen and broaden its appeal. He also re-affirmed his belief in the right of self-determination of the entire state as it existed before 14 August 1947, a stand which he shared with numerous other pro-independence organisations existing on both sides of the line of control, including the JKLF. Whilst he refused to condemn militancy, Shabir Shah continued to reiterate his earlier position: that the gun was no solution to Kashmir's problems and that the issue should be resolved by involving the 'real' representatives of Kashmir.[56]

Hurriyat supporters were also disappointed that the Hurriyat 's voice was not carrying the necessary political weight. Neither able to form an alternative 'government' to challenge Farooq Abdullah in the state of Jammu and Kashmir nor able to counter the dominance of the Azad Jammu and Kashmir government in Muzaffarabad, the Hurriyat found that its influence was being increasingly marginalised. 'Look at the Azad government of Jammu and Kashmir. They have a Prime Minister, a President and government officials, whereas the Hurriyat has no such organisation,' stated Dr Ayub Thakar of the World Kashmir Freedom Movement. Part of the concern lay in the belief that both the Pakistani government and that of Azad Kashmir were projecting themselves as spokesmen for the Kashmiri movement for self-determination. 'It should have been the leadership from the valley fighting the movement. We need to tell the world our voice is the real one,' stated Thakar. As a valley Kashmiri, in exile since 1981, Thakar was also critical of any real desire that those from Azad Jammu and Kashmir would have to change the status quo. 'If the valley were joined to Pakistan, they would have to defer to the valley politicians; if the valley became independent, and they became independent too, they would also have to defer to the valley, which they do not want.'[57] In order not to weaken their movement, however, the APHC and the Azad government of Jammu and Kashmir, continued to present a united front over the issue of independence or unification with Pakistan as well as papering over the cracks of their dissent. According to the former prime minister of Azad Jammu and Kashmir, Sardar Abdul Qayum Khan, what all the Kashmiris continued to want was freedom. 'People are more concerned with freedom than the shape of the thing; whether it is independence or Pakistan will not be decided on the battlefield but through institutional means.'[58]

After over two years in government, Farooq Abdullah had achieved neither 'maximum autonomy' nor a substantial economic package. As in his previous administration, Abdullah's critics accused him of authoritarianism and corruption. He was further embarrassed when his 80 year-old mother, Begum Jehan, said that she would enter politics if corruption was not eliminated from his administration, a charge he refuted.[59] Abdullah was also criticised for his 'woeful dependence on administrative measures and including security forces' operations' as opposed to maintaining a dialogue with the political activists who could be an important link between the people and the administration.[60] Ladakhis remained discontented with the way in which their interests were still subservient to those of the valley. 'Abdullah bargained hard in New Delhi for the economic grant to be increased because of the problems of administering difficult terrain in Ladakh; but when the grant was given, he then distributed it according to population density, which benefited the valley and not Ladakh.'[61] The inhabitants of Jammu continued to fear the dominance of the valley; their discomfort has been compounded by the influx of the Kashmiri Pandits, with whom they have had to compete for professional employment and who have become increasingly assertive of their 'national', Panun Kashmir, identity.[62]

As chief minister, Farooq Abdullah still retained his ability to speak passionately in international fora about the rights of the Kashmiri people and the wrongs perpetrated against them: 'In Kashmir we need development, roads, bridges, clean drinking water; when the people have nothing then of course they say, why not fight?' Contrary to official Indian policy, Abdullah also continued to state that the only solution was for the LOC to be recognised as the international border between the one-third of the state controlled by Pakistan and that controlled by India.

People are asking themselves the question: 'What are we fighting for?' The line [of control] is in exactly the same place. Nothing has changed. We are just killing innocent people on both sides of the line. Take the Siachen glacier – 75 miles of ice. We fire hundred of shells across the line on the ice. Operations on Siachen cost 9 to 10 crores of rupees per day.[63] Couldn't the money be better spent?[64]

Nuclear tests and Lahore

In March 1998 Gujral's United Front government fell after Congress withdrew its support. For the first time in India's political history, a coalition government of the Hindu nationalist, Bharatiya Janata Party (BJP) assumed office with Atal Behari Vajpayee as Prime Minister.[65] Whilst the Pakistani government continued to talk in international fora about the need for solving the core issue between the two countries – Kashmir – and their preference for an international mediator, the BJP government evolved a policy which was more pro-active than any of its predecessors. Firstly, the government repeatedly noted that the whole of the former princely state belonged to India, including Azad Jammu and Kashmir 'forcibly occupied by Pakistan'; secondly, it brought its nuclear programme back into public awareness. The UF government of Deve Gowda had been pursuing a similar line in an attempt to challenge the monopoly which the five members of the 'nuclear club' – US, UK, France, Russia, China – had on nuclear issues, by blocking the adoption of a draft Comprehensive Test Ban Treaty in August 1996. But no Indian government had dared to carry out a nuclear test since 1974. On 11 and 14 May, without warning, the Indian government conducted five underground tests in the western desert state of Rajasthan. The reaction of the international community was immediate and outraged. A serious of punitive actions were announced, which included the imposition of sanctions by the United States, the suspension of a $26 million dollar annual grant by Japan, the freezing of development aid by Germany; in addition, Sweden curtailed a three-year aid agreement and Denmark froze aid at $28 million per year.[66] The Government of Pakistan was immediately requested by President Clinton to show restraint. Nawaz Sharif responded, however, by telling the American President that Pakistan would have no option but to take 'appropriate measures' to protect its sovereignty and security.

Pakistan's nuclear capability was an open secret, but, under continuing pressure from the United States to prevent nuclear proliferation in South Asia, Pakistan had refrained from detonating a nuclear device. Although some commentators believed that Pakistan's interests would be better served by using the nuclear issue to bargain for greater pressure on India from the international community to make some concessions over Kashmir, the force of Pakistan's own public opinion eventually proved too great. On 28 May the Pakistani government announced that it had conducted five tests in the remote Chagai area in the deserts of Balochistan. On 30 May there was a further announcement of one more explosion in order to complete its series of tests. Following Pakistan's detonation, the international community again expressed its disapproval by imposing economic sanctions. The G8 meeting in Britain condemned the tests, stating that they had affected 'both countries' relationships with each of us, worsened rather than improved their security environment, damaged their prospects of achieving their goals of sustainable economic development, and run contrary to global efforts towards nuclear non-proliferation and nuclear disarmament.'[67]

Although Pakistani commentators attempted to portray its economy as robust and able to withstand the effect of sanctions, Pakistan was far more vulnerable economically than India and, consequently the effect of sanctions was assessed as being far greater. 'Whatever measures Sartaj Aziz, Pakistan's finance minister, introduces in the country's budget today to pre-empt the damage from sanctions, there are already signs the government believes they may not be enough,' wrote Mark Nicholson of the *Financial Times* in June 1998.[68] In fact, once both countries agreed to a moratorium on nuclear testing and a commitment to sign the Comprehensive Test Ban Treaty by September 1999, economic sanctions were relaxed. On 11 November 1998 a statement by the press secretary at the White House explained that President Clinton had decided to ease sanctions against India and Pakistan in response to the 'positive steps both countries had taken to address our non-proliferation concerns . . . we and many other countries are very concerned about Pakistan's financial crisis. The International Monetary Fund is working actively with Pakistan to develop a programme to forestall default on its international debt.'[69] Following a decision in January 1999 of the Paris Club, representing 20 OECD countries, loan instalments and interest payments becoming due at the end of 1999 amounting to $3.3 billion were rescheduled. New inflows of $4 billion from the IMF, World Bank and Asian Development Bank were also promised.

Amidst the renewed belligerency between India and Pakistan, the demands of the Kashmiri activists were rapidly receding from international consciousness. As both countries continued to test their long range missiles, which were capable of carrying nuclear warheads, the fear of a renewed arms race between India and Pakistan appeared to be far more alarming than the undefined and apparently unrealisable demands for self-determination of the Kashmiris. Even so in the opinion of the Pakistani government, India's nuclear policy was firmly attached to the Kashmiri issue and its pledge to retake Azad Kashmir. 'Two things aggravated the situation following India's recent tests,' stated Sardar Qayum Khan in July 1998. 'Firstly, Pakistan's information sources told us that the Indian army had brought its attacking forces, paratroopers, helicopter gunships and artillery – up to the ceasefire line in Jammu and Kashmir. Their purpose was to try and overrun Azad Kashmir which could then have been used as a bargaining chip in return for Pakistan's agreement to some accommodation over the valley of Kashmir.'[70] The Indian government, however, denied any such aggressive intentions; Prime Minister

Vajpayee stated that 'there is no tension between the two countries as a result of our tests'.[71]

At government level there was also the realisation that tensions needed to be eased. When the prime ministers of India and Pakistan met at SAARC in Sri Lanka in July, they both agreed to resume formal talks. Once again the Pakistanis hoped to draw in the international community as a mediator. 'These weapons have been made by both the countries and are not meant to display in parades, oil and clean them and apply polish on them,' stated foreign minister Gohar Ayub at the summit. 'There is a possibility of war, there is a flashpoint, the world leadership must come as a third party and encourage them to resolve the Kashmir dispute.'[72]

On 23 September 1998 the two prime ministers agreed 'that an environment of peace and security is in the supreme national interest of both sides and that resolution of all outstanding issues, including Jammu and Kashmir, is essential for this purpose.' In October 1998 Indian foreign secretary K. Ragunath met his Pakistani counterpart, Shamshad Ahmad, in Islamabad. In keeping with the mood of reconciliation, the Pakistani foreign secretary again referred to Kashmir in the light of their changed nuclear status. 'In this drastically changed environment, it is important that we join together for durable peace and durable solution.'[73] The culmination of these discussions was Atal Vajpayee's historic visit on the inaugural run of the Delhi–Lahore bus service on 20 February 1999. In one of the most symbolic meetings between the two prime ministers, Nawaz Sharif welcomed Atal Vajpayee to a banquet at the Lahore Fort. Vajpayee also visited the Minar-e-Pakistan, from where Mohammad Ali Jinnah first announced the League's proposal for an independent Pakistan. Their respective foreign secretaries signed an eight-point memorandum of understanding, pledging to 'engage in bilateral consultations on security concepts and nuclear doctrines' as well as reviewing their communications links, confidence building measures, consultation on security, disarmament and non-proliferation issues.[74] In a document which became known as the Lahore declaration, Prime Ministers Nawaz Sharif and Atal Vajpayee agreed to 'intensify their efforts to resolve all issues, including the issue of Jammu and Kashmir.' They further agreed to 'refrain from intervention and interference in each other's internal affairs.'[75]

Despite the enthusiasm over Vajpayee's visit to Pakistan, it was clear that the Lahore declaration would have no significance if, in reality, neither side could move ahead on the Kashmir issue. Relations between India and Pakistan could not be improved, stated Syed Ali Shah Gilani, chairman of the APHC, without a lasting solution of Jammu and Kashmir being the core issue.'[76] His sentiments were echoed by AJK Prime Minister, Sultan Mehmood: 'We demand that dialogue for solving the Kashmir issue should not be on a bilateral basis between Pakistan and India, but trilateral as Kashmiris are also a party who should decide about their future.'[77] Moreoever, at Lahore, India and Pakistan had reiterated their determination to implement the Simla agreement 'in letter and spirit'. Since, in the opinion of the Kashmiri activists, Simla had already failed, there was every expectation that, yet again, the Lahore declaration would not achieve for the Kashmiris the extent of their demands. Soon after his visit to Lahore, Vajpayee stated that 'Kashmir was an integral part of India and not a single area of Indian soil would be given away.' Following the BJP coalition government's defeat in the April 1999 vote of confidence in the Lok Sabha, Vajpayee remained as caretaker Prime Minister, pending the elections scheduled for September 1999.

Undeclared war?

At Lahore, Nawaz Sharif and Atal Vajpayee had also agreed 'to continue to abide by their respective unilateral moratorium on conducting further nuclear test explosions, unless either side, in exercise of its national sovereignty decides that extraordinary events have jeopardised its supreme interests.' Foreign military analysts were still fearful that the next war between India and Pakistan could be a nuclear one and both countries were under continuing pressure to sign the Comprehensive Test Ban Treaty. Since their 1998 nuclear tests, US deputy secretary of state, Strobe Talbott, had held nine rounds of talks with officials in both India and Pakistan in order to urge them to sign the CTBT. The issue, however, remained sensitive. Analysts suggested that it would be inappropriate for India or Pakistan to appear to be 'rewarded' for their tests by being accepted as formal members of the 'nuclear club' which, according to Strobe Talbott, might then encourage other countries to 'blast their way into the ranks of the nuclear weapons states.' One of the US's areas of basic concern was progress in bilateral discussions to resolve the dispute over Kashmir.[78]

Barely three months after the Lahore declaration, the two countries found themselves closer to war than they had been since 1971. As the winter snows melted, and the Indian and Pakistani armies adopted their forward positions, artillery exchanges between the Indian and Pakistani armies along the LOC increased; villages were evacuated. Over the past two years, the Kargil district close to the line of control, north-east of Srinagar, had been the target of particularly severe attacks. Following intensive cross-border shelling in October 1997, I. K. Gujral had warned Nawaz Sharif that if any country had evil designs 'it will become our duty to defend our nation'.[79] In August 1998 nearly 100 people were reported as being killed during shelling and artillery fire along the lne of control.

In the Spring of 1999, under cover of heavy artillery and mortar fire, about 600 militants[80] moved into the 16,000 ft mountains in the Kargil area. Unlike the regular skirmishes, however, this operation, which resembled the surprise airlift of Indian troops onto the Siachen glacier in April 1984, involved occupation of 130 previously held Indian picquets. Unobserved by the Indians, the militants had succeeded in taking over defensive positions, which the Indians manned in summer but vacated during winter and had failed to patrol. According to Indian intelligence sources, a lack of co-ordination between India's Research and Analysis Wing (RAW) and military intelligence officials 'and the absence of mutual confidence between them led to the situation in Kashmir assuming such serious proportions.'[81] From these strategic vantage points, the militants claimed that they had 'liberated' 120 square miles of 'Indian' Kashmir. Not only were they able to threaten the security of the road from Srinagar to Leh but Indian supply routes to the Siachen glacier as well. The Indian government maintained that the militants were Afghan 'mercenaries', including Pakistani regular soldiers and reportedly some British Muslim volunteers,[82] all of whom had crossed the line of control after being trained by the Pakistani army in high altitude fighting and armed with US stinger missiles. The Pakistani government, however, denied any involvement in the incursion and stated that the militants were indigenous 'freedom fighters' fighting for the liberation of Kashmir.

In late May, for the first time since the insurgency began and with the West 'too busy' to focus on Kashmir,[83] India resorted to aerial bombardments of the militants in the Kargil district. Pakistan immediately retaliated to the aerial activity so close to the line of control by shooting down two MiG fighter planes which had reportedly crossed the LOC into Pakistani airspace One pilot was killed, the other was captured as a prisoner of war (and later returned to India).[84] A day later, an Indian helicopter gunship was also shot down. The danger of such 'incidents' leading to an escalation of hostilities was demonstrated when a school on the Pakistani side of the line of control was accidentally hit. Ten children were killed and there were popular calls for 'revenge'. Tempers also ran high in India when the bodies of six Indian soldiers, which were returned to the Indian government by the Pakistani army, appeared to have been mutilated, a charge which the Pakistani government denied.

In an attempt to reduce mounting tensions, Nawaz Sharif at once used the hotline telephone to speak to Vajpayee. 'Sending planes will only make matters worse,' he reportedly told the Indian prime minister. The airstrikes, however, continued and India also announced plans to send in ground troops. In view of the difficult terrain in which the militants had taken up their positions, Pakistan's assertions that they were entirely indigenous 'freedom fighters' met with considerable scepticism. They were clearly well-trained and well-armed. 'You cannot venture up there in shorts and a singlet. The conditions under which they are operating mean they need back up. Food rationing alone is an ongoing commitment. A force of 600 men would need a ton of food a day. The only people who could supply that sort of back up are the Pakistanis and they could not do so without the assistance of the army,' commented Brian Cloughley, former deputy commander of UNMOGIP.[85]

Whether the incursion had been sanctioned by Prime Minister Nawaz Sharif was initially unclear. It seemed hardly credible that, soon after shaking hands with Vajpayee over the Lahore declaration in February 1999, Sharif could have covertly sanctioned an operation across the line of control which

was bound to have far-reaching repercussions for their attempts at reconciliation. George Fernandes, the Indian defence minister, chose to exonerate
both the Pakistani Prime Minister and the ISI, as well as offering safe passage
to the infiltrators to return back across the LOC (an offer, which he later
denied). Fernandes's political opponents in the Congress Party believed that
he had been misled by the Pakistani prime minister's denials and at once called
for Fernandes's resignation. The head of the ISI, Lt General Zia Ud Din, had
been nominated by Nawaz Sharif; it did not therefore seem possible for either
the ISI or Sharif not to have known about – and consequently sanctioned – the
incursion. Nawaz Sharif also appeared well in control of the army. In October
1998 he had obliged the army chief, General Jehangir Karamat, to resign after he
had openly criticised the government and installed General Pervez Musharraf, in
supersession to other more senior generals.

The Kargil offensive also appeared to have the characteristics of a well-
planned military operation which was orientated not towards the valley and
the Kashmiris' right of self-determination but towards taking up the offensive
in order to pressurise the Indians on the Siachen glacier. It was no secret that
the Pakistanis were still annoyed at the incursions which the Indians had made
north of map coordinate NJ9842, where the demarcation of the line of control
ended. Instead, however, of giving any explanations, the Government of Pakistan
became involved in a series of implausible denials which no one believed and
which were all the more confusing since they were not consistent.

Whilst the obvious motivation behind the incursion was obscured behind
Pakistani denials of involvement, analysts looked to the reasons why Pakistan
should try yet again to 'internationalise' the Kashmiri issue. 'Sharif is
attempting to consolidate his personal power in the face of considerable
opposition, particularly from the regions. He may believe that his position
could be significantly bolstered if he spearheaded the drive to achieve a deeply
felt national goal,' commented *Oxford Analytica*.[86] Sharif was also believed to be
trying to please the small but influential Islamic orthodox lobby in Pakistan as
well as appeasing the cross-border influence of the Taliban in Afghanistan.
Was this, commentators speculated, a repeat of the ill-advised 1965 war, where
a coterie of advisers had persuaded their superiors to undertake what
Pakistan's own journalists were calling an adventurist war?

In support of Indian allegations of Pakistani complicity, the Indians
publicised the fact that they had found a Pakistani identity card and army pay
papers in an abandoned rucksack following their recapture of stategic
positions on the mountains.[87] In June 1999 the Indian government also
released the transcript of two taped telephone conversations allegedly recorded
on 26 and 29 May between Pakistani chief of army staff, General Pervez
Musharraf, who was on a visit to Beijing, and the chief of general staff,
General Mohammed Aziz, in Islamabad. In addition to being proof of
Pakistani involvement, the Indians believed that the conversations demonstrated
how the Pakistani generals were keen to use the operation as a public relations

exercise. As Aziz was recorded as saying to Musharraf: 'Today for the last two hours the BBC has been continuously reporting on the air strikes by India. Keep using this – let them keep using this – let them keep dropping bombs. As far as internationalisation is concerned, this is the fastest this has happened.' In an attempt to bolster their argument that the Indians were the aggressors, the two generals allegedly agreed that no mention should be made of the bombs which were dropped on the Indian side of the LOC, only of those dropped on the Pakistani side.[88] When the transcripts were released to the press, the Government of Pakistan described the conversations as 'fabricated'.

There was also no shortage of militants who – even though belatedly – claimed that their organisations were involved. On 31 May Lashkar-i Toiba gave a statement saying that 1,000 of its mujaheddin were in Kargil. On 9 June, their spokesman, Abdullah Montazir, stated that they had begun planning the Kargil operation last year. On 14 June, Fazlul Rehman Khalil of the Harkat-ul Mujaheddin said that their cadres were in Kargil and that they would welcome all Muslims for the jihad from Egypt, Chechnya and Sudan. Lashkar-i Toiba even warned the Sharif government that, if under foreign pressure, they were asked to withdraw from Kargil, they would destroy the government.[89] In an attempt to give substance to the assertion that 'indigenous' Kashmiris were in the Kargil mountains, sympathisers described how they were surviving on a diet of uncooked barley flour combined with sugar and water as well as foodstuffs left in the bunkers by the Indian army.[90] From the Indian perspective, however, even if the insurgents included members of the militant organisations, they were in Kargil with the assistance of the Pakistani military in order to carry out directives which clearly accorded with Pakistan's irredentist foreign policy objectives.

Seven weeks after its offensive began, Indian officials were admitting that they had lost 251 men, with 420 wounded at an estimated cost of $4 million a day.[91] They also stated that they had killed approximately 467 'Pakistani soldiers' and 120 insurgents in the operation against Kargil.[92] As was recognised by Indian Air Force chief Amal Yaswant Tipnis, it would, however, take time to dislodge the infiltrators. 'Pushing the intruders back is a slow process. It is difficult terrain and they are holding positions on high ground.'[93] Described by the Indian government as 'one-third effective', it was also evident that India's costly aerial bombardment would not be sufficient to flush out the insurgents. 'Flying amidst mountain peaks in such treacherous conditions poses tremendous problems; bombs which do not hit their targets would have no impact because they would be immediately absorbed by the snow,' stated Brian Cloughley.[94]

Large numbers of civilians were once more the casualties of the conflict. According to Lord Ahmed, a Kashmiri of Mirpuri orgin, who had settled in Britain, twenty thousand people had been displaced from villages in and around Kargil and Dras because of the offensive and were currently in Ladakh because they had nowhere else to go. His aim, as Vice Chairman of 'Justice for Jammu and Kashmir' in the UK, was to have them recognised officially as international refugees, as opposed to displaced persons, so that they could be the recipients of humanitarian aid.[95]

At a political level, the atmosphere between India and Pakistan remained hostile. At the end of May, UN Secretary-General, Kofi Annan, had offered to send an envoy to New Delhi and Islamabad to defuse tensions, but Vajpayee rejected the offer. If an envoy needed to be sent to discuss peace, he said, he should be sent to Islamabad and not to New Delhi. Following the visit to New Delhi by Pakistani foreign minister, Sartaj Aziz, Indian foreign minister, Jaswant Singh, was sceptical about the benefits of any talks. 'The conduct of Pakistan raises serious doubts about the professed aim of "defusing tension" as averred by Aziz.'[96]

A day after the talks collapsed, during a visit to the Kargil district, Prime Minister Vajpayee accused Pakistan of 'betraying India's friendship'. In Srinagar, the APHC organised a strike to protest against the Indian prime minister's visit in order to warn India that 'it could not be kept in bondage for long by the use of brute military force'.[97] Yet again, endorsing Pakistan's position that the insurgents were 'indigenous' and that their actions reflected the Kashmiris' demand for self-determination, their leaders appealed to the international community to take note of India's 'crime of trampling all principles of liberty'. But it was also clear that the focus of the international community's interest in the Kashmir conflict had been transferred from the situation in the valley to Kargil. That the Kashmiris were no further advanced in their demand for self-determination was temporarily forgotten amidst concern about escalating tensions between India and Pakistan. Kashmiri activists believed, from reading the enormous coverage given to Kosovo in the western press, compared with the sporadic mention of Kashmir, that the international community was still far too preoccupied with Kosovo to take on another humanitarian issue.

The shift in focus to Kargil also provided the opportunity for the Indian security forces in the valley to continue to crush political dissent with relative impunity. 'There is a massive contradiction here. In the far north, India is fighting the good fight,' reported journalist Peter Popham. 'But 125 miles down the road, India is behaving like the most heavy-handed sort of occupying power.' As was reported at the time, in mid-June three militants came to a village in the northwest corner of the Kashmir valley, where they took refuge in a house. The following day, the Border Security Forces came and surrounded the area and set fire to the house, burning two of the militants. 'Then they didn't stop there,' related one of the villagers, Ghulam Kadar, 'and set the entire area on fire, a student was burnt alive, schoolbooks in hand ...' Fifty houses were also destroyed. 'Everywhere were heaps of bricks and stones and blackened timber and scorched corrugated iron roofing. The newly homeless ex-residents stood about mutely poking at what was left of their lives,' wrote Popham, who visited the area.[98] Ghulam Kadar also pointed to the dilemma of civilians, as always, caught between the Indian security forces and the militants: 'The militants come to our villages, what can we do? We've no connection with them but if someone points a gun and says we are going to stay in your house.'[99] In another incident, the police were reported as setting fire to more than fifty stalls in the market in Srinagar in retaliation for the killing of one of their colleagues.[100]

The Indian government also did not want the APHC leaders making political capital out of the Kargil operation. When Shabir Shah tried to visit Kargil, he was arrested. APHC leaders, including Yasin Malik, who took out a protest march in Srinagar, requesting the international community to address the Kashmir issue, were detained for a day.[101] New Delhi also imposed a temporary ban on Pakistan TV cable transmissions within India in order to stop an abnormal level of 'propaganda'. Pakistan's minister for information, Mushahid Hussain, described the ban as an attempt by India 'to hide facts both from its own people and from the international community.'[102] Viewers in Pakistan, however, who watched the Indian channel, Zee-TV, were also branded as unpatriotic.

Despite the attempts of both countries to counteract the news statements emanating from each other's television networks, they were unable to prevent the spread of a 'cyber-war' on the internet. 'The battle of electronic propaganda, or cyber-war, has become the latest mode of attack as an increasing number of people from both sides of the conflict churn out inflammatory e-mails and set up jingoistic web pages,' reported Charu Lata Joshi of the BBC. On 12 June, 'India Votes.com' posed a question to web-surfers: 'After the barbaric act of Pakistan what should India do now?' As Joshi reported: 'Heated responses flew back to the site, as each person tried to be more nationalistic than the other.... The tragedy is that while many hardline attitudes can now easily be accessed on the internet, there appear to be few sites which advocate a breaking down of the barriers that divide the two countries.'[103]

Throughout the Indian offensive against the infiltrators in the Kargil district, the Pakistani government called on the international community to assist in a resolution of the Kashmir dispute. Unconvinced by Pakistan's denials of involvement, the western response was far more supportive of India's demands for a withdrawal than Pakistan's request for discussions to solve the core issue of Kashmir. At the June G8 summit in Cologne, in their statement on regional issues, the member countries expressed their concern about:

> the continuing military confrontation in Kashmir following the infiltration by armed intruders which violated the line of control. We regard any military action to change the status quo as irresponsible. We therefore call for an immediate end to these actions, restoration of the line of control and for the parties to work for an immediate cessation of the fighting, full respect in the future for the line of control and the resumption of the dialogue between India and Pakistan in the spirit of the Lahore declaration.[104]

President Clinton put the blame squarely on Pakistan in a message to Nawaz Sharif, advising him to withdraw the infiltrators, whom the Americans believed were Pakistani soldiers from the Northern Light Infantry. Although the

Pakistani government protested at the American description of the 'Kashmiri mujaheddin' as 'infiltrators from Pakistan', international opinion continued to accept that the militants in Kargil had come from Pakistan. 'Pakistan is the instigator here,' said a senior US administration official. 'Pakistan has to figure out how to restore the status quo ante.'[105] In Moscow, deputy foreign minister, Grigory Karasin called on Pakistan's ambassador, Mansoor Alam, and also asked Islamabad to withdraw the infiltrators. At the end of June, US General Anthony Zinni, commander in chief of the US Central Command (CENTCOM), accompanied by a senior American diplomat, Gibson Lanpher, visited Islamabad for talks. Instead, however, of agreeing to bring pressure on India to change the status quo, the Americans reportedly repeated President Clinton's request to Nawaz Sharif to put pressure on the infiltrators to withdraw.

As a traditional ally, China had assured Pakistan of its 'deep and abiding interest in and support for the sovereignty, territorial integrity, independence and security of Pakistan'.[106] This did not mean, however, encouraging ideas of 'self -determination' amongst the Kashmiris and during Nawaz Sharif's visit to Beijing in late June, the Chinese leaders were noticeably cool towards accepting Pakistan's claim that the insurgents in Kargil were 'freedom fighters'. 'China is worried that it could be Kosovo today, Kashmir tomorrow and then Tibet the next day,' commented a western analyst.[107] China had also been working towards improved relations with India. In 1993, the two countries had signed a Peace and Tranquility agreement as well as another pact to lessen tensions along the disputed Sino-Indian border. China had also begun to hint that Pakistan should consider accepting the LOC as the international border.[108] Elsewhere numerous other diplomatic initiatives took place. Indian foreign secretary, K. Raghunath, went to France and Britain to lobby support for the Indian position on Kashmir. Pakistani diplomats tried to gain support for their position at the conference of the Organisation of Islamic Countries (OIC) in Burkino Faso.

In the initial weeks of the conflict, the fear of escalation, leading to a nuclear war appeared more real than ever before. Pakistan's intimation that the war could lead to the use of nuclear weapons if a solution were not forthcoming on the Kashmir issue was regarded as tantamount to 'nuclear blackmail'. Although India had declared that it would not use nuclear weapons in a first strike, military analysts continued to ask whether, in view of Pakistan's inability to win a conventional war against India's superior forces, it would be tempted into making a nuclear weapon attack on India's military installations? Although Pakistan's minister for information, Mushahid Hussain, described the prospect of nuclear war as 'outlandish', his refusal to state categorically that Pakistan would not use nuclear weapons in a first strike enhanced the perception that Pakistan was the aggressor.[109]

Rumours of a possible attack by India across the international border in the Punjab also caused apprehension on both sides of the frontier. Although the Indian government repeatedly announced that it did not want the war to escalate, India's Strike Corps, comprising about 10,000 mechanised troops, armoured formations and infantry divisions were warned to make preparations to leave their bases. The Indian navy was also put on high alert.[110] American spy satellite photographs also revealed tanks, heavy guns and other material on trains at a base in Rajasthan. Although the Indian ambassador in Washington described the arrangements as 'precautionary', in view of the fact that the Indians would be unlikely to use tanks in the mountains of Kashmir, the Americans deduced that India was preparing to invade Pakistan across the international border.[111] On the Indian side of the international frontier, the population of Khem Karan, scene of intense fighting in the 1965 war, dropped from 16,000 to 5,000. Despite the cross-border hostility, however, visitors continued to make the journey both ways on the twice-weekly train between Delhi and Lahore.[112] In Pakistan, those living close to the international frontier and the LOC also feared the consequences of an escalation in fighting. In Azad Jammu and Kashmir more than 25,000 people reportedly fled the Mangla area in Mirpur to escape cross-border shelling.[113]

Pakistanis, who did not believe their government's explanations, were cynical about what, if anything, the offensive in Kargil would achieve. 'With each passing day,' wrote Ayaz Amir in *Dawn* on 25 June, 'it should be coming clear even to the benighted that in Kashmir we are allowing ourselves to get caught in a bind. While the ultimate objective of the venture under way remains shrouded in a mist of confusion and conflicting statements, the western powers, whose opinion matters to us because they are our creditors, are not buying the line that the Pakistani army has nothing to do with the occupation of the Kargil heights and the fighting which this has sparked.'[114] Since the Pakistani government was not admitting its involvement, no explanation could be given on the possible outcome of pressurising the Indians on the Kashmir issue. Amongst Indians, who were measuring the force of Vajpayee's reactions as a yardstick of his possible electoral success, attitudes were hardening. As one commentator observed: 'The Kargil infiltration and the body bags have been brought home to all parts of India through the widespread ownership of television sets. Prior to the Kargil infiltration it would have been possible for the Indian prime minister to settle the Kashmir issue by recognising the line of control as the international border and not asking for the third of Kashmir which India calls Pakistan Occupied Kashmir. Now that concession by India is politically very difficult. There is a feeling that Pakistan has shot itself in the foot in Kargil and delayed any rapprochement for a very long time.'[115]

Considerable publicity was given by the Indians to the recapture of strategic locations along the 85-mile battlefront. The recapture of Point 5140 on the Tololing height, described as 'unparalleled in the history of mountain warfare'[116] marked the beginning of a series of victories claimed by the Indian government, in what was known as 'Operation Vijay'; the battle for Tiger Hill in July was described by India as 'a turning point' since the 16,500 ft peak overlooked the main road from Kargil to Leh. A Pakistani army press briefing, however, described the Indian claim of capturing Tiger Hill as 'makebelieve'. Analysts believed, however, that due to the difficult conditions in which the Indians were fighting and their own unpreparedness for a high-altitude campaign, the victories were less glorious than their spokesmen liked to portray. 'It is more than likely that the forces holding Tiger Hill scuttled their operations and then the Indians came in and claimed their positions,' commented Brian Cloughley.[117] Local inhabitants of the area also criticised the Indian government for its conduct of the war: 'They send soldiers up here from places like Rajasthan which are at sea level, and order them to climb a mountain.'[118] What was given less publicity was the extent to which Indian forces on Siachen were feeling the pinch on their supplies during the occupation of the Kargil heights. In June Vajpayee had also warned Clinton of the disastrous effect which the body bags were having on public opinion.

Victory or defeat?

In the tense atmosphere of the continuing conflict in early July, Prime Minister Nawaz Sharif requested an urgent meeting with President Clinton in Washington. Following their meeting Clinton and Sharif issued a statement which affirmed the Pakistani Prime Minister's commitment to take 'concrete steps' for the restoration of the line of control in accordance with the Simla agreement. Known as the Washington agreement, Clinton agreed to take 'a personal interest in encouraging an expeditious resumption and intensification' of Indo-Pakistani bilateral efforts, once 'the sanctity' of the line of control was fully restored.'[119] But, as numerous commentators pointed out, how could the Pakistani Prime Minister honour his pledge to Clinton to put pressure on the infiltrators to withdraw, if, as he had earlier maintained he did not control them? How also could Clinton's 'personal interest' in the Kashmir issue be binding on any incoming US government once Clinton had left office?

On 12 July, Nawaz Sharif broadcast to the nation, explaining his reasons for requesting the militants to withdraw. 'Our decision to give diplomacy another chance has not been taken out of any pressure, haste or worry.' Without explaining the ambiguity of Pakistan's earlier denials insofar as concerned Pakistan's control of the infiltrators, Sharif told a nationwide audience that the objective of the militants in capturing the Kargil heights was to draw the attention of the international community to the Kashmir issue. 'Their action has vindicated our stand that Kashmir is a nuclear flashpoint.'[120] With the promise by the United States to assist in a resolution of the Kashmir issue, the attention of the international community had been drawn towards the Kashmir issue; it was therefore no longer necessary for the insurgents to remain in the Kargil mountains.

Nawaz Sharif's commitment to request the infiltrators to withdraw was immediately rejected by the Kashmiri activists and militants who stated that they were not bound to honour any accord between Pakistan and the United

States without their consent. The Hizb again affirmed that it would not rest until the 'illegal' rule in 'Indian-held' Kashmir was overthrown. 'Kargil is our own land and why should we be asked to withdraw?' asked Kaleem Siddiqui, spokesman for the Hizb. Members of the Jamaat-i Islami in Azad Jammu and Kashmir staged a protest rally in Muzaffarabad.[121] Jamaat leader, Munawwar Hassan, criticised Nawaz Sharif for letting down the army, the mujaheddin and dashing the hopes of 140 million people of Pakistan. 'He will not escape this.'[122] In a departure from Gilani's usual pro-Pakistani stance, the chairman of the APHC made it clear that although Pakistan had been supporting 'the indigenous struggle of the people of Jammu and Kashmir morally, diplomatically and politically . . . this does not mean Pakistan can take a decision on our behalf.'[123] The JKLF criticised the Pakistani government for its 'misadventure' in Kargil, condemning it as a wrong action for a right cause.[124]

Former President, Farooq Leghari, chairman of the Millat Party in Pakistan, demanded Sharif's immediate resignation for what former foreign minister Sardar Aseff Ali, called a 'complete diplomatic surrender.'[125] Former prime minister, Benazir Bhutto, however, was critical of the decision to send infiltrators into Kargil in the first place. Kargil, she said, was the 'biggest blunder in Pakistan's history, which has cost Pakistan dearly. Those who were killed were sent back quietly because the Pakistani government did not have the courage to own them.'[126] In an interview with the BBC, she said that she was sure Nawaz Sharif had authorised the intrusion to divert attention from his domestic failures and charges of corruption.[127] Bhutto had earlier suggested an open border policy between India and Pakistan (as had occurred between Israel and Jordan) in order to resolve the Kashmiri crisis. She also recognised that, as prime minister, she was wrong in 'holding Indo-Pakistan relations hostage' to the single issue of Kashmir in the hope of highlighting the cause of the Kashmiri people. 'That policy certainly did not advance the cause of peace in South Asia.'[128]

In India, the withdrawal of the insurgents was hailed as a victory. At a BJP rally in New Delhi, Indian home minister, L. K. Advani, reminded his audience that the Kargil infiltration must have been underway at the same time as Pakistan 'talked peace' in Lahore and that the Indian military operation in Kargil would continue until the 'last intruder' was evicted.[129] 'Guns' said defence minister, George Fernandes 'will answer' any infiltrators who remained in their positions. Jaswant Singh, India's foreign minister, ruled out any early resumption of talks.[130] Prime Minister Vajpayee, however, referred again to the Lahore declaration as 'a firm commitment between India and Pakistan to resolve all issues bilaterally.. let us see if Pakistan is ready to make a fresh beginning.'[131] In order to highlight the consequences of Pakistan's 'warmongering' even further, the India League, paid an estimated £25,250 for a full-page advertisement in *The Times* (London)[132] (as well as an additional sum for an advertisement in *The New York Times*): 'A State within a State – a modern Rogue Army with its finger on the nuclear button', which described:

'A five decades long legacy of lies ... and lawlessness.'[133] The Pakistani High
Commission in London protested at the malicious 'propaganda' against its
army, which had 'an impeccable record of professionalism and excellence'. It
was, however, becoming increasingly difficult for the Pakistani government to
keep up the pretence that neither it nor the army had had anything to do with
the incursion. (On 14 August, the NLI was inducted into the regular army and
64 personnel, mostly from the NLI, were given gallantry awards for their role
in Kargil.)[134]

The withdrawal of the infiltrators in mid-July also coincided with a strike in
the valley called by the Hurriyat in order to commemorate the 1931 'martyrs' –
those who had been killed in the Abdul Qadir incident nearly seventy years
ago. The National Conference and the APHC observed 13 July as a day of
homage. The APHC urged for a solution to the Kashmir issue in order to
avert 'a dangerous holocaust' in Kashmir.[135] Militant activity in the state again
hit the headlines. In Doda district, north of Jammu, an attack was made on a
village defence committee, set up to protect remote villages from such attacks.
The villagers engaged the militants in a shoot out, after which ten villagers and
five mlitants were dead.[136] In another attack four construction workers were
killed in Poonch. On 21 July, a hand grenade attack in a crowded vegetable
market in Baramula killed two civilians and wounded another sixteen.
Habibullah Wani, a local Congress Party supporter was shot dead in Srinagar.
On 27 July a bomb exploded on a bus travelling from Rawalpindi to
Muzaffarabad in Azad Kashmir. At least seven people were reported killed
and 19 injured. It was the first such incident to occur in AJK.[137]

Nawaz Sharif faced continuing domestic criticism for sanctioning the
withdrawal. Hardline Islamist parties in Pakistan remained outraged that he
had 'caved in' to US pressure. On 25 July, according to the BBC's Islamabad
correspondent, Owen Bennett-Jones, 'the most significant' street protest
against the government of Nawaz Sharif took place in Lahore, during which
tens of thousands of protesters shouted 'Down with America' and burnt effigies
of President Clinton. The Jamaat again called for Sharif to be overthrown.
Other militant groups vowed to keep fighting in Kashmir, with the threat that
they would carry out suicide attacks.[138] From the Indian perspective, the fact
that Nawaz Sharif had failed to follow through an unofficial peace initiative
conducted by a respected former Pakistani high commissioner in India, Niaz
Naik, and R. K. Mishra, a confidante of India's national security adviser,
demonstrated that he was playing 'both sides of the fence.' Had he agreed to
the Indian offer of a phased withdrawal of the infiltrators three weeks before
the withdrawal actually took place, many lives could have been saved. But, the
Indians believed, it was not until the infiltrators started to encounter military
reversals that he made his visit to Clinton in the United States.[139]

In the weeks following the withdrawal, there were conflicting reports of
militants still operating across the line of control. Fighters were reported as
holding positions in the Mushkoh valley, Dras and Batalik sectors. Finally, on

26 July – ten weeks after India's aerial bombardment began and the news hit international headlines – Lieutentant-General N. C. Vij, Indian head of military operations, announced that the last of the Kashmiri infiltrators had been expelled. 'There is no Pakistani presence on Indian territory.'[140] At the end of July Indian sources confirmed that their casualties were 417 soldiers dead, 570 wounded and 15 missing. On the Pakistani side they stated that 690 Pakistani soldiers and 150 'guerillas' were reported as dead.[141] Actual figures for casulaties are believed to be much higher.

The lives of thousands in Kargil and the surrounding villages were devastated. At the height of the shelling, Dr Zohara Bannu, one of only three doctors left in the district hospital in Kargil, told journalist Peter Popham: 'We get many cases of premature deliveries due to the shock of constant shelling, tension-induced abortions, depression, insommia.'[142] When the hospital was hit, shattering the windows in the nurses' quarters, the nurses fled. According to the BBC's Delhi correspondent, Daniel Lak, more than 30,000 people had left their homes during the fighting. 'The departing helicopters and truck convoys of the Indian armed forces go home amid a feeling of victory, a job well done evicting intruders from across the line of control. But a few months away from Kargil's unbelievably harsh winter, it is clear that the battle to rebuild shattered lives and avoid hunger and disease will be an even greater challenge for India.'[143] In the valley, the tourist industry again had to face the repercussions of the fighting: 'The houseboat owners, egged on by the Tourism Department, splashed out on paint and fairy lights this year in the hope that the bad times were over,' wrote the Frontline correspondent of *The Independent*. 'And up to mid-May they were. Nearly 150,000 tourists came to Kashmir in the spring – more than for the whole of 1998. But then the Kargil war broke out and they all disappeared.'[144]

The Indian army also prepared to maintain a year round watch of about 8,000 to 10,000 soldiers at an estimated cost of £1.8 million a day along the LOC in Kargil district. 'The task is formidable and the costs astronomical,' said an army officer stationed in Dras.[145] On an earlier visit to Kargil, General V. P. Malik, the Indian army chief, had also pointed to the difficulties of securing the LOC, stating that it was too long and too rugged for the army to defend it perfectly.[146] As the Indian armed forces realised, even after the Kargil operation, militancy in the valley remained. On 1 August, official Indian sources reported an encounter with 'heavily-armed Pakistani-backed fighters' in Kupwara district, 120 miles south-west of Kargil; they killed six 'infiltrators' and were working to flush out the rest.[147]

With a general election scheduled for September, Vajpayee worked hard to counteract criticism from the opposition parties in India, which condemned the BJP government for a massive failure of intelligence which had facilitated infiltration from across the LOC in the first place. A reshuffle in RAW was immediately announced. The formation of a committee, under veteran defence analyst, K. Subramanyam, to investigate how there had been such a lapse of security was greeted with some scepticism. 'Generally speaking, official committees in India have not succeeded in shedding much light on the subject of their enquiry,' commented the *Times of India*.[148] In an attempt to win the propaganda war with Pakistan, India's information and broadcasting minister, Pramod Mahajan, announced that about $100m would be spent to improve the state-run TV networks in Kashmir. During a visit to Kashmir, local people had told Mahajan that the reception of Pakistani television was better than that of India's state-run Doordarshan network.

Despite the official Pakistani perception of 'victory' in internationalising the Kashmir issue in Kargil, the loss to Pakistan's international credibility was significant. The financial cost, the loss of life, the loss of India's trust in future peacemaking initiatives, the boost to the Indian government's position over the state of Jammu and Kashmir, was also considerable. India also benefited from a thaw in relations with the United States, which had strongly criticised the Indian government for its nuclear tests in May 1998. On 20 July Clinton had made a surprise telephone call to Vajpayee applauding India's 'restraint' in Kargil. He also reaffirmed his interest in making a visit to India, which had been cancelled the previous year.[149] U.S. Secretary of State, Madeleine Albright, spoke out against the militancy: 'Acts of terrorism must stop immediately because such actions make the Kashmir conflict more, not less, difficult to resolve.'[150] When Albright met Indian foreign minister, Jaswant Singh, in Singapore on the eve of the ASEAN regional forum, according to a senior US official, 'the Indian foreign minister expressed appreciation and gratitude for the US role in helping to bring the Kargil problem to a satisfactory resolution which it is not quite at yet, but is heading in that direction.' An Indian spokesman called the talks 'very good and can-did.'[151] In a move destined to please the United States, Singh also confirmed Delhi's commitment to signing the Comprehensive Test Ban Treaty. Nawaz Sharif, meanwhile, was seeking support from amongst Pakistan's Islamic friends. During his July visit, he described the 'important role' which Saudi Arabia was playing in the resolution of the conflict over Kashmir.[152]

That both India and Pakistan could claim 'victory' after Kargil, demonstrated, yet again, how far from resolution the Kashmiri conflict was. A decade after the insurgency in the valley began – over fifty years since the partition of the sub-continent led to the contest between India and Pakistan over ownership of the state – there was still no consensus amongst the main protagonists. How therefore could there be victory? Those Kashmiris who had grown old in their fight for political liberty and whose sons had taken up the struggle were still pawns on the Indo-Pakistani chessboard of diplomatic rivalry.

After Kargil

On 10 August, a Pakistani naval aircraft was shot down by two Indian MiG-21 fighter planes in the Rann of Kutch. The Indian government claimed that the plane had violated Indian airspace and, when challenged, had acted in an 'evasive and offensive' manner. Accusing the Indians of 'cold-blooded murder', the Pakistani government stated that the plane, whose 16 crew and passengers all died, was on a routine training exercise and had been shot down over Pakistani territory. The Indian government, however, maintained that the aeroplane was on a spying mission and alleged that, since May, Pakistani aircraft had already violated Indian airspace eight times. The precise location of the plane before it was shot down was more sensitive than at first appeared; although the border between Sindh and Kutch had been settled by arbitration in 1965, the 38 mile estuary of Sir Creek, rich in oil and natural resources, which separates the Pakistani province of Sindh from the Indian state of Gujarat , was still not demarcated. A day later, the Indian government alleged that Pakistani forces had fired at three Indian helicopters which were visiting the site of the downed plane, whose wreckage had landed on both sides of the international frontier. The Pakistanis said that they were not firing at heli-copters but two MiG fighter jets, which were accompanying the helicopters and were in Pakistani airspace. Once more, fearful that renewed hostility be-tween the two countries could escalate into armed conflict, the United States called for restraint and urged India and Pakistan to respect their 1991 commit-ment not to fly within six miles of their common frontier. The US also called for a resumption of the stalled peace dialogue initiated six months previously.

Although the shooting down of the plane was not directly related to the Kashmir issue, the continuing antagonism between India and Pakistan, following a tit for tat pattern of claim and counter-claim, meant that any hope of reconciliation, and consequently any resumption of political dialogue, was impossible. 'It is hard to be optimistic at this stage,' stated James Rubin, US State department spokesman, after the plane was shot down. 'If anything, today's events are an indication that we're going in the wrong direction.'[153] Militant leaders based in Azad Jammu and Kashmir were reported as threatening to take revenge on India for the attack 'such that India will remember for years to come'.[154] Yet again the Pakistani government requested international mediation to assist in resolving its differences with India. On the basis that Indians and Pakistanis 'spoke the same language' and therefore did not need an interpreter, the Government of India continued to reject any third party involvement, either by the United States or the United Nations.

Within the Indian-administered state of Jammu and Kashmir, there was a noticeable increase in militant activity throughout the summer. The Indian authorities believed that over 1,000 militants had recently succeeded in crossing the LOC, most of whom had entered the valley near Kupwara, a poor region where support for the militancy remained strong. 'They crawled through forests described by a brigadier as so thick that "a man could pass under your nose on a cloudy day and you wouldn't see him",' reported Julian West from Kupwara in the *Sunday Telegraph*.[155] Daring attacks by militants, reportedly belonging to the Harkat-ul Mujaheddin and the Hizb-ul

Mujaheddin, on the camps of the 30,000 strong Rashtriya (National) Rifles –
the counter-insurgency force on whom responsibility had devolved for
fighting the militancy in the valley – sent 'shock waves' throughout the entire
security set up of the country.[156] In early August, about 40 militants occupied
houses surrounding an army post in Kupwara district. At dawn they opened
fire with automatic weapons and rockets, killing five Indian soldiers and
injuring 12. The following day, Colonel Balbir Singh, who was investigating
the attack, and four of his men were ambushed and killed. According to Julian
West, the militants were remarkably brazen. Before the attack in Kupwara
district, they had played cricket on a tightly guarded pitch near the army post.
Throughout August there were numerous other incidents, including a
landmine explosion which killed four policemen and injured more than ten.
The Indian authorities believed that the resurgence of militant activity was a
'now or never' initiative on behalf of the Pakistani government to rekindle the
insurgency in the valley after having failed to 'internationalise' the issue in
Kargil. The Indians also noted increased activity on the Siachen glacier. In
poor visibility, a Pakistani patrol attempted unsuccessfully to capture an Indian
post. Five Pakisani soldiers were reported dead.

In response to the upsurge in violence and following a high-level meeting
of the Intelligence Bureau (IB), the Special Secretary (Security) and the
Director, Special Protection Group (SPG), it was agreed to increase security
forces in the state, 'denuded' on account of Kargil, with special emphasis on
'synergising' the operations against the militants as well as restructuring
intelligence networks. As reported by Rahul Bedi for the BBC, the diversion
of 40,000 troops 'overnight' from the valley to Kargil had 'gravely weakened
the security grid in the Kashmir valley'. With an armed rebellion which was
'no where close to ending', and with the LOC requiring constant supervision,
army officials admitted that the security vacuum had been inadequately filled
by the overstretched Rashtriya Rifles. They also conceded that frequent
deployment had led to mental breakdowns and 'fraggin', when soldiers went
beserk, shooting their comrades and then themselves.[157]

Both Pakistan and India celebrated their 52nd year of independence in a
sombre atmosphere. In his independence day speech on 14 August, Nawaz
Sharif accused India of being a threat to regional peace and security, following
the downing of the Pakistani plane in the Rann of Kutch. India's independence celebrations on 15 August were held amidst heavy security. Atal
Vajpayee made it clear that there would be no resumption of dialogue with
Pakistan while Kashmiri 'separatists' were trained in camps on Pakistani soil.
'How can meaningful talks be held in this atmosphere? Pakistan must
understand that by encouraging terrorist activities, it can't resolve problems.'[158]
In the valley, independence day was observed as a black day. Most shops in
the valley were closed and traffic was reduced.

The Indian government also believed that the objective of the sudden
increase in militant attacks was in order to create panic by acts of sabotage in

the run up to the September general election. In a move likely to appeal to electors, and contrary to his statement at the independence day celebrations, Vajpayee affirmed that, if re-elected, in addition to strengthening the country's armed forces, a BJP government would try and re-open talks with Pakistan. 'A meeting ground will have to be found.'[159] Sonia Gandhi, leader of the Congress Party, who likewise pledged talks with Pakistan, began her campaign by accusing the BJP government of 'dozing' at the outbreak of the Kargil crisis. As with previous elections since 1991, the APHC instituted 'an anti-polls campaign' in Jammu and Kashmir in an attempt to encourage people to boycott what their leaders called 'sham' polls. In fact, the boycott was surprisingly successful and the turnout was generally low with the exception of voters in the Kargil area. The government responded to the anti-polls campaign by arresting the APHC leaders, Syed Ali Shah Gilani, Maulana Abbas Ansari, Yasin Malik and Javed Mir as well as Shabir Shah. In view of the APHC's boycott, of the six candidates, who were elected to the Lok Sabha from the state of Jammu and Kashmir, two were BJP members and four National Conference. Farooq Abdullah retained his position as chief minister and Girish Saxena, who had replaced Krishna Rao as governor in May 1998, remained in office. At a national level, as expected, following closure of the polls in early October, Atal Vajpayee announced the BJP-led coalition election victory. Try as it might to point to the government's lack of vigilance over Kargil, the Congress Party could not undermine the political mileage which the BJP had been able to gain over the war.

Domestically, both countries kept highlighting the 'positive' elements of Kargil. The Indian government continued to congratulate itself on its successful campaign against Pakistan, which, the Indians believed, had exposed itself as the true instigator of the insurgency in Kashmir. From the Pakistani perspective, India's increased expenditure on patrolling the line of control was highlighted as a positive benefit to Pakistan's position. Both at home and abroad, the Pakistani government insisted that the only solution to the Kashmir issue was the implementation of the UN resolutions to hold a plebiscite. The referendum in East Timor in September 1999 also drew strongly opposing reactions from the Indian government and the Kashmiri political activists. Whilst the activists instantly drew parallels, the Indian government stated that there was no similiarity between the Kashmir issue and East Timor, an opinion with which the US concurred.

At the diplomatic level, during the UN General Assembly session at the end of September, both Pakistan and India sought to lobby in favour of their respective positions, yet again claiming victory. The Pakistani government welcomed the call put forward by 40 members of the House of Representatives requesting Clinton to appoint a special envoy to mediate in Kashmir. Indian officials, however, pointed to their victory over the Kashmir issue because President Clinton had repeatedly refused to mediate. Likewise, on the ground in the valley of Kashmir, both Pakistan and India saw the situation working to their advantage. Whilst the Indians maintained that the insurgency was in decline, the Pakistanis believed that its persistence would continue to use up valuable Indian resources making eventual compromise inevitable. In early October, the Pakistani government was once more embarrassed by the determination of JKLF leader, Amanullah Khan, to try and cross the line of control with thousands of supporters. As with his earlier attempts in 1992, he was arrested before he could reach the LOC, and the march was called off.

On 12 October the history of relations between Pakistan and India took a new turn, when General Musharraf staged a bloodless military coup ousting Nawaz Sharif as prime minister. For weeks, rumours had been rife that a military coup was imminent, causing President Clinton to give a stern warning that the US would oppose any alteration in the constitutional position of Pakistan. Relations between Sharif and Musharraf had evidently soured after Kargil. In addition to having to concede near bankruptcy of the country, Sharif was continuing to face domestic opposition to the Kargil withdrawal by those who believed that, whatever the reason – (American concerns that the Government of India would respond to domestic pressure to cross the international border or the LOC in 'hot pursuit' and the possibility that the US would 'pull' the IMF plug) – the Pakistani prime minister had given in too easily to American pressure. In order to put an end to speculation of a rift between the chief of army staff and the prime minister, Sharif reaffirmed Musharraf's position as COAS until his term ended in 2001. Days later, while Musharraf was visiting Sri Lanka, Sharif announced his retirement and replacement by Lt Gen Zia Ud Din, head of the ISI. With the support of the army, Musharraf was immediately able to return to Pakistan and stage a counter-coup. All elected officials were dismissed, the constitution was put in abeyance and, without declaring martial law, Musharraf assumed the position of chief executive.

Although the general's actions received severe criticism from the international community for breaching democratic institutional procedure, the coup appeared to be welcomed by the majority of the citizens of Pakistan. Without specifying any date for returning the country to elected civilian rule, General Musharraf announced a 7-point plan which included a commitment to improve relations with India and to de-escalate forces along the international frontier. Predictably, there was no suggestion of a withdrawal along the line of control nor of a compromise with the Indian government over Kashmir. By the end of 1999, given Pakistan's need to balance domestic compulsions with an equally compelling need for international support, it was difficult to determine how the leaders of Pakistan would proceed with their 'unfinished war' over the state of Jammu and Kashmir; nor was it clear how the disaffected Kashmiris could win theirs.

CHAPTER 10

New Century, New Vision?

I do believe we will live in peace. The question is how much pain we will have to go through to get there.[1]

Salman Arif, Khidmet Seminar

Mind sets will have to be altered and historical baggage will have to be jettisoned.

Prime Minister Atal Vajpayee to President Pervez Musharraf.[2]

By the beginning of the 21st century, there was no indication that the conflict over Kashmir was any nearer resolution; the Kashmiri political activists and militants who were demanding either independence or accession to Pakistan still felt they had not been granted their 'right of self-determination' and were pressing for dialogue which involved India in tripartite talks with Pakistan. Mindful of their inability to gain the ascendancy, either politically or militarily, against the Indian government, they were also looking to the international community to support their cause. The Indian government was still attempting to normalise the situation in the valley, at the same time as accusing Pakistan of facilitating 'cross-border terrorism'. Although it was willing to enter into a dialogue with the Kashmiri activists, it saw no advantage in discussing the situation in the valley of Kashmir with Pakistan or in contemplating the secession of all or part of the state, whose retention, as a predominantly Muslim state, was considered essential for India's secular identity.[3] The Indian government also saw no role for the UN either as a peacekeeping force or as a mediator or indeed for any country to become involved in discussing the issue.

Officially, the Pakistani government was still talking about determining the will of the people with reference to the United Nations resolutions, in the belief that a majority Muslim population would be unlikely to choose to remain as part of India. It was still caught in the ambiguous position of supporting the Kashmiris' right of self-determination and yet refusing to concede the 'third option' of independence. Unofficially, Pakistanis were divided in their support of the Kashmir cause; on the one hand, they wanted to show solidarity with their Muslim brothers and sisters in the valley; on the other, they were faced with the futility of a struggle which appeared to be unwinnable.

As in the past, and especially since India and Pakistan tested nuclear weapons, the international community viewed the Kashmir issue as the most likely source of conflict between the two countries. But, in view of India's insistence that no third party mediator was required, it felt powerless to take a more active role in settling the dispute. It was also widely recognised that, although the threat of all out war had been averted at Kargil in 1999 and Pakistan had not used the nuclear weapons it was subsequently reported as having deployed[4], it needed only another spark to re-ignite the ideological and territorial debate over the state of Jammu and Kashmir.

Hijacking

The barometer of international awareness regarding Kashmir shot up again when, on 24 December 1999, a group of men, armed with grenades, pistols and knives, hijacked an Indian Airlines airbus, with 178 passengers and 11 crew members, on its way from Nepal to New Delhi.[5] The plane tried to land in Lahore, but was denied permission by the Pakistani government. Instead, the hijackers forced the plane to land at Amritsar where it spent forty minutes on the ground, before making an emergency landing at Lahore, in order to refuel and to take on food; it then took off for Kabul. When the Afghan authorities stated that it was impossible to land safely at night, the plane went on to Muscat, the capital of Oman, but was refused permission to land. It then headed for the United Arab Emirates in order to refuel again, during which time 27 hostages were released. The hijackers also off-loaded the body of a 25 year-old Indian, who was returning from his honeymoon in Katmandu and had been killed by the hijackers. According to a released hostage, he had not kept his eyes covered, as all the hostages had been ordered to do and had looked at the hijackers. After refuelling, the plane flew on to Kandahar where it arrived on the morning of 25 December.

Lashkar–i Toiba immediately condemned the hijacking and denied any involvement; instead a group calling itself the Islamic Salvation Front claimed responsibility. Once the plane reached Afghanistan, the hijackers issued their first public demand, requesting the release, amongst others, of Maulana Masood Azhar, a Pakistani religious leader, who had gone to Kashmir in 1994 to help in the insurgency and was captured soon afterwards and imprisoned in a high security jail near Jammu. Azhar was an ideologue and fundraiser for the Harkat-ul Ansar (reformed in 1997 as Harkat-ul Mujaheddin) and his release had also been demanded by the Al Faran group who kidnapped the western tourists in 1995. Despite the presence of the plane on Afghan soil, the Taliban foreign minister insisted that they would not mediate. 'It is up to the UN to intervene and end this,' he said in a telephone interview with the Associated Press.[6] Although the UN stated that it had not received an official request by the Taliban to mediate, Erick de Mul, UN coordinator for Afghanistan, was designated to deal with the hijacking.

While the plane remained on the ground, bearded Taliban troops, wearing black turbans stood guard, armed with assault rifles in armoured personnel carriers. Although the identity of the hijackers was unknown, one called himself Ibrahim, Azhar's brother. As negotiations continued from the airport control tower, Prime Minister Vajpayee insisted that his government would not bow to their demands, which were increased to include 35 more Kashmiri militants, and a £125 million ransom. But after three days, the hijackers reduced their demands and the Indian government eventually agreed to release three militants, including Azhar. The crisis finally ended when the five masked hijackers, holding their guns high, left the airport in a van with a driver provided by the Taliban. Both they and the three released militants immediately disappeared into the Afghan countryside. In addition to Azhar, those released were Mushtaq Zargar, founder member of the Al Umar militant group, and Sheikh Omar Saeed, who had been involved in the kidnapping of three Britons (later released) in New Delhi in 1994. A British passport holder, it seemed an odd twist of fate, that, after his release, he was legally free to return to Britain. Both he and Azhar re-surfaced in Pakistan where Azhar openly held public rallies accompanied by rifle-toting guards.

Subsequently the US government informed the Pakistani government that it believed that Harkat-ul Mujaheddin was responsible for the hijacking and questioned Pakistan's involvement in supporting its activities through its military and intelligence agencies. But the US did not accede to India's demands to place Pakistan on the State Department's list of countries that sponsor terrorism.[7] At the same time, the Indian government was criticised for 'sending a signal to Kashmiri militants that India is a soft state which can be manipulated through terrorist activity'. The Indian government excused its capitulation by saying that it had reduced the number of militants from that originally demanded and 'saved 160 lives'.[8]

Core issue?

In Pakistan, as General Musharraf grew into the office he had assumed for himself, he took an appeasing attitude towards India. He also continued the policy of his predecessors by describing Kashmir as the 'core issue' affecting relations between the two countries. 'We have been trying all kinds of bus diplomacy and cricket diplomacy… why has all of it failed? It has failed because the core issue was not being addressed… because there is only one dispute, the Kashmir dispute… others are just aberrations, minor differences of opinion which can be resolved,' he said in his first interview with an Indian journalist.[9] Domestically, he talked about reforms and promised to hold elections in October 2002 following the Supreme Court's validation of his tenure of power for three years from the date of the coup; internationally, he requested investment and asked the world community to understand the compulsions which had made him overthrow Nawaz Sharif, who, after being tried and convicted for conspiracy to kill the chief of army staff, was later exiled for ten years to Saudi Arabia.

Despite his conciliatory statements towards India, Musharraf also continued with Pakistan's traditional policy of supporting the Kashmiri movement for 'self-determination'. On 5 February 2000, a day celebrated in Pakistan as 'Kashmir Solidarity Day', he visited a refugee camp outside Muzaffarabad. Amidst slogan raising during his speech, he distinguished between terrorism and those 'freedom fighters' who were fighting for their self-determination against the Indian government. 'There are some splinter groups, some misguided people who bring a bad name to the mujaheddin. Those people should desist from any form of terrorism, whether it is hijacking of planes, killing of innocent civilians or bomb blasts.'[10] Politically, however, Musharraf was still insisting that the UN resolutions were the acceptable way to resolve the conflict. He also adopted an injured tone towards India, saying that he was prepared to talk 'anywhere at any time' with Prime Minister Vajpayee and that he was 'sorry to say' that the major obstacle to re-starting the dialogue was Indian intransigence.[11] The Indian prime minister remained unmoved, indicating that although the Pakistani ruler may have forgotten about Kargil, the Indian people had not and there was no point in holding talks while 'terrorists' continued to infiltrate across the line of control.[12]

Internationally, the Government of India appeared to have gained the upperhand in the publicity stakes. In March, President Clinton made the first visit to India by an American head of state for twenty-two years. But his visit was overshadowed by news of a massacre of Sikhs in Kashmir. On the evening of 20 March, a group of about fifteen men, dressed in army battle fatigues and armed with grenades and assault rifles, went to the village of Chittisinghpura in Anantnag district, fifty miles south-west of Srinagar. After the villagers had finished their evening prayers, the men were separated from their families and made to sit in two groups against the walls of the temple, ostensibly to check identification papers. 'After ordering the women and children to leave, they shot dead all the males at point-blank range in firing that continued for at least ten minutes,' said Gurmukh Singh, an eyewitness.[13] Described as the worst massacre in the state since the insurgency began, 34 men were shot, one later dying of his wounds[14]. It was also the first attack on Kashmir's 80,000 Sikh community, which had remained as a neutral party throughout the insurgency. Indian officials immediately blamed the Lashkar-i Toiba and the Hizb-ul Mujaheddin for the attack, stating that their intention was to 'internationalise' the Kashmir dispute on the eve of Clinton's visit. But when three human rights activists investigated the incident, they concluded that the finger pointed towards 'renegades' rather than the militants. It was also noted that a unit of Rashtriya Rifles was stationed nearby but did nothing to help the villagers and only visited the scene the following day. The inquiry did not, however, believe that the perpetrators were from the security forces.[15]

During his high-profile visit to India, President Clinton dismayed the Kashmiri activists by neither referring to Kashmir during his address to the Indian Parliament nor in the 'vision statement' which he signed with the Indian Prime Minister. In their discussions, Vajpayee assured the Americans that, despite appearances, the region was not a 'nuclear flashpoint'. 'We have a problem of cross-border terrorism, but there is no threat of war.'[16] In view of the United States' condemnation of Musharraf's military takeover, the US president made only a token visit to Pakistan. His message in a televised address to the Pakistani people was sombre: democracy must be restored and Musharraf must take steps to control the insurgent groups, based in Pakistan, whose fighters were crossing the line of control to fight in Jammu and Kashmir. He also cautioned his listeners that 'no grievance, no cause, no system of belief can ever justify deliberate killing of innocents'. In a statement far removed from the 'personal interest' he had promised to take after Kargil in 1999, he announced that the United States could not mediate or resolve the dispute in Kashmir. 'Only you and India can do that through dialogue.'[17] The effect of Clinton's cordial five-day visit to India, compared with his unfriendly stopover in Islamabad engendered a mixed reaction in Pakistan. Whereas some analysts believed it was time for Pakistanis to rescue their longstanding friendship with Washington, in military circles it was recognised that, if Pakistan wanted to continue to pursue its Kashmir policy, it might need to rediscover its traditional friends in the region. 'We don't need to enter into an arms race with India, but we cannot let Kashmir go. Let Kashmir become a bleeding wound for India,' stated former chief of army staff, Aslam Beg. 'The costs will be heavy on both sides, but heavier for India.'[18]

Meanwhile, the repercussions of the massacre of the Sikhs were continuing to be felt in the valley. Shortly after the attack, the state government of chief minister Farooq Abdullah announced that every effort would be made to find those responsible. But when a joint unit of the army and a special operations group killed five men in a village in Anantnag district, stating that these men were responsible for the massacre of the Sikhs, the local people did not believe the official account. Protest demonstrations were held claiming that the dead men were innocent civilians. Although the state government promised exhumations and a further inquiry, the strikes continued. At the beginning of April, several thousand demonstrators marched on Anantnag in order to submit a memorandum to the deputy commissioner. The situation turned ugly when the protesters started to throw stones at a police post. Later, when the crowd reached the village of Brakpora, the police opened fire, killing seven people and injuring another fifteen, leading to yet another sequence of recrimination and inquiry.

Autonomy, ceasefire and census

On the political front, Farooq Abdullah was attempting to make good his pledge to restore the state to its pre-1953 autonomy. According to recommendations of the Kashmir Autonomy Report[19], New Delhi's authority should be once more restricted to defence, foreign policy and communications, as was the case before 1953. The report also suggested that the state should have its own Prime Minister and Supreme Court. But

Abdullah was opposed not only by the government in New Delhi, but also by the 8 BJP opposition members in the state assembly. Wearing black headbands, they chanted slogans accusing the National Conference of being pro-Pakistan. When, after five days of heated debate, the resolution was passed, they walked out. Although the Congress (I) opposition members opposed autonomy during the debate, stating that the government should instead fight poverty and the militants, they abstained from voting. The Buddhist and Hindu communities also opposed Abdullah's autonomy plan, criticising it as a first step towards secession. In New Delhi, the government indicated that it was not opposed to giving the state some measure of autonomy, although granting the pre-1953 status would weaken India's national integrity.[20] The Hurriyat rejected autonomy as a solution to the Kashmir dispute. Syed Ali Shah Gilani, chairman of the APHC, said that the struggle for the right to self-determination and for a permanent solution to the problem would continue.

Throughout 2000, militant attacks on government buildings and personnel continued to follow their seasonal pattern. Unexpectedly, in July, Majid Dar, the valley commander of the Hizb-ul Mujaheddin, announced a unilateral ceasefire for three months and offered to open a dialogue with the Indian government. 'Within days, HM militants were playing cricket with Indian security force units (and winning),' wrote Alexander Evans.[21] New Delhi responded by instructing the security forces to reciprocate and accepted the offer of dialogue. But the ceasefire was not respected by the other militant organisations, especially Lashkar-i Toiba and Al Jehad. On 1 August, 105 civilians were killed in seven separate incidents. In the largest attack, 23 Hindu pilgrims were shot dead in Pahalgam when unidentified gunmen went into a market place and threw grenades, opening fire with automatic weapons. In this attack, eyewitnesses later suggested that the security forces had panicked when the attack began and had themselves indiscriminately fired into the crowd, leading to more deaths and injuries. An inquiry later concluded that members of the security forces had used 'excessive force' in retaliation against the attack by two militants. The report, however, was not made public and those identified were not arrested.[22]

By the first week of August the ceasefire had broken down. From Muzaffarabad, Syed Salahuddin, leader of the Hizb in Pakistan, was insisting that any talks should include Pakistan as an equal participant which was not acceptable to the Indians. The APHC had also not given the ceasefire its political support. 'The opportunity was there but it was lost,' said Abdul Qadri, general-secretary of the JKLF based in Muzaffarabad. 'We had certain differences with the method it was taken out. It should have been a collective decision.'[23] From Rawalpindi, JKLF leader Amanullah Khan had produced a five-phase formula, yet again reaffirming his belief that the only way to bring peace was for the state to be re-united and given its complete independence so that, instead of being 'a bone of contention', Kashmir would become 'a bridge of friendship' between India and Pakistan. 'This change will, on the one hand save South Asia from the horrors of a nuclear or a conventional war and rid the two countries of so heavy defence budgets and, on the other hand, herald the dawn of a peaceful, prosperous and dignified future for India, Pakistan and Kashmir.'[24] Although he claimed to have widespread support across the line of control, his position as Chairman of the JKLF was weakened by the continuing rift with Yasin Malik.

Within the Indian-administered state of Jammu and Kashmir, attention was also focused on holding a census[25]. Publicised as an exercise in the interest of the people in order to help the government with drawing up its development plans, in May over 20,000 government workers were deployed across the state, marking houses, industrial and commercial buildings as well as recording the availability of electricity, water and other basic amenities. In September, the actual counting of the population was held. As in 1991, when the militant groups forced the census to be cancelled, a ban was imposed on the grounds that it was not possible to hold a credible census because thousands of Kashmiris had either been displaced, had migrated or were in jail. The Hizb-ul Mujaheddin described the census as 'a futile exercise' and warned all Muslim officials that they would face 'dire consequences' if they took part. Even though counting went smoothly in Ladakh and Jammu, it remained problematical in the valley and the deadline for the conclusion of the census had to be extended beyond 30 September. Although the Indian authorities eventually announced that the census was completed, for a number of areas figures were reportedly based on assumptions, since the enumerators did not dare to move door to door because of the militant ban.[26]

Meanwhile, there were daily reports of militants apprehended, attacks and counter-attacks. In 2000, the number of insurgency-related killings in Jammu and Kashmir increased in comparison with the previous year. As recorded by the US State Department's Human Rights Report on India, extrajudicial killings by government forces, which included deaths in custody and 'faked encounter killings', continued to occur frequently.[27] Although the National Human Rights Commission, appointed and financed by the Indian government, directed that all encounter deaths be investigated immediately, it was widely recognised that members of the security forces were rarely held accountable for the killings. In addition, the NHRC had no statutory power to investigate alleged security force abuses if it was not satisfied with the responses to its inquiries. The Indian government continued to rely on the activities of the counterinsurgents both to track and also allegedly to perpetrate 'extrajudicial' killings of the militants. But it was recognised that their overall utility was diminishing because they no longer had the same intelligence as when they first came over to the side of the government.[28]

Despite the fact that the Terrorist and Disruptive Activities (Prevention) Act (TADA) had been allowed to lapse in 1995, over 1,000 people were reported as remaining in detention without trial. Several thousand more were believed to be held in interrogation centres for periods of short-term confinement, which could last up to six months. Most of those detained were held under the Jammu and Kashmir Public Safety Act dating from 1978. The Jammu and Kashmir Disturbed Areas Act and the Armed Forces (Jammu and Kashmir) Special Powers Act, both passed in July 1990, still gave the security forces wide-ranging powers, including authority to shoot those suspected of breaking the law or disturbing the peace as well as to destroy buildings in which militants and/or their weapons were believed to be hidden. The judiciary still functioned with difficulty.

Even though Abdullah said he would institute inquiries which were 'even-handed', he was criticised for using language which was not conducive to improving relations between the disaffected elements of society and paving the way for a dialogue. When, on 15 January 2001, a near-miss grenade attack was made on Abdullah's life, he was reported as stating that militants should be shot down at any cost. As Amnesty International reported, 'such language incites further violence and contributes to an atmosphere of impunity in which state agents may feel entitled to commit extrajudicial executions on the assumption that they will not be held accountable.'[29] An example of this was the arrest, in February 2001, of Jalil Ahmad Shah. Described by the government as 'a militant commander', a spokesman of the JKLF refuted this allegation, instead insisting that he was only a district secretary of the party, whose manifesto was non-violent. His death in an 'encounter' once again set in motion a series of connected incidents with protest demonstrations, indiscriminate shooting into the crowd by the security forces, leading to more deaths and recrimination.

At the same time, the Indian government was persisting with attempts to start a dialogue in the spirit, described by Prime Minister Vajpayee, of *insaniyat* (humanity). In November 2000, he stated that 'combat operations' would not be carried out against militants during the Muslims' holy month of fasting, Ramadan. Pakistan reciprocated by announcing that troops along the line of control would exercise 'maximum restraint'. But, although the Indian 'ceasefire' remained in force for over six months, there was overall scepticism amongst the local Kashmiris regarding its genuine impact. There was also little enthusiasm for the dialogue instigated in the name of Shri K.C. Pant, a senior politician and former minister in the Indian government. Although for the first time, the Indian government indicated that it was prepared to talk to militants who had given up the gun, the sticking point remained the government's insistence that discussions should take place within the framework of the Indian Union.

To Agra

As the people of the United States elected their 43rd president in the most fiercely contested election in US history, the eye of the United States' administration was temporarily averted from events in South Asia. But, even before the new president, George W. Bush, was confirmed in office, state department officials were anticipating that the new administration would carry on the policy initiated by Clinton at the beginning of his second term of office: that South Asia was of increasing importance for US interests and it was therefore important for the US to enhance its relationship with the countries of the region. In December 2000 Karl Inderfurth, assistant secretary of state for South Asia, had also indicated that the US would continue to play the role of 'facilitator' rather than mediator in order to help India and Pakistan resolve their problems, including Kashmir. When he assumed office, Bush immediately made it clear that his administration would encourage India and Pakistan to resume a dialogue.

In the spring of 2001, Vajpayee relaxed his position by inviting Musharraf to India. Overnight, newspaper columns became full of encouraging statements from analysts looking to a bright new future where the Kashmir issue was resolved and Pakistan and India could live in peace. Even the inhabitants of the Northern Areas seemed to think that Musharraf's visit would resolve their anomalous position by which they had no status under the constitution of Pakistan and yet, for all practical purposes, were considered to be part of Pakistan.[30] Others in Pakistan were more sceptical, believing that Vajpayee's sudden *volte-face* was because of pressure from the United States, which would in turn put pressure on Pakistan to rein in the militants in Kashmir. 'If General Musharraf is to avoid being bullied by Washington and fêted to death in Delhi, he has to make his stand clear now. His Foreign Office has to learn to protest and stage walk-outs whenever the words 'cross-border terrorism' or 'Kashmiri separatists' are used by any Indian official,' stated a retired Brigadier.[31] Kashmiri political activists based in the valley were also not convinced that anything would come of Musharraf's meeting with Vajpayee. Yasin Malik, who made his first ever visit to the United States and Britain for medical treatment, was adamant that any deal made over the heads of the Kashmiris would be rejected. Kashmir, he said, is not 'an animal to be carved up.'[32]

Prior to the visit, in a move which was not altogether unexpected, Musharraf also assumed the office of president. As with the 1999 coup, his arbitrary assumption of additional power was not welcomed by the international community. But it gave him the prospect of remaining in office beyond the period of three years, for which the Supreme Court had validated his military takeover. The Indo-Pakistani talks, scheduled to take place in mid-July, were held at Agra, and also included a nostalgic visit to Musharraf's ancestral home in Old Delhi. But, despite the display of cordiality between the two leaders, no mutually acceptable outcome could be achieved during the talks. Subsequently Musharraf claimed that he had succeeded in obtaining Vajpayee's agreement on admitting the centrality of the Kashmir issue to their relationship, but, when it came to signing the communiqué, the wording had been revised to include a mention of 'cross-border terrorism' which Musharraf was not prepared to concede.[33] After first postponing his departure in order to try and agree an acceptable text, Musharraf concluded the summit by returning abruptly to Islamabad in the middle of the night.

Immediately after the talks, both sides tried to vindicate their respective positions as well as maintain an upbeat attitude about the outcome. 'We are of course disappointed that the two sides could not arrive at an agreed text,' stated the Indian external minister, Jaswant Singh. 'This was on account of the difficulty in reconciling our basic approaches to bilateral relations. India is convinced that narrow, segmented or unifocal approaches will simply not work. Our focus has to remain on the totality of the relationship.' Pakistan's foreign minister, Abdul Sattar, also pointed to the 'meeting of minds'. Both sides held wide-ranging discussions on a number of issues, he stated, but it was unfortunate 'that the expected consummation did not materialise.'[34] Musharraf refused to call the talks a failure; instead he said that they were inconclusive. Vajpayee later said the Agra summit was a failure because Musharraf refused to recognise that there was terrorism in Jammu and Kashmir[35].

International reaction to the outcome of the talks was reserved. UN Secretary-General Kofi Annan encouraged the two leaders to regard the Agra summit as a 'first step' towards establishing a sustainable bilateral dialogue in order to resolve their differences. The US was also restrained. 'The two sides were grappling with very difficult issues that have divided them for over 50 years,' stated assistant secretary of state for South Asia, Christina Rocca. 'Yet the serious and constructive atmosphere of these talks tells me that both sides are committed to resolving their differences.'[36] The response of the militant groups was less sympathetic. 'The failure of the talks has proved the correctness of the mujaheddin's stance that India never wants to solve the issue through negotiations. The resolution of this issue is only possible through jihad,' stated Ahmad Hamza, vice-chief of the militant group, Al Badar.[37]

Meanwhile in Azad Jammu and Kashmir, there was a flurry of interest as Amanullah Khan's JKLF announced that it would participate in the forthcoming elections in AJK. But the requirement was for them to declare that they believed in 'the ideology of Pakistan, the ideology of the state's accession to Pakistan and the integrity and sovereignty of Pakistan'. When they refused to do so, their nomination papers were rejected.[38] To those who were fighting for the independence of the state, it was another indication of Pakistan's ambiguous support of the Kashmiris' right of 'self-determination'.

September 11

When, on Tuesday 11 September, four planes were hijacked, two of which were flown into the World Trade Center in New York, another into the

Pentagon, while a fourth crashed into a field in Pennsylvania, no immediate connection was made with Pakistan and the Kashmiris' 'freedom struggle' in Jammu and Kashmir. But as soon as the United States government became convinced that the terrorist attacks were instigated by Saudi dissident, Osama bin Laden, based in Afghanistan since 1996 and supported by the Taliban regime of Mullah Omar, which was in turn supported by Pakistan, the Pakistani government found itself in the spotlight once more. After brief deliberation and acting against the radical Islamic segments of public opinion, President Musharraf effected a complete U-turn in his Afghan policy. He announced his alliance with President Bush against the Taliban in a 'war on terrorism' and his support of the United States' plan to destroy Osama bin Laden's 'Al Qaeda' network in a series of airstrikes on targets within Afghanistan. This immediately gave him the warmth of a new US-Pakistani relationship but it also meant that Pakistan's Kashmir policy would come under critical observation. The Indian government, in particular, was disturbed at the prospect of Pakistan's collaboration with the United States and its allies in waging a war against terrorism in Afghanistan while continuing its support of 'cross-border terrorism' into Jammu and Kashmir.

The distinction was further blurred by the knowledge that some Kashmiris had trained in Afghanistan and some Afghans had fought in Kashmir; Musharraf therefore found himself under increasing international pressure to condemn all acts of terrorism, wherever they took place. He did not have to wait long: on 1 October there was a suicide attack on the Srinagar assembly in which 38 people died; realising how sensitive the situation was, Musharraf immediately telephoned Vajpayee to condemn the act of 'terrorism'. Far more serious in terms of the reaction it engendered from the Indian government, was the attack on the Indian parliament on 13 December, when 14 people were killed. The Indians lost no time in blaming Pakistan for harbouring the terrorists, who were alleged to be from Lashkar and Jaish-e Mohammed, a radical group formed in 2001 by Azhar, one of the militants released after the December 1999 hijacking. Vajpayee immediately ordered the closure of the border between India and Pakistan and suspended all flights from Delhi to Lahore. The bus service, which he had inaugurated in 1999 with former Prime Minister Nawaz Sharif, was also stopped. The only point of entry and exit which remained open was the border crossing on foot at Wagah – midway between Lahore and Amritsar – which was for the use of foreigners and nationals 'on official business' only.

The United States, which was still heavily engaged in its operations in Afghanistan, supported the Indian reaction; at the same time, the administration was clearly anxious not to embarrass Pakistan unduly. At the end of December, it designated the Lashkar-i Toiba and Jaish-e Mohammed as 'foreign terrorist organisations' under US law and requested Pakistan to shut the groups down. 'These groups, which claim to be supporting the people of Kashmir, have conducted numerous terrorist attacks in India and Pakistan,' stated secretary of state, Colin Powell. 'As the recent horrific attacks against the Indian parliament and the Srinagar State Legislative Assembly so clearly show, the Lashkar-i Toiba, Jaish-e Mohammed and their ilk seek to assault democracy, undermine peace and stability in South Asia, and destroy relations between India and Pakistan.'[39] On 29 December the Indian defence minister, George Fernandes, announced that India's armed forces were fully mobilised. Pakistan immediately followed suit by announcing that its mobilisation was complete on 1 January 2002.

In order to convince both the Pakistani people and the international community that Pakistan was serious about countering terrorism, on 12 January President Musharraf made a keynote speech which ordered a crackdown on extremism in the country. But in a significant part of the speech, he voiced Pakistan's continuing support of the Kashmiris' freedom struggle. 'Kashmir runs in our blood. No Pakistani can afford to sever links with Kashmir. The entire Pakistan and the world knows this. We will continue to extend our moral, political and diplomatic support to Kashmiris.'[40] Whilst the international community accepted the speech at face value and welcomed his commitment to take action against 'any Pakistani individual, group or organisation found involved in terrorism within or outside the country', the Government of India was not convinced. The international border remained closed and the expectation was that the Indians would continue to monitor the situation, until the snows melted, in order to determine whether more militants crossed from any of the estimated 72 points of entry across the line of control.[41]

For those watching how Musharraf handled the situation two questions were uppermost in their minds: how much control did he have over the militants and how genuinely did he and those in the wings – his army corps commanders and the ISI – intend to restrain incursions into the state of Jammu and Kashmir? There was also a third question: how much control did Musharraf actually have over extremism in his own country? The answer to this last question was tragically provided when *Wall Street* correspondent, Daniel Pearl was kidnapped in Karachi on 23 January. Throughout February there was intense speculation as to whether he was dead or alive. Finally, a month after his kidnap, his death was confirmed when the kidnappers sent a videotape to the US Consulate in Karachi showing Pearl having his throat cut. Although his abduction was unrelated to the ideology of the Kashmir issue, the fact that Sheikh Omar Saeed, released after the December 1999 hijacking, confessed to his involvement in the kidnap, yet again demonstrated how acts of terrorism could no longer be compartmentalised.[42]

Valley view

In the valley of Kashmir, security was tightened following the 13 December attack on the Indian Parliament. Yet again, the Kashmiri people were at the receiving end. All STD dialling out of the state and internet facilities, introduced in 1998, were immediately cut off. Only people in hotels and offices who could get a connection through New Delhi were able to use e-mail, which was both slower and more expensive. No longer able to use the cyber booths with their new computers, young men stood idle, playing billiards and talking. 'If the Indian government wants to win back their allegiance,' said a Kashmiri student from Britain visiting his family in Srinagar in April 2002, 'then this is no way to do it.'[43]

Even before this, the normalisation, which had been promised to the valley, had not yielded the necessary dividends. Although the fruits of Kashmir's orchards continued to be harvested, agriculture had been affected by lack of investment and poor management and marketing. As Governor Saxena admitted, the injection of funds into the state had not always reached those to whom it was destined.[44] In the Spring of 2002, with the Indian and Pakistani armies still menacingly positioned along the international frontier, and shelling taking place regularly across the line of control, the valley was a sad place. Especially in the rural areas, the Kashmiris were still waiting for a miracle to happen which would free them from the occupying forces of the Indian government as well as attacks from the militants and restore general peace and prosperity. Behind closed doors, many Kashmiris regretted that the insurgency had ever started and wished that they could return to the way things were. But these were not views which they dared to express publicly. Others remained adamant that they could not go back to the situation pre-1989 after all the suffering, abuse of human rights and lives which had been lost.[45] After thirteen years of insurgency, women were described as the 'invisible' losers. An estimated 5,000 were widows, with an equal number, possibly more, of women whose husbands had disappeared, leaving them as breadwinners, neither free to grieve nor re-marry; over 50,000 children were orphans. Levels of domestic violence had also risen 'but when the nation is at stake, violence at home seems unimportant.'[46] In recent years, in order to escape from the trauma of crackdown and cordon and search operations in the rural areas, there had been a steady movement of people wanting to live in the more secure surroundings of Srinagar. The Pandit community, however, still remained exiled from their homes. Their demand for a 'Panun Kashmir' for the Hindu community in the valley demonstrated their feeling of alienation but it was not an answer either to their troubles or those of the Kashmiri community as a whole.

Strikes continued to be held as a weapon of protest against the actions of the Indian government. On 6 April shops were again shut in protest at the introduction of a new act, the Prevention of Terrorism Act (POTA). Amnesty immediately warned that the ordinance would undermine human rights because of the wide powers of detention which it gave to the police. 'But,' said a Kashmiri journalist based in Srinagar, 'there are far worse laws, like the Disturbed Areas Act, which gives the security forces wide-ranging powers, including authority to shoot those suspected of "disturbing" the peace.'[47] Although the local newspapers had greater freedom than in the past, they were still subject to intimidation. At the end of June 2002, three men entered the Srinagar offices of *Kashmir Images*, one of several local English language newspapers. After talking for twenty minutes with sub-editor, Zafar Iqbal, one of them pulled out a gun and shot him. In mid-July, there was a serious attack on Shahid Rashid, a former militant and founder of the Urdu-language newspaper, *State Reporter*. In addition, supporters of the National Conference were always liable to be targeted by the militants. In one month alone five National Conference activists were killed. Even so, people continued to try and lead normal lives. An oasis of calm for the more fortunate has been provided by the Tyndale-Biscoe School in central Srinagar. Hidden behind huge gates erected during the height of the insurgency in order to keep out intruders, the Principal Pervez Kaul, regarded the role of the school as a 'beacon of light' during difficult times.[48]

The tourist industry was still a fraction of what it had been in its heyday, although the richer Pandits and Punjabi elite were less afraid than in previous years of returning to their houseboats, guarded by their Muslim servants during the height of the insurgency.

Older established houseboat owners, like Gulam Butt on Naseem Bagh, had managed to survive by prior diversification into selling carpets and handicrafts. Those who could get outlets in India's major cities and abroad suffered less than the average Kashmiri. The world-wide boom in the sale of pashmina shawls in the mid-1990s also benefited some traders, but inevitably the Kashmiri weavers were not the people who profited but the middlemen.[49] 'And,' says author Justine Hardy, who set up her own business importing pashminas from Kashmir into England, 'most of the huge demand was met by the Nepalese. The Kashmiri weavers were just not able to produce enough shawls.' Their potential business was also affected by the Kargil crisis in 1999. 'The goats producing the fine quality pashmina wool graze in the hills of Ladakh, and because of Kargil, Indian troops were stopping all traffic from going up there.'[50] In addition, Kashmiri weavers were adversely affected by the ban on weaving shahtoosh from the protected Tibetan antelope.

Even though the curfew had been relaxed, Srinagar still lacked the vitality of the old days. The lakes were cleaner, but the streets were still dirty. Shopkeepers stood expectantly at the entrance to their shops, eager to attract the few westerners who came to Srinagar, who were inevitably journalists. 'I thank God for a little bread and butter,' said Gulzar, a tailor in Srinagar, whose only customers in recent years were foreign journalists, UN officials and diplomats, 'but now I would like some jam.'[51] As Mark Tully so aptly illustrated in a documentary shown on British television in June 2002, Kashmir may be one of the most beautiful places in the world, but the latest guide book on India does not contain a chapter on it. Instead, it warns that the valley of Kashmir is a warzone and tourists are advised not to visit.

Politically, the Hurriyat had enhanced its profile by visits abroad. Yasin Malik's stay in the United States and Britain in 2001 had given him more exposure to foreign media than he had ever experienced in Srinagar. Attempts by the APHC to visit their counterparts in Azad Kashmir were, however, still thwarted by the Indian government's control over their passports.[52] In the spring of 2002, in an effort to answer the government's accusation that the APHC had no representation because it had never contested elections, Malik initiated an alternative 'election commission' which would oversee elections of candidates who might be considered representative spokesmen. But, before the initiative took off, he was arrested for allegedly receiving $100,000 in contravention of India's foreign exchange regulations. Although he denied the allegation, he was kept in jail which removed him from the political scene at a critical juncture as the APHC was preparing to elect a new chairman in place of the outgoing chairman, Abdul Gani Bhat.[53]

The APHC was also attempting to re-think its election strategy prior to the September elections to the state legislative assembly. Rumours persisted that its executive council members were split between those who wanted to contest the elections in order to try and prevent Farooq Abdullah, or his son and heir apparent, Omar, from perpetuating the National Conference's tenure of office and those who were still refusing to do so because of the requirement to recognise the state's allegiance to the Indian Union.[54] In April, Omar Farooq visited Dubai with Abdul Gani Lone, where they held an 'accidental' meeting with the former prime minister of Azad Jammu and Kashmir, Sardar Abdul Qayum Khan. Yet again, they affirmed their belief that dialogue amongst the Kashmiris on the both sides of the line of control was the best way to resolve the Kashmir issue. They also discussed the forthcoming elections and decided that they should continue with their proposed boycott, while trying to create 'an atmosphere conducive to a peaceful process'.[55] Subsequently, Lone's assassination on 21 May, deprived the movement of one of its 'elder' statesmen who had been part of the movement of protest before the insurgency began. Pending identification of his assassin, the finger was pointed at Islamic extremists who had already issued death threats because of the more moderate stance he was adopting towards India.[56] His son, Bilal, was immediately inducted onto the APHC executive council in his father's place as president of the Supreme Council of the People's Conference.

Eyeball to eyeball

Throughout the winter months, while Srinagar was still enshrouded in snow and the mountain passes were closed, the Government of India reserved its judgement regarding Pakistan's sincerity in stopping movement across the line of control. But there was annoyance that Musharraf would not hand over the 20 Indians whose extradition the government had requested. Rumours also persisted that thousands of fighters were waiting to cross into northern

Kashmir as soon as spring came. In Pakistan, terrorist attacks were still shaking the confidence of the international community in Musharraf's ability to control extremist elements in his own country while remaining in the frontline of the war against terrorism in Afghanistan. In March, there was a grenade attack on a church in the diplomatic enclave in Islamabad which killed five including two Americans and wounding others; at the beginning of May, a car bomb exploded near the Sheraton Hotel in Karachi killing 11 French technicians and three Pakistanis. And although the referendum which Musharraf held on 30 April was orchestrated to show the international community that he still enjoyed the people's continued support, it was a reminder that he was not an elected leader and therefore had no real mandate from the people.

Across the international border, the BJP government was also facing its own domestic problems. In February it had lost four by-elections, most importantly in Uttar Pradesh. Within days, 'state-backed' violence tantamount to a 'deliberate pogrom' erupted against the Muslim population in Gujerat, which left 900 officially confirmed dead in scenes reminiscent of partition[57]. As the Indian government attempted to deflect attention from its internal situation by condemning Pakistan again for sponsoring 'cross-border terrorism' in Jammu and Kashmir, both the Indian and Pakistani armies went on high alert. By the beginning of May, the ISI chief, Eshanul Haq, was warning that there was 'an all-time high risk' of conflict in the coming weeks. What immediately attracted international attention were the inflammatory statements which emanated from both countries about the potential use of their nuclear weapons. In view of its belief, that it could not win a conventional war, Pakistan continued to reserve the right of a first strike. Almost without realising the gravity of what it was saying, the Government of India maintained that it could 'absorb' a first strike and still be in a position to retaliate. Yet again, mirroring Kargil, what concerned international opinion most was not the Kashmir issue, but the fact that India and Pakistan were still arguing over it and that this could lead to all out war. Even the immediate humanitarian aspects gained little news coverage. But, as shelling and exchange of artillery fire continued across the line of control, the lives of thousands in the border areas were once more convulsed.

In mid-May, a militant attack on an army base in Jammu left over 30 people dead, including 19 women and children, yet again adding to the heightened tensions. Amidst tight security, Vajpayee made a three-day visit to the state of Jammu and Kashmir, undeterred by the strike called in protest against his presence. He also visited the wounded from the army base attack in the hospital in Jammu. More ominously, he went to Kupwara district to address the troops on the frontline, promising, in uncharacteristically belligerent tones for the mild-mannered mid-septuagenarian, that India must prepare to for 'a decisive fight' with Pakistan. In response to Indian moves along the international frontier, which included the deployment of its warships in the vicinity of Karachi, Pakistan prepared to draw back its forces from the UN peace-keeping mission in Sierra Leone and from its western frontier, bordering Afghanistan.[58] As international observers and commentators waited expectantly for a declaration of war, analysts were assessing their armies' relative strength in what would obviously be a bloody fight, pitting the Indian army's greater numbers against the Pakistan army's superior quality. They also continued to assess the impact of a possible nuclear strike, with maps publicised of potential targets.[59]

In order to explain the hostility in India, Vajpayee informed both President Bush and Prime Minister Blair that India was losing patience with Pakistan. 'There is a national anger,' explained Vajpayee 'because Musharraf has not translated into reality the promises he made in his January 12 speech to stop cross-border terrorism.'[60] Regardless of Musharraf's denials, the Indians remained convinced that the ISI was continuing to assist the insurgents according to an agenda which had changed little since the insurgency began. Indian journalist, Deepak Sharma reported how Musharraf continued to 'hoodwink' his allies in fighting terrorism. 'On the one hand, the General vows to stop infiltration in 30 days, while on the other, his men in the ISI continue to fund terrorist groups active in Kashmir.' Sharma's report stated that Indian intelligence had enough evidence to corroborate the involvement of top ISI officials funding terrorists through banks in London and New Delhi.[61] More damaging was British foreign secretary Jack Straw's subsequent assertion in the House of Commons that there was 'a clear link' between the ISI and the Kashmiri militant groups.[62] Kashmiri activists were also dismayed when Straw said that the Kashmiris were not engaged in a 'freedom' struggle. His statement, said Dr Ayub Thukar of the World Kashmir Freedom Movement, 'put a nail in the coffin of Kashmiris' hopes.'[63]

As Britain and the United States took the lead in announcing the withdrawal of all their citizens from India and Pakistan, President Bush appealed personally to both Musharraf and Vajpayee to think about where their respective belligerence would lead. Whereas his message to Musharraf related to stopping all support for 'terrorism', his request to Vajpayee was to de-escalate. The US State Department also warned that even if the leaders were not intending to start a war, 'irresponsible elements' could do so against their apparent wishes. During early June, Islamabad and New Delhi saw a stream of high-level visitors: after Jack Straw visited India and Pakistan in late May, US deputy secretary of state, Richard Armitage, went to Islamabad and Delhi. Following his discussions with Musharraf, Armitage said that he felt 'very heartened' by the Pakistani president's assurance that he would not initiate war. Although Armitage had confronted the Pakistanis with the suggestion that Al Qaeda fighters might be operating in Kashmir, he was obliged to admit that there was no 'hard evidence' and the Pakistanis denied the allegation. Armitage's visit was followed shortly afterwards by US defence secretary, Donald Rumsfeld, who spent two days in Delhi before reaching

Islamabad. Soon after his visit, a car bomb exploded outside the American consulate in Karachi, next to the Marriott Hotel, killing 11 Pakistanis and injuring over 50 people. The attack, unrelated to the Kashmir issue, was another indication, following the murder of Daniel Pearl, of anti-western feeling amongst extremist groups, exacerbated by US actions in Afghanistan. Since the fall of the Taliban regime, numerous Taliban and Al Qaeda supporters had found refuge with their natural sympathisers in Pakistan, who continued to oppose the US's 'war on terror' and Pakistan's assistance of it. That Pakistan was so exposed to the fallout from the prevailing chaos in Afghanistan meant that peace with India was even more imperative.

In view of their interests in South Asia, China and Russia had also expressed concern about the Indo-Pakistani stand-off. President Vladimir Putin of Russia had even offered to perform an intermediary role when Vajpayee and Musharraf attended a scheduled regional summit conference in Almaty, Kazakhstan. Both Putin and the Chinese president, Jiang Zemin, met Vajpayee and Musharraf separately. But the atmosphere between the two leaders was glacial and they used their public pronouncements at the summit to protest at their opposite number's continuing belligerence. Subsequently, the only positive development appeared to be the Indian government's proposal for joint patrolling of the line of control by India and Pakistan. The suggestion, however, was rejected by the Pakistani government, which preferred to 'bolster' a third party force.

By the middle of June, a measure of restraint entered the statements of both Pakistani and Indian leaders on the use of nuclear weapons. Vajpayee attributed the improvement in relations to Musharraf's commitment to put an end to movement across the line of control, but US pressure and attention on the region had evidently contributed to the cooling of tempers.[64] Weather conditions and the arrival of the monsoon also meant that, although both countries retained their capability to fight a conventional war across the international frontier in the Punjab, it was no longer practical. But, even though India and Pakistan withdrew verbally from the deadly game of brinkmanship which had kept the world in suspended animation for weeks, the underlying grievances between India and Pakistan and the Kashmiri people were unresolved. The only outcome – a lesson which should already have been learnt at Kargil – was the realisation that the Kashmir dispute had become too dangerous to neglect.

Visionary solutions?

Numerous commentators and analysts have written thousands of words suggesting how to resolve the Kashmir issue in order to bring peace and prosperity to South Asia. They have examined the state of Jammu and Kashmir as an independent state, the valley as part of India, part of Pakistan, as an autonomous region, as a joint protectorate, the state permanently divided along the line of control, demilitarised, with or without UN peacekeeping forces, the issue resolved through a unitary plebiscite, a regional plebiscite, elections, bilateral negotiations, tripartite dialogue, with or without mediation. No specific proposal, however, has ever left the drawing board.[65]

The reasons are self-evident. Firstly, the Indian government is in physical possession of the valley of Kashmir, which is the main area of contention. It has therefore not felt the imperative to engage in dialogue beyond that it has so far unsuccessfully pursued with the disaffected Kashmiris in the valley. Secondly, despite their stated desire to improve their relationship, India and Pakistan still have far too great a legacy of mistrust, dating back to partition, to be able to jettison their historical and emotional 'baggage'. As time has passed, the Indian attitude towards Pakistan has, if anything, hardened. Contrary to longstanding descriptions of the state of Jammu and Kashmir as 'disputed territory', Indian officials are now attempting to move away from calling the Kashmir issue a 'dispute' at all. 'A dispute,' Governor Saxena said to me in April 2002, 'is about two people having the potential right to something. In this instance you have a situation where we have a house; another person wants the house; they come in, occupy one third of it and then tell me we have a dispute.'[66] And, although privately many Indians admit their mistakes in handling Kashmir, the government continues to blame Pakistan whole-heartedly for the insurgency. In the hostile climate of 2002, defence minister, George Fernandes' more enlightened statement in 1990 seems to have been forgotten: 'I do not believe that any foreign hand engineered the Kashmir problem. The problem was created by us, and if others decided to take advantage of it, I do not believe that one should make that an issue; given the nature of the politics of our sub-continent, such a development was inevitable.'[67]

Across the border in Pakistan, despite the warmth which exists between Pakistanis and Indians at a social and intellectual level, the Pakistani establishment has likewise fallen victim to the belief that India is committed to destabilising Pakistan and seeing the country fragment. This has become especially true since the advent to power in 1998 of the BJP government, under the dominant influence of home minister, L.K.Advani, appointed deputy prime minister in July 2002. Mirroring the extremism of the radical Islamist groups in Pakistan, India's fundamentalist Hindu organisations have been alarmingly 'rewriting' Indian history in order to define India as a Hindu rather than a secular country. This sort of propaganda has made Pakistanis even more concerned about the fate of their Muslim brethren across the line of control in the valley of Kashmir. At the same time, Pakistanis have also been adept at re-writing their own history, whether it is analysing the causes of the Kargil conflict or conceding the extent to which they have aided the insurgency militarily for their own objectives.

Until there is a complete change of heart in both countries, it is therefore going to be impossible for any leader to sit down and discuss an issue in good faith which has such deep-rooted historic, religious and emotional overtones. Even at Simla, when the international community believed that a breakthrough had been achieved by India's acceptance of Pakistan as a 'bilateral' negotiating partner, both countries were operating from different premises. India believed that Pakistan had tacitly accepted the line of control as the international border, Pakistan denied that it had. Moreover, if they are to make any headway, both India and Pakistan need to a adopt a policy of national consensus on Kashmir; otherwise any concessions either side ever feels able to make are likely to be torpedoed by an opposition eager to elicit an emotional response from the people. And if decisions are to be taken on behalf of the people, they also need to fill their vacuum of knowledge about the issues at stake – not by reading biased textbooks or jingoistic websites – but through informed debate. An end to the Vietnam war was accelerated because Americans, realising the implications, protested on the streets. The conflict over Kashmir might also be ended by the peoples of South Asia understanding what a tremendous negative impact it has had on their lives.

But even if Pakistan and India were to agree to discuss Kashmir in greater sincerity, it would only be producing a short-term solution to think that the issue could be resolved without the representative participation of the millions of inhabitants of the state of Jammu and Kashmir, for whom elections in the state – arguably never free and fair – have been no substitute to a genuine dialogue and process of 'self-determination'. That some, frustrated by the lack of political freedom, burdened by economic and social grievances, took up arms in order to fight for their vision of the future has made the issue more deadly and its resolution more pressing. 'You talk of these men as terrorists,' said a veteran political and former militant activist, 'but they are a collection of wounded people.'[68] While their grievances remained unaddressed, others, using a politicised version of Islam, started a 'jihad', which gained a momentum of its own. The Indian government urgently needs to recognise the depths of those wounds, firstly, by acknowledging that the Kashmiris' grievances arose long before they took up arms in the 1990s, and that using terror to counter terror only breeds more hatred and violence;[69] secondly, by admitting that Pakistan does have a role to play, and that India needs Pakistan to play that role in order for the two countries to live in harmony as neighbours. While India continues to blame Pakistan for waging a 'proxy' war, there is always the chance that another serious militant attack will again send India and Pakistan to the brink of war (and beyond).[70]

Regrettably, those who have spent long years fighting for the independence of the entire state of Jammu and Kashmir are bound to be disappointed. Unless the national boundaries of both India and Pakistan change as dramatically as those of the former Soviet Union in 1991, there is no likelihood of either India or Pakistan agreeing to an independent state of Jammu and Kashmir. Even changes in structure envisaged by intermittent 'track 2' discussions or Vajpayee's suggestion of 'devolution' of powers would still leave the valley as part of the Indian Union.[71] And so the challenge for the Kashmiri 'freedom fighters' struggling against 'occupation' by Indian forces is to understand that without Indian agreement, no change in their political status will take place. After September 11, the distinction between freedom fighting and terrorism has been virtually obliterated. As many Kashmiri politicians themselves have begun to realise, whatever gains they make must now be at the negotiating table.

The Pakistani government also needs to see where the Kashmir issue is taking its country and its people, caught up in their own cyclical trauma of domestic unrest, religious extremism and military takeovers. Could its leaders also not acquire some vision to see where continued belligerence and brinkmanship can lead? Do they really want to fight even a conventional war with India because India continues to administer an area, centred on the valley, which it believed over fifty years ago it should have been able to control? At the height of the crisis, no one seemed to notice the bitter irony of President Musharraf's warning that Pakistan would use its nuclear weapons to preserve its sovereignty, without recognising that the use of them would be the surest way not only of destroying Pakistan's sovereignty but the country and probably the region as well.

In a situation where the alternative is potential nuclear war, there is ample scope for visionary gestures. The Indian government could start by indicating that it has no claim over the Northern Areas and Azad Jammu and Kashmir, whose inhabitants have never shown any desire for union with India. Discussions relating to the Siachen glacier, where more men die of frostbite and avalanches than in battle, could be resumed at once. Demilitarisation could take place in order to free Kashmiris from their constant feeling of being 'occupied'. The sooner borders become 'soft' the better, so that people whose families have been divided for over half a century can meet, attend weddings, go to funerals and learn to understand and respect each other's divergent viewpoints. If there could be a checkpoint Charlie in the dark days between East and West Berlin, then why not, as an initial step, a checkpoint Chakoti on the line of control? If there can be a bus from Delhi to Lahore, then why not a bus from Srinagar to Muzaffarabad?

Pakistanis may find that it is too great a climb-down to accept the line of control, whose 'sanctity' President Clinton confirmed after Kargil in 1999, but the government could at least begin by indicating which areas of the state it has no claim over. In the past, Pakistanis argued forcefully for the plebiscite to be held as agreed by India and Pakistan in 1947 and as recommended by the UN resolutions. It may be understandable that, lacking any other official plan or agreement to retain its standing as a party to the debate, Pakistan has not admitted that holding a unitary plebiscite, whose outcome would undoubtedly create disaffected minorities, may not now be the best way forward. But, in reality, Pakistanis no longer expect that they will take possession of the whole state, including those areas of Buddhist Ladakh and Hindu Jammu, whose inhabitants are obviously content with their status within India. Perhaps now is the time to say so.[72] Pakistan might also consider removing the ambiguity in its statements concerning the Kashmiris' right of self-determination. Is Pakistan fighting so that the valley becomes part of Pakistan, or, in the event India did agree to devolve power, would Pakistan be prepared to see the valley, too small to be completely independent, constituted with autonomous status? And, if the line of control is not acceptable as an international border, perhaps now might also be the time to indicate where, realistically, adjustments could be made. After half a century, Pakistan may feel that without the Kashmir issue to unite its public opinion, its *raison d'être* is somehow diminished. But this is just a state of mind which reasoned debate has quietly but steadily already begun to erode. Even before the heightening of tensions in May and June 2002, President Musharraf was conceding that both countries needed to move away from their 'stated' positions.[73]

Kashmir is now one of the most dangerous situations in the world, not so much because of the issue itself but because of India and Pakistan's failed relationship in dealing with it. Although Indian leaders have complained bitterly that any third party involvement is 'interference' in its internal affairs, Prime Minister Vajpayee has now accepted that the United States may play a useful role as a 'facilitator'.[74] Perhaps, provided the outcome does not merely benefit India because it suits the United States's geo-strategical and economic interests, such 'facilitation' might at least begin to break the deadlock. If our advent into the 21st century has taught us anything, it is that, when world peace is threatened or human rights are abused, the affairs of nation states are not sacrosanct. The revolution in electronic media, digital and satellite communication means that it is no longer possible to isolate issues as though they have no impact in the larger context. That the world can be held in thrall because India and Pakistan, after over half a century, are still arguing about their respective positions on Kashmir, invokes international concern at the highest level.

As we shall surely see in the decades to come, the future is not the rigidity of nation states but the fluidity of cross-cultural and regional communication. At the beginning of the next century, the 'unending war' of words and weapons over the state of Jammu and Kashmir may appear as a small entry in our electronic information packs, when South Asia will have long since become the new economic union of the east. Only then perhaps will people realise how great the tragedy was that so many lives were lost and so much time and money wasted arguing about ownership of land, which would have prospered far more if its people had been allowed to live peacefully, moving as geography determined their passage, long before political divisions were erected to circumscribe the inevitable interaction of humanity.

Glossary

Militant organisations:

In 1989 there were reported to be 130 militant organisations; there are now about 20, most of which have only a few hundred members. In the late 1990s several counter-insurgent groups were also set up.

Al-Umar Mujaheddin: Founded by Mushtaq Zargar from Awami Action Commmittee, political party which supports Mirwaiz Omar Farooq; small indigenous membership.

Al Badar: Off-shoot of Hizb-ul Mujaheddin.

Al Barq: Established in 1990 as militant wing of Abdul Gani Lone's political party, the People's Conference (which supported independence).

Al Fateh: Pro-Pakistan. Led by Zain-ul Abdeen, a former contestant in the 1987 elections. Established as an off-shoot from Al Jehad with a few hundred members.

Al Faran: Splinter of Harkat-ul Ansar. Held responsible for kidnapping five western tourists in 1995; no longer operative.

Al Jehad: Established in 1991 as militant wing of Shabir Shah's Peoples League. Pro-Pakistan (although Shah came out in favour of independence).

Allah Tigers: Islamic group which forced the closure of bars, video parlours and cinema halls as being anti-Islamic. No longer operative.

Dukhtaran-e Millat (Daughters of Islam): Fundamentalist womens' group, led by Asyia Andrabi. Supported Allah Tigers. Limited activity. No armed attacks.

Harkat-ul Mujaheddin: Formerly called Harkat-ul Ansar.

Hizb-ul Mujaheddin: Founded in Sept 1989. Militant wing of Jamaat-i Islami. Official objective is re-unification with Pakistan. Led by Syed Salahuddin, 50s, (a MUF candidate in 1987 elections). Assessed as the largest 'indigenous' militant group, with several thousand members.

Harkat-ul Ansar: Founded in 1993 from two groups set up in 1980 to run Afghan refugee camps. Radical Islamist group which is pro-Pakistan. In 1997 following a ban by the US it was re-named Harkat-ul Mujaheddin. Banned by Pakistan in December 2001.

Hizbul Momineen: The only Shia group, with a small following, founded in early 1990s as militant wing of Maulvi Abbas Ansari's political party, Ittehad-ul Muslimeen.

Hizbullah: No longer operative. Political wing is the Muslim League of Kashmir.

247

Ikhwan ul Muslimeen: Pro-independence. Started as Student's Liberation Front in 1989 with a few hundred members. After its leader, Ghulam Nabi Azad, was killed, it became a counter-insurgent outfit, called Ikhwan ul Muslimoon.

Ikhwan-ul Muslimoon: Largest counter-insurgent group, led by Kukka Parrey. Established in late 1990s. Created a political wing, the Awami League: two candidates contested the 1996 state elections but both lost.

Jaish-e Mohammed: Radical Islamic group, founded in Jan 2001 by Mohd Azhar. Based in Pakistan and responsible for numerous suicide attacks in Kashmir. It was banned by the US in Dec 2001 and by Pakistan in Jan 2002. Azhar was arrested in Pakistan in Dec 2001.

Jammu and Kashmir Liberation Front (JKLF): Favours independence. Founded by Maqbool Butt in 1964. Led by Amanullah Khan, based in Rawalpindi. In 1995 JKLF split between its Pakistani and Indian-based wings led by Yasin Malik in Srinagar. The APHC recognised Malik, who had renounced militancy, as the legitimate leader of the JKLF.

Lashkar-i Toiba: Founded in 1993. Radical Islamist group based in Pakistan. Many members are ex-mujaheddin from Afghanistan. Banned by the United States in Dec 2001 and by Pakistan in Jan 2002.

Muslim Janbaaz Force: Formed as militant group from the Peoples League (Shabir Shah); only a few hundred members. No longer operational.

Muslim Liberation Army: Oldest Gujar counter-insurgent group.

Muslim Mujaheddin: Pro-Pakistan. A splinter group of the Hizb-ul Mujaheddin and supports the Muslim Conference.

Operation Balakote: Set up by Azam Inquilabi, with membership of a few hundred. In the 19th century, Syed Ahmed of Balakote, near Abbottabad, in NWFP Pakistan, had fought a losing battle against the Sikhs. Inquilabi chose the name to signify the uneven struggle they were fighting against the Indian government. In 1995 Inquilabi returned to Srinagar and gave up the armed struggle.

Taliban: Gujar counter-insurgent group.

Kashmir Liberation Jehad: Established by Border Security Force from surrendered militants.

Tehrik-ul Mujaheddin: Small indigenous militant group, belonging to the Jamaat Al Hadith school of thought.

United Jihad Council: Umbrella organisation of all the indigenous militant groups, set up in 1990. Originally led by Azam Inquilabi; now led by Syed Salauddin.

Note: In this book I have used the names by which the respective governments call that part of the state which they control: thus 'Azad Jammu and Kashmir' for that part administered by Pakistan and 'Jammu and Kashmir' for that part administered by India. When I refer to Kashmiris, I generally mean the inhabitants of the valley, although all inhabitants of the state of Jammu and Kashmir are, politically speaking, Kashmiris.

Notes

Chapter 1 Introducing Kashmir

1. M. A. Stein, preface to Kalhana, *Rajatarangini* (Chronicle of Kings), 1900, p. xxiv.

2. A Brahmin Kashmiri praised as the Herodotus of Kashmir, Kalhana wrote his Chronicle of Kings in the mid-12th century. Sir Aurel Stein made the first English translation in 1900. After searching for the original manuscript, which had been divided between three owners, it took him over a decade to translate and annotate the work.

3. Kashmiri is classified as a member of the Dardic or north-western group of Indo-Aryan languages. It is the only language in the Dardic group to have a script and a literary tradition.

4. François Bernier, *Travels in the Mogul Empire*, AD 1656–1668, Delhi, 1969, p. 400.

5. The highest caste of Hindu social hierarchy.

6. Henry Sender, *Kashmiri Pandits*, Delhi, 1988, p. 34.

7. Prithivi Nath Kaul Bamzai, *A History of Kashmir from earliest times to the present day*, 1973, p. 426.

8. The honorific title of Pandit to Kashmiri Hindus arises from their status as the official 'learned' class of the society. It is generally applied, somewhat loosely, to upper caste Hindus living in the valley, although they are not always Brahmins.

9. William Moorcroft, *Travels in the Himalayan Provinces, of Hindustan and the Punjab*, London, 1841, p. 123.

10. Moorcroft, *Travels*, p. 293.

11. Victor Jacquemont, *Correspondence inédite, 1824–32*, Paris, 1867, p. 97.

12. Godfrey Vigne, *Travels in Kashmir, Ladakh, Iskardo*, 1842, Vol. 1, p. 257.

13. Mohammad Saraf, *Kashmiris fight for freedom*, Lahore, 1977, Vol. 1, p. 65.

14. Gulab Singh obtained Jammu in 1820; the ceremony conferring the title of Raja took place in 1822.

15. At the rate of 51 rupees to the dollar, 75 lakhs – 7.5 million rupees – was $150,000.

16. An expedition in 1841 to conquer Tibet failed.

17. B.S. Singh, *The Jammu Fox*, Southern Illinois, 1974, p. 162.

18. Adoption Sunnad to Maharajah Runbeer Singh, Cashmere, 5 March 1862.

19. Colonel Ralph Young, *Journal of a trip to Cashmere, 1867*, MSS Eur, B 133, p. 16.

20. Robert Thorp, *Cashmere Misgovernment*, Longmans, Green & Co. 1870, p. 8–9.

21. Lord Kimberly to the Government of India, as quoted in Alastair Lamb, *Kashmir: A Disputed Legacy 1846–1900*, Roxford, Herts, 1991, p. 13.

22. Margaret Fisher, Leo E. Rose, Robert A. Huttenback, *Himalayan Battleground*, London, p. 69.

23. Teng, Bhatt, Kaul, *Documents on Constitutional History, India,* 1977, p. 27.

24. Walter Lawrence, *The Valley of Kashmir,* Henry Frowde, 1895, p. 2.

25. Pratap Singh to Lord Lansdowne, in Teng, Bhatt & Kaul, *Documents,* p. 39.

26. *Tyndale-Biscoe in Kashmir,* an Autobiography, London, 1951, p. 52.

27. See Sher Ali Pataudi *The Elite Minority, The Princes of India,* Lahore, 1989, p. 1; 565 is normally given as the number of princely states, but it is also put at 584 or 562.

28. Montagu & Chelmsford, *Report on Indian Constitutional Reform,* 22 April 1918, MSS Eur C 264/42, IOIC, p. 141.

29. As quoted in Montagu & Chelmsford, *Report,* p. 5.

30. Montagu & Chelmsford, *Report,* p. 76.

31. Allama Iqbal, as quoted in Sheikh Mohammad Abdullah, *Flames of the Chinar,* New Delhi, 1993, tr. from Urdu by Khushwant Singh, p. 3.

32. Representation to the Viceroy, Lord Reading by Khadmans of Khanqah Muallah, Shah Hadman, Srinagar, 29 Sept 1924 as quoted in *Muslims of Kashmir,* R1/1/1474, OICI.

33. G.K.S. Fitze, to Syed Mohsin Shah, 1 July 1925, *Muslims of Kashmir.*

34. Major Searle, assistant political agent, Chilas, 'Diary 1924–25', MSS Eur A 165, OIOC, p. 27.

35. Founded by Sir Syed Ahmed Khan, a prominent educationalist, in the 19th century. Aligarh was the leading Muslim educational establishment in British India.

36. Prem Nath Bazaz says that he made 'a violent speech advocating massacre of Hindus', *History of the Struggle for Freedom,* New Delhi, 1954, p. 152.

37. Abdullah, *Flames,* p. 24.

38. Maharaja of Bikaner, *Round Table Conference,* Madras, 1931, p. 32.

39. H.V. Hodson, *The Great Divide,* London, 1969, p. 78.

40. As quoted in Hodson, *The Great Divide,* p. 79.

41. See Ayesha Jalal, *The Sole Spokesman,* Cambridge, 1985, p. 12 fn. 14.

42. Pranay Gupte, *Mother India,* New York, 1992, p. 270, footnote mentions the unsubstantiated rumour that Sheikh Abdullah was the illegitimate son of Nehru's father, Motilal Nehru.

43. Congress Working Committee, 29 July–1 August 1935, as quoted in Akbar, *Behind the Vale,* p. 81.

44. Mohammad Ali Jinnah, 17 June 1947, *Speeches and Statements, Gov. of Pakistan,* 1989, p. 17.

45. See Patrick French, *Liberty or Death,* Flamingo, 1998, pp. 256–6.

46. Karan Singh, *Heir Apparent,* Oxford, 1982, p. 41.

47. Karan Singh, *Heir Apparent,* p. 42.

48. Karan Singh, *Heir Apparent,* p. 53.

49. Karan Singh, *Heir Apparent,* p. 38.

Chapter 2 Independence

1. Mountbatten, as quoted in Michael Edwardes, *The Last Years of British India,* p. 89.

2. Hodson, *The Great Divide,* p. 83.

3. Wavell, *The Viceroy's Journal,* London, 1973, p. 199–200.

4. Attlee, quoted in Philip Ziegler, *Mountbatten,* London, 1985, p. 359.

5. Mountbatten, quoted in Hodson, *The Great Divide*, p. 289.

6. Mountbatten, quoted in ibid., p. 293.

7. Alan Campbell-Johnson, 'Address to Pakistan Society', 12 October 1995.

8. W. H. Morris-Jones, 'Thirty-six Years Later: the Mixed Legacies of Mountbatten's Transfer of Power', *International Affairs*, Autumn 1983, p. 624.

9. Ibid., p. 625; he was constitutional adviser to Mountbatten from June–August 1947.

10. Sir Conrad Corfield, *Some Thoughts on British Policy and the Indian States, 1935–47*, as quoted in Philips & Wainwright, *The Partition of India*, p. 531.

11. Nehru to Mountbatten, 17 June 1947, in *Transfer*, Vol. XI, Doc. 229, p. 443–4.

12. Mountbatten to Saraf, 3 November 1978, as quoted in *Kashmiris Fight*, Vol. II, p. 1395.

13. V. P. Menon, *The Story of the Integration of the Indian States*, Calcutta, 1956, p. 394.

14. Singh, *Heir Apparent*, p. 48.

15. Captain Dewan Singh, interview, Jammu, 11 April 1994.

16. Alan Campbell-Johnson, *Mission with Mountbatten*, London, 1977, p. 120.

17. Nehru to Mountbatten, 27 July 1947, in *Transfer*, Vol. XII, Doc. 249, p. 368.

18. Ismay, *The Memoirs of General the Lord Ismay*, London, 1960, p. 433.

19. Menon, *Integration*, p. 395.

20. Campbell-Johnson, *Mission*, p. 120.

21. Patel to Hari Singh, 3 July 1947, in *Patel Correspondence*, Vol. I, Doc. 34, p. 33.

22. Lord Mountbatten, *Time Only to Look Forward*, London, 1949, p. 52.

23. Mountbatten in *Transfer*, Vol. XI, Doc. 319, p. 593.

24. Mountbatten to Webb, 28 June 1947, *Transfer*, Vol. XI, Doc. 387, p. 720.

25. Viceroy's Report, 1 August 1947, No. 15, *Transfer*, Vol. XII, Doc. 302, p. 449.

26. Saraf, interview, Rawalpindi, March 1994.

27. Shahid Hamid, *Disastrous Twilight*, Great Britain 1986, p. 273.

28. Mir Abdul Aziz, interview, Rawalpindi, March 1994.

29. Mohammad Ali Jinnah, *India News*, 13 July 1947, in *Transfer of Power*, Vol. XII, Doc. 87, p. 128.

30. Mohammad Ali Jinnah, 17 June 1947, *Speeches and Statements*, p. 17.

31. Sir Walter Monckton to Lord Ismay, 9 June 1947, *Transfer*, Vol. XI, Doc. 112, p. 216.

32. Ismay to Mountbatten, 7 April 1948, Dr Kirpal Singh (ed.), *The Partition of the Punjab*, New Delhi, 1991, Doc. 238, p. 706.

33. Mountbatten, *Time Only*, p. 30.

34. Chaudhri Muhammad Ali, *The Emergence of Pakistan*, New York, 1967, p. 218–9.

35. Quoted in Hugh Tinker, 'Pressure, Persuasion, Decision: Factors in the Partition of the Punjab, August 1947', *The Journal of Asian Studies*, August 1977, p. 702.

36. Lord Wavell to Lord Pethick-Lawrence, 7 February 1946, *Transfer*, Vol. VI, Doc. 406, p. 912.

37. 'Draft Statement to be made by Parliamentary Spokesman', as quoted in Hugh Tinker, 'Pressure, Persuasion, Decision', p. 704.

38. Abell to Abbott, 8 August 1947, *The Partition of the Punjab, 1947*, Lahore, 1983, Vol. 1, Doc. 198, p. 245.

39. Ismay to Mountbatten, 7 April 1948, *Partition of the Punjab, 1947*, ed. Kirpal Singh, Delhi 1991, Doc. 238, p. 706.

40. Ali, *Emergence*, p. 213.

41. 'Report of the interview between Mountbatten and Nawab of Bhopal and Nawab of Mysore', 4 August 1947, *Transfer*, Vol. XII, Doc. 335 , p. 509.

42. Wavell, *Viceroy's Journal*, p. 384.

43. Letter to Peter Scott, 17 July 1947, *Transfer*, Vol. XII, Doc. 151, p. 214.

44. Lord Birdwood, *Two Nations and Kashmir*, London, 1956, p. 74.

45. Ali, *Emergence*, p. 215.

46. Akbar, *Behind the Vale*, p. 98.

47. Christopher Beaumont, correspondence with the author, 10/17 October 1995.

48. Campbell-Johnson, 'Address'.

49. Professor Zaidi, interview, Islamabad, April 1994.

50. Ibid.

51. Morris-Jones, 'Thirty-six Years Later', p. 628.

52. Suhrawardy, A. H., *Kashmir: The Incredible Freedom Fight*, Lahore, 1991, p. 36.

53. As quoted in ibid., p. 37.

54. Mountbatten to Listowel, 8 August 1947, *Transfer*, Vol. XII, Doc. 383, p. 586–7.

55. Singh, *Heir Apparent*, p. 55.

56. Lamb, *Birth of a Tragedy*, p. 52.

57. Viceroy's Personal Report, No. 17, *Transfer*, Vol. XII, Doc. 489, para 51, p. 757.

58. Menon, *Integration*, p. 395.

59. Suhrawardy, *Incredible Freedom Fight*, p. 25.

60. Muhummad Saraf, interview, April 1994.

61. See Korbel, *Danger in Kashmir*, p. 54.

62. Horace Alexander, *Kashmir*, Friends Peace Committee, London, 1953, p. 7.

63. Richard Symonds, as quoted in Korbel, *Danger in Kashmir*, p. 68.

64. Sardar Muhammad Ibrahim Khan, interview, Islamabad, 24 March 1994.

65. Sardar Abdul Qayum Khan, interview, Islamabad, March 1994.

66. Singh, *Heir Apparent*, p. 54.

67. George Cunningham, 23 September 1947, 'Diary', MSS Eur D 670/6, OIOC.

68. Alexander, *Kashmir*, p. 7.

69. Ian Stephens, *Pakistan*, London, 1963, p. 200.

70. Lamb, *Disputed Legacy*, p. 123.

71. Lamb, *Birth of a Tragedy*, p. 70.

72. Bhattacharjea, *Wounded Valley*, p. 177.

73. Korbel, *Danger in Kashmir*, p. 66.

74. Nehru to Patel, *Patel Correspondence*, 27 September 1947, Vol. I, Doc. 49, p. 45.

75. Abdullah, 'Speech at Huzoori Bagh', 2 October 1947, in *Flames*, p. 86.

76. Kachru to Nehru, 4 October 1947, *Patel Correspondence*, Vol. I, Doc. 57, enclosure, p. 54–5.

77. Patel to Nehru, 8 October 1948, ibid., Vol. I, Doc. 58, p. 56.

78. Lamb, *Birth of a Tragedy*, p. 67.

79. Taseer, *Sheikh Abdullah*, pp. 50 & 271.

80. Abdullah, *Flames*, p. 88.

81. Recorded by Cunningham, 'Diary', 18 October 1947.

82. Mehr Chand Mahajan, *Looking Back*, London, 1963, p. 133.

83. Quaid-i Azam, Mohammad Ali Jinnah, *Speeches and Statements, 1947–48*, Government of Pakistan, 1989, p. 91–2; see also Korbel, *Danger in Kashmir*, p. 69–70.

84. Patel to Mahajan, 21 October 1947, *Patel Correspondence*, Vol. I, Doc. 65, p. 62.
85. Mahajan to Patel, 23 October 1947, ibid., Doc. 66, p. 63.
86. Press note, 23 October 1947, ibid., Vol. I, Doc. 67, p. 65.
87. As quoted in Taseer, *Sheikh Abdullah*, p. 145.
88. Faiz as quoted in ibid., p. 145.

Chapter 3 Accession

1. Singh, *Heir Apparent*, p. 57.
2. Maj-Gen Akbar Khan, *Raiders in Kashmir*, Karachi, 1970, p. 11.
3. Sardar Muhammad Ibrahim, interview, Islamabad, 24 March 1994.
4. Akbar Khan, *Raiders*, p. 17.
5. Sir George Cunningham, 15 October 1947, Diary, MSS Eur D 670/6, OIOC; Cunningham is probably referring to the Pakistan National Guard set up on 7 October under Major-General Shahid Hamid as a voluntary force to supplement the Pakistani armed forces. 'Many' units took part in the Kashmir operations; see Shahid Hamid, *Early Years of Pakistan*, Lahore, 1993, p. 62.
6. Cunningham, 'Diary', 20 October 1947.
7. Ibid., 22 October 1947.
8. Stephens, *Pakistan*, p. 202.
9. Alexander, *Kashmir*, p. 8.
10. Ayesha Jalal, *The State of Martial Rule*, Cambridge, 1990, p. 58.
11. Professor H. Zaidi, interview, Islamabad, 18 April 1994.
12. Muhammad Saraf, interview, Rawalpindi, March 1994; *Kashmiris Fight*, Vol. 2, p. 988.
13. K. H. Khurshid as quoted in Rajendra Sareen, *Pakistan: The India Factor*, New Delhi, 1984, p. 221.
14. Cunningham, 'Diary', 26 October 1947
15. See Bhattacharjea, *Wounded Valley*, p. 136.
16. Menon, *Integration of the Indian States*, p. 410.
17. *Dawn*, 7 December 1947.
18. Lamb, *Disputed Legacy*, p. 131.
19. Menon, *Integration of the Indian States*, p. 397.
20. There are conflicting reports on whether or not this was because of an attack by the tribesmen.
21. Korbel, *Danger in Kashmir*, p. 77.
22. Singh, *Heir Apparent*, p. 57.
23. Campbell-Johnson, *Mission with Mountbatten*, p. 224.
24. Gopal, *Nehru*, p. 19.
25. Menon, *Integration of the Indian States*, p. 397–8.
26. Captain Dewan Singh, interview, Jammu, 11 April 1994.
27. Singh, *Heir Apparent*, p. 59.
28. Mehr Chand Mahajan, *Looking Back*, London, 1963, p. 151.
29. Indian White Paper, 3 March 1948, in 'Kashmir, Internal Situation', L/P & S/13, OIOC.
30. Menon, *Integration of the Indian States*, p. 400; Captain Dewan Singh, interview, Jammu, April 1994.
31. Dewan Singh, interview, Jammu, April 1994.

32. Menon, *Integration of the Indian States*, p. 400.

33. *Documents on Kashmir Problem*, Vol. XIV, New Delhi, 1991, as quoted in Bhattacharjea, *Wounded Valley*, p. 150.

34. Korbel, *Danger in Kashmir*, p. 84.

35. Mahajan, *Looking Back*, p. 152.

36. Ibid. p. 154.

37. Lamb, *Birth of a Tragedy*, p. 96.

38. Collins and Lapierre say the journey took seventeen hours; see *Freedom at Midnight*, p. 355.

39. Singh, *Heir Apparent*, p. 58–9.

40. Mahajan, *Looking Back*, p. 152.

41. Ibid., p. 150.

42. Ibid., p. 276; see also Campbell-Johnson, *Mission with Mountbatten*, p. 224.

43. Collins & Lapierre, *Freedom at Midnight*, p. 356.

44. Alexander Symon to Sir Archibald Carter, 27 October 1947 in 'Kashmir Internal Situation', L/P&S/13, OIOC.

45. *Selected Works of Jawaharlal Nehru*, Vol. 4, 2nd edition, ed S. Gopal, New Delhi, 1986, p. 278.

46. B. G. Verghese, 'Lamb's Tales from Kashmir', *Sunday Mail*, 14–20 June 1992, as quoted in *The Kashmir Issue*, High Commission of India, London, 1993, p. 155.

47. See Lamb, *Birth of a Tragedy*, p. 99–100.

48. Ibid., p. 102–3.

49. Korbel, *Danger in Kashmir*, p. 79.

50. Ziegler, *Mountbatten*, p. 446.

51. Quoted in Korbel, *Danger in Kashmir*, p. 76.

52. Major Khurshid Anwar's account, as reported in *Dawn*, 7 December 1947.

53. Cunningham, 'Diary', 10 November 1947.

54. Brigadier L. P. Sen, as quoted in Rajesh Kadian, *The Kashmir Tangle*, New Delhi, 1992, p. 93.

55. Stephens, *Pakistan*, p. 202.

56. Muhammad Saraf, interview, Rawalpindi, March 1994.

57. Prem Nath Bazaz, *Azad Kashmir*, Lahore, p. 33.

58. Commonwealth Relations Office Note, 1 December 1947, in 'Kashmir Internal Situation', L/P. &S/13, OIOC.

59. Mahajan to Mountbatten, 27 October 1947. *Patel Correspondence*, Vol. I, Doc. 70, p. 69.

60. Hamid, *Disastrous Twilight*, p. 278.

61. Cunningham, 'Diary', 28 October 1947.

62. Ibid., 7 November 1947.

63. Ali, *Emergence*, p. 293.

64. Mountbatten to Nehru, 2 November 1947, *Patel Correspondence*, Vol. I, Doc 72, p. 71–81.

65. Liaquat Ali Khan to Nehru, *White Paper on Jammu and Kashmir*, as quoted in Korbel, *Danger in Kashmir*, p. 96.

66. As quoted in Menon, *Integration of the Indian States*, p. 406.

67. Ibid., p. 400.

68. 'Status of Hunza, Nagar and Political Districts', OIOC.

69. Menon, *Integration of the Indian States*, p. 393.

70. Chenevix-Trench, *Frontier Scouts*, p. 273.
71. Major William Brown, as quoted in *The Scotsman*, 22 March 1994.
72. Chenevix-Trench, *Frontier Scouts*, p. 276.
73. Major William Brown, as quoted in *The Scotsman*, 22 March 1994.
74. Chenevix-Trench, *Frontier Scouts*, p. 269.
75. Muhammad Saraf, interview, Rawalpindi, 24 March 1994.
76. Arif Aslam Khan, interview, en route to Baltistan, 17 April 1995.
77. Menon, *Integration of the Indian States*, p. 410.
78. Mountbatten, quoted in Hodson, *The Great Divide*, p. 462–3.
79. Mountbatten, quoted in ibid., p. 465.
80. Commonwealth Relations Office, note, 1 December 1947, in Kashmir Internal Situation', L/P&S/13, OIOC.
81. British High Commissioner's opdom No. 3, 8 January 1948, as quoted in Jalal, *State of Martial Law*, p. 58.
82. *The Times*, 13 Jan 1948, quoted in Korbel, *Danger in Kashmir*, p. 84.
83. Akbar Khan, *Raiders*, p. 13. The INA fought against the British in World War 11.
84. *Dawn*, 7 December 1947.
85. Akbar Khan, *Raiders*, p. 100.
86. Eas Bokhari, *Kashmir Operations 1947–48*, ISPR forum, Lahore, August 1990.
87. En route to Leh, April 1995.
88. Nehru to Patel, 30 May 1948, *Patel Correspondence*, Vol. I, Doc 152, p. 190–1.
89. Patel to Nehru, 4 June 1948, ibid., Vol. I, Doc 153, p. 192–3.
90. Patel to Ayyangar, 4 June 1948, ibid., Vol. 1, Doc 156, p. 199.
91. Sher Ali Pataudi, *The Story of Soldiering and Politics*, Lahore, 1988, p. 119.
92. General Sher Ali Pataudi, interview, Islamabad, 14 April 1995.
93. Mountbatten, as quoted in Hodson, *The Great Divide*, p. 465.
94. Hodson, *The Great Divide*, p. 466
95. Jawaharlal Nehru, as quoted in Korbel, *Danger in Kashmir*, p. 98.
96. Sir Zafrullah Khan, 'Speech to Security Council', 16 January 1948, as quoted in Khan, *Troubled Frontiers*, p. 281.
97. See Gopal, *Nehru*, Vol. II, p. 23.
98. V. Shankar, unpublished memoirs, p. 607.
99. *Patel Correspondence*, 3 July 1948, Vol. VI, Doc. 327, p. 387.
100. Resolution 39, 20 January 1948, Doc No S/654, quoted in *Kashmir in the Security Council*, Government of Pakistan, Islamabad, p. 2.
101. Resolution 47, 21 April 1948, Doc S/726, quoted in *Kashmir in the Security Council*, p. 7.
102. Resolution, 13 August 1947, Doc No S/1100, dated 9 November 1948, quoted in *Kashmir in the Security Council.*
103. Nehru to Patel, 27 October 1948, *Patel Correspondence*, Vol. VII, Doc. 576, p. 665.
104. Resolution, 5 January 1949, Doc No S/1196, dated 10 January 1949, as quoted in *Kashmir in the Security Council*, p. 16.
105. Akbar Khan, *Raiders*, p. 155.
106. Colonel Abdul Haq Mirza, *The Withering Chinar*, Islamabad, 1991, p. 173.
107. Pataudi, *Soldiering*, p. 119–120.
108. Menon, *Integration of the Indian States*, p. 412.
109. Kashmir Papers, Reports of the United Nations Commission for India and

Pakistan, June 1948–December 1949, Government of India, New Delhi, 1952.
110. As quoted in UN Commission's Report, Government of India, 1952.

Chapter 4 Special Status

1. Singh, *Tragedy of Errors*, p. xi.
2. Captain Dewan Singh, interview, Jammu, 11 April 1994.
3. Quoted in Akbar, *Behind the Vale*, p. 135.
4. Singh, *Heir Apparent*, p. 83.
5. Nehru, IV, p. 325, as quoted in Bhattacharjea, *Wounded Valley*, p. 166 and Singh, *Heir Apparent*, p. 83.
6. Nehru to Mahajan, 1 Dec 1947, *Patel's Correspondence*, Vol. I, Doc. 88, p. 101.
7. Singh, *Heir Apparent*, p. 85.
8. Mahajan to Patel, 24 Dec 1947, *Patel's Correspondence*, Vol. I, Doc. 103, p. 128.
9. Mahajan to Patel, 11 Dec 1947, ibid., Vol. I, Doc. 92, p. 113.
10. Hari Singh to Patel, 31 Jan 1948, ibid., Vol. I, Doc. 124, p. 162–3.
11. Patel to Hari Singh, 9 Feb 1948, ibid., Vol. I, Doc. 127, p. 166.
12. Nehru to V Shankar, private secretary to Sardar Patel, 3 April 1948, ibid., Vol. I, Doc. 138, p. 175.
13. Nehru to Patel, 12 May 1948, ibid., Vol. I, Doc 149, p. 189.
14. Nehru to Patel, 5 June 1948, ibid., Vol. I, Doc. 157, p. 200.
15. Hari Singh to Patel, 9 September 1948, ibid., Vol. I, Doc. 180, p. 225.
16. Singh, *Heir Apparent*, p. 92.
17. Quoted in Singh, *Heir Apparent*, p. 96.
18. Captain Dewan Singh, interview, Jammu, 11 April 1994.
19. Singh, *Heir Apparent*, p. 101.
20. Ibid., p. 104.
21. Abdullah, *Flames*, p. 108.
22. As quoted in Akbar, *Behind the Vale*, p. 137.
23. Akbar, *Behind the Vale*, p. 139.
24. See Bhattacharjea, *Wounded Valley*, p. 181, note 26.
25. Taseer, *Sheikh Abdullah*, p. 51.
26. Ayyangar, as quoted in Abdullah, *Flames*, p. 113.
27. Krishan Mohan Teng & Santosh Kaul, *Kashmir's Special Status*, Delhi, 1975, p. 45.
28. Patel to Nehru, 27 June 1950, *Patel Correspondence*, Vol. X, Doc. 247, p. 353.
29. Patel to Nehru, 3 July 1948, ibid., Vol. X, Doc. 250, p. 357.
30. Abdullah, as quoted in Teng & Kaul, *Kashmir's Special Status*, Appendix IV, p. 198.
31. Sheikh Abdullah, 10 April 1952, Ranbir Singhpura, Jammu, as quoted in Balraj Puri, *Triumph and Tragedy*, New Delhi, 1981, p. 99.
32. Abdullah, *Flames*, p. 118.
33. Balraj Puri, *Kashmir: Towards Insurgency*, London, 1993, p. 27.
34. Balraj Puri, *Jammu: A Clue to the Kashmir Tangle*, Delhi, 1966, p. 7–8.
35. Puri, *Triumph and Tragedy*, p. 94.
36. Puri, *Jammu*, p. 11.
37. Lamb, *Disputed Legacy*, p. 197.
38. Puri, *Kashmir Tangle*, p. 93.
39. Ibid., p. 98.
40. Janet Rizvi, *Ladakh*, Oxford, 1983, p. 70.

41. Abdullah, *Flames*, p. 121.

42. As quoted in P. S. Verma, *Jammu and Kashmir at the Political Crossroads*, New Delhi, 1994, p. 42.

43. Puri, *Triumph & Tragedy*, p. 93.

44. Singh, *Heir Apparent*, p. 92.

45. Patel to Nehru, 27 June 1950, *Patel Correspondence*, Vol. X, Doc. 247, p. 353.

46. Gopal, *Nehru*, Vol. II, p. 90.

47. Letter dated 15 September 1950 from Sir Owen Dixon to the Security Council quoted in Korbel, *Danger in Kashmir*, p. 172–3.

48. Resolution 91 (1951) Doc No S/2017/REV.I, quoted in *Kashmir in the Security Council*.

49. Korbel, *Danger in Kashmir*, p. 179.

50. Jalal, *The State of Martial Law*, p. 120.

51. Ibid., p. 117.

52. Ibid., p. 132.

53. Nehru to Bakshi Ghulam Muhammed, 18 August 1953, quoted in Gopal, *Nehru*, Vol. II, p. 182.

54. Gowher Rizvi, 'Nehru and the Indo–Pakistan Rivalry over Kashmir', *Contemporary South Asia*, March 1995, Vol. IV, No. 1, p. 27.

55. Nehru to Muhammed Ali Bogra, 10 November 1953, as quoted in Gopal, *Nehru*, Vol. II, p. 185.

56. Nirad C. Chaudhri, as quoted in Sam Burke, *Mainsprings of Indian and Pakistani Foreign Policies*, Minneapolis, 1974, p. 143.

57. Jain, ed. *Soviet–South Asian Relations*, Vol. I, p. 4.

58. Khrushchev, as quoted in Abdullah, *Flames*, p. 134.

59. Burke, *Indian and Pakistani Foreign Policies*, p. 148.

60. B. L. Kak, *The Fall of Gilgit*, New Delhi, 1977, p. 31.

61. Stanley Wolpert, *Zulfi Bhutto of Pakistan*, Oxford, 1993, p. 64.

62. Louis D. Hayes, *The Impact of U.S. Policy on the Kashmir Conflict*, Texas, 1971. p. 28.

63. The Karakoram highway was opened in 1978.

64. Resolution 126, 2 December 1957, quoted in *Kashmir in the Security Council*, p. 38.

65. Morozov, 21 June 1962, as quoted in Jain, *Soviet–South Asian Relations*, Vol. 1, p. 45.

66. Leo Rose, 'The Politics of Azad Kashmir', in *Perspectives on Kashmir*, ed. Raju G. C. Thomas, Colorado, 1992, p. 237.

67. Saraf, *Kashmiris Fight*, Vol. II, p. 1289–90.

68. Mir Abdul Aziz, interview, 24 March 1994.

69. Rose, 'The Politics of Azad Kashmir', p. 238.

70. Korbel, *Danger in Kashmir*, p. 200.

71. See Ian Stephens, *Horned Moon*, London, 1953, p. 138.

72. Saraf, *Kashmiris Fight*, Vol. II, p. 1294.

73. Lamb, *Disputed Legacy*, p. 189.

74. Abdullah, 10 April 1952, as quoted in Saraf, *Kashmiris Fight*, Vol. II, p. 1200.

75. Abdullah, *Flames*, p. 122.

76. See Puri, *Towards Insurgency*, p. 20.

77. Verma, *Crossroads*, p. 46.

78. Abdullah, *Flames*, p. 127.

79. Singh, *Heir Apparent*, p. 160.
80. Gopal, *Nehru*, p. 133.
81. Nehru to G. S. Bajpai, 30 July 1953, as quoted in Gopal, *Nehru*, p. 132.
82. See Lamb, *Disputed Legacy*, p. 199.
83. *The Times*, 8 May 1952, as quoted in Taseer, *Abdullah*, p. 148.
84. Stephens, *Horned Moon*, p. 210–11.
85. Taseer, *Abdullah*, p. 23.
86. Kak, *Fall of Gilgit*, p. 27.
87. *New York Times*, 28/30 July 1955, as quoted in Korbel, *Danger in Kashmir*, p. 319.
88. Abdullah, *Flames*, p. 128.
89. Abdullah, February 1958, as quoted in Lamb, *Disputed Legacy*, p. 203.
90. As quoted in Korbel, *Danger in Kashmir*, 1966, p. 322.
91. Saraf, *Kashmiris Fight*, Vol. II, p. 1322.
92. Excerpts from Sheikh Abdullah's latest statements, *Kashmir & the Peoples Voice*, 1964.
93. Abdullah, *Flames*, p. 143.
94. *Daily Express*, 5 February 1957, as quoted in Saraf, *Kashmiris Fight*, Vol. II, p. 1226.
95. Mir Qasim, p. 82, as quoted in Verma, *Crossroads*, p. 52.
96. Nehru as quoted in Gopal, *Nehru*, Vol. 3 1956–1964, p. 262.
97. Prem Nath Bazaz, *The Shape of Things in Kashmir*, New Delhi, 1965.

Chapter 5 Diplomacy and War

1. John Kenneth Galbraith, US Ambassador in New Delhi, 19 January 1963, as quoted in Altaf Gauhar, *Ayub Khan*, Lahore, 1993, p. 227 fn. 41.
2. Burke, *Indian and Pakistani Foreign Policies*, p. 187.
3. Nehru, quoted in Gopal, *Nehru*, Vol. III, p. 223.
4. Burke, *Indian and Pakistani Foreign Policies*, p. 166, p. 169.
5. President Kennedy, as quoted in Gauhar, *Ayub Khan*, p. 215 fn. 28.
6. Kak, *Fall of Gilgit*, p. 43.
7. Gopal, *Nehru*, Vol. III, p. 256.
8. Ziegler, *Mountbatten*, p. 601.
9. Kak, *Fall of Gilgit*, p. 47.
10. Gopal, *Nehru*, p. 258.
11. James, *Pakistan Chronicle*, p. 97.
12. State Department telegram, dated 9 March 1963, as quoted in James, *Pakistan Chronicle*, p. 96.
13. Rostow was chairman of the Policy Planning Council at the US State Department; see James, *Pakistan Chronicle*, p. 98.
14. See Sisir, Gupta, *Kashmir: A Study of India–Pakistan Relations*, London, 1966, p. 355.
15. James, *Pakistan Chronicle*, p. 102.
16. See James, *Pakistan Chronicle*, p. 101.
17. Kak, *Fall of Gilgit*, p. 48–9.
18. Zulfikar Ali Bhutto, as quoted in Wolpert, *Bhutto*, p. 74.
19. Amanullah Khan, interview, Rawalpindi, April 1995.
20. Zulfikar Ali Bhutto, as quoted in Wolpert, *Bhutto*, p. 77.
21. Document dated 18 May 1964, S/PV 1117, *Kashmir in the Security Council*, p. 42.

22, 23. Bazaz, *The Shape of Things in Kashmir*.

24. *Observer*, 16 December 1960, as quoted in Abdullah, *Flames*, p. 144.

25. Abdullah, *Flames*, p. 144.

26. Sheikh Abdullah, reported by *The Times of India*, 10 April 1964, as quoted in *Kashmir and the Peoples Voice*.

27. Krishna Menon, 13 April 1964, as quoted in ibid.

28. *Indian Express*, editorial, 13 April 1964, as quoted in ibid.

29. *The Times of India*, editorial, 16 April 1964, as quoted in ibid.

30. Gopal, *Nehru*, p. 264.

31. Abdullah, *Flames*, p. 152.

32. Ibid., p. 154.

33. Gauhar, *Ayub Khan*, p. 257.

34. Ibid., p. 260.

35. Ibid., p. 265.

36. Abdullah, *Flames*, p. 155.

37. James, *Pakistan Chronicle*, p. 114.

38. See Wolpert, *Bhutto*, p. 78.

39. Abdullah, *Flames*, p. 157.

40. Ibid., p. 158.

41. Abdullah, as quoted in Burke, *Indian and Pakistani Foreign Policy*, p. 186.

42. Abdullah, *Flames*, p. 160.

43. Burke, *Indian and Pakistani Foreign Policy*, p. 186-7.

44. Gauhar, *Ayub Khan*, p. 290.

45. Johnson was annoyed that Pakistan's US Patton tanks were moving towards the Indo–Pakistani border. They had been sold to Pakistan on the understanding that they would not be used against India.

46. Gauhar, *Ayub Khan*, p. 301.

47. James, *Pakistan Chronicle*, p. 126.

48. Ibid., p. 129.

49. Gauhar, *Ayub Khan*, p. 312.

50. Shahid Hamid, *Early Years of Pakistan*, Lahore, 1993, p. 177.

51. Gauhar, *Ayub Khan*, p. 493.

52. Karim, *Troubled Frontiers*, p. 80.

53. Lamb, *Disputed Legacy*, p. 261.

54. Gauhar, *Ayub Khan*, p. 326.

55. Hamid, *Early Years of Pakistan*, p. 177.

56. Ayub Khan, 29 August 1965, as quoted in Wolpert, *Bhutto*, p. 90.

57. Akbar, *Behind the Vale*, p. 171.

58. Gauhar, *Ayub Khan*, p. 330.

59. Ibid., p. 334.

60. James, *Pakistan Chronicle*, p. 136.

61. Burke, *Indian and Pakistani Foreign Policy*, p. 190.

62. James, *Pakistan Chronicle*, p. 141.

63. Gauhar, *Ayub Khan*, p. 342.

64. As quoted in Gauhar, *Ayub Khan*, p. 347.

65. See James, *Pakistan Chronicle*, p. 144.

66. *The Times*, London, 18 Sept 1965 as quoted in Gauhar, *Ayub Khan*, p. 348.

67. Gauhar, Ayub Khan, p. 352-3.

68. Hamid, *Early Years of Pakistan*, p. 184.

69. Zulfikar Ali Bhutto, 22/23 Sept 1965, as quoted in Wolpert, *Bhutto*, p. 94.

70. James, *Pakistan Chronicle*, p. 150.

71. Korbel, *Danger in Kashmir*, p. 347.

72. James, *Pakistan Chronicle*, p. 166.

73. Feldman, *From Crisis to Crisis*, p. 159.

74. James, *Pakistan Chronicle*, p. 157.

75. *Dawn*, 16 March 1966, as quoted in Gauhar, *Ayub Khan*, p. 404.

76. See Maleeha Lodhi, 'Bhutto, the Pakistan Peoples Party and Political Development in Pakistan, 1967–77', PhD thesis, 1981, London School of Economics.

77. Justice Abdul Majeed Mallick, interview, Mirpur, 30 March 1995.

78. *Washington Post*, 14 August 1965, as quoted in Korbel, *Danger in Kashmir*, 1966, p. 341.

79. Inder Gujral, interview, New Delhi, 9 April 1994.

80. Dharma Vira, interview, New Delhi, April 1994.

81. Saraf, *Kashmiris Fight*, Vol. II, p. 1378.

82. Amanullah Khan, interview, Rawalpindi, March 1994.

83. Maqbool Butt, as quoted in B. L. Kak, *The Untold Story of Men and Matters*, Jammu, 1987, p. 76.

84. Kak, *Untold Story*, p. 77.

85. Saraf, *Kashmiris Fight*, Vol. II, p. 1379.

86. Jai Prakash Narayan, confidential letter to Mrs Gandhi, 26 June 1966, as quoted in Akbar, *Behind the Vale*, p. 183.

87. As quoted in Verma, *Crossroads*, p. 53.

88. See Lamb, *Disputed Legacy*, p. 290–4.

89. Amanullah Khan, interview, Rawalpindi, March 1994.

90. Akbar, *Behind the Vale*, p. 173.

91. Inder Malhotra, *Indira Gandhi*, London, 1989, p. 133.

92. J. N. Dixit, interview, New Delhi, April 1994.

93. Gandhi to Nixon, 15 Dec 1971, in Indira Gandhi, *India*, London 1975, p. 173.

94. Simla is now written Shimla; I have retained the original spelling as it was at the time of the agreement.

95. White Paper, 1977, as quoted in Lamb, *Disputed Legacy*, p. 27.

96. Simla agreement, sub-clause 4 (ii), as quoted in Lamb, *A Disputed Legacy*, p. 297 and other publications.

97. T. N. Kaul, *Sunday Times of India*, 17 October 1993.

98. Zulfikar Ali Bhutto, *If I am Assassinated*, New Delhi, 1979, p. 130.

99. Ibid., p. 131.

100. P. N. Dhar, *The Times of India*, 4 April 1995.

101. J. N. Dixit, *The Times of India*, 7 April 1995.

102. Saraf, interview, March 1994.

103. P. N. Haksar, telephone interview, New Delhi, April 1995.

104. Bhattacharjea, *Wounded Valley*, p. 232–3.

105. Girish Saxena, interview, New Delhi, 16 April 1994.

106. Z. A. Bhutto, speech in the National Assembly, as quoted in the *Pakistan Times*, 19 July 1972.

107. Farooq visited Pakistan during negotiations for the Kashmir accord.

108. Farooq Abdullah, as quoted in Akbar, *Behind the Vale*, p. 186.

109. Farooq Abdullah, interview, Srinagar, 5 April 1995.

110. Wolpert, *Bhutto*, p. 192.

111. Interview, Muzaffarabad, March 1994.

112. Figures from *Azad Kashmir at a Glance, 1993*, Planning & Development Dept, Azad Govt of the State of Jammu and Kashmir.

113. Farooq Abdullah, interview, Srinagar, 5 April 1995.

114. Rose, 'The Politics of Azad Kashmir', p. 241.

115. Sheikh Abdullah, *Hindustan Times*, 5 March 1972 in Verma, *Crossroads*, p. 122.

116. Mir Qasim, *Hindustan Times*, 18 March 1972, ibid., p. 122.

117. Mir Qasim, *My Life and Times*, New Delhi, 1992, p. 132.

118. Sheikh Abdullah, interview with *The Times*, London, 8 March 1972, as quoted in Bhattacharjea, *Wounded Valley*, p. 234.

119. Sheikh Abdullah, *Flames*, p. 164.

120. Ibid., p. 165.

121. Akbar, *Behind the Vale*, p. 188.

122. Kashmir accord, as quoted in Verma, *Crossroads*, p. 58 Saraf, *Kashmiris Fight*, Vol. II, p. 1276.

123. Verma, *Crossroads*, p. 57.

124. Lamb, *Disputed Legacy*, p. 309.

125. See Akbar, *Behind the Vale*, p. 189.

126. Mir Qasim, *My Life and Times*, p. 145.

127. Prem Nath Bazaz, as quoted in Lamb, *Disputed Legacy*, p. 312.

128. Sheikh Abdullah, *Flames*, p. 168.

129. Verma, *Crossroads*, p. 129; interviews with APHC in Islamabad, March 1995.

130. Interview, Muzaffarabad, March 1994.

131. Ali, interview, Srinagar, March 1981.

132. Verma, *Crossroads*, p. 62.

133. Azam Inquilabi, interview, Islamabad, April 1994.

Chapter 6 Bravado and Despair

1. Sheikh Abdullah, Iqbal Park, 21 August 1981, as quoted in Akbar, *Behind the Vale*, p. 197.

2. Farooq Abdullah, 24 September 1989, as quoted in Puri, *Towards Insurgency*, p. 57.

3. Bhutto was executed on 4 April 1979 on a charge of conspiracy to murder a political opponent.

4. Sheikh Abdullah, as quoted in Singh, *Tragedy of Errors*, p. 16.

5. Singh, *Tragedy of Errors*, p. 18.

6. Bhattacharjea, *Wounded Valley*, p. 241.

7. Singh, *Tragedy of Errors*, p. 19.

8. Ibid., pp. 20–2.

9. As quoted in Taseer, *Sheikh Muhammad Abdullah*, Lahore, p. 67.

10. Prime Minister Sardar Abdul Qayum, interview, Islamabad, 25 March 1994.

11. Amanullah Khan, interview, Rawalpindi, 24 March 1944.

12. Singh, *Tragedy of Errors*, p. 24.

13. Mir Abdul Aziz, interview. Rawalpindi, 24 March 1994.

14. M. J. Akbar, *Behind the Vale*, p. 199.

15. When Indira Gandhi broke with the old guard of the Congress Party in 1969 it split into several factions. In 1978 she formed her own party, known as Congress(I) i.e. Indira.

16. Farooq Abdullah, interview, New Delhi, April 1994.

17. Singh, *Tragedy of Errors*, p. 34.

18. Ibid., p. 30.

19. Inder Malhotra, *Indira Gandhi*, London, 1989, p. 278.

20. Supporters of the Mirwaiz were called 'goats' because of the tradition of wearing a beard.

21. Akbar, *Behind the Vale*, p. 202.

22. Ibid., p. 205.

23. Verma, *Crossroads*, p. 129 & 143.

24. Tavleen Singh, interview, New Delhi, April 1994.

25. Singh, *Tragedy of Errors*, p. 38.

26. Ibid., p. 40.

27. Malhotra, *Indira Gandhi*, p. 279.

28. Bhattacharjea, *Wounded Valley*, p. 245.

29. Akbar, *Behind the Vale*, p. 207.

30. Ibid., p. 206.

31. Singh, *Tragedy of Errors*, p. 53.

32. Bhattacharjea, *Wounded Valley*, p. 246.

33. Singh, *Tragedy of Errors*, p. 54.

34. Malhotra, *Indira Gandhi*, p. 295.

35. Bhattacharjea, *Wounded Valley*, p. 248.

36. Singh, *Tragedy of Errors*, p. 68.

37. Jagmohan, *Frozen Turbulence*, p. 286.

38. Singh, *Tragedy of Errors*, p. 68.

39. Abdullah, *My Dismissal*, p. 11.

40. Ibid., p. 32.

41. Mir Qasim, *My Life and Times*, p. 163.

42. Singh, *Telegraph*, India, 11 July 1984, as quoted in *Tragedy of Errors*, p. 74.

43. Malhotra, *Indira Gandhi*, p. 297.

44. Singh, *Tragedy of Errors*, p. 79.

45. Jagmohan, *Frozen Turbulence*, p. 346.

46. Singh, *Tragedy of Errors*, p. 98.

47. Akbar, *Behind the Vale*, p. 213.

48. See Verma, *Crossroads*, p. 74.

49. As quoted in Verma, *Crossroads*, p. 159.

50. Verma, *Crossroads*, p. 137.

51. *Times of India*, 26 March 1987, as quoted in Verma, *Crossroads*, p. 141.

52. As quoted in Verma, *Crossroads*, p. 141.

53. Farooq Abdullah, interview, New Delhi, 15 April 1994.

54. Singh, *Tragedy of Errors*, p. 102.

55. Mir Abdul Aziz, interview, March 1994.

56. As quoted in Verma, *Crossroads*, p. 79.

57. Farooq Abdullah, interview, New Delhi, 1994; Bhattacharjea, *Wounded Valley*, p. 253.

58. Amanullah Khan, interview, Rawalpindi, March 1995.

59. Rodney Cowton, *The Times*, 27 December 1985.

60. Edward Desmond, 'The Insurgency in Kashmir (1989–91), *Contemporary South Asia*, March 1995, Vol. IV, No. 1, pp. 6–7.

61. Yasin Malik, *Our Real Crime*, Srinagar 1994, p. 1.

62. Singh, *Tragedy of Errors*, p. 108.

63. Ibid., p. 107.

64. Jagmohan, *Frozen Turbulence*. p.111–13.

65. Verma, *Crossroads*, p. 229.

66. Bhattacharjea, *Wounded Valley*, p. 255.

67. Verma, *Crossroads*, p. 208.

68. Rajendra Sareen, *Pakistan: the India Factor*, New Delhi, 1984, p. 40.

69. Desmond, 'The Insurgency in Kashmir', p. 8.

70. Singh, *Tragedy of Errors*, p. 204.

Chapter 7 Vale of Tears

1. *Sunday Observer*, 10 August 1990 quoted in Kadian, *The Kashmir Tangle*, p. 147.

2. Reeta Chowdhari Tremblay, 'Kashmir: The Valley's Political Dynamics', *Contemporary South Asia*, March 1995. Vol. IV, No. 1, p. 81.

3. Verma, *Crossroads*, p. 230.

4. Ibid., p 236.

5. Jagmohan, *Frozen Turbulence*, p. 125.

6. Bhattacharjea, *Wounded Valley*, p. 257.

7. Puri, *Towards Insurgency*, p. 58.

8. Singh, *Tragedy of Errors*, p.110.

9. Puri, *Towards Insurgency*, p. 56.

10. Farooq Abdullah, interview, New Delhi, 15 April 1994.

11. *Peace Initiatives*, ed. Sundeep Waslekar, Vol. I, No. 2, Sept–Oct 95, p 16–18.

12. Jagmohan listed 44 'terrorist organisations' at the beginning of 1990; see *Frozen Turbulence*, Appendix XV, p. 751–2.

13. Azam Inquilabi, interview, Islamabad, 25 March 1994.

14. Ibid.

15. Mufti Muhammed Sayeed, as quoted in Singh, *Tragedy of Errors*, p. 120.

16. Dr Major (retd) Muzafar Shah, interview, Lahore, 7 April 1994.

17. Jagmohan, *Frozen Turbulence*, p. 373.

18. Farooq Abdullah, interview, New Delhi, 15 April 1994.

19. See Akbar, *Behind the Vale*, p. 281.

20. Jagmohan, *Frozen Turbulence*, p. 342.

21. Singh, *Tragedy of Errors*, p. 131.

22. See Puri, *Towards Insurgency*, p. 60.

23. Haseeb, interview, Srinagar, 7 April 1995.

24. See Singh, *Tragedy of Errors*, p. 132.

25. Tony Allen-Mills, *The Independent on Sunday*, 28 January 1990.

26. *Daily Telegraph*, 22 January 1990.

27. Puri, *Towards Insurgency*, p. 60.

28. Akbar, *Behind the Vale*, p. 219.

29. Haseeb, interview, Srinagar, April 1995.

30. Desmond, 'The Insurgency in Kashmir', p. 8.

31. Inder Gujral as quoted in *Newsline*, May 1990, p. 17.
32. Puri, *Towards Insurgency*, p. 63.
33. Singh, *Tragedy of Errors*, p. 205.
34. Jagmohan, *Frozen Turbulence*, p. 34.
35. Ibid., p. 364.
36. Ved Bhasin, interview, Jammu, 10 April 1994.
37. See *Asia Watch*, May 1991, p. 57.
38. Jagmohan, *Frozen Turbulence*, p. 419.
39. Shiraz Sidhva, 'Present Insurgency is a Peoples Movement', as quoted in *Kashmir Bleeds*, p. 34.
40. *The Guardian*, 24 February 1990.
41. Singh, *Tragedy of Errors*, p.144.
42. Jagmohan, *Frozen Turbulence*, p. 21.
43. Ibid., p. 465.
44. George Fernandes, 'India's Policies in Kashmir', quoted in *Perspectives on Kashmir*, ed. Raju G. C. Thomas, p. 288.
45. The figure of 250,000 has also been given out of a total of 300,000 Kashmiri Pandits in the valley ('Report of a Mission', International Commission of Jurists, 1994).
46. Jawaharlal, interview, Mishriwalla camp, Jammu, 10 April 1994.
47. Dr Pamposh Ganju, interview, London, February 1996.
48. Jagmohan. *Frozen Turbulence.* p. 492.
49. Fernandes, 'India's Policies in Kashmir', p. 291.
50. Puri, *Towards Insurgency*, p. 65.
51. Report of Tarkunde, Sachar, Singh, Puri, as quoted in Bhattacharjea, *Wounded Valley*, p. 267.
52. Omar Farooq, interview, London, 9 November 1995.
53. Singh, *Tragedy of Errors*, p. 152.
54. Punjab Human Rights Organisation, Report, 1990.
55. Satish Jacob, 'Interview with Punjab Human Rights Organisation', 1995.
56. Punjab Human Rights Organisation Report, 1990.
57. Jagmohan, *Current. 26 May–1 June. 1990*, as quoted in PHRO Report, 1990.
58. Ashok Jaitley, as quoted in Desmond, 'The Insurgency in Kashmir', p. 6.
59. Singh, *Tragedy of Errors*, p. 157.
60. Girish Saxena, interview, New Delhi, 16 April 1994.
61. Derek Brown, *The Guardian*, 14 February 1990.
62. David Housego, *The Financial Times*, 6 June 1990.
63. Azam Inquilabi, interview, Islamabad, 25 March 1994.
64. V. M. Tarkunde, *Radical Humanist*, New Delhi, March 1990.
65. As quoted in Kadian, *The Kashmir Tangle*, p. 141.
66. Kadian, *The Kashmir Tangle*, p. 142.
67. Mian Zahid Sarfraz, interview, *Friday Times*, 6–21 June 1991.
68. Asia Watch, *Human Rights in India, Kashmir Under Siege*, May 1991, p. 5.
69. Desmond, 'The Insurgency in Kashmir', p. 15.
70. Christopher Thomas, *The Times*, 4 April 1991.
71. *Response of the Indian Government*, p. 17.
72. *Human Rights in Kashmir, Report of a Mission*, ICJ, 1994.
73. David Housego, *The Financial Times*, 22 April 1991.
74. Tony Allen Mills, *The Independent*, 2 June 1991.

75. Tim McGirk, *The Independent*, 17 September 1991.

76. Anwar Iqbal, *The News*, 8 February, 1992.

77. Puri, *Towards Insurgency*, p. 67.

78. Asia Watch, *The Human Rights Crisis in Kashmir*, June 1993, p. 45.

79. Dr Farida Ashai, as quoted in Asia Watch, *Human Rights Crisis*, p. 44.

80. *Asia Watch*, June 1993, p. 45.

81. Girish Saxena, interview, New Delhi, 16 April 1994.

82. Interview, Karachi, 1 April 1994.

83. *Asia Watch*, June 1993. p. 55.

84. Aditya Sinya, *The Pioneer*, 11 April 1994.

85. Mirwaiz Umar Farooq, telephone interview, Srinagar. April 1995.

86. Saxena, interview, New Delhi, 16 April 1994.

87. Ibid.

Chapter 8 Hearts and Minds

1. Farooq Abdullah, interview, New Delhi, 15 April 1994.

2. Mirwaiz Omar Farooq, interview, London, 9 November 1995.

3. *The Economist*, 'Kashmir: Another Try', 27 March 1993, p. 81.

4. The members of the mission were: Sir William Goodhart, UK, Dr Dalmo Dallari, Brazil, Ms Florence Butegwa, Uganda, Professor Vitit Muntarbhorn, Thailand. Their report was issued in November 1994.

5. Amnesty International, *Torture and Deaths in Custody in Jammu and Kashmir*, 31 January 1995, p. 8.

6. Journalist, interview, London, September 1995.

7. Azam Inquilabi, interview, Islamabad, 25 March 1994.

8. M. N. Sabharwal, director-general of J&K police, interview, Srinagar, April 1994.

9. *Response of the Government of India to Report of Amnesty International on Torture and Deaths in Custody in Jammu and Kashmir*, p 22.

10. Amnesty, *Torture and Deaths in Custody*, p. 7.

11. Yasin Malik, interview, Srinagar, 6 April 1995.

12. UN Commission for Human Rights, Geneva, February 1994, E/CN.4/1994.

13. Shekhar Gupta, 'On a Short Fuse', *India Today*, 15 March 1994, p. 26.

14. Narasimha Rao, 'Don't Underestimate Us', *India Today*, 15 March 1994, p. 34.

15. Shekhar Gupta, *India Today*, 15 March 1994, p. 29.

16. Ahmad, Sajjad, *Greater Kashmir*, 12 April 1994.

17. Dr Karan Singh, in *The Times of India*, Bangalore, 11 April 1994.

18. Tim McGirk, *The Independent*, 31 October 1994.

19. Haroon Joshi, interview, Srinagar, April 1995.

20. Yasin Malik, interview, Srinagar, 6 April 1995.

21. Shabir Shah, interview, Srinagar, 5 April 1995.

22. Abdul Gani Lone, interview, Srinagar, 5 April 1995.

23. Professor Abdul Ghani, as quoted in *Asian Age*, 12 April 1994.

24. Mian Abdul Qayum, advocate, interview, Srinagar, 14 April 1994.

25. Governor General (retd.) Krishna Rao, 'Statement on Doordashan', Jammu, 3 April 1995.

26. Farooq Abdullah, interview, Srinagar, 5 April 1995.

27. Mirwaiz Omar Farooq, interview, London, 9 November 1995.

28. Brigadier Arjun Ray, General Staff, Corps HQ, interview, Srinagar, April 1995.

29. *Peace Initiatives*, ed. Sundeep Waslekar, Vol. I, No. 2, Sept–Oct 1995, p. 13.

30. As quoted in 'Faltering Steps' by Shiraz Sidhva, *Frontline*, New Delhi, 9–22 April 1994, p. 4.

31. Kaleem Omar, 'Special Report on Kashmir', *The News on Friday*, 28 July 1995.

32. Rahul Bedi, 'On the Kashmir Beat', *Jane's Defence Weekly*, 21 May 1994, p. 19.

33. *Response of the Indian Government*, p. 21.

34. *Human Rights in Kashmir, Report of a Mission*, International Commission of Jurists, Geneva, November 1994.

35. Amnesty, *Torture and Deaths in Custody*, January 1995, p. 2.

36. *The Observer*, London, 13 November 1994, as quoted in Amnesty, *Torture and Deaths in Custody*, January 1995, p. 19.

37. Asia Watch, 'The Human Rights Crisis in Kashmir, A Pattern of Impunity', Rawalpindi, June 1993, p. 58.

38. *Response of the Government of India*, p. 22–3.

39. Amnesty International, *India: Analysis of the Government of India's response to Amnesty International's Report on Torture and Deaths in Custody in Jammu and Kashmir*, March 1995, p. 1.

40. Amnesty, *Torture and Deaths in Custody* January 1995, p. 60–1.

41. Ibid., p. 10.

42. Section 8(1) as quoted in *Human Rights in Kashmir*, ICJ report.

43. *Human Rights in Kashmir*, ICJ report.

44. Section 4, as quoted in *Human Rights in Kashmir*, ICJ report.

45. *Human Rights in Kashmir*, ICJ report.

46. Ibid.

47. Mian Abdul Qayum, interview, Srinagar, April 1994.

48. *Response of the Indian government*, p. 10.

49. Brigadier Arjun Ray, interview, Srinagar, April 1995.

50. M. N. Sabharwal, director-general J & K Police, interview, Srinagar, April 1994.

51. Indian High Commission, London, February 1996.

52. Puri, *Towards Insurgency*, p. 78.

53. Dinesh Kumar, *The Times of India*, August 1993.

54. Governor Gen (retd) K. V. Kirshna Rao, 'Statement on Doordashan', Jammu, 3 April 1995.

55. Student, interview, Srinagar, April 1995.

56. Businessman, interview, Srinagar, April 1995.

57. Houseboat Owner, interview, Srinagar, April 1995.

58. Amnesty, *Torture and Deaths in Custody*, January 1994, p. 59.

59. Asia Watch, *The Human Rights Crisis in Kashmir*, June 1993, p. 98.

60. Girish Saxena, interview, New Delhi, 16 April 1994.

61. Farooq Abdullah, interview, Srinagar, 5 April 1995.

62. See *Human Rights in Kashmir*, ICJ report.

63. Interview, Srinagar, April 1995.

64. Mirwaiz Omar Farooq, interview, London, 9 November 1995.

65. Yasin Malik, interview, Srinagar, 6 April 1995.

66. Amanullah Khan, telephone interview, February 1996.

67. Siddiqi was amongst 32 killed in police firing in March 1996 when the mosque at Hazratbal was once more placed under siege.

68. Interviews, Srinagar, April 1995.

69. Indian High Commission, London, February 1996.

70. Statistics to end March 1995, supplied by Ram Mahan Rao, Adviser to Government of J&K, New Delhi, April 1995.

71. Indian High Commission, London, February 1996.

72. Interview, Srinagar, April 1994.

73. Girish Saxena, interview, New Delhi, April 1994.

74. Desmond, 'The Insurgency in Kashmir', p. 15.

75. Interview, New Delhi, 1995.

76. *Response of the Government of India*, p. 5.

77. Prime Minister Sardar Abdul Qayyum Khan, interview, Islamabad, March 1995.

78. *Human Rights in Kashmir*, ICJ report .

79. 'The Islamic Blowback', BBC 2, 11 November 1995.

80. Muhammad Saraf, interview, Rawalpindi, March 1994; he died in November 1994.

81. Mirwaiz Omar Farooq, interview, London, 9 November 1995.

82. Yasin Malik, interview, Srinagar, April 1995.

83. Anthony Davis, *Jane's Intelligence Review*, Vol. VII No 1.

84. Indian High Commission, London, February 1996.

85. Sheikh Jamaluddin, interview, Srinagar, April 1994.

86. Izhar Wani, *The Daily Telegraph*, 12 May 1995.

87. Master Gul's role was publicised in the documentary, 'The Islamic Blowback', broadcast on BBC 2 on 11 November 1995.

88. Nazimuddin Sheikh, interview, Islamabad, 29 March 1995.

89. Prime Minister Sardar Abdul Qayum, interview, Islamabad, 25 March 1994.

90. Mirwaiz Omar Farooq, interview, London, 9 November 1995.

91. Ambore camp, interview, Muzaffarabad, 29 March 1994.

92. Nayyar Malik, interview, Muzaffarabad, 29 March 1994.

93. Masood Kashfi, Station Director, interview, Muzaffarabad, 29 March 1994.

94. Interview, Rawalpindi, April 1995.

95. Prime Minister Sardar Qayum Khan, interview, Islamabad, March 1994.

96. Azam Inquilabi, interview, Islamabad, March 1994.

97. Yasin Malik, interview, Srinagar, April 1995.

98. Raja Nisar Wali, interview, Gilgit, 16 April 1994.

99. Wazir Firman Ali, interview, Islamabad, 14 April 1995.

100. See Verdict on Gilgit & Baltistan (Northern Area) Mirpur, 1993.

101. Student, interview, Sopore, April 1994.

102. Amnesty, *An Unnatural Fate*, December 1993, p. 7.

103. Dr Rashid, interview, Srinagar, April 1994.

104. *Peace Initiatives*, ed. Sundeep Waslekar, New Delhi, September–October 1995, Vol. I, No. 2, p. 15.

105. *Peace Initiatives*, p. 11.

106. Indian government figures for 1995 are 2,796 persons killed; for 1994, 2,899 killed. This compares with 31 killed in 1988, 92 killed in 1989, 1,177 killed in 1990. Indian High Commission, London, February 1996. Unofficial statistics are much higher.

107. Amnesty, interview, London, October 1995.

108. Bone and Joint hospital, interview, Srinagar, April 1994.

109. Brigadier Arjun Ray, interview, Srinagar, April 1995.

110. Ashok Jaitley, telephone interview, New Delhi, 11 April 1995.

111. Farooq Abdullah, interview, Srinagar, 5 April 1995.

112. Ram Mahan Rao, interview, New Delhi, 10 April 1995.

113. Pinto Narboo, interview, New Delhi, 10 April 1995; also P. K. Triparthi, District Commissioner, interview, Leh, 12 April, 1995.

114. Congress politician, interview, Jammu, April 1995.

115. Indian High Commission, London, February 1996: in 1995 45 per cent were killed, compared with 20 per cent in 1994.

116. Stephen Humphrey, interview, Srinagar, April 1994.

117. Iqbal Chapra, interview, Srinagar, April 1994.

118. Muhammed Kotru, interview, Srinagar, April 1994.

119. David Mackie, *The Daily Telegraph*, 24 June 1994.

120. Kim Housego in ibid.

121. Martha Fichtinger, interview, Srinagar, April 1995.

122. Sam Valani, interview, Srinagar, April 1995.

123. Gary Lazzarini, interview, Srinagar, April 1995.

124. Manager, Ahdoo's Hotel, interview, Srinagar, April 1995.

125. Kaleem Omar, Special Report on Kashmir, *The News on Friday*, 28 July 1995.

126. K. Padmanabhaiah in *The News on Friday*, 28 July 1995.

127. Omar Farooq, interview, London, 9 November 1995.

Chapter 9 Conflict or Consensus?

1. Edward Desmond, 'The Insurgency in Kashmir (1989-91)' in *Contemporary South Asia*, March 1995, Vol 4, No 1, p 8.

2. Yasin Malik, interview, Srinagar, 6 April 1995.

3. James Woolsey, as quoted in *The Economist*, 7 January 1994.

4. Private conversation, March 1995.

5. Robin Raphel, as quoted in *The Financial Times*, 1 November 1994.

6. Strobe Talbott, press conference, New Delhi, 8 April 1994.

7. A. H. Suhrawardy, interview, Rawalpindi, March 1994.

8. See Sumantra Bose, *The Challenge in Kashmir*, 1997, p.195.

9. India Human Rights Abuses in the Election Period in Jammu and Kashmir, *Amnesty International*, ASA20/39/96.

10. Dev P. Kumar, *Kashmir, Return to Democracy*, New Delhi, 1996, p. 11.

11. Christopher Thomas, *The Times*, 24 May 1996.

12. As quoted in Kumar, *Return to Democracy*, p. 13.

13. Interview Farooq Abdullah, New Delhi, 14 Dec. 1998.

14. http://jammukashmir.nic.in/normalcy/welcome.html.

15. *The Statesman*, 3 October 1996.
    http://jammukashmir.nic.in/normalcy/welcome.html.

16. Sumantra Bose, *The Challenge in Kashmir*, Delhi, 1997, p. 177.

17. Agencies, New Delhi, as quoted in *The News*, 6 March 1997.

18. India-Pakistan Foreign Secretary-level Talks, Joint Statement, 23 June 1997.

19. Private information, Islamabad, Karachi, May 1997.

20. as quoted in *The Observer*, 17 August 1997.

21. 'Even the Queen's departure from India stirs up trouble '– Madras, India, CNN, 18 October 1997.

22. *Indian Express,* New Delhi, 10 October 1997.

23. *Business Standard Newspaper,* 14 October 1997.

24. John Kampfner, *Robin Cook,* Victor Gollanz, 1998, p. 175–8.

25. *The News,* 15 August 1997.

26. APP, Muzaffarabad, as quoted in *The News,* 27 January 1998.

27. Despite the death of the Norwegian, Hans Christian Ostro, as a matter of principle the Norwegian government stayed involved in discussions throughout..

28. Sir Nicholas Fenn, GCMG, correspondence, 9 July 1999.

29. Hilary Synnott, conversation, 26/27 July 1999.

30. Farooq Abdullah, interview, New Delhi, December 1998.

31. Alexander Evans, as quoted in 'Kashmir: the past ten years', *Asian Affairs,* Feb. 1999, p. 30.

32. Danny Summers, correspondence, July 1999.

33. M. J. Gohel, correspondence, London, 28 June 1999.

34. Statement by Lord Avebury, member of the UK Liberal Democrat Foreign Affairs Team and Vice-Chair, UK Parliamentary Human Rights Group, New Delhi, 29 November 1998.

35. Jonathan Harley, *The Herald,* June 1999, p. 49.

36. Survey, India and Pakistan, *The Economist,* 22 May 1999.

37. 'If they are dead, tell us.' 'Disappearances' in Jammu and Kashmir, Amnesty International, ASA 20/02/99, February 1999.

38. Survey, India and Pakistan, *The Economist,* 22 May 1999.

39. Human Rights Watch, http://news.bbc.co.uk/hi/english/world/south asia/.

40. M. J. Gohel, correspondence, 28 June 1999.

41. See Alexander Evans, unpublished research material, 1999.

42. Amnesty International, ASA20/09/96, September 1996.

43. Amnesty International, ASA 20/02/99, February 1999.

44. Iftikhar Gilani, *Kashmir Times,* dateline 24 January 1999.

45. Iftikar Gilani, *Kashmir Times,* 24 January 1999: Report of Union Home Ministry.

46. Editorial, *Kashmir Times,* 30 September 1998.

47. See Alexander Evans, unpublished research material, 1999.

48. See Isambard Wilkinson, 'Pakistan funds Islamic terror', *The Sunday Telegraph,* 16 May 1999; Alexander Evans, *Asian Affairs,* p. 32;.

49. Fact sheet: 'U.S. strike on Facilities in Afghanistan and Sudan' US Dept of State, 21 August 1998.

50. Private information.

51. Mirwaiz Omar Farooq, interview, London, 9 November 1995.

52. APHC spokesman quoted in Kashmir Global Network, *Kashmir News Report,* 12 July 1997 quoted in John D. Cockell, *Ethnic Nationalism and Subaltern Political process: exploring autonomous democratic action in Kashmir,* September 1998.

53. Azam Inquilabi, Jama Masjid, Srinagar, 21 July 1995 as quoted in John Cockell, *Ethnic Nationalism and Subaltern political process: exploring autonomous democratic action in Kashmir,* September 1998.

54. Alexander Evans, unpublished research material; BBC News, 'Kashmiri separatist wants talks with India' 25 May 1998..

55. *The Pioneer,* 27 October 1997.

56. Srinagar, NNS, *The Nation,* London, 5–11 Feb 1999.

57. Dr Ayub Thakar, World Kashmir Freedom Movement, 26 July 1999.

58. Sardar Abdul Qayum Khan, interview, London, 6 July 1999.

59. Agencies, New Delhi, as quoted in *The Nation*, London, 4–10 June 1999.

60. *The Kashmir Times,* 30 September 1998.

61. Private conversation, July 1999.

62. Sumantra Bose, *The Challenge in Kashmir,* New Delhi, 1997, p. 95.

63. $700,000 per day (approx.).

64. Farooq Abdullah, interview, New Delhi, 14 December 1998.

65. Vajpayee was foreign minister in the Moraji Desai government 1977–79.

66. Washington, NNS, as quoted in *The Nation*, London, 15–21 May 1998.

67. http://www/library.utoronto.ca/97/foreign, 12 June 1998.

68. 'Pakistan's economy looks too weak to stand many internatinal sanctions,' Mark Nicholson, *The Financial Times,* 12 June 1998.

69. 'Easing of Sanctions on India and Pakistan', Statement by the Press Secretary, The White House, 7 November 1998.

70. Interview, Sardar Abdul Qayum Khan, 4 July 1998.

71. Vajpayee in New Delhi, as quoted in *The Nation*, 27 July 1998.

72. *The Nation,* London, 31 July 1998.

73. As quoted in *The Nation,* London, 17/18 October 1998.

74. Memorandum of Understanding signed by the Indian Foreign Secretary, Mr K. Raghunath, and the Pakistani Foreign Secretary, Mr Shamshad Ahmad, Lahore, 21 February 1999.

75. Lahore declaration signed by the Prime Ministers of India and Pakistan on 21 February 1999.

76. As quoted in *The Nation*, London, 5/11 March 1999.

77. As quoted in *The Nation*, London, 25 March 1999.

78. 'Pakistan, India set for fresh N-talks', Peter Montagnon, *The Financial Times,* 27 January 1999.

79. 'Stern Gujral cautions Pak', *The Asian Age,* 3 October 1997.

80. Figures are conflicting; in mid-May the Srinagar-based, Excelsior newspaper, stated that an Indian army patrol had seen 200-300 'foreign' militants who 'seemed to have infiltrated' from the Pakistani side of the line of control. This number was later put at about 600. It is now clear that they were mostly from the NLI, based in Skardu.

81. As reported by Rahul Bedi, *The Daily Telegraph,* 28 May 1999.

82. Julian West, 'British guerillas blamed for border conflict with India,' *The Sunday Telegraph,* 30 May 1999.

83. Ahmed Rashid, *The Daily Telegraph,* 28 May 1999.

84. Reports varied as to whether the planes were actually shot down or developed engine trouble. One report stated that the MiG-21 had strayed across into Pakistani airspace and was hit by a surface-to-air missile while the MiG-27 developed engine trouble and crashed.

85. Brian Cloughley, former deputy commander of UNMOGIP, author of 'A History of the Pakistan Army: Wars and Insurrections', interview, June 1999.

86. In Perspective – the Weekly Column from *Oxford Analytica.* 9 June 1999.

87. See report by Julian West, *Sunday Telegraph,* 30 May 1999.

88. As quoted in *Asian Age,* 12 June 1999.

89. Press reports, Embassy of India, Press, Information & Culture Wing, Washington DC. May–June 1999.

90. Private information, July 1999.

91. Institute of Defence Studies , as quoted in *The News*, 16 June 1999; Krishnan Guruswamy, 'India Takes Strategic Kashmir Peak', *Associated Press*, 5 July 1999.

92. *Kashmir Times*, 26 June 1999; Krishnan Guruswamy, 'India Takes Strategic Kashmir Peak, *Associated Press*, 5 July 1999.

93. As quoted in *The News*, 17 June 1999.

94. Brian Cloughley, June, 1999.

95. Lord Ahmed, interview, London, 30 June 1999.

96. New Delhi, NNS, as quoted by *The Nation*, 4–10 June 1999.

97. Agencies, as quoted in *The News*, 13 June 1999.

98. 'India uses "dirty war" tactics in Kashmir, Peter Popham, *The Independent*, 20 June 1999.

99. Susannah Price, http://news.bbc.co.uk/hi/english/world/south asia, June 1999.

100. BBC News, South Asia, 23 June 1999.

101. Srinagar, NNS, *The Nation,* London, 25 June–1 July 1999.

102. http://news.bbc.co.uk/hi/english/world/monitoring, 4 July 1999.

103. Kashmir's cyberwar by Charu Lata Johsi, http://news.bbc.co.uk/hi/english/world/south asia, 28 June 1999.

104. Text: G8 statement on regional issues. G8 Cologne Summit Documents, Transcripts June 18-20 1999, http://www/usia/gov/topical/econ/g8koln/g8region.htm.

105. Thomas Lippman, *The International Herald Tribune*, 28 June 1999.

106. As quoted in *The Nation*, London, June 1999.

107. Private information, July 1999.

108. Survey, India and Pakistan, *The Economist*, 22 May 1999.

109. BBC 24 News, Hard Talk with Tim Sebastian, 23 June 1999.

110. *The Sunday Telegraph*, 20 June 1999.

111. 'India was set to invade Pakistan,' Brian Fenton, *The Daily Telegraph*, 27 July 1999.

112. http://.bbc.co.uk/hi/english/world/south asia, 4 June 1999.

113. Pamela Constable, *International Herald Tribune*, 7 June 1999.

114. Ayaz Amir, *Dawn,* 25 June 1999.

115. Private correspondence, June 1999.

116. Rahul Bedi, *Daily Telegraph*, 22 June 1999.

117. Brian Cloughley, July 1999.

118. As quoted by Peter Popham, *The Independent*, 1 July 1999.

119. http://.bbc.co.uk/hi/english/world/monitoring/newsid, 5 July 1999.

120. Prime Minister Nawaz Sharif, 12 July 1999, Islamabad, NNS, as quoted in *The Nation,* London, 16-22 July 1999.

121. Muzaffarabad, NNS, *The Nation,* London, 9–15 July 1999.

122. http://.bbc.co.uk/hi/english/world/sout asia, 5 July 1999.

123. *Greater Kashmir*, Srinagar, dateline 20 July 1999.

124. Islamabad, NNS, *The Nation,* London, 16–22 July 1999.

125. Rahul Bedi & Christopher Lockwood, 'Pakistanis protest over Kashmir retreat', *The Daily Telegraph,* 13 July 1999.

126. Benazir Bhutto, former Prime Minister and leader of the opposition, London, 20 July 1999.

127. http://.bbc.co.uk/hi/english/world/south asia, 23 July 1999.

128. Benazir Bhutto, *The New York Times*, as quoted in *The Nation*, London, 11–17 June 1999.

129. New Delhi, Agencies, *The Nation*, London, 9–15 July 1999.

130. Srinagar, Agencies, *The Nation*, London, 16–22 July 1999.

131. New Delhi, Agencies, *The Nation*, London, 9–15 July 1999.

132. Standard cost for a full page black & white advertisement in *The Times* (advertising dept.).

133. *The Times*, 13 July 1999.

134. Islamabad, NNS, *The Nation*, London, 20–26 Aug 1999.

135. As quoted in *The Nation*, London, 23–29 July 1999.

136. There are conflicting reports over numbers dead.

137. http://.bbc.co.uk/hi/english/world/south asia, 27 July 1999.

138. Owen Bennett-Jones, http://news.bbc.co.uk/hi/english/world/south asia, 25 July 1999.

139. 'Early deal to end Kashmir conflict was ignored', Suzanne Goldenberg, *The Guardian*, 22 July 1999.

140. http://.bbc.co.uk/hi/english/world/south asia, 26 July 1999.

141. *Daily Telegraph*, 27 July 1999.

142. Peter Popham, Frontline, *The Independent*, 1 July 1999.

143. http://.bbc.co.uk/hi/english/world/south asia, 23 July 1999.

144. Frontline, *The Independent*, 22 July 1999.

145. 'Year-round watch put on border in Kashmir', Rahul Bedi, *The Daily Telegraph*, 20 July 1999.

146. http://news.bbc.co.uk/hi/english/world/south asia, 19 July 1999.

147. http://.bbc.co.uk/hi/english/world/south asia/newsid, 1 August 1999.

148. http://.bbc.co.uk/hi/english/world/south asia/newsid, 26 July 1999.

149. http://news.bbc.co.uk/hi/english/world/south asia, 20 July 1999.

150. http://news.bbc.co.uk/hi/english/world/south asia, 20 July 1999.

151. http://news.bbc.co.uk/hi/english/world/south asia, 25 July 1999.

152. Jeddah, NNS, *The Nation*, London, 23-29 July 1999.

153. http://news.bbc.co.uk//hi/english/world/south asia/newsid, 12 August 1999.

154. as quoted in *The Nation*, London, 13-19 August 1999.

155. Julian West, *The Sunday Telegraph*, 15 August 1999.

156. Iftikar Gilani, *The Kashmir Times*, dateline 7 August 1999.

157. http://news.bbc.co.uk//hi/english/world/south asia/newsid, 15 August 1999.

158. http://news.bbc.co.uk//hi/english/world/south asia/newsid, 15 August 1999.

159. http://news.bbc.co.uk//hi/english/world/south asia/newsid, 16 August 1999.

Chapter 10 New Century, New Vision

1. Salman Asif, Khidmet seminar, 'Indian & Pakistani relations in the 21st century', SOAS, London, 24 July 1999.

2. As quoted in President Musharraf's speech to the nation, 12 January 2002.

3. This belief is being challenged by Hindutva ideology, propagated by some urban middle class Hindus that India is a Hindu country and that Muslims should leave or recognise their status as foreigners.

4. Bruce Riedel, 'American Diplomacy and the 1999 Kargil Summit at Blair House,' Policy Paper Series 2002, Center for the Advanced Study of India, University

of Pennsylvania, May 2002, as reported in *The Sunday Times*, 12 May 2002 and on bbc.co.uk/hi/english/world/south asia/ May 2002.

5. Most of the passengers were Indian; there were 12 Europeans and two Americans.

6. Telephone interview, *Associated Press*, Kabul, 25 December 1999.

7. Among the nations on the list are Iran, Iraq and Syria. Such a designation would end all loans to Pakistan from the World Bank and the IMF which could push Pakistan into economic collapse.

8. Rahul Bedi, 'Hostages released in bargain with India', *The Daily Telegraph*, 1 January 2000.

9. Gen. Pervez Musharraf, interview with *The Hindu*, 16 January, 2000.

10. Gen. Pervez Musharraf, Ambore refugee camp, February 2000.

11. Gen. Pervez Musharraf, interview, Karachi, February 2000.

12. See Shaukat Qadir, 'An Analysis of the Kargil Conflict 1999', *RUSI Journal*, April 2002.

13. Gurmukh Singh, as quoted in *The Daily Telegraph*, 22 March 2000.

14. Some reports state that two men later succumbed to their injuries, bringing the total dead to 36.

15. They included retired Justice Ajit Singh Bains, Chairman of the Punjab Human Rights Organisation, Sardar Inderjit Singh Jaijee, Convener of the Movement Against State Repression and Lt Gen Kartar Singh Gill, Advisor to the PHRO and MASR.

16. Prime Minister Atal Vajpayee, as quoted in *The Daily Telegraph*, 22 March 2000.

17. President Clinton's address to the people of Pakistan, *Dawn*, 25 March 2000.

18. General Aslam Beg, as quoted by Pamela Constable, *International Herald Tribune*, 28 March 2000.

19. The panel of experts was convened in October 1996; the report was finally presented before the state assembly in June 2000.

20. Governor Saxena confirmed this to me in an interview in Jammu, April 2002.

21. Alexander Evans, 'Reducing Tension is Not Enough', *Washington Quarterly*, Spring 2001.

22. Amnesty International, 'India: Impunity must end in Jammu and Kashmir', April 2001, ASA 20/023/2001.

23. Abdul Qadri, General-Secretary, JKLF, interview, Muzaffarabad, October 2000. Dar is now believed to be under Indian protective custody.

24. JKLF Formula to solve Kashmir Issue, 1–2 July 2000. In November 2000, Amanullah Khan's daughter married Abdul Gani Lone's son Sajad in Islamabad in a wedding 'uniting families' across the line of control.

25. A census is held in India every 10 years. The last census was held in Indian J & K in 1981.

26. According to the Indian government, regardless of the ban, the census was completed in all districts. No breakdown figures are yet available for 2001.

27. US State Department, Human Rights Report on India, 2000. Indian government figures indicate 1,520 militants were killed in encounters in the first nine months of 2000, compared with 1,082 in 1999.

28. Gov. Saxena, interview, Jammu, April 2002.

29. Amnesty International April 2001, ASA 20/023/2001.

30. Private information, Hunza, June 2001. The Balawaristan National Front, which calls for the independence of the Northern Areas, does not have a significant following. Support for the movement came from those who were disappointed that

men from the Northern Light Infantry, who had fought in Kargil, were initially 'disowned' by the Pakistani government. Later they were honoured as 'martyrs'.

31. Usman Khalid, leader of Al Ansaar, based in the UK, as quoted in *The Pakistan Post*, 31 May 2001.

32. Yasin Malik, interview, London, 20 June 2001.

33. President Musharraf, interview, Rawalpindi, April 2002; additional private information.

34. Jaswant Singh and Abdul Sattar, Agra, NNS, as quoted in *The Nation*, London, 20/26 July 2001.

35. Prime Minister Vajpayee, interview with *Newsweek*, June 2002.

36. Washington Online. July 2001.

37. ANI, Rawalpindi, July 2001.

38. Interview, Amanullah Khan, Rawalpindi, June 2001. This clause in the nomination papers was inserted by Sardar Qayum Khan in the 1970s as an 'interim' measure pending a plebiscite under the auspices of the UN.

39. Secretary of State Colin L. Powell, 26 December 2001, US State Department.

40. President Musharraf, speech to the nation, 12 January 2002. He expressed similar sentiments in his speech to the nation on 27 May 2002.

41. The Indian government also started discussing with the United States the positioning of sensors to monitor the line of control.

42. Sheikh Omar Saeed later withdrew his confession. He was sentenced to death in July 2002.

43. Private information, Srinagar, April 2002. E-mail and STD facilities were reconnected in May 2002.

44. Gov. Saxena, interview, Jammu, April 2002.

45. Private information, London & Srinagar, 2002.

46. Uravashi Butatia, 'Speaking Peace. Womens' Voices from Kashmir' *Sunday Times of India*, 7 April 2002.

47. Interview, Srinagar, 2002.

48. Pervez Kaul, Principal, Tyndale-Biscoe school, Srinagar, April 2002.

49. The quality of the wool depends on the altitudes at which the goats grazed. See Justine Hardy's *Goat: From Kashmir to Notting Hill* (John Murray, 2000) for a discussion of the origins of pashmina.

50. Justine Hardy, interview, London, June 2002.

51. Gulzar, of K.Salama & Sons, interview, Srinagar, April 2002.

52. Malik's passport was 'country specific' permitting him to travel only to the US and the UK. In early 2001 five members of the APHC executive council wanted to visit Pakistan to have talks with Gen Musharraf but the Indian government refused passports to Syed Ali Shah Gilani and Sheikh Abdul Rashid.

53. As of September 2002 Yasin Malik remains in jail. Election of a new APHC Chairman was postponed.

54. In Britain the requirement is to take an oath after being elected before taking one's seat. In order to encourage participation of disaffected individuals in elections, both India and Pakistan might consider adopting this system. Interview, Lord Avebury, July 2002

55. Sardar Abdul Qayum Khan, interview, London, June 2002; Sardar Qayum is now Chairman of the President's National Kashmir Committee with status of a Cabinet Minister.

56. Allegations were also made against Hindu extremists and supporters of Farooq Abdullah who would have opposed Lone's challenge to Abdullah's virtual monopoly of power. Lone had been badly beaten up at a press conference by a Hindu extremist on 1 April. He had also received death threats from militants.

57. Gujerat Carnage 2002, A Report to the Nation by an Independent Fact Finding Mission, April 2002. Unofficial figures: more than 2,000

58. Approximately 8,000 troops were deployed to assist the US against Al Qaeda and Taliban fighters. The regime had fallen in Dec 2001 but the location of Mullah Omar and bin Laden was still unknown.

59. Pakistan was estimated to have 25-50 nuclear warheads, India 100-150, 20 each deliverable by fighter planes, the remainder to be fitted to Shaheen, Ghauri, Hatf missiles (Pakistan) or Agni, Prithvi missiles (India). Source: Jane's Strategic Weapon Systems.

60. Prime Minister Vajpayee to Prime Minister Blair, as reported in *The Nation*, London, 6 June 2002

61. Deepak Sharma, *The Pioneer*, 26 May 2002

62. Jack Straw, text of parliamentary debate in the House of Commons, June 2002. Straw's allegation was denied by Pakistan's interior minister, Moin Hyder. The USA, Japan and Russia have also accepted the link between the ISI and Kashmiri militant groups.

63. Dr Ayub Thukar, World Kashmir Freedom Movement, interview, London, July 2002.

64. On 10 June, Vajpayee had lifted the ban imposed on Pakistani flights flying over its territory. Flights to and from Lahore/Delhi remained suspended. (Colin Powell also visited the region in Jan and July 2002).

65. See Kashmir Study Group: *The Kashmir Dispute at 50*, USA, 1997 & Kashmir: *The Way Ahead*, 1999

66. Governor Saxena, interview, Jammu, April 2002. India and Pakistan are still arguing about the validity of the Instrument of Accession. See Prem Shankar Jha's rebuttal of Professor Alastair Lamb's assertion that the state did not accede to India before Indian troops arrived on 27 October 1947, which Lamb in return rebutted, due to the unreliability of the testimony produced by the Indian writer.

67. George Fernandes, 12 October 1990, 'India's Policies in Kashmir: an Assessment and Discourse', in *Perspectives on Kashmir*, ed. Raju G.C.Thomas, Colorado, USA, 1991, p.286.

68. Interview, Srinagar, April 2002. Syed Salahuddin, the hardline leader of the Hizb-ul Mujaheddin and the United Jihad Council, was a former contestant of the 1987 elections.

69. See Sumit Ganguly, *The Crisis in Kashmir*, CUP & Woodrow Wilson Centre, 1997, p. 42, for an application of Samuel Huntingdon's argument that in a situation where there is institutional decay and political mobilisation, instability often arises. See also: John Ray, 'Kashmir 1962 to 1986: A footnote to history', *Asian Affairs*, June 2002.

70. In mid-July, armed men attacked Qasimnagar, a shanty town near Jammu, killing over 20 Hindus, mostly women, and wounding at least 30 more.

71. In July 2002 the Indian government announced that it would begin 'autonomy' talks with the state government. It later stated that talks would relate to a 'devolution of powers' but not full autonomy. In Jammu discussions were related to creating a regional council. Opponents warned of the dangers of 'trifurcation'.

72. A MORI poll held in major cities of Srinagar, Jammu and Leh in the Indian administered state of Jammu and Kashmir in late April 2002 revealed that 61% believed they were better off politically and economically as part of India; 6% as part of Pakistan; 33% did not know. 70% wanted a relaxation in restrictions crossing the line of control. The option of independence was not given although 55% said they would like greater political freedom in both Pakistani and Indian-administered parts of the state. The survey was commissioned by Lord Avebury who believed that within the limitations they were able to operate, without being able to include any rural representation, its findings were fair. It would require a fully participational referendum, without constraints, to indicate the true wishes of the people.

73. President Pervez Musharraf, interview, Rawalpindi, April 2002

74. Prime Minister Vajpayee, *Newsweek*, June 2002

Bibliography

Unpublished sources

THE BRITISH LIBRARY, ORIENTAL AND INDIA OFFICE COLLECTION

'Adoption by the Maharaja of the Second Son of the Raja of Poonch, 1906–7'.
Chelmsford Collection, 'Report on Indian Constitutional Reforms', 22 April 1918.
Christie, John, 'W.H.J. Christie Collection', 1947.
'Copies of Selected Documents Relating to Sir Muhammad Iqbal'.
Crown Representatives' Records, 1923.
Cunningham, Sir George, 'Diary', 1947'.
'Death of His Highness the Maharaja of Kashmir', 1925.
'Documents Relating to Raj Kumar Jagat Dev Singh', For & Pol Dept, 1924.
'Documents Relating to a Suitable Occupation for Raja Hari Singh', For & Pol Dept, 1918.
'Enclosures to Secret Letters in India', Vol. 103.
'Fortnightly Reports of the Resident in Kashmir 1924, 1925–26, 1927'.
General Reports by Colonel Ramsey, C. I. E., Resident in Kashmir, 1910.
'Kashmir Internal Situation', 1947–1948.
'Kashmir Reforms Scheme', For & Pol Dept, 1922.
Lawrence, Henry, 'Henry Lawrence Collection, Jan 1846–Feb 1847'.
Lorimer, David Lockhart, 'Lorimer Papers'.
Luard, Dr Hugh Bixby, Personal Memoirs, 1890–99.
'Memorandum on the Future of the Gilgit Agency, 1930'.
'Muslims of Kashmir', For & Pol Dept, 1924.
Poonch State Affairs, 1892.
Searle, Major, 'Diary', 1924.
'Sedition in Kashmir', Foreign Dept, 1907.
'Status of Hunza and Nagar and Political Districts', For & Pol Dept, 1941.
Young, Colonel Ralph, 'Journal of a Trip to Cashmere, 1867'.

OTHER UNPUBLISHED DOCUMENTS AND MANUSCRIPTS

Alder, Garry, 'British Policy on the Roof of the World, 1865–95', PhD thesis, Sept 1959, University of Bristol.
Evans, Alexander, draft research thesis, SOAS.
Lodhi, Maleeha, 'Bhutto, The Pakistan Peoples Party and Political Development in Pakistan, 1967–77', PhD thesis, London School of Economics, 1981.
Shankar, V., 'Memoirs' (by kind permission of Miss Rashmi Shankar).
United Nations Commission for Human Rights, Geneva, February 1994, E/CN.4/ 1994, (UN Library, London).

Interviews and briefings

Abbasi, Fayyaz Ali, Assistant Commissioner: Mirpur, March 1995.
Abdullah, Dr Farooq, former Chief Minister of Jammu and Kashmir: Srinagar & New Delhi, 1994, 1995, 1998, 2002.
Afridi, Amjad, lawyer: Jammu, April 2002.

Afzal, S.M., JKLF: Rawalpindi, March 2002.

Ahdoo's Hotel, Manager: Srinagar, April 1995.

Ahmad, Sardar Riaz, Secretary Agriculture, Chattar, AJK: March 1994.

Ahmed, Lord: London, June 1999.

Ahmed, Nasir, Deputy Commissioner: Gilgit, April 1994.

Advani, Muhstaq Ahmed, Muslim Conference: Rawalpindi, March 1995.

Akbar, Chaudhri Latif, advocate and former minister, PPP: Muzaffarabad, March 1994.

Akhtar, Prof. Sharifa, J & K Action Committee: Karachi, April 1994.

Akhtar, Miss Rumina, J. & K Action Committee: Karachi, April 1994.

Akhtar, Miss Shahbina, J & K Action Committee: Karachi, April 1994.

Ali, Wazir Firman, former Joint Secretary, Ministry of Kashmir Affairs: Islamabad, April 1995.

Alvi, Syed Ghulam Mustafa: Rawalpindi, March 2002.

Ansari, Abdul Khaliq, advocate: Mirpur, March 1995.

Ansari, Maulvi Abbas, Ittehad-ul Muslimeen: Srinagar, April 2002.

Ashraf, Malik Muhd, Inspector-General Police: Gilgit, April 1994.

Asif, Salman: Khidmet seminar, London, July 1999.

Atta, Mrs Saleema, Associate Professor Economics, University College, Muzaffarabad: March 1994.

Avebury, Lord: London, June 1999, July 2002.

Azim, Muhammed, advocate: Mirpur, March 1995.

Aziz, Mir Abdul, journalist: Rawalpindi, March 1994.

Aziz, Sartaj, former Pakistani foreign minister: Birmingham, 2002.

Aziz, Tahir, research officer, Azad government of Jammu and Kashmir: Islamabad, March 1995.

Balti, Iqbal, journalist: Islamabad, April 1995.

Bandey, Abdul Majid, advocate, Srinagar: London, April 1996.

Bano, Dr Hamida, University of Kashmir, Srinagar: London, 1996, Srinagar 2002.

Beaumont, Christopher, former Secretary to the Boundary Commission, correspondence: October 1995.

Bedi, Rahul, journalist: New Delhi April 1994/1995.

Bhasin, Ved, journalist: Jammu, April 1994, 2002.

Bhutto, Benazir, as Prime Minister: Islamabad, 1994 & 1995; London, 1999, 2002.

Bercha, Sher Baz Ali Khan, assistant librarian and writer: Gilgit, April 1994.

Bhattacharya, Subhabrata, journalist: New Delhi, April 1994.

Bone & Joint Hospital: Srinagar, doctors & patients, April 1994.

Brown, Mrs Margaret: Islamabad, April 1994.

Butt, Gulam, houseboat owner, Srinagar: March 1981, April 1994, April 1995, 2002.

Campbell-Johnson, Alan, Address to Pakistan Society: London, October 1995.

Chapra, Iqbal, Houseboat Owners Association: Srinagar, April 1994.

Chaudhri, Dr Muhd Khairyat, Dean of Arts Faculty, University of Azad Jammu and Kashmir, March 1994.

Cloughley, Colonel Brian: former deputy cdr UNMOGIP, London, 1999, 2000, 2002.

Dar, Ghulam: JKLF: Srinagar, April 2002.

Dar, Shabir Ahmed, Muslim Conference: Srinagar, April 2002.

Dhar, Vijay: New Delhi, April 1994/1995.

Dixit, J. N., former Foreign Secretary for the Government of India: New Delhi, April 1994, Oxford, 2001.

Dongola, Abdul Hamid, taxi driver: Srinagar, April 1994 & 1995.

Doucet, Lyse, journalist: February 1996.
Evans, Alexander, independent analyst: 1999, 2001, 2002.
Fai, Gulam Nabi, Kashmir American Council: Islamabad, 2000.
Fenn, Sir Nicholas, GCMG, former UK High Commissioner for India: 1999.
Farooq, Mirwaiz Omar, Srinagar/London: April/November 1995.
Farooqi, Siddique, Secretary, AJK government: Muzaffarabad, March 1994.
Fichtinger, Martha, tourist: Srinagar, April 1995.
Ganju, Dr Pamposh, Indo-European Kashmir forum: London, February 1996.
Ghanie, Mohd Sidiq, Peoples League: Muzaffarabad, October 2000.
Gohel, M.J., Asia-Pacific Foundation: London, 1999, 2002.
Gujral, Inder, former Foreign Minister of India, New Delhi, April 1994.
Guru, M. R., Srinagar: April, 1994.
Haksar, P. N., civil servant: telephone interview, New Delhi, April 1995.
Hamilton, Mollie Kaye, author: Surrey, June 1995.
Hardy, Justine, author: London, 2000, 2002.
Haseeb, medical student: Srinagar, April 1995.
Hayat, Colonel Zubair, Military Adviser, Pakistan High Commission: London, 2002.
Hijazi, Dr Haider, JKLF: Rawalpindi, March 1995.
Humphrey, Stephen, tourist: Srinagar, April 1994.
Husain, Irfan, journalist: Islamabad/London 2002.
Hussain, Altaf, journalist: Srinagar, April 2002.
Hussain, Shahmat, medical student: Srinagar, April 1995.
Inquilabi, Azam, Jammu and Kashmir Plebiscite Front/Operation Balakote: Islamabad, March 1994, Srinagar, April 2002.
Jaitley, Ashok, civil servant: New Delhi, April 1995, Jammu 2002.
Jaleel, Muzamil, journalist: Srinagar, April 2002.
Jamaluddin, Sheikh, Afghan prisoner, former militant: Srinagar, April 1994.
Jameel, Yusuf, journalist: Srinagar, April 1994.
James, Wing-Cdr A. G.: London, 1994.
Jawaharlal, teacher and refugee: Jammu, April 1994.
Joshi, Haroon, journalist: Srinagar, April 1995.
Karamat, General Jehangir, former Pakistani chief of amy staff: Birmingham, 2002.
Kashfi, Masood, radio station director: Muzaffarabad, March 1994.
Kaul, H. K. Librarian, India International Centre: New Delhi, March 1994.
Kaul, Pervez, Principal, Tyndale-Biscoe School: Srinagar, April 2002.
Khalid, Dr Nazir A., J. & K Action Committee: Karachi, April 1994.
Khan, Sardar Abdul Qayum Khan, Prime Minister of the Azad government of Jammu and Kashmir: Islamabad, March 1994, March 1995, London, July 1999, June 2002.
Khan, Abdul Wahid, ex-Joint Secretary: Gilgit, April 1994.
Khan, Aftab Ahmed, Secretary, Northern Areas: Islamabad, March 1994.
Khan, Amanullah, JKLF: Rawalpindi, March 1994, March 1995, February 1996, June 2001.
Khan, Arif Aslam: en route to Baltistan, April 1995.
Khan, Farooq Ahmed, Secretary for Tourism, AJK: Muzaffarabad, March 1994.
Khan, Habib, Inspector General Police: Muzaffarabad, March 1994.
Khan, Khalid Ibrahim, son of Sardar Mohammad Ibrahim Khan: Islamabad, 1994.
Khan, Muhammad Afzal, Minister, Northern Areas: Islamabad, March 1995.
Khan, Mahmood, Chief Commissioner: Gilgit, April 1994.

Khan, Nisar Hussain, Joint Secretary, Ministry of Industries and Production: Islamabad, April 1995.

Khan, Riaz Ahmed, Secretary, Dept of Agriculture & Livestock: Muzaffarabad, 1994.

Khan, Sardar Mohammad Ibrahim, Founder/President of Azad Government of Jammu & Kashmir: Islamabad, March 1994.

Khan, Sardar Muhd Latif Khan, Secretary for Education, AJK: Muzaffarabad, 1994.

Khan, Shaharyar Muhammad, former Foreign Secretary to the Government of Pakistan: Islamabad, March 1994, Oxford, May 2001.

Khan, Tanveer Ahmed, Foreign Secretary to the Gov of Pakistan, Islamabad, 1994.

Khashif, Zahid Amin, Chairman of Development Authority: Muzaffarabad, 1994.

Khel, Shefqat Kaka, Ministry of Foreign Affairs: Islamabad, March 1994.

Koker, A. S., advocate: Mirpur, March 1995.

Kotru, Muhammad, Houseboat Owners Association: Srinagar, April 1994.

Khwaja, Mrs Faiza: Islamabad, March 1994.

Lamb, Prof. Alastair, Address to Pakistan Society, London: March 1996, 2001, 2002.

Latif, Mr Ch. Muhammad and Mrs Tanveer: Muzaffarabad, March 1994.

Lazzarini, Gary, tourist: Srinagar, April 1995.

Lone, Abdul Gani, Peoples Conference: Srinagar, April 1995.

Malik, Mrs Nayyar, social worker: Muzaffarabad, March 1994.

Malik, Yasin, JKLF: Srinagar, 1995, London, 2001.

Mallick, Justice Abdul Majeed: Mirpur, March 1995.

Masood, Khalid, Agricultural Training Institute, Ghari Dopatta, AJK: March 1994.

Masood, Tahir, Ittehad-ul Muslimeen: Rawalpindi, March 1995.

Masud, Tariq, Kashmir House: Islamabad, March 1994/1995.

Mehmood, Khwaja Ahsan, J & K Action Committee: Karachi, April 1994.

Militants from JKLF, Hizb-ul Mujaheddin, Harkat-ul Ansar: Srinagar, April 1995.

Muhammad, Noor, Regional Programme Officer, Agha Khan Project: Hunza, 1994.

Musharraf, General Pervez, CEO of Pakistan: Karachi, 2000; as President: 2002.

Mushtaq, Dr Muhammed, Jamaat-i Islami: Muzaffarabad, March 1994.

Mustafa, Gulam, Assistant Commissioner: Muzaffarabad, March 1994, October 2000.

Naik, Niaz, former Foreign Secretary to the Gov of Pakistan: Islamabad, 1994.

Narboo, Pinto, former minister, Ladakh: New Delhi, April 1995.

Naseem, Syed Yousuf, Peoples Conference: Rawalpindi, March 1995.

Naqshbandi, Fez, research officer, Azad Government of Jammu and Kashmir: Islamabad, March 1994, February 2000.

Naqvi, Jawed, journalist: London/New Delhi, 2002.

Pataudi, General Sher Ali: Islamabad, April 1995.

Peters, Philip, tourist: Srinagar, April 1995.

Powell, Colin, Statement by Secretary of State, US Dept of State, 26 December 2001.

Puri, Balraj, author: telephone interview, Jammu, April 1995.

Qadri, Altaf, JKLF: Muzaffarabad, October 2000.

Qayum, Mian Abdul, advocate: Srinagar, April 1994.

Quereshi, Khalil Ahmad, Board of Revenue and Secretary to AJK Government: Muzaffarabad, March 1994.

Rao, Ram Mahan, adviser to Government of J & K: New Delhi, April 1995.

Raphel, Robin, US assistant secretary of state: Islamabad, 1995.

Rashid, Doctor: Srinagar, April 1994.

Rashid, Malik Abdul, Secretary Kashmir Cell: Muzaffarabad, March 1994.

Rathore, Mr and Mrs Mohd Amin, J & K Action Committee: Karachi, April 1994.

Ray, Brigadier Arjun, General Staff, Corps Headquarters: Srinagar, April 1995.

Sabharwal, M. N., Director-General of J & K Police: Srinagar, April 1995.

Safi, Ghulam Muhammad, APHC: Rawalpindi, March 1995, London, April 1996.

Saghar, Mehmood Ahmed, Peoples League: Rawalpindi, March 1995.

Salama & Sons, K, tailor: Srinagar, April 2002.

Saraf, Chief Justice (retd) Muhammad Yusuf: Rawalpindi, March/April 1994.

Saraf, Mohd Ashraf, Muslim Conference: Muzaffarabad, October 2000.

Sattar, Abdul, Pakistani foreign minister: press briefing, London, 2001.

Saxena, Girish, New Delhi, April 1994; as Governor of Jammu & Kashmir, Jammu, 2002.

Sen, Gautam, lecturer, LSE: Khidmet seminar, London, July 1999.

Shah, Major Hussain, Northern Areas Joint Platform: Gilgit, April 1994.

Shah, Dr Major (retd) Muzaffar, Kashmir Action Committee: Lahore, April 1994.

Shah, Shabir, Peoples League: Srinagar, April 1995.

Shah, Syed Fazil, Director, Pakistan Information Dept: Gilgit, April 1994.

Shankar, V., former private secretary to Sardar Patel: New Delhi, March 1981.

Sheikh, Nazimuddin: Foreign Secretary to the Gov of Pakistan: Islamabad, 1995.

Sidhvar, Shiraz, journalist, New Delhi, April 1994.

Singh, Mrs Arjun, New Delhi, April 1995.

Singh, Captain Dewan, former ADC to Maharaja Hari Singh: Jammu, April 1994.

Singh, Dr Karan Singh, son of Maharaja Hari Singh, former Sadar-i-Riyasat: New Delhi, April 1994.

Singh, L. P., former Indian Home Secretary: New Delhi, April 1994.

Singh Tavleen, journalist: New Delhi, April 1994.

Suhrawardy, Abdul H., author: Rawalpindi, March 1994.

Swarup, Vikas, Counsellor, Indian High Commission: London, 2002.

Symonds, Richard, author: Kashmir roundtable, London, 2001.

Synnott, Hilary, former High Commissioner in India: London, 1999.

Talbott, Strobe, US Deputy Secretary of State, press conference: New Delhi, 1994.

Talib, Rasheed, journalist: New Delhi, April 1994.

Thapar, Karan, journalist: New Delhi, April 1994.

Thapar, Romila, Professor Emeritus, Jawaharlal Nehru University: London, July 2002.

Thukar, Dr Ayub, World Kashmir Freedom Movement, London, 1994, 1996, 1999, 2002.

Triparthi, P. K., District Commissioner: Leh, April 1995.

Vajpayee, Prime Minister Atal: reception, London, October 2001.

Valani, Sam, tourist: Srinagar, April 1994.

Vira, Dharma, civil servant: New Delhi, April 1994.

Wali, Raja Nisar, Northern Areas Joint Platform: Gilgit, April 1994.

Wani, Dr Ghulam Qadir, J & K Islamic Conference: Rawalpindi, March 1995.

Wani, Mumtaz Ahmed, advocate, Srinagar: London, April 1996.

Wani, Muhstaq Ahmad, Muslim Conference: Rawalpindi, March 1995.

Waverley, Viscount: London, October 1995.

Wirsing, Robert, Asia Pacific Center for Security Studies, Hawaii: Islamabad, 2000.

Zafar, Colonel, Line of Control: Chakoti, March 1994.

Zaidi, Professor Z. H.: Islamabad, March/April 1994.

Zahir-ud Din, journalist: Srinagar, April 2002.

Note: Positions and professions relate to the dates of interviews. Numerous additional people have contributed to my analyses. I have also consulted newspapers and periodicals in Britain, India and Pakistan as well as BBC and linked websites.

Books, articles and published papers

Abdullah, Farooq, *My Dismissal*, New Delhi, 1985.

Abdullah, Sheikh Mohammad, *Flames of the Chinar*, New Delhi, 1993. tr. from the Urdu by Khushwant Singh.

Aitchison, C. U., ed. *A Collection of Treaties, Engagements and Sanads*, Vol. XII Part I, Calcutta, 1931.

Alexander, Horace, *Kashmir*, Friends Peace Committee, London, 1953.

Ali, Chaudhri Muhammad, *The Emergence of Pakistan*, New York, 1967.

Akbar, M. J., *Kashmir: Behind the Vale*, New Delhi, 1991.

Amnesty International Reports, December 1993, Jan 1995, March 1995, Sept 1996, Feb 1999, June 2000, April 2001.

Asia Watch, Reports, May 1991, June 1993.

Azad Govt of the State of Jammu and Kashmir, *Azad Kashmir at a Glance*, 1993.

Bamzai, Prithivi Nath Kaul, *A History of Kashmir, Political, Social, Cultural from the Earliest Times to the Present Day*, New Delhi, 1973.

Bazaz, Prem Nath, *Azad Kashmir*, Lahore, 1951.

—— *History of Struggle for Freedom*, New Delhi, 1954.

—— *The Shape of Things in Kashmir*, New Delhi, 1965.

Bedi, Rahul, 'On the Kashmir Beat', *Jane's Defence Weekly*, 21 May 1994.

—— 'Casualties Rise in Kashmir', *Jane's Defence Weekly*, 28 January 1995.

Beg, Mirza Afzal, *Sheikh Abdullah Defended*, Srinagar, 1962.

Bergen, Peter, *Holy War Inc. Inside the secret world of Osama bin Laden*, London, 2001.

Bernier, François, *Travels in the Mogul Empire, AD 1656–1668*, ed. Archibald Constable, Delhi, 1969.

Bhattacharjea, Ajit, *Kashmir: The Wounded Valley*, New Delhi, 1994.

Bhutto, Zulfikar Ali, *If I am Assassinated*, New Delhi, 1979.

Bikrama Jit Hasrat, (ed.) *The Punjab Papers*, Punjab, 1970.

Birdwood, Lord, *Two Nations & Kashmir*, London, 1956.

Bose, Sumantra, *The Challenge in Kashmir*, New Delhi, 1997.

Burke, Samuel M., *Mainsprings of Indian and Pakistani Foreign Policies*, Minneapolis, 1974.

Campbell-Johnson, Alan, *Mission with Mountbatten*, London, 1972.

Chenevix-Trench, Charles, *The Frontier Scouts*, London, 1985.

Chopra, Pran, *India, Pakistan and the Kashmir Tangle*, New Delhi, 1994.

Cloughley, Brian, *A History of the Pakistan Army, Wars and Insurrections*, Oxford 1999.

Cockell, John, *Ethnic Nationalism and subaltern political process*, September 1998.

Collins, Larry & Lapierre, Dominique, *Freedom at Midnight*, London, 1975.

Cooley, John K., *Unholy Wars*, London, 2001.

Corfield, Sir Conrad, 'Some Thoughts on British Policy and the Indian States, 1935–47', in C. H. Philips & Mary Doreen Wainwright (eds) *The Partition of India*, 1970.

Cunningham, J. D., *The History of the Sikhs*, London, 1849.

Dasgupta, C., *War and Diplomacy*, New Delhi, 2002.

Davis, Anthony, 'The Conflict in Kashmir', *Jane's Intelligence Review*, Vol. 7, No. 1, 1995.

Desmond, Edward W., 'The Insurgency in Kashmir 1989–1991', in *Contemporary South Asia*, Vol. 4, No. 1, March 1995.

Drew, Frederic, *The Northern Barrier of India*, London, 1877.

Durand, Colonel Algernon, *The Making of a Frontier*, London, 1900.

Dutt, Dr Nalinaksha, *Buddhism in Kashmir*, Delhi, 1985.

Edwardes, Herbert & Merivale, Herman, *The Life of Sir Henry Lawrence*, London, 1872.

Edwardes, Michael, *The Last Years of British India*, London, 1963.

Enriquez, Captain C-M, *The Realm of the Gods*, London, 1915.

Evans, Alexander, 'Kashmir: the past ten years', *Asian Affairs*, February 1999.

—— 'Reducing Tension is Not Enough', *The Washington Quarterly*, Spring 2001.

—— 'Why Peace Won't Come to Kashmir', *Current History*, April 2001.

Feldman, Herbert, *From Crisis to Crisis, Pakistan 1962–1969*, Oxford, 1972.

Ferguson, James P. *Kashmir: an Historical Introduction*, London, 1961.

Fernandes, George, 'India's Policies in Kashmir: An Assessment and Discourse' in Ragu G. C. Thomas (ed.) *Perspectives on Kashmir*, Colorado, 1992.

Fisher, Margaret, Rose, Leo E., Huttenback, Robert A., *Himalayan Battleground*, 1963.

French, Patrick, *Sir Francis Younghusband*, London, 1994.

—— *Liberty or Death*, London. 1998.

Gandhi, Indira, *India*, London, 1975.

Ghose, Dilip Kumar, *Kashmir in Transition*, Calcutta, 1975.

Ganguly, Sumit, *The Crisis in Kashmir*, CUP & Woodrow Wilson Center, 1997.

Gauhar, Altaf, *Ayub Khan, Pakistan's First Military Ruler*, Lahore, 1993.

Gopal, Sarvepalli, *Jawaharlal Nehru*, Vols, 1,2,3, London, 1975, 1979, 1984.

Government of India, Foreign Dept, *Visitor's Rules for Jammu and Kashmir*, 1916.

—— White Paper (India), 3 March 1948.

Government of India, 'Response of the Government of India to Report of Amnesty International titled *An Unnatural Fate*', December 1993.

Government of Pakistan, *Kashmir in the Security Council*, Islamabad, March 1990.

Gupte, Pranay, *Mother India*, New York, 1992.

Hamid, Shahid, *Karakuram Hunza*, Karachi, 1979.

—— *Disastrous Twilight*, Great Britain, 1986.

—— *Early Years of Pakistan*, Lahore, 1993.

Hayes, Louis D., *The Impact of US Policy on the Kashmir Conflict*, Arizona, 1971.

Hewitt, Vernon, *Towards the Future? Jammu and Kashmir in the 21st Century*, 2001.

History of the Sikhs: A Concise Account of the Punjaub & Cashmere, compiled from authentic sources, Calcutta, 1846.

High Court of Judicature, Azad Jammu and Kashmir, 'Verdict on Gilgit and Baltistan (Northern Area)', Mirpur, 1993.

Hodson, H. V., *The Great Divide*, London, 1969.

International Commission of Jurists, *Report of a Mission*, Geneva, 1994.

Ismay, *The Memoirs of General the Lord Ismay*, London, 1960.

Jacquemont, Victor, *Correspondence inédite*, 1824–32, Paris, 1867.

Jaffar, S. M., *Kashmir Sold and Resold*, Lahore, 1992.

Jagmohan, *My Frozen Turbulence*, New Delhi, 1994.

Jain, R. K., *Soviet–South Asian Relations, 1947–78*, Vols 1 & 2, New Delhi, 1978.

Jalal, Ayesha, *The Sole Spokesman*, Cambridge, 1985.

—— *The State of Martial Rule*, Cambridge, 1990.

James, Sir Morrice, *Pakistan Chronicle*, London, 1993.

Jha, Prem Shankar, *Kashmir 1947*, Delhi, 1998.

Kadian, Rajesh, *The Kashmir Tangle, Issues & Options*, New Delhi, 1992.

Kak, B. L., *The Fall of Gilgit: the Untold Story of Indo-Pak Affairs from Jinnah to Bhutto*, New Delhi, 1977.

—— *The Untold Story of Men and Matters*, Jammu, 1987.

Kalhana, *Rajatarangini, The Chronicle of the Kings of Kashmir*, tr. M. A. Stein, 1900.

Kalla, Aloke, *Kashmiri Pandits and Their Diversity*, Delhi, 1985.

Kampfner, John, *Robin Cook*, London, 1998.

Kapur, M. L., *Eminent Rulers of Kashmir*, New Delhi, 1975.

Karim, Maj. Gen. Afsir, *Kashmir: The Troubled Frontiers*, New Delhi, 1994.

Kashmir Study Group: *The Kashmir Dispute at 50*, USA, 1997.

—— *Kashmir: The Way Ahead*, USA, 1999.

Khan, Akbar, *Raiders in Kashmir*, Karachi, 1970.

Khan, Amanullah, 'Oppressor v/s Oppressed', Court of Appeal, Brussels, 16 December 1993, Rawalpindi, 1993.

Khanna, Professor D. D., *Defence Studies Papers*, No. 1, University of Allahabad, 1981.

Khurshid, K. H., *Memories of Jinnah*, ed. Khalid Hasan, Karachi, 1990.

Knight, E. F., *Where Three Empires Meet*, London, 1893.

Korbel, Joseph, *Danger in Kashmir*, Princeton, 1955 & 1966.

Lamb, Alastair, *Crisis in Kashmir*, London, 1966.

—— *Kashmir: A Disputed Legacy 1846–1990*, Herts, 1991.

—— *Birth of a Tragedy*, Herts, 1994.

—— *Incomplete Partition, The Genesis of the Kashmir Dispute 1947–1948*, Herts, 1997.

Lawrence, Walter, *The Valley of Kashmir*, London, 1895.

Lumby, E. W. R., 'British Policy Towards the Indian States, 1940–7' in C. H. Philips & Mary Doreen Wainwright (eds) *The Partition of India*, London, 1970.

Mahajan, Mehr Chand, *Looking Back*, London, 1963.

Malhotra, Inder, *Indira Gandhi*, London, 1989.

Malik, Yasin, *Our Real Crime*, Srinagar, 1994.

Mansbergh, Nicholas, (editor-in-chief), *The Transfer of Power*, 1942–47, Vols I–XII. London, 1970–83.

Masani, Zareer, *Indira Gandhi*, London, 1975.

Menon, V. P., *The Story of the Integration of the Indian States*, Calcutta, 1956.

—— *The Transfer of Power in India*, New Delhi, 1957, 1981.

Mirza, Colonel Abdul Haq, *The Withering Chinar*, Islamabad 1991.

Moorcroft, William, *Travels in the Himalayan Provinces of Hindustan and the Punjab*, 1841.

Moore, Thomas, *Lalla Rookh*, London, 1986.

Morris-Jones, W. H., 'Thirty-six Years Later, The Mixed Legacies of Mountbatten's Transfer of Power', *International Affairs*, Autumn 1983.

Mountbatten, Lord, *Time Only to Look Forward*, London, 1949.

Napier, Lt Gen. Sir Charles, *Defects, Civil & Military of the Indian Government*, 1853.

National Documentation Centre, Lahore, *The Partition of the Punjab*, 1947, Lahore, 1983.

Nehru, Jawaharlal, *Selected Works*, ed. Sarvepalli Gopal, Vol. 4, 2nd ed., New Delhi, 1986.

Neve, Arthur, *Thirty Years in Kashmir*, London, 1913.

—— *The Tourist's Guide to Kashmir, Ladakh, Skardo, etc.*, Lahore, 1938.

Neve, Ernest, *A Crusader in Kashmir*, London, 1928.

Nugent, Nicholas, *Rajiv Gandhi*, London, 1990.

Panikkar, K. M., *The Founding of the Kashmir State*, London, 1953.

Pant, Kusum, *The Kashmiri Pandit*, New Delhi, 1987.

Parmu, Dr Radha Krishnan, *Muslim Rule in Kashmir, 1320–1819*, New Delhi, 1969.

Pataudi, Sher Ali, *The Story of Soldiering and Politics*, Lahore, 1988.

—— *The Elite Minority, The Princes of India*, Lahore, 1989.

Patel, Sardar, *Correspondence*, ed. Durga Das, Ahmedabad, 1971.

Punjab Human Rights Organisation, *The Kashmir Massacre, A Report on the Assassination of Mirwaiz Mauvi Farooq and its Aftermath*, Punjab, 1990.

Punjabi, Riaz, 'Kashmir Imbroglio: the Socio-political Roots', *Contemporary South Asia*, Vol. 4, No. 1, March 1995.

Puri, Balraj, *Jammu: A Clue to the Kashmir Tangle*, New Delhi, 1966.

—— *Triumph and Tragedy*, New Delhi, 1981.

—— *Kashmir: Towards Insurgency*, London, 1993.

—— 'Kashmiriyat: the Vitality of Kashmiri Identity', *Contemporary South Asia*, Vol. 4., No. 1, March 1995.

Qadir, Shaukat, 'An Analysis of the Kargil Conflict, 1999', *RUSI Journal*, April 2002.

Qasim, Mir, *My Life and Times*, New Delhi, 1992.

Rashid, Ahmed, *Taliban, Islam, Oil and the New Great Game*, London, 2000.

Ray, John, 'Kashmir: 1962–1986: A footnote to history', *Asian Affairs*, June 2002.

Ray, Hermen, *How Moscow sees Kashmir*, Bombay, 1985.

Rivzi, Gowher, 'Nehru and the Indo-Pakistan Rivalry Over Kashmir, 1947–1963', *Contemporary South Asia*, Vol. 4, No. 1, March 1995.

Rivzi, Janet, *Ladakh*, Oxford, 1983.

Rose, Leo E., 'The Politics of Azad Kashmir', in Ragu G. C. Thomas, (ed.) *Perspectives on Kashmir*, Colorado, 1992.

Round Table Conference, *India's Demand for Dominion Status: Speeches by the King, the Premier, the British Party Leaders and the Representatives of the Princes and People of India*, Madras, 1931.

Sanya, Dr Shanka, *The Boats and Boatmen of Kashmir*, New Delhi, 1979.

Saraf Muhammad, *Kashmiris Fight for Freedom*, Lahore, 1977.

Sareen, Rajendra, *Pakistan: The India Factor*, New Delhi, 1984.

Sedgwick, W., *India for Sale: Kashmir Sold*, Calcutta, 1886.

Sender, Henry, *The Kashmiri Pandits*, Delhi, 1988.

Sharma, Dewan, *Kashmir under the Sikhs*, Delhi, 1983.

Singh, B. S., *The Jammu Fox*, Southern Illinois, 1974.

Singh, Karan, *Heir Apparent*, Oxford, 1982.

Singh, Dr Kirpal, (ed.) *Partition of the Punjab – 1947, Select Documents*, New Delhi, 1991.

Singh, Raghubir, *Kashmir: Garden of the Himalayas*, London, 1983.

Singh, Tavleen, *Kashmir: A Tragedy of Errors*, New Delhi, 1995.

Stephens, Ian, *Horned Moon*, London, 1953.

—— *Pakistan*, London 1963.

Suhrawardy, A. H., *Kashmir: The Incredible Freedom Fight*, Lahore, 1991.

Talbot, Ian, *Pakistan: A Modern History*, London, 1998.

Tarkunde, V. M., 'Kashmir for Kashmiris', *Radical Humanist*, New Delhi, March 1990.

Taseer, C., Bilqees, *The Kashmir of Sheikh Muhammad Abdullah*, Lahore, 1986.

Teng, K. M. and Kaul, S., *Kashmir's Special Status*, Delhi, 1975.

Teng, K. M., Bhatt, Kaul, R. K. and Kaul, S., *Kashmir: Documents on Constitutional History*, India, 1977.

Thomas, Raju G. C. (ed.) *Perspectives on Kashmir*, Colorado, 1992.

Thorp, Robert, *Cashmere Misgovernment*, London, 1870.

Tinker, Hugh, *India and Pakistan*, London, 1962.

—— 'Pressure, Persuasion, Decision: Factors in the Partition of the Punjab, August 1947, *Journal of Asian Studies*, Vol. XXXVI, No. 4, August 1977.

Torrens, Lieut.-Col. Henry, *Travels in Ladak, Tartary & Kashmir*, London, 1862.

Tremblay, Reeta Chowdhari, 'Kashmir: the Valley's Political Dynamics' in *Contemporary South Asia*, Vol. 4, No. 1, March 1995.

Trotter, Lionel, *History of the British Empire, 1844–1862*, London, 1866.

Tyndale-Biscoe, Canon C. E. *An Autobiography*, London, 1951.

United Nations Commission for India and Pakistan, Kashmir Papers: *Reports of UNCIP, June 1948–December 1949*, Government of India, New Delhi, 1952.

Verghese, B. G., 'Lamb's Tales from Kashmir', in *The Kashmir Issue*, High Commission of India, London, 1993.

Verma, P. S., *Jammu and Kashmir at the Political Crossroads*, New Delhi, 1994.

Vigne, Godfrey, *Travels in Kashmir, Ladak, Iskardo*, London, 1842.

Von Huegel, Baron Charles, *Travels in Kashmir and the Punjab*, ed. T. B. Jervis, 1845.

Wakefield, William, *The Happy Valley*, London, 1879.

Walker, Annabel, *Aurel Stein*, London, 1995.

Wani, Dr Nizam-ud din, *Muslim Rule in Kashmir (1554–86)*, Jammu, 1987.

Waslekar, Sundeep, (ed.) *Peace Initiatives*, Vol. 1, No. 2, Sept–Oct 1995, New Delhi, 1995.

Wavell, *The Viceroy's Journal*, ed. Penderel Moon, London, 1973.

Wirsing, Robert, *India, Pakistan and the Kashmir Dispute*, London, 1998.

—— *Boundary & Territory Briefing*, ed. Clive Schofield, University of Durham, Vol. 2, No. 5, 1998.

—— 'Kashmir in the terrorist shadow', *Asian Affairs*, February 2002.

Wolpert, Stanley, *Jinnah of Pakistan*, Oxford, 1984.

—— *Zulfi Bhutto of Pakistan*, Oxford, 1993.

Wylie, Sir Francis, 'Federal Negotiations in India 1935–39 and After' in C. H. Philips & Mary Doreen Wainwright (eds) *The Partition of India*, London, 1970.

Yasin, Madhavi, *British Paramountcy in Kashmir*, New Delhi, 1985.

Yasmeen, Samina, 'The China Factor in the Kashmir Issue' in Ragu G. C. Thomas (ed.) *Perspectives on Kashmir*, Colorado, 1992.

Younghusband, Francis, *Kashmir*, London, 1924.

Zaidi, Professor Z. H., (ed.) *Jinnah Papers, Prelude to Partition*, National Archives of Pakistan, 1993.

Ziegler, Philip, *Mountbatten, The Official Biography*, London, 1985.

Zutshi, N. K., *Sultan Zain-ul Abidin of Kashmir*, Jammu & Lucknow, 1976.

Index

→ Gender
→ Aid
→ Violence/conflict
→ Identity, class, etc
→ Terrorism

Security
→ Terrorism

Books ⊥

⊗ DDR SSR
⊛ Aid (Socio-Economic)
⊕ Peacebuilding